AMERICAN PRIESTESS

The Extraordinary Story

of Anna Spafford

and the

American Colony

in Jerusalem

JANE FLETCHER GENIESSE

ANCHOR BOOKS

A Division of Random House, Inc.

New York

Frontispiece: In Jerusalem Anna Spafford came to question the established church and
its revered sites, such as the famous Via Dolorosa.

FIRST ANCHOR BOOKS EDITION, SEPTEMBER 2009

Copyright © 2008 by Jane Fletcher Geniesse

The author gratefully acknowledges permission from Valentine Vester to quote from
Our Jerusalem: An American Family in the Holy City, 1881–1949, by Bertha Vester,
Garden City, N.Y.: Doubleday, 1950; from Odd Karsten Tveit to quote from
Annas Hus: En beretning fra Stavanger til Jerusalem, Oslo: Cappelen, 2000,
which was translated and privately published in 2007 by Peter Scott-Hansen,
who also gave his permission to quote from this work, as well as to quote from
his translation of *Dala-Swedes in the Holy Land,* by Edith Larsson;
and from Cecily Dewing to quote from the unpublished memoir,
"Jerusalem Before Zionism," by her uncle Lars Lind.

The Library of Congress has cataloged the Nan A. Talese edition as follows:
Geniesse, Jane Fletcher.
American priestess : the extraordinary story of Anna Spafford and the American Colony
in Jerusalem / Jane Fletcher Geniesse.—1st ed.
p. cm.
1. American Colony (Jerusalem)—History. 2. Christian communities—Palestine.
3. Spafford, Anna T., 1842–1923. 4. Americans—Jerusalem—History.
5. Lay missionaries—Jerusalem—History. 6. Jerusalem—Church history. I. Title.
BV4406.9.G46 2008
266.0092—dc22
[B] 2007041233

Anchor ISBN: 978-0-307-27772-5

Author photograph by Joe Arcidiacono
Book design by Donna Sinisgalli
Maps designed by Jeffrey L. Ward

www.anchorbooks.com

Printed in the United States of America
10 9 8 7 6 5 4 3 2 1

This book is dedicated to the youngest generation,

my three grandchildren:

Joe, named for the wonderful Joes;

Rob, for the special grandfathers;

and Julia, for her great-great-grandmother and her aunt.

As they decide the future, may they also study the past.

Praise, therefore, be to Him who hath made the
histories of the Past an admonition unto the Present.

—Sir Richard Burton, *The Arabian Nights*

Contents

Principal Characters   xiii

ONE   *A Beginning*   1

TWO   *Anna*   12

THREE   *Spafford*   23

FOUR   *Thrilling Ideas*   33

FIVE   *The Calamity of the Age*   42

SIX   *Collision at Sea*   53

SEVEN   *"You Must Give Yourself to My Work"*   61

EIGHT   *Return to Chicago*   67

NINE   *The Overcomers*   80

TEN   *"Amelikans" in Yerushalayim*   91

ELEVEN   *The Gadites*   108

TWELVE   *Bad News and Good Works*   116

THIRTEEN   *Friends and a Foe*   125

FOURTEEN   *Overcoming Temptation and the Dangers of Attachment*   134

FIFTEEN   *Struggling On*   141

SIXTEEN   *The Whiting Affair*   151

SEVENTEEN *The Trial*   157

EIGHTEEN *The Chicago Swedes*   166

NINETEEN *The Swedes from Nås*   173

TWENTY *A Cemetery War Begins*   183

TWENTY-ONE *The Sultan, the Emperor,
the Zionist—and Buried Bodies*   197

TWENTY-TWO *The Novelist*   210

TWENTY-THREE *The New Dispensation*   214

TWENTY-FOUR *Triumph*   221

TWENTY-FIVE *War*   233

TWENTY-SIX *Suffering*   245

TWENTY-SEVEN *Surrender*   260

TWENTY-EIGHT *The Lion and the Lamb*   274

TWENTY-NINE *Death*   287

THIRTY *Epitaph*   297

Afterword   310

Acknowledgments   314

Notes   317

Bibliography   349

Index   365

Photo Credits   379

Principal Characters

Chicago Overcomers

Anna and Horatio Spafford, and their daughters Bertha and Grace

Cousin Rob Lawrence, Horatio's nephew

Aunt Maggie Lee, Horatio's sister

Amelia Gould, Anna's rich friend, recently widowed

William Rudy, mill owner

Caroline Merriman, Rudy's foster mother

John and Mary Whiting, and their daughter Ruth. Their son John
was born in Jerusalem, and the children would soon receive a
substantial inheritance

Otis and Lizzie Page, and their daughter, Flora

Captain William and Mary Sylvester, who joined the group in London

Annie Aiken, the Spafford baby nurse, although only fourteen years old
herself

Dr. Samuel Hedges, who did not sail with the group to Jerusalem

Members Who Joined the American Colony in Jerusalem

Elias Habib, Arab dragoman

Johanna Brooke, teacher

Jacob Eliahu, adopted by the Spaffords

Rev. Herbert Drake, companion of "Chinese" Gordon, and Anna's
"tempter"

Elijah Meyers, inventor, who recorded Anna's messages

Rev. Edward F. Baldwin, former missionary to Morocco

Furman Baldwin, who attempted suicide over Grace Spafford

Professor John Dinsmore, educator; his wife, Mary; and their
daughter, Ruth

Principal Swedes from Chicago and Nås

Olof Henrik Larsson, founder of Chicago's Swedish Evangelical Church;
 his wife, Mathilda; and their daughter, Edith
Olaf, Lars, Nils, and Eric Lind, brothers orphaned when their parents died
 in Jerusalem
Lewis Larsson, who married Edith, daughter of Olof Henrik Larsson

Jerusalem Friends of the American Colony

Rolla Floyd, tour operator, and his wife, Docia
Ali Bey Juzdar, the Overcomers' landlord
Eliezer Ben-Yehuda, Hebrew scholar
Ismail Bey Husseini, director of public education, Jerusalem
Frederick Vester, who married Bertha Spafford

Principal Diplomatic Antagonists

U.S. Consul Selah Merrill
U.S. Consul Edwin S. Wallace
U.S. Consul General Charles M. Dickinson

Other Antagonists

Rev. A. Hastings Kelk, London Jews Society
P. H. Winterstein, correspondent for *Our Rest and Signs of the Times*
Alice E. Davis, correspondent for the *Age to Come*
T. J. Alley, printer of the defamatory tract "The Spaffordite Fraud"
John and Amelia Adamson, former members who "escaped"
Regina Lingle, Mary Whiting's mother
Professor David Lingle, Mary Whiting's brother
John S. Gould, Amelia Gould's brother-in-law in charge of her estate
Rev. William K. Eddy, Presbyterian Board of Missions

Evangelists

Dwight L. Moody, leading evangelist
Ira Sankey, Moody's singing partner
Major D. W. Whittle, whose daughter married Moody's son
William E. Blackstone, author of the Blackstone Memorial

Influential Millennialists in Great Britain

John Nelson Darby, founder of the Plymouth Brethren
Lord Shaftesbury, reformer
Dr. Charles Piazza Smith, astronomer royal

Tomb and Mosque of Sheikh Jarrah

Detention HQ

Stables for Horses, Cows/Pigsty

Hol Brita's Chicken Coop

Dungeon for Storing Canned Goods

Outhouses

Tennis Court

Brother Joseph's Blacksmith Shop

Ladies' Dormitory

Selim Effendi House

"Upper Room"

Bread Bakery/ Carpenter Shop

Tin Shop of O.H. Larsson

Men's Dormitory

"Big House"

Photo Studio

Palm House"

Bedrooms

Bedrooms

Lewis Larsson's House

Nablus Road

Salah al-Din Street

Bertha and Frederick Vester's House

To Damascus Gate

To Herod's Gate

© 2008 Jeffrey L. W

JERUSALEM

area of detail

American Colony Compound

Bertha and Frederick Vester's House

St. George's Cathedral and Boys' School

▲ Mt Scopus

"New" American Cemetery

Augusta Victoria Hospital

Saladin al-Din Street

Nablus Road

Garden Tomb

"Skull" Cliff

"Old House" on Bezetha Hill

Herod's Gate

Damascus Gate

Muslim Quarter

Lion's Gate

Via Dolorosa

Muslim Cemetery

New Gate

Via Dolorosa

HARAM AL-SHARIF

Golden Gate

Jaffa Road

Christian Quarter

Holy Sepulcher

DOME OF THE ROCK

Mt. of Olives ▲

David Street

Jericho Road

Jaffa Gate

Wailing Wall

Grand New Hotel

Frederick Vester's Store

Jewish Quarter

Maghribi Quarter

Jewish Cemetery

Armenian Quarter

Dung Gate

Zion Gate

"Old" American Cemetery

Mosque of King David and Room of the Last Supper

Church of The Virgin's Dormition

Anglican Protestant Cemetery

▲ Mt. Zion

| 0 Yards | 250 | 500 |
| 0 Meters | 250 | 500 |

To German Colony

© 2008 Jeffrey L. Ward

AMERICAN
PRIESTESS

CHAPTER ONE

A Beginning

The world to an end shall come
In eighteen hundred and eighty-one.
—Prophecy by an anonymous author, 1488

On a windy September day in 1881, the captain ordered the anchor dropped while the ship was still far offshore. This was routine procedure, as the port of Jaffa in Palestine was notoriously unsafe. Until that moment, however, not one of the eighteen pilgrims assembled on deck had been aware of just how difficult disembarkation might be. In their haste to leave Chicago, none had thought to pack a guidebook, and they now strained to make out details of the scene before them. The town of Jaffa seemed pretty in the morning sunlight. A mosque crowned a picturesque riot of domed houses tumbling down to the sea. There was an inviting waterfront, lined with handsome brick and stone warehouses, and orange trees abounded in the countryside around the town. But the foaming waves that crashed against a circular belt of sunken boulders between them and the shore were distinctly intimidating.[1]

Neither their own steamer nor any of the other large ships anchored nearby could get close to shore. This had been so since 1345, when the Egyptian Mamluks had destroyed Jaffa's venerable harbor, determined that no infidel crusaders would ever again invade the Eastern lands after Sultan Baybars had expelled the last Western knights in 1271. Tradition had it that Andromeda was chained to one of these jagged rocks, and it was from Jaffa—or ancient Joppa—that Jonah had fled to escape being sent to Nineveh, and then was swallowed by a whale. Hiram of Tyre sent his Lebanese cedars on floats to this port for Solomon to build his great temple in Jerusalem, and in the town itself Simon the tanner had been host to Saint Peter.

The pilgrims knew these stories. Though they lacked a guidebook, they each carried a Bible, and biblical names and characters were as familiar to them as those of their families. They were both weary and excited. They had been voyaging since August 17, when they left Chicago abruptly, after nightfall. If some had not been completely ready, none could have hesitated. The glorious message for which they had been waiting had come at last. Eagerly, they obeyed the summons. The Resurrection was at hand and they were prepared to meet the Messiah.

Thus, via Quebec by train, then by steamer to London, six women, four men, a nineteen-year-old youth, two young girls, and three babies had sailed by the northern route to Liverpool. With the addition of a retired British army captain and his wife who had asked to join them in London, the little band was now close to their hearts' desire. Soon they would be in Jerusalem to greet their Savior personally when He alighted on the Mount of Olives.

Within moments, a motley fleet of rowboats and little barges surging through the rock barrier threw their lines over the ship's side and were bobbing against its hull. A rabble of barefooted Arabs, hoisting themselves up with ropes and chains, clambered swiftly aboard, shouting incomprehensibly. Many had daggers thrust into their wide red sashes, and all seemed enormous and frightening to the startled passengers whom the captain had only recently warned of Jaffa's famously unceremonious custom of disembarkation. Clad in baggy trousers and wearing red fezzes, the boatmen fell upon passengers and baggage like a swarm of hornets, scooping men, women, children, trunks, valises, and hatboxes up in a viselike grip, and half-tossed, half-handed them over to their waiting comrades below. Finding themselves breathless and disarranged but at least safe in the heaving tenders, the ladies patted their bonnets and skirts back into order while the gentlemen offered a steadying hand. Once past the rock barrier, they were again seized by the Arab longshoremen, who carried them through the surf and up the beach, and finally set them down on Canaan's sacred soil.

Little did the pilgrims guess, as they waited for their ride over the sultan's new carriage road from Jaffa to Jerusalem, that filth, illness, and sorrow awaited them. Nor could they know of the singular friendships and rapturous moments that also lay ahead. In Chicago, the newspapers had called them the "Overcomers." Their doctrines were strange. They had been rebuffed and ridiculed for their beliefs, and for their unwavering faith in their spiritual leaders, Horatio Spafford and his blue-eyed wife, Anna. Yet educated, attractive, mostly well-to-do, and some socially prominent, these pilgrims were moved by the absolute conviction that they had been called to their journey.

The second half of the nineteenth century, often called America's Gilded Age, was known as "Bible drenched," and for good reason. After the recent and bloodily divisive Civil War, America had become rich, but the new wealth, resulting from an agrarian way of life giving way to an industrialized society, brought stress to many. A grand network of railroads and the Erie Canal, completed in 1825, had fueled a westward migration. Travel and the creation of new businesses had become easier, but massive dislocations followed. Suddenly there were crowded cities and an urban poor. Moreover, vast numbers of immigrants seeking work and a better life continued to arrive, bringing with them new ideas that disturbed rural America. By the middle of the tumultuous century that gave birth to the Overcomers, many made anxious by the secularism and Enlightenment thinking of the old Continent had turned to religion for reassurance and certitude.

This impulse was hardly new to America, which had already enjoyed two waves of religious "awakenings" in the past. The first had occurred four decades before the American Revolution, the second began at the start of the nineteenth century and lasted into the 1830s. Although the founding fathers, valuing freedom of conscience, had separated church from state, the country was overwhelmingly Protestant. Central to Protestantism was the belief that man needed no interceding church hierarchy to save his soul: justification was by faith, and salvation thus the responsibility of the individual alone. This liberating notion had given rise over the years to schismatic groups breaking off from mainstream churches to found their own denominations, develop their own creeds, and evangelize those in need of being "saved."

Alexis de Tocqueville, touring the country in 1831, had observed that "the prevailing passion" seemed to be "acquiring the good things of the world," but he had also been fascinated by a second powerful theme. "In the midst of American society you meet with men full of fanatical and almost wild spiritualism . . . From time to time strange sects arise which endeavor to strike out extraordinary paths to external happiness. Religious insanity is very common in the United States."

As the firewall between church and state prevented the creation of a state-supported church of the kind that existed in many European countries, individual preachers in America had to create and sustain their own congregations and develop techniques to bind them close. Conditions, therefore, were ripe for preacher-prophets to roam the land, look for converts, and win them away to their own special visions. Nothing, it seems, served as well as a revival to satisfy the Protestant's desire to embrace the Lord and lay down his burdens of sin and guilt. The country had long seen multitudes of eager seekers traveling long distances to gather in tents to be exhorted, to shout "Amen!" and to be born again. Longing to "feel" God's presence in their bodies as well as in their hearts and minds, many Protestants yearned for a dramatic baptism in the Holy Spirit. Accordingly, flourishing pentecostal movements had long been part of the American scene where overwrought believers engaged in strange, even shocking behaviors.*

In August 1801, at Cane Ridge, Kentucky, twenty-five thousand farmers and their families converged from their lonely mountain farms in search of religious communion. At a gathering larger than most cities of the period, and held under the auspices of Presbyterians but drawing masses from the faster-growing Methodist and Baptist denominations,

---

* In a telephone interview in November 2007, the distinguished scholar George M. Marsden noted that Pentecostalism as a distinct entity originated in 1901 with the outbursts inspired by Charles F. Parham. (See Marsden's *Fundamentalism and American Culture*, 72.) My reference to "pentecostal" here is not to an organized movement as such but to behaviors in which some believers have engaged since the first Pentecost was mentioned in the Book of Acts.

men, women, and children laughed, sang, twirled, and barked like dogs until they collapsed unconscious on the ground in a trance. "These were rough people, profane, heavy drinkers, violent, who had never before attended night camp meetings. Conversion and love-making intermingled in an orgy of Pentecostal enthusiasm."[2] Reports of the bacchanal ignited a flurry of similar revivals elsewhere in the country among people equally lonely, ignorant, devoid of other entertainments, and above all bewildered by the social and economic upheavals marking the times.

The fervor famously scorched upper New York state, aptly named "the Burned-Over District" for its consecutive religious enthusiasms. Horatio Spafford was born and raised in Troy, New York, and had seen the impact of thousands of foreign immigrants converging to dig the 363-mile-long Erie Canal and rub their strange habits against staid old ways. Suddenly mills and factories stood where farms had been, and shantytowns sprawled with noisy pubs, drinking, and crime. Itinerant preachers arrived to offer consolation and their personal interpretations of Protestantism—if in fact these could be called Protestant at all—and the more sensational they were, the greater the number of adherents gathering to be consoled. Multitudes of sects arose. Perhaps among the best known were the celibate dancing Shakers who followed "Mother" Ann Lee in 1776, then, in 1830, Joseph Smith's polygamous Mormons, and, finally, the Oneida Perfectionists who practiced "free love" as preached by John Humphrey Noyes in 1848. Like most other sects, these products of the Burned-Over District revolved around a charismatic leader who drastically reordered traditional family relationships.

As nineteenth-century revivalism gathered momentum, expectations became common among Protestants in America for an imminent Second Coming. For many, the decades of violence in Europe had surely heralded that the end was near. William Miller, a New York state farmer and Baptist lay preacher, was one who twice preached a specific date for the return. When Christ disappointed Miller in 1843, he recalculated the date for precisely October 22, 1844, an exactitude that was his undoing. When some forty thousand Millerites gathered for the fateful day and again nothing happened, derision sent him to an early grave, while the believers who had sold their homes and businesses to don ascension robes were left to sorrow in bankruptcy.[3]

For many Protestants, preachments from a Sunday pulpit by their Episcopal, Presbyterian, Congregationalist, Baptist, or Methodist pastors could never adequately answer their craving for an intense spiritual experience, which was for these seekers more important than scriptural guidance. So many turned to sects that offered unbridled and ecstatic practices, and over the years a wide variety of different strains blossomed from Protestantism. Among them were the Christian Scientists, the Churches of Christ, the Fourierists, Swedenborgians, and Seventh-Day Baptists, the Keswick movement, the Holiness movement, the Plymouth Brethren, Pietists and Quietists, Spiritualists, and Inner-Lightists, as well as endless other denominational divisions, branches, sects, and cults dedicated to satisfying "religious desire."[4] Ever curious and experimental, Americans have tried everything from animal magnetism and healing machines to table rapping and magnetic fluids in their quest for communion with the saving God and a favorable reception in the world to come.

It was from this creative current in Protestant thinking that the Overcomers were born, inspired by their prophets, Horatio and Anna Spafford, in Chicago. Above all, they were convinced millenarians, awaiting the cataclysm in which God would destroy the ruling power of evil and raise the righteous into the heavenly kingdom.[5] Unlike so many of their fellow citizens, however, who considered America itself to be the new Zion—the place for a fresh and godly start where they could build a new "City on a Hill"[6]—the Spaffords and their followers turned eastward to the old Zion: Jerusalem, in Ottoman Palestine. Here they would establish themselves as the first permanent and longest-lasting American settlement in the holy city. All the while, they looked for the "signs" that would herald the Messiah's return, constructing a personal theology that incorporated much of evangelical thinking at that time, including the necessity of the Jews' return to the land of their fathers, according to the ancient prophecies. As they waited and watched, they would bear witness to the titanic events that ultimately formed the modern Middle East. Surviving war, famine, plagues, and revolution, these ardent believers participated in the death throes of the Ottoman Empire, witnessed the arrival of the victorious British in 1917, and eventually saw a second generation grow up. Their colony flourished through the British mandate period as Jews arrived in ever-increasing numbers to fulfill their own Zionist dream. A smaller group stayed on through World War II and eventually saw the creation in 1948 of the powerful new Jewish state, Israel.

The pilgrims became known almost immediately as the American Colony, although in due course their expanding membership would include British, Indian, Canadian, Scottish, French, Turkish, Romanian, Polish, Serbian, Spanish, Danish, Norwegian, and especially Swedish additions. From the start, they were viewed as cranks and degenerates by Jerusalem's Protestant missionaries, and particularly by two successive U.S. consuls who ascribed to them immoral practices and sexual license. Yet to many Jews, Muslims, Greeks, Latins, Armenians, Copts, and sundry others who contended often viciously in the City of Peace, their reputation was quite the opposite—one of unsurpassed goodness and generosity to the poor and the needy around them. Notable visitors to Jerusalem who stayed under their hospitable roof returned home singing paeans to the American Colony even as it was quietly evolving into a business for the profit of the strongest of the surviving members, a business that exists today as one of the most celebrated hotels in the Middle East. As one contemporary wag observed, "They came to do good and they stayed to do well."

If the process crushed the lives of some weaker members unable to escape the cruelty, emotional blackmail, and discrimination that buttressed the pilgrims' utopian dream, the story is a very human one. In times of confusion, suffering, or dread of the future, otherwise reasonable men and women have willingly handed over their freedom to another deemed stronger and endowed with greater certainty—usually a leader they believe to be in touch with a "higher" authority. Certainly it happened when the Overcomers came to Jerusalem in 1881 and settled down as an active and integral part of one of the most fiercely divided and emotional places on earth. Their contribution to the social and political life of Jerusalem was to leave an indelible imprint. Even today there is not a map of Jerusalem that does not show the visitor how to find his way to the famous American Colony Hotel, just a short walk outside the walls.

On the bustling Jaffa quay, the sun beat down on the well-dressed and apparently affluent pilgrims as they moved toward the throng of Turkish soldiers, custom officers, and longshoremen. An agent for the British tourist agency Thomas Cook & Son identified himself to Horatio Spafford. Tall, silver-haired, and dignified, Horatio inquired about what arrangements had been made for them. The agent said he had two spring wagons to take them to Jerusalem. Surveying the ladies in their handsome traveling costumes, their guide added that he hoped it would not be too rough a ride. In the meantime, he suggested that they wander a bit in the streets.

"You've been lucky," said the agent, assuring them that he would steer them through Turkish customs as quickly as he could. "We've just finished a cholera quarantine. If you had come earlier, the Turks would have kept you in one of their prisons until it was over."

Horatio glanced at his wife standing beside him. Erect, her lovely Scandinavian complexion pale in the morning glare but her eyes as brilliant as the sea, she was as beautiful and necessary to him as she had been when he had fallen in love with her, a mere girl of fifteen and he a practicing attorney of twenty-nine. Now she was thirty-nine and had borne him seven children. They were close to their goal; they were standing on the very ground Christ's feet had touched. Like other Protestant Americans encountering the Holy Land for the first time, they looked with misty eyes at turbaned and sandal-footed Arabs dressed, they believed, in the same robes Christ and his apostles had worn. To them, the scene seemed profoundly familiar. This was the place, as Horatio had said, "where my Lord lived, suffered, and conquered. And I wish to learn how to live, suffer, and especially to conquer."[7]

In the American imagination, Palestine held a mythic place. Bible-reading Protestants envisioned its landscape and its sacred sites, familiarizing themselves with its geography as intimately as they knew their own cities. As de Tocqueville had noted, the habit of the American businessman was to go home at night, not to review his ledgers, but to read his Bible to his family. Some viewed it as a dreamland, lacking reality. Others recognized it as a real place, which they yearned for and felt they must eventually visit.[8] In the second half of the nineteenth century especially—when personal prosperity, a brisk steamship trade, and relaxed regulations issued by the Ottoman sultan under whose rule the shabby province of Palestine lay made the trip more feasible—Americans streamed here by the thousands. Even President Lincoln, on that fateful day when he went to Ford's theater, told his wife that he intended to visit the Holy Land. For all, it was the "spot on earth where the beauty and the majesty of God have been revealed to man," as one rhapsodic visitor wrote in 1867.[9]

Soon the Overcomers would be in Jerusalem. And as it invariably was for all the other pilgrims, tourists, missionaries, officials, archaeologists, and hopeful entrepreneurs initially exposed to this city of their dreams, it would be a shock. "It is the most hopeless, dreary, heartbroken piece of territory out of Arizona," wrote Mark Twain, who declared after a visit in 1867 that even "the sun would skip it if he could make schedule by going around."[10] The optimistic, determined, and cheerful American spirit was usually incredulous at witnessing the squalor, lassitude, incompetence, and medieval wretchedness of Ottoman Palestine, and yet adored it—unless, of course, the visitor's spirit was as sardonic as Mark Twain's. If Jerusalem's streets were narrow, the smells intolerable, and the water polluted, nevertheless earnest Americans wandered the sacred ruins in a state of exaltation, confirmed in their belief that all the Bible told them was true. As to the pathetic nature of the place, they concluded that Zion was "suffering for its sins," that the Lord had "punished his wayward people" who had committed deicide and were now paying penance. Every diligent student of the New Testament was familiar with Saint Paul's prophecy that the conversion of the Jews to Christianity would precede the Messiah's return. And if they were millenarians like the Overcomers, they believed that God had postponed the final judgment until the Jews were returned to Zion to repent their sins.

The Overcomers had long been on the lookout for "signs" heralding the end of days. They believed that they were living in a pre-apocalyptic pause. For them, this was the last chapter of a long history in which mankind had consistently ignored God's commands from the time that Adam and Eve had eaten of the forbidden fruit. To the Overcomers, these chapters or eras were known as "dispensations." In this, the final dispensation, it had been revealed to Horatio that their little band was none other than the "Bride" of Christ, the "Bridegroom."

Signs were always important to millenarians, and the Overcomers took them very seriously. Earthquakes, tidal waves, meteor showers, and similar alarming phenomena were indicators that Armageddon approached. Newspapers had carried stories of the fire in Vienna's Ring Theater earlier in 1881, when 860 opera lovers perished—surely a punishment on pleasure seekers. On March 13 in Russia that year, in the sanctity of a church, Czar Alexander II had been felled by an assassin, and in America a madman shot President James A. Garfield on July 2, just a month and a half before the Overcomers left Chicago.

On September 4, 1881, two weeks after the papers announced that Mrs. Garfield was pregnant and expecting a baby in November, an article in the *New York Times* mentioned that "a new sect has arisen in Chicago, whose members call themselves the Overcomers. They assume to have a peculiar inheritance in the promises which were made to the seven churches of Asia, claim to work miracles, and believe in the salvation of all, even of the Devil; but many will first have to pass through purgatory. Their leader and some of their most advanced saints are said to be on their way to Jerusalem to inaugurate the new dispensation."[11]

It was nightfall when the pilgrims at last arrived in Jerusalem, exhausted but exhilarated. They had been bounced for hours and choked by clouds of billowing white dust. As the Cook's agent promised, the day had been long, and now the sky was bright with distant stars. They climbed stiffly out of the spring wagons and walked beneath the Jaffa Gate. The streets were only dimly lit by the glow of kerosene lamps from inside stone houses.

They had very little luggage. The Spaffords themselves had brought only one trunk. Material possessions were insignificant with the end so near. Horatio had told Cook's that they could not afford the more expensive alternative of camping in tents outside the walls, where the air was less foul than in the city. Had the Overcomers not vehemently rejected the teaching of the established Christian churches, they might have been comfortable in one of the pilgrim hostels sponsored by various Christian orders. Instead, the band of eighteen pilgrims followed the agent to a squalid caravanserai, the Mediterranean Hotel, near the Coptic convent on the Street of the Patriarch, off David Street. There, with mixed emotions and quiet prayer, they spent their first night in Jerusalem.

The following morning they arose to find themselves a house. Mark Twain had said, "What Palestine wants is paint. It will never be a beautiful country while it is unpainted. Each detachment of pilgrims ought to give it a coat."[12] The Overcomers intended to do just that—find themselves a house, broom out the vermin, and paint it. Anna would make sure it was as pretty and welcoming as the lovely place she had abandoned in Chicago. And when the whispers began, swelling to a muffled roar, that all was not right with this singular American household, the gaze of Horatio's beautiful wife never wavered, nor did she cease to work her abundant charm on Jerusalem's susceptible citizenry.

CHAPTER TWO

Anna

I stood ready to say to my fatherland, my kin-
dred, my parish and my parents, farewell.
　　　　—A Norwegian who left Stavanger in 1855

Norway and Sweden have already sent large
colonies to this country, who have settled princi-
pally in Wisconsin and Illinois. They prove to
be most valuable and exemplary citizens, sober,
chaste, industrious, and intelligent.
　　　　—Knoxville Republican, *May 13, 1856*

High over the rocky coast gulls circled freely, mocking the hardship of the Stavanger people. This Norwegian port was not the
only town that had fallen on hard times. All of Norway, indeed all of
Scandinavia, was still suffering from the deprivations inflicted by the
Napoleonic Wars. Always proud, traditionally stoic, inured to hard work
and long dark winters, the Norsemen felt they had been tested enough.
The majority of Norwegians, like most Scandinavians, were deeply
religious, and many agreed that their stern Lutheran ministers were interested less in their spiritual needs than in maintaining a rigidly class-
conscious status quo. Increasingly, they were attracted to the more
satisfying new Protestant faiths spreading across the ocean from America. For some time now, they had been welcoming Baptist, Mormon,
and Methodist missionaries into their homes to preach. In Stavanger a
community of Quakers had been quietly developing ever since hundreds

of Norwegian merchant seamen imprisoned by the British had been assisted, and then converted, by British Quakers.

In 1842, less than thirty years after the seamen returned home with their new faith, a baby girl was born to a family of Quaker sympathizers living just outside Stavanger's city limits. When Anne Tobine Larsdatter Øglende arrived on March 16, 1842, her father and mother had been hurriedly married only six months before.[1] Her father, Bjarne Lars Larsen Øglende, was a widower struggling to raise two children.[2] Although a farmer as well as a carpenter skilled in making violins and somewhat better off than some, he found it difficult to be alone. He sought comfort in the warm embrace of a girl from southern Norway, Gurine Tobine Andersdatter. When he learned she was pregnant, he did the honorable thing and made her his wife.[3] Their blue-eyed, flaxen-haired baby was baptized in Stavanger's old Domkirke in the presence of family friends. Many were Quakers, although Lars himself had not embraced Quakerism; it was a dangerous thing to do. The state-supported Lutheran Church had denounced this increasingly popular new faith as heretical. To be a dissenter risked persecution as the Lutheran hierarchy fought to stanch the flight of its parishioners. One could be imprisoned simply for gathering privately with friends to pray and read the Bible. Small wonder that thrilling letters telling of liberty in America were secretly passed from family to family and gave pause to men like Øglende.

"I can tell you that here we do not live frugally," crowed one happy immigrant. "One has eggs and egg pancakes and canned fish and fresh fish, and fruits of all kinds, so it is different from you who have to sit and suck herring bones."[4]

Another letter boasted of chickens and hogs apparently for the taking. "We can cut all the hay we want—all free! All our bread is white, being made from bolted wheat flour. This is surely the Promised Land."[5]

But beyond such unheard-of abundance, the news that mattered most was the descriptions of a democratic society in American which allowed freedom of worship: "All are alike, the farmer, the minister, and the judge. One does not need to go and bow and nod, hat in hand," which was the expected behavior of a Norwegian man to his social superior.[6]

It would not be long before such reports persuaded Anne's father and his friends. Having heard that carpenters in America were scarce, Lars decided to take the risk, but to leave behind his seven-year-old son, Edvard, and older daughter, Rachel. If things worked out, they could follow later. On May 10, 1846, the Øglendes, including four-year-old Anne, and 150 other Norwegians set sail for New York on the 290-ton sailing vessel *Norden*. The trip took two months, the passengers bedded on straw, and each woman cooked her family's dinner in an improvised galley, with little to eat but porridge and an occasional codfish caught off the Newfoundland Banks.[7]

New York, however, was not their real destination; they were eager to follow in the wake of their countrymen who were establishing Scandinavian communities in Chicago, a boomtown growing faster than any city in the country. Formally organized only thirteen years earlier and the gateway to the west, the Chicago of 1846 was already called "the boss city of the Universe."[8] Shipping traffic through the Great Lakes brought trade to Lake Michigan's southern shore, where goods and people could be off-loaded to resume the trek farther west or south. The completed Erie Canal contributed to an explosion of commerce powering a great wave of westward migration to a frontier rich in timber, minerals, and farmland for the taking if one did not fear hard work.

The gently flowing and dreadfully polluted Chicago River was the six-mile-long city's convenient artery, branching off in two directions. Tall-masted ships moved along it, and at points where the streets crossed the river, swinging bridges manned by two men swung out to let them pass. Mud was the problem in the low-lying shore land. Water stood in the streets for most of the year. A brown bog in winter, it turned to choking dust in summer, so the new city was building a network of elevated wooden sidewalks. Most of Chicago, in fact, seemed constructed of wood, easily obtained from surrounding forests. As a result, citizens were vigilant about fire and divided the city into districts, each known by its number. "In some central and conspicuous place in each," an admiring young English visitor wrote his family, "is a box containing an apparatus by which a bell may be rung in a room in City Hall. In this room there are men constantly watching the bells. As soon as the bell of any district is rung, the watchers reply with a hurried kind of chime on the large bell of the City Hall, which can be heard in every part of the city. This is to announce that there is a fire."[9]

Fire was not the only hazard. The air was thick with smoke from the burning of bituminous coal, which blackened new buildings practically before they were built. Lake Michigan's swampy shore bred mosquitoes, so malaria, or "ague fever," as it was called, swept the city at regular intervals. The Chicago River was an open sewer, and while steps were already being taken to ensure a clean water supply by driving a pipeline deep into Lake Michigan, there were also periodic outbreaks of scarlet fever, diphtheria, smallpox, typhoid, and cholera.

Funerals were common in the various congested enclaves where Germans or Irish or Scandinavians composed the largest portion of the city's foreign-born. It was they who took on the low-paying jobs that native-born Americans disdained. Germans worked in breweries, distilleries, and factories. Their beer gardens, scandalously open on Sunday, rang with boisterous merriment. The Irish claimed the area southwest of downtown near the stockyards and lumberyards. Merry and feckless to disapproving Protestants, they gathered to dance and play cards all night in their pubs and sallied forth in prodigious numbers on Saint Patrick's Day. The Scandinavians were more dispersed, more circumspect, and far more inclined to observe Protestant taboos against drinking, dancing, and cards. They stuck together in wards near the North Side, worked in shipyards and manufacturing, and provided the city with tailors, dressmakers, and milliners.

There could be no doubt that Chicago was a religious town. "Sunday in Chicago," said one visitor, "though not observed as it is in New England, is, I think, more respected than any town of 20,000 inhabitants or upwards, south of Philadelphia. The movement of the people is generally churchward, and the churches are well filled . . . Crime and immorality exist to an alarming extent; yet the Puritan element so far predominates in the population of the place, that wickedness is neither popular nor respectable."[10] Almost daily, it seemed, a new church spire thrust skyward to compete along a horizon of bristling ships' masts. Unlike the Roman Catholic Irish, who resisted integration into this intensely Protestant society, the conservative-minded Scandinavians endorsed the Calvinist values of frugality, hard work, and sober living. To the degree they saw fit, they also strove to cast off the customs of the Old Country to better fit in as Americans.[11]

The Øglende family was as adaptive as the rest. It was quickly apparent that they would have to not only learn English but drop their strange Norwegian names. So Lars became Lars Lawson, his wife Tanetta, and Anne simply Anna Tubena Lawson. Anna's half brother and half sister, Edvard and Rachel, had arrived, and he became Edward. A new baby brother was christened Hans, and the family settled down to reap the benefits of the new land.

Three years later, in 1849, cholera struck. It came on April 29 with an emigrant boat, the *John Drew*, and raged until late October. That year 678 persons died, the worst death rate from any cause since Chicago began keeping health statistics.[12] Yellow notices were tacked on doors, warning people away from infected homes.[13] The contagion was unsparing, but crowded tenement areas bore the heaviest losses. When Tanetta and little Hans fell sick, harsh reality interrupted the Lawsons' lives. Much later Anna told her daughter that she remembered the sounds of groans and grieving emerging from thin walls as she hurried through deserted streets to fetch medicine and brandy.[14] The baby died, and then shortly afterward Anna's mother succumbed.

Once more Lars Lawson was a widower. Although his daughter Rachel was old enough to assume some of the housekeeping responsibilities, Edward was only ten, and Anna seven. The burdens were heavy. For six years the family struggled on, until Lars realized he, too, might die. In his case it was a debilitating "consumption" that caused him to cough up blood. However, there was one hope. The harsh winter air of Minnesota, people were saying, killed germs.

In 1854 the Chicago and Rock Island Railroad completed a line from Chicago to St. Paul, Minnesota. The former president Millard Fillmore agreed to use the line for a rail and riverboat journey as a "coming-out party" for the newly established Minnesota Territory.[15] In early June 1854, Fillmore's "Grand Excursion," described as "by far the most brilliant event of its kind that the West has ever witnessed," took off in the company of twelve hundred revelers.[16]

In warm weather the journey to Minnesota from Chicago could be made in about thirty hours, and so a spectacular landgrab was launched. In April 1855 the steamer *War Eagle* disgorged 814 eager speculators and would-be settlers in a mad scramble to squat on as much U.S. government land as possible until their claims were formally assigned and, after that, on any land that had not already been taken from the helpless and deracinated Sioux and Dakota Indian tribes. To stake a claim, one simply had to build a house. Even single women, unable to stake a claim unless they were widowed or "head of a family," could show equal enterprise simply by borrowing a house and a neighbor's baby—to be returned when their claim was registered.[17]

Through the spring and summer of 1855 untold numbers of native Yankees, English, Irish, Dutch, Germans, and assorted others streamed to Minnesota to take advantage of "a good state—one of the most fertile, best timbered, best watered, of all the New States," as Horace Greeley, editor of the *New-York Tribune* and a great booster of western migration, enthusiastically put it.[18] But especially Norwegians came. Over the years, more Norwegians were to settle in Minnesota than in any other state in the country—some 850,000 between 1825 and 1928.[19] In particular, the Norwegians were attracted to the developing township of Wanamingo, named after a Native American heroine, which offered good water, forests in the north, and a grassy plain stretching to the south as far as the eye could see.

It was to Wanamingo that Lars and Edward headed. Like all other hopefuls, they arrived in an ox-drawn "screech wagon," so called because "the poorly-lubricated wheels and axles emitted a penetrating wail never to be forgotten by those who heard it."[20] Little did they realize that the sound was a mourning dirge for their little family, already stunned by loss and now splitting further apart, soon to break up forever.

Emphatically, Anna did not want to leave Chicago. Some rather nice things had begun to happen to the lovely thirteen-year-old, and she was loath to abandon these glimmerings of good fortune. A neighbor, Sarah Ely, whose children were grown, had taken a fancy to the motherless girl.[21] When she proposed that the child come to live with her, and promised to pay her tuition at Dearborn Academy, it was a relief to Lars, despite a lurking fear that a fancy school might cause his daughter to forget the "old ways" or the proper respect she owed him. She might even think herself superior to her less educated family. But pressed strongly by Mrs. Ely and his older daughter, Rachel, Lars gave in. To Anna, admittance to this good private school was unqualified joy. She quickly made friends with the children of prominent Chicago citizens and established herself as "a brilliant scholar." She also showed a natural gift for music. "Her voice was lovely, and people predicted that when it was trained a great future lay before her," a schoolmate wrote years later.[22]

Still, a grim thought intruded. Her father, in the stern tradition of Old World parents, had promised her hand in marriage to a friend his age. Anna loathed the prospect, but obedience was expected. Norwegian immigrants generally opposed "blending," resisted "mixed marriages," demanded their children retain the language, and especially emphasized Sabbath worship in a Lutheran church. Lutheran ministers made it clear from the pulpit that they frowned on sending children to the fast-developing American public school system, urging instead attendance at parochial schools. American children, they warned, were "wild animals" and behaved "much worse than the children of . . . the fatherland."[23]

Reluctantly preparing to leave, Lars had warned Anna that she must be pious, pure, and submissive.[24] Lately she had been defiant, refusing to attend either church or Sunday school. She even refused to pray. This behavior worried Lars. He was unaware that Anna had had "an unfortunate experience with a so-called Christian," as Anna's daughter wrote much later about something mysterious that had turned Anna against religion in general.[25] The man had been "outwardly a church pillar, inwardly mean. She had seen this person behave cruelly to defenseless dependents who had no means of retaliation. She herself had been subjected to his petty tyranny," Anna's daughter concluded enigmatically. She did not go into the exact nature of the abuse—whether it was "tyranny" or a worse sexual exploitation—but whatever happened undoubtedly influenced Anna's subsequent behavior.

The summons to Minnesota arrived as Anna flourished at Dearborn, barely a year after her father and half brother had departed. Edward, seventeen, lacking Anna's exciting prospects, had left willingly to seek a better life than what he could find in Chicago. But he was not able to manage the care of his rapidly sickening father alone. Their sister, Rachel, was married to a ship's carpenter and beginning a family, so, painful as it was, the duty fell to Anna. It was a wrench to leave school, but she had no choice. At least, she thought, she might escape her aged suitor.

In the fall of 1856, Anna found herself sharing a tiny log cabin in a wilderness where the next neighbor was seven miles away. Instead of studies, friends, and music, she toiled in the backbreaking work of a frontier woman: cooking, canning, churning, mending, washing, and ironing. Such crops as her father and half brother had been able to plant in the spring had to be harvested, the cow had to be milked, and the chickens had to be tended. She loathed the brutal work and came to hate the very sound of the Norwegian language.

Then winter came. The two stoic children had early learned the necessity for self-reliance; however, no new homesteader was ever prepared for the ferocious blizzards that blanketed Minnesota until late spring. As one man who lived through many winters in Wanamingo remembered: "The silence of death rests on the vast landscape, save when it is swept by cruel winds that search out every chink and cranny . . . Neighborly calls are infrequent because of the long distances which separate farm houses . . . An alarming amount of insanity occurs in the new prairie states among farmers and their wives." Another wrote about the "crying spells" that wives and daughters were subject to.[26]

The winter of 1856–57 turned out to be the worst in fourteen years.[27] Temperatures regularly plummeted into double digits below zero as arctic air and blistering winds raked the area. No visitors came. Wolves howled near the cabin. For food all Edward could do was shoot an occasional deer. Anna had heard stories of Indian massacres, and while such dangers were exaggerated, the silence and isolation lent them credence. As a child, she had been frightened by Norwegian tales a caretaker had told her of demons and ghosts poised to destroy her, and now these satanic creatures seemed to hover just outside the stranded cabin. It was a long, harrowing, and lonely winter, and all the while Anna's father weakened. His anxious children did their best to make him comfortable, but as the first new buds of spring finally appeared, Lars died.

Neighbors came from miles around to help them make a coffin. Edward stained it, and Anna lined and padded it with straw covered with a white linen sheet. The remorseless cold continued into late April, so there were no flowers. Instead, they collected fragrant branches of fir and laurel and wove wreaths for their father's grave.[28] They buried him a short distance from their cabin on a treeless height overlooking woods along the banks of the Zumbro River.

Now Anna could think only of returning to Chicago. She waited impatiently for the frozen river to reopen to traffic, but it was not until May 1 that the first boat through Lake Pepin finally docked in St. Paul— the latest date for the river to open that had ever been recorded.[29] She was determined never to suffer through such an experience again. She was fond of her half brother, but life in a frontier cabin was not for her. Besides, her father had deeded the property solely to Edward, who would register it with the census taker later that year.[30] Therefore, when Anna heard that a Norwegian pastor was in the area and intended to drive to Red Wing, where she could catch the ferryboat to La Crosse or Prairie du Chien and from there take the train to Chicago, she eagerly sent a message asking to accompany him.

Brother and sister were quiet as they drove to the farm where the pastor was staying. Unspoken between them was a sense that this parting might be final. Nothing, Anna vowed to herself, would ever bring her back to this forsaken wilderness. Yet when Edward wheeled the wagon around to go home, she ran beside it and tears flowed down her cheeks. Edward bade her turn back. "Goodbye!" she gasped breathlessly, and that was the last Edward and Anna saw of each other. She walked slowly to the farmstead, where the minister was waiting.

Although she had understood that the preacher would leave for Red Wing immediately after he held a service, she found that the farm was packed with Norwegians eager to shake off winter isolation and have a festive gathering. As it had been nearly impossible to travel in the winter, the minister's presence suddenly made long-delayed marriages, baptisms, and a celebration of Holy Communion possible and the excuse for a grand occasion. Men and women carried food to long tables from laden wagons. Gossip and news of deaths and births were exchanged. The excitement was enormous. But for Anna this was a time of sorrow. She felt a deep aversion to being encased again in the Norwegian language, Norwegian customs, Norwegian piety. She wanted to leave, to be back in Chicago with her sophisticated classmates at Dearborn Academy. But here these immigrants from Norway seemed unable to think or talk about anything but God's presence and their Lutheran faith.

Nothing had changed in her disdain for religion, so Anna was crushed to discover that the pastor was lingering on in the area in order to baptize some hundred babies born over the winter. It meant at least another week at the farm, as it was too late to return to Edward in Wanamingo. Frustrated, she watched as the preacher drove off with the last of the guests, and as night closed over the prairie, she joined the farmer and his wife in the farmhouse's single cavernous room, where the couple apparently cooked, worked, and slept. The husband lit a lamp, then leered at Anna. With a shock, Anna realized that his wife was blind. Mercifully, however, the woman immediately climbed a rickety stepladder, leading Anna to a small, dirty attic with a pile of straw in the corner. Exhausted, Anna lay down and immediately fell asleep.

She must have been sleeping for several hours when she felt something or someone pawing at her face. She could see nothing. Rigid with fear, not daring to scream, she lay motionless. It was not an animal, she realized, as the creature was mumbling in incoherent Norwegian. After several minutes, it shuffled away into another corner, and Anna could breathe again. She sensed it settling down and eventually heard loud snoring. Wide awake and miserable, Anna found herself praying. "O God," she cried softly to herself, "deliver me, and I will never be discontented again."[31]

When Anna opened her eyes the next morning, she saw a young woman lying across the dimly lit attic. Filthy, disheveled, and still asleep, the girl seemed more animal than human. Terrified that she would wake her, Anna crept downstairs, where the farmer and his wife were eating breakfast. Shortly afterward the strange creature lumbered down to join them, gulped a bowl of porridge, then ran into the woods, where she stayed until evening. As if she owed no special explanation, the farmer's wife casually mentioned that the girl was their daughter.

The thought of another night in the attic was nearly unendurable. Yet all day the farmer continued to make suggestive gestures under the vacant eyes of his wife. Avoiding him fearfully, Anna knew she could not stay downstairs. That evening as she curled up again in her corner, the girl returned. Anna whispered soothingly to her, and to her surprise the poor soul responded gratefully. The girl was not dangerous after all, only feebleminded or insane, and as the endless days wore on, Anna sought to win her trust. By the time the pastor finally returned to collect her, there was affection in the girl's wild eyes. When Anna left, her pitiful companion croaked a mournful and inarticulate goodbye.

Later, Anna would remember the year in Minnesota as her "Gehenna," a time when she surmounted despair and survived.[32]

Returning at last to Chicago, Anna embraced the city and all it represented as if it were a reprieve from Hades itself. Mercifully, her suitor had married someone else and she was free. With help from Mrs. Ely, and by earning money as a part-time waitress, she reentered Dearborn Academy.[33] Strong, determined, mature beyond her years, Anna resolved to seize what other good opportunities might fall her way. She took up schoolwork with a vengeance—and excelled. She worked hard at her music lessons, and equally hard at consolidating the friendships she recognized were useful if she did not want to slip back into an immigrant's existence. It was not yet clear what lay ahead for her, but she was confident that she could shape that future along lines far removed from the backbreaking life of the frontier.

When her friend Jenny Simpson suggested she accompany her to Sunday school, Anna emphatically turned her down. She had no interest, she said, in getting involved with a church.

"Come just once and see," urged Jenny. "Our Sunday school teacher is different. He doesn't talk down to us. He gives us a chance to express our opinions, and he loves an argument. Annie," Jenny said, "it will do you good to hear Mr. Spafford."[34]

CHAPTER THREE

Spafford

*Oh Christian! time, time is passing away! op-
portunities are going, will soon be gone! We
shall soon be at the bar of God. The Christian
who means to do all he can, will say—"what
can I do this week—this day—this hour?" This
is the genius of earnestness. Are there any sick to
be visited? Are there any poor to be relieved? . . . Delay not to speak a word of encouragement—direct that soul to Christ . . .
"Whatsoever thy hand findeth to do, do it with
thy might."*

—From a Congregationalist tract, 1853

In 1856, the year Anna went to Minnesota, a twenty-eight-year-old lawyer had arrived in Chicago from Troy, New York, to seek his destiny. Horatio Gates Spafford was shy, intellectually inclined, deeply devout, and interested in public policy. A member of the Republican Party, he was attracted to this vibrant metropolis-in-the-making, which by mid-century had a population of eighty thousand, was growing and prospering by the hour, and was experiencing one of its periodic religious revivals. It was just the place for a man like Spafford. Like so many others who believed that the nation's soul was in jeopardy, he was dismayed by the problems of a rapidly growing industrial society. Something, he felt, must be done quickly about illiteracy, overcrowding, and especially the "wicked" customs—such as card playing, drinking, and ignoring the Sabbath—that the immigrants, who composed over half of Chicago's population, were bringing with them to the city. Horatio had attended some of the revivals that had swept the Burned-Over District. Now, in Chicago, he believed that the reforms he sought to remedy the city's problems could only occur through renewed Christian faith. He wanted to be a soldier in a vibrant Christian militancy. And so he hung out his shingle as an attorney, looked for a Presbyterian church to join, plunged into politics, and connected with a group who wanted to open a Young Men's Christian Association in midtown.

Chicago thrived on making money, and no institution better reflected the confluence of business and evangelical objectives than the YMCA, a fact demonstrated in Boston when young businessmen had founded the first YMCA in America four years earlier. Chicago's young leaders who followed suit were connected to evangelical churches winning American Protestants by the thousands. This new YMCA was up and running by 1858, and immediately assumed an important role in the life of the city. Its purpose was to provide a social organization offering meeting rooms, a library, public lectures, and "literary classes" to attract promising and lonely young men newly arrived in town and provide them with "good Christian influences." The founders tended to be rather vague on theological positions but strong on personal earnestness, piety, and especially diligence in the pursuit of business opportunity. In every way, their YMCA promoted the values dear to the evangelical's heart: individualism, religious enthusiasm, social activism, and above all an unabashed admiration for the American cult of success that was not in the least incompatible, in their view, with good Christian living.

For Horatio Spafford, these were congenial goals. Moreover, participation in the YMCA linked him to Chicago's business community, to the wealthy merchants, leaders of society, and growing numbers of industrialists whose stately mansions lined Michigan and Wabash avenues. Horatio lost no time diving into politics, swiftly gaining a reputation as an up-and-coming figure. "On last Saturday the Republicans of Laporte, Indiana, had a rousing meeting. Bonfires were lit and the greatest enthusiasm prevailed. The principal speaker was H. G. Spafford of Chicago, who made a telling and able address," observed the *Chicago Tribune* on September 3, 1856.[1]

It was at the YMCA that Horatio met an extraordinary young man who, for a critical period, would exert an enormous influence over him. Dwight Lyman Moody, a poor shoe salesman from Northfield, Massachusetts, was only nineteen when he had stepped off the train from New England in the same year that Spafford arrived from Troy. Like Spafford, he envisioned a career and even a personal fortune in Chicago's vibrant melting pot. While he was dismayed to see stores open on the Sabbath— a custom "enough to sicken anyone"—he was impressed with the abundant evidence of prosperity, noting admiringly that the city had "about the nicest dwelling places I ever see."[2] Unlike Spafford with his law degree, Moody was minimally educated and never managed a firm grasp on the King's English. It would always be part of his charm. To both these men, who soon became friends, the business of moneymaking and the business of religion were intertwined and equally important. It made perfect sense that the YMCA became the center of their social lives.

While Moody made friends easily with his bumptious, warm, and unaffected manners, Spafford was more reserved and was treated with careful respect. A tall handsome man with an arching, patrician nose, thick dark hair, and deep-set eyes, he was quite nearsighted but vain enough to avoid being caught wearing spectacles. Romantically inclined and idealistic, he loved literature, music, and especially poetry, and did not share the anti-intellectualism of many evangelists. Moody, on the other hand, never considered the possession of books important. He "abhorred" novels as "trashy" and paid little or no attention to scientific and historical developments. "I have one rule about books," he said. "I do not read any book unless it will help me to understand *the* book."[3] Short, stocky, with full lips and a short curly beard, Moody had an open and kindly face. Possessed of a phenomenal memory for names and a flair for anecdote as he strategized to win converts, he had the instincts of a natural orator and would be likened to his flamboyant contemporary P. T. Barnum. He soon earned the sobriquet "Crazy Moody," as he thought nothing of crashing newspaper offices to tell the editors about his success in recruiting urchins off the street, feeding and clothing them, and winning them for Jesus in his Sunday school.[4]

Sunday schools were key. The evangelicals agreed that it was essential to Christianize the hordes of immigrants daily entering the city, and thus co-opt the rowdier elements. "We consider the Sabbath school as the only hope for city heathenism. The church has no other means by which she can enlighten its darkness or penetrate its interior," as one leader put it. It was a barely concealed method of social control, particularly aimed at the young. On August 27, 1856, the *Northwestern Christian Advocate* urged: "Let Sunday schools be sustained, and let the children of foreigners be looked up and sent to school, if we wish well to our country."[5]

This was a summons to which Spafford and Moody responded enthusiastically, and both devoted their Sundays to teaching the Bible. Spafford was a Presbyterian, while his friend Moody, previously a Congregationalist, joined the Methodists, whose bent, he felt, was more evangelical. What mattered for both men was belonging to a church committed to Christian activism and outreach. Encouraged by the YMCA and especially by its noon prayer meetings, they answered the call to teach and to exhort.

Although desire for a humane society was part and parcel of evangelical thinking at this time—at least until the fractious divisions of the late nineteenth and early twentieth century divided Protestantism into fundamentalist and liberal camps—evangelicals looked to social improvement through individual conversion. Although they generally deplored slavery, and advocated temperance, prison reform, and rights for women, the evangelist agenda at this time stressed personal moral reform coupled with hard work, rather than an analysis or a coming to grips with the underlying causes or deep-seated institutional problems that plagued the day. "Shun speculative piety," one evangelical preacher urged in 1869. "Meditate, but meditate in order that you may do . . . Be diligent in Business. This will help you to be fervent in Spirit and better to serve the Lord."[6] This was the theme of the daily YMCA noon prayer meetings and the Sunday schools that both new friends regularly attended. At the same time, they sought to take what advantage they could of the seemingly unstoppable economic boom.

By 1856 land speculation had reached a fever pitch, and both Spafford and Moody were eager investors. As an attorney, Spafford was making a good income, so for him property investment was easy; Moody saved his earnings, loaned small amounts to new acquaintances at usurious rates—as was the prevailing custom—and bought land when he could. A brief crash, known as the Panic of 1857, when the Ohio Life Insurance and Trust Company of New York suspended payment and forced its creditors to default, caused financial entities throughout the country to fail and banks to call their loans. It sobered both men, as it did the nation, but not for long. As the speculative rush became an irresistible force in both their lives, Horatio had an important encounter.

It was on a Sunday afternoon in his Presbyterian class, some time after Anna's return from Minnesota, that Horatio watched a slender young woman enter his classroom with one of his students, Jenny Simpson. Instantly, he was struck by her beauty, the steady gaze of her remarkable blue eyes, and an apparently guileless and detached attitude. She was tall and wore her golden hair in a crown of braids around her head. Right away, he understood she must be a Scandinavian immigrant, and he was fascinated.

To Horatio's disappointment, however, Anna did not return to his class the next week, or the week after. He found himself thinking about her, and reviewed the surprise he had felt over some searching comments she had volunteered. He was intrigued that she seemed to have no interest in church matters. Clearly she was both bright and thoughtful. He had no idea how old she was and certainly did not guess that she was a mere fifteen. Finally, when it was evident that she was not going to return, he inquired about her and found that she was living with her sister. He decided to pay a call on Mr. and Mrs. Charles Frederickson. Soon it became one of many visits, and Anna, flattered and pleased by the attention from the attractive lawyer, looked forward to them. She responded to the conversations they had about poetry, about the evils of slavery, and especially about music. She was interested but still far from convinced when he casually raised the subject of getting oneself right with God. Religion, apparently, had little allure for the striking immigrant.

Anna approved, however, of Horatio's gentle demeanor and was touched by the shyness she detected under his formal good manners. He continued to call on her and after a time told her of his background. He was a direct descendant, he confided, of a certain Gamelbar de Spof-forth, mentioned in the Domesday Book. He explained that his deceased father had been a man of broad interests ranging from history to horti-culture and his enthusiasm for history had prompted him to write an early gazetteer of New York. Horatio also had two cousins who were gov-ernors of Idaho and Nevada. His grandfather Colonel John Spafford had played a minor but heroic role in the American Revolution.[7] She could not help being impressed, and while he was aware that she worked as a waitress, he seemed unaffected by any sense of class difference. However, he was much older, and to Anna their backgrounds seemed a yawning gulf too wide to bridge.

Still, after a year of such visits, a day came when Anna found herself dressing with particular care. Her sister, Rachel, teased her, but cooper-ated by baking a cake and brought a tea tray to the parlor.[8] Horatio, however, did not show up. The evening wore on, and still Anna waited. Finally, Rachel put away the refreshments and withdrew for the night. Anna sat alone, listening carefully for footsteps, convinced that he would come. Just as she, too, had decided that she might as well go to bed, there was a faint knocking at the door. Horatio stood on the porch, grin-ning shyly.

"Would you mind," he asked, "coming for a little walk?" Unable to decide if she was more annoyed or elated by his late arrival, Anna threw a shawl around her shoulders and stepped into the evening air. They strolled for several blocks together, but Horatio remained silent until they had turned back and were close again to the house. Suddenly he blurted out: "Would you consider taking a trip with me to Patagonia?"

Anna looked up at him, assuming this was an announcement that he was intending to go to South America as a missionary. The idea ap-palled her, yet she replied softly, "I will go anywhere with you."

"So you love me, Anna?"

She stared at his face, waiting. "Will you be my wife?" he asked.

"Yes," she replied.[9]

Although Rachel Frederickson liked Horatio, she had some reserva-tions about a union between her sister and the older lawyer. Anna was too young. She had not finished her schooling. Rachel also felt that it was her responsibility to keep her sister within the tight Norwegian community. She was well aware that her clever younger sibling had enjoyed opportunities no one else in the family had been offered, and she did not want them thrown lightly away. But Anna knew her own mind. A future with Horatio would confer status and security, and she made it clear that she was determined to marry her eligible, well-to-do suitor. A family discussion followed. Horatio, astonished to discover that Anna was only sixteen, resolved the issue by offering to pay for her completed education if she were to attend the Young Ladies' Seminary at Ferry Hall, a select boarding school north of the city in fashionable Lake Forest.[10] He would wait for her, he promised.

"I wish you were acquainted with Mr. Spafford," Anna wrote Sarah Ely on December 6, 1860. "He is a respectable and noble man. I owe him a great deal, but I will not get married out of gratitude. I have often wondered what he sees in someone like me, because I am so plain and ignorant, while he is so strong and knowledgeable. I pray to God that I will be worthy of him," she added with becoming modesty. "It is strange to think back to when I lived with you as a little girl. How little I ever thought about what might happen in the future."[11]

Anna had chosen well, but so had Horatio. His lovely blond wife-to-be with her dazzling smile, beautiful white teeth, and dainty ears "had a merry, kind, and affectionate disposition that won the hearts of many people," as a friend wrote later, noting that "she could be mischievous too, with a keen sense of humor."[12] Anna applauded his ambitions and rejoiced in his triumphs, both professional and speculative. In 1859 the faculty of Lind University made Spafford their professor of medical jurisprudence.[13] He brought her with him to rallies in support of Abraham Lincoln's candidacy and confided in her about some exciting land deals he had invested in.

By 1860 Moody had quit the shoe business to devote himself entirely to evangelism. His aggressive tactics—preaching in the red-light district, plunging into saloons and brothels, and even barging inside miserable shanties to demand that their astonished occupants accept Jesus—were criticized at first by fellow evangelicals. Yet his sincerity, gusto, and commitment, and his evident concern for the welfare of the city's neglected, steadily won over his critics. Horatio was one of Moody's greatest admirers. This was the sort of Christian militancy that Horatio believed necessary to solve the nation's problems. Soon Moody's school for poor children was the second largest in the city, packed with noisy and intensely loyal followers from the poorest districts, and Moody was no longer ridiculed as "Crazy Moody."

Horatio was not the only one to admire the hard-driving missionary for an "earnestness so great and a personal appeal so forcible that everyone felt Moody was talking to him alone."[14] When Moody declared that he wished to dedicate himself solely to God's work, Horatio was glad to join in an illustrious company that included such prominent YMCA members as Philip Armour, the meatpacking magnate; Cyrus H. McCormick, the reaper king; John V. Farwell, who made a fortune in dry goods and real estate; Joseph Medill, publisher of the *Chicago Tribune*; and Victor Lawson, soon to be publisher of the *Chicago Daily News*—all of whom undertook to guarantee the young evangelist financial support. When his budget fell short, Moody had no qualms about letting them pick up the slack.

At the YMCA, Horatio listened with the others to Moody outline his evangelical strategies that fit so neatly with the aims of a business community concerned with maintaining social stability. To the end of his life businessmen would be Moody's closest friends and most ardent supporters. These relationships would, in due course, make it difficult for him to criticize the inclination of big business to exploit the poor, and as Moody's career blossomed, he would forge an alliance with the very newspaper publishers who had once mocked him. The nineteenth-century tycoons who later competed to finance his spectacular revivals would trumpet his success in bringing millions of dollars into the coffers of their cities as millions of people came to know the warmhearted evangelist as the "best-loved man in America."

To Chicago's evangelically inclined businessmen, making as much money as possible was an absolute good. Monetary success was a sign of diligence, not of corruption, and had God's approval. Neither Horatio nor any of the others meeting regularly at the YMCA had any difficulty with the notion that a good Christian was a steward of his money and should use it beneficially. For them, the worst sin was laziness. As Moody explained: "There is no hope for a man's reformation who does not go to work. Laziness belongs to the old creation. I don't know what to do, and I don't see what God can do, with a lazy man."[15] No other ethos could have been more in tune with a vibrant America powering and prospering itself into its Gilded Age. The idea prevailed that piety revealed itself "by its fruits." Inevitably, "justification by works" was becoming the standard by which not just evangelicals lived but the country as a whole. This was a change from the old Calvinist determinism of earlier Protestants—the belief that God had selected an elect to be saved and no amount of good works could alter the fate of those not included among the chosen.

With the entrepreneurial instincts they all shared, Moody welcomed investment tips from his rich supporters. And so it happened that the ambitious young preacher joined his ambitious friend Horatio, the city's wealthiest grandees, and countless eager others in land speculations that each and every one was convinced could only redound in magnificently swollen portfolios. And in fact, there is little doubt that this would have been the case, if only, somehow, an extraordinary event could have been averted.

Finally, after three long years of waiting, Anna and Horatio were married on September 5, 1861, in the recently built Second Presbyterian Church on the city's South Side. The Civil War had begun, and Union forces were not doing well. In July, the Confederates had smashed the Union at the first Battle of Bull Run, and again in August, at the Battle of Wilson's Creek in Missouri. It would have been unthinkable to have a large wedding, so they invited very few friends, sending announcements to the rest. Anna wore a wedding gown she had created herself, thriftily designing it so that it could be useful in her wardrobe afterward. A dark blue taffeta frock with a hooped skirt showed off her slim waist, and a matching bonnet trimmed with pink roses and shirred pink chiffon covered her blond hair. When the bridal couple arrived at the church, they were surprised and touched to see that it had been decorated with white flowers and packed with smiling people. Although a few matrons whispered that it was a pity to waste Horatio on an immigrant girl who had once been a waitress and whose family had no standing in the city, most welcomed her as Horatio's bride.[16]

Afterward, the newly married pair drove straight to a new house they had rented in Lake View. Five and a half miles north of the city limits, bounded by Lincoln Park on the south, Lake View was a beautiful township in the midst of what was still farmland where handsome houses had been set on rolling lawns. Already it was stamped as the right place for Chicago's more prosperous citizens anxious for clean air and magnificent views of the lake. Their new home was adorned with Victorian fretwork and shaded by enormous trees. Three years later, Horatio felt himself in a position to buy it, paying $3,000 with a mortgage of $2,500 at 7 percent interest. It was a shrewd purchase. A local author writing an overview of Chicago and its suburban real estate ten years later cited the Spafford house as "one of the most attractive spots in Lake View" and gave its value at $75,000.[17]

Soon their home became the center of musical gatherings and earnest religious discussions. Four daughters were born in this pleasant suburb. Horatio traveled daily to his office in the city on a newly built commuter rail line, frequently bringing home friends for dinner and to spend the night. As there was no such thing as a telephone to warn her, Anna refused to be surprised and, aided by three servants and a houseboy, kept her larder well provisioned. Less than a decade and a half later, the vine-covered house would gain a reputation as the hub of a new religion. But by that time the Spaffords had found compelling reasons to see heaven and hell through a rather special light of their own.

CHAPTER FOUR

Thrilling Ideas

*I believe with perfect faith in the coming of the
Messiah, and though he tarry, I will wait daily
for his coming.*

—The Twelfth of Maimonides's
Thirteen Principles of Faith

The 1860s was a defining decade for America. By its end, a
Gilded Age was under way that made abundantly clear to Europe
just how powerful America had become. The terrible Civil War fought
between 1861 and 1865 saw slavery abolished and spelled the downfall
of the aristocratic planter life of the South. Now there was a new economic order dominated by big business and big government.[1] Fought by
three million Americans, the war saw more than 600,000 die—2 percent
of the population—including President Abraham Lincoln, assassinated
on Good Friday, April 14, 1865. As the awesome struggle concluded, the
South was poor and the North was very, very rich. Not least among the
cities that had profited was the dynamic metropolis of 300,000 souls on
Lake Michigan's windy and mud-covered southwestern tip.

All through the war, Spafford, Moody, and countless others had contributed to relief efforts for the Northern army. Spafford, by then a partner in the prominent firm of Spafford, McDaid, and Wilson, helped
found the Christian Commission. An instrument of the YMCA, and
dedicated to Christianizing the nation, the commission sent agents like
Dwight Moody to battlefield areas to exhort the troops to "reconstitute"
their souls while distributing cheap Bibles and religious tracts printed in

the hundreds of thousands by the YMCA. His work with the commission put Moody in touch with a larger venue, and the business leaders and newspaper publishers he met around the nation later funded and publicized his spectacular revivals in the next decade.

Anna joined Chicago's wives in feverish relief work of their own at the U.S. Sanitary Commission, which gathered women from seven thousand local auxiliaries to raise money for camp inspectors and medical care. A hugely successful fund-raiser was organized that brought in over $100,000, and to which Lincoln himself had contributed his personal copy of the Emancipation Proclamation. "I had some desire to retain the paper," the president told the commission, "but if it shall contribute to the relief and comfort of the soldiers, that will be better."[2]

After the blood-drenched pastures reverted once more to working farms, life in Chicago resumed a more normal pace. One after the other, three daughters were born to Anna and Horatio: Annie in 1862; a year later, Maggie; and then little Elizabeth, called Bessie, who arrived in 1866. Often at Lake View, the Spaffords entertained men whose dreams were big. It was a matter of pride to Anna that her husband was so highly regarded by these evangelical visionaries and that her house had become a comfortable center for them to congregate. She poured tea and tried to listen—although, privately, theological passion still eluded her. Her children, home, and friends were her true religion. Benignly, like the good hostess she was, she beamed and patiently refilled cups as her guests urgently discussed the goals, tactics, and doctrine necessary for winning the nation to Christ.

To these architects of evangelism, it was clear by now that Moody, young as he was, was their leader. Horatio, reveling in these exchanges, was among the first to recognize that his friend's singular energy and organizing skills made him the man the growing movement needed. Horatio applauded with the rest of the listening circle when Moody emphasized the need for interdenominational cooperation. "We need lay preachers like all of you," Moody said as his eyes burned with enthusiasm. "God calls each and every one of us to preach His word."

Not one of these gentlemen had ever passed through the portals of a theological seminary, but that did not dampen their ardor for devising a theology of their own. They were devouring evangelical periodicals and drinking thirstily of current trends—in particular an appealing doctrine drawn from the work of a seventeenth-century Dutch divine, James Arminius. Arminianism challenged the predestination of traditional Calvinism and by mid-century had seeped into the fabric of Protestantism.[3] Salvation, according to Arminius, was available to all, not merely to an elect chosen by God. These evangelicals believed that any man could save himself through the exercise of his free will. When a man repented his sinful ways and let the Holy Spirit enter his heart, redemption would follow. Moody called this consoling and inclusive message "the Glad Tidings." It freed believers from the fearful notion that they might not be among the elect and was welcomed by those seeking an emotional outlet within a buttoned-up culture in which Puritan constraints still whispered reproving messages.

Like many other American evangelists, Horatio, Moody, and their evangelical fellows were inheritors of postmillennialism, which anticipated the millennium as a result of the good works of Christians the world over, to be followed by the Last Judgment and blessed by the second appearance of Christ on earth. This cheerful vision had long been the prevailing view, and fit beautifully with the unshakable American faith in endless improvement and limitless possibilities, and dated from late colonial days. Mankind was surging upward toward "the long-awaited kingdom of the spirit." A previous generation of preachers had spurred this eschatology during the Second Great Awakening, urging a "quickening" in the settled eastern churches and bringing a "muscular Christianity" to the unchurched of the western frontier.[4]

The evangelical fraternity had grown up with postmillennialism. Adding the anti-determinist Arminianism to the mix suited Horatio and Moody. In the meantime, they had become intrigued with news from England that a vigorous debate was under way over whether or not the Church of England should be shorn of the ecclesiastical and liturgical ornamentations that were "corrupting" it and be returned to its original simplicity. Accompanying these recommendations were ominous predictions of the imminent bodily return of Christ, who would bring down a fiery destruction upon sinners before God rendered the Last Judgment.[5] To Horatio and Moody working over their Bibles, these preachments were irresistible—and inevitably both men wanted to travel to England to see for themselves what the excitement was all about. In 1870, confident that his wife and daughters were well taken care of, pleased with his flourishing law practice, and wishing to attend to several business affairs in London, Horatio decided that the time was ripe for an investigation and departed for a four-month stay.

No sooner had he set foot in London than he encountered the full blast of the doctrinal debates raging around John Nelson Darby. A lean, shabbily dressed, wild-haired Irishman, Darby had trained in law but after an intense religious experience sought ordination in the Anglican communion. He was the leader of a bold reform movement called the Plymouth Brethren that was turning the English church on its head. In every conversation with fellow evangelicals, it seemed, Horatio was told of Darby's railings against the Anglicans for their inclination to "popish" ritual and liturgical "trappings." His demand that the Church of England return to its apostolic origins was provoking anxious introspection among Protestants, and even the Catholic faithful were affected.

This was a time when burgeoning British industrialism, allied with scientific advances, threatened many time-honored assumptions, and Darby was not alone in condemning those segments of society that toyed with the heretical views offered by a scientist named Charles Darwin. Darby's was one of the loudest voices insisting that faith prevail over reason. All knowledge came from the Bible, the fiery-eyed preacher thundered to his rapt listeners. Reprovingly, he repeated that the Bible was "inerrant." It was the only and single source of all truths.

A powerful preacher, despite an absence of rigorous theological training, whose "fallen cheek, bloodshot eye . . . seldom shaven beard" never ceased to awe admirers and critics alike, Darby had found God while recuperating from a riding accident. In Plymouth, England, he had gathered around him others willing to believe that conversion came through "ecstatic experience." Roving the country, exhorting in London and on the Continent, "the will of God seldom blurred before his vision," Darby encouraged his congregation into eruptions of pentecostal gibberish and physical contortions.[6] He offered them a radical, pessimistic, yet peculiarly seductive doctrine that he termed "dispensational premillennialism." His voice trumpeting from his pulpit, Darby inveighed against a world already in the last and final "dispensation."

Mankind, he warned, was corrupt, vice-ridden, and vulnerable to the machinations of a deceitful Antichrist. "Prepare yourselves!" Darby would thunder, predicting that at any moment unbelievers would be beset by a seven-year tribulation of writhing torment. If the Jews did not embrace Jesus, they would be burned with other apostates in the fires of hell while the returning Christ would snatch the repentant "up in the clouds" in a glorious "Rapture." God would then defeat Satan in the Battle of Armageddon and establish a kingdom on earth. Few listening to Darby's terrifying fulminations did not fervently hope that they would be among the snatched-up blessed whose hats, shoes, and satchels would scatter as they soared to heaven in their Savior's arms. Although Darby's massive writings were "almost uniformly unintelligible,"[7] his fevered message nonetheless captivated many seekers, and soon dispensational premillennialism swept from England to America, where it was to have a far more lasting impact.[8]

To Horatio's impressionable ear, Darby's emphasis on the biblical prophecies, on the Book of Revelation as a source for his theories, and particularly on the belief that the Jews must be returned to Zion in order to speed the millennium seemed as timely as it did to the growing ranks of Darby's Plymouth Brethren. Horatio was well versed in the calls of Old Testament prophets for the Jews to return to their ancient homeland in Palestine; they must rebuild the temple destroyed by Titus in A.D. 70, which in turn, according to Darby, would spark a chain of events ultimately culminating in the apocalypse.[9] This vision, however, required that Jews be converted to Christianity as Saint Paul had foretold in the New Testament. At least in the eyes of scattered Orthodox Jewry—who desired the return as ardently as their Christian advocates—this was not only preposterous but anathema. But their opinion on the matter was not invited.

Spafford heard a similar theme from still another quarter. No self-respecting evangelical visiting from America could miss the flurry of discussion surrounding the dignified figure of Anthony Ashley Cooper, 7th Earl of Shaftesbury. This marble-faced peer, whose views cast a long shadow over Victorian England's notions of rectitude, had been entreated for decades by both Whigs and Conservatives to join their cabinets. Instead, Shaftesbury, whose "every separate dark lock of hair seemed to curl from a sense of duty," remained steadfastly aloof from party affiliation, devoting his energies to succoring the poor and the downtrodden of industrial England.[10] Appalled by the plight of children and women pulling coal carts deep in mines, sympathetic to lunatics chained and raving in filthy asylums, indignant at the squalor that turned boys into thieves, he was responsible for driving through a number of reform acts that paved the way for eventual government regulations.[11] But Shaftesbury was also a biblical literalist who despised the dangerous new Darwinism as vehemently as Darby, and of all the causes that he championed, summoning "God's ancient people" to England to be converted to Christianity and then restored to Zion was almost a mania.

As it happened, Shaftesbury's obsession fit neatly with British foreign policy, and he had the sympathetic ear of his stepfather-in-law, Lord Palmerston. The shapers of the vast British Empire on which the sun never set became convinced that Palestine was better off in friendly hands lest the French, Germans, or, heaven forbid, the Russians slip in ahead to impose their influence on a vulnerable Turkish sultan and obstruct the route to India. There were many, therefore, who supported Shaftesbury's dream even if it was for less pious reasons, and increasingly the notion of helping Jews settle in Palestine became a focus of both religious and secular conversations.

As for Horatio, he was thrilled with the idea of a Hebrew return. Slowly, it became paramount in his eschatology. Stimulated and energized by his exposure to these various ideas, he traveled to Edinburgh to hear yet another noteworthy voice in the religious cacophony of the day. Professor Charles Piazza Smith, the astronomer royal for Scotland, was an enthusiastic promoter of the British-Israelite theory—that the Anglo-Saxons are descended from the lost tribes of Israel.[12] Compelling as Horatio found this idea, even more was he attracted to a second theory of the good professor. Dr. Piazza Smith had recently returned from Egypt, where he had labored for months measuring the Great Pyramid of Giza inch by inch and had concluded that it was built by "divine inspiration." Each passage, chamber, and gallery revealed a cryptic message in the Old Testament. Through careful analysis of biblical prophecies coordinated with his astronomical surveys and measurements, he believed that

Christ's return could be predicted with precision. Spafford and Dr. Piazza Smith were introduced; Horatio was dazzled, the astronomer delighted, and the two agreed to stay in touch. Before Horatio returned to Chicago, he had obtained Dr. Piazza Smith's promise that when he had divined the exact year of the anticipated cataclysm, he would let Horatio know immediately.

During this same post–Civil War period, Dwight Moody also traveled to England, where he, too, was drawn into the scintillating exchanges stirring British evangelical circles. Eager to explore developments, he tested the waters for a future evangelical tour. Efficient and forceful, he promptly established his headquarters at the London YMCA, introduced the noon prayer meetings that had been such a useful recruiting tool in Chicago, and quickly found his ambitions fulfilled as a wildly successful guest attraction at evangelical gatherings. As had become his pattern, he lost no time connecting with the business and newspaper leaders whose support he would need for what he wanted to be—and which became—a triumphal tour of the British Isles that would win the admiration of the Protestant world.

The thirty-year-old evangelist was a breath of fresh air to the British who came in droves to hear his "heartfelt testimony" and enjoyed his high-spirited emotionalism, which contrasted so happily with their own restrained British style.[13] While Moody might wave his arms, shout, and frequently weep as he exhorted sinners to repent and open themselves to "the inrush of the Holy Spirit," his sermons had a sweetness and revealed a profound concern for his listeners' daily struggles that was different from Darby's fearful messages. Moody liked to give advice. He told instructive tales of prodigal sons, patient mothers, and drunken fathers who had found Jesus and were saved.

A few critics declared themselves "disgusted" by the mixing of social classes at Moody's swollen meetings that brought in tradesmen, washerwomen, and factory workers as readily as ministers and the highborn. Moody was pioneering a new and uniquely American brand of evangelism that was democratic and inclusive. He ignored denominational distinctions as well as social ranking, declaring that he welcomed all: "the backslidden, the intemperate, the skeptical, the rich and the poor, the educated and the uneducated, the wounded and the burdened."[14] A few in the British circles that cared were taken aback, considering it an "impertinence" that Moody would ask a man to confess his sins in public. One observer dismissed his sermons as "extremely diffuse . . . unconnected, rambling and given to repetition."[15] But in general the "round-shouldered, beetle-browed" former shoe salesman from Chicago, who peppered his sermons with "stray Americanisms," gripped them, astonished them, and ultimately endeared himself to them for "his wonderfully simple and winning style."[16]

In his turn, Moody listened to the debates inflaming British clerics and plucked from them whatever appealed. Not analytically disposed or trained in systematic theology, this inspired young orator collected doctrinal bits and pieces, patched them together, and captivated his listeners. Because Moody was unwilling to publish a statement of his beliefs, his audiences (who probably didn't care) and his later biographers (who did) were never clear precisely what his theology was; his contribution was that of a thrilling energizer of the multitude. He gave himself infinite slack to respond to the requirements of any particular audience, and this remained the secret of his power as he brought recruits to God.

Although it seems that Moody may have met John Nelson Darby when he visited the United States in the late 1860s, he apparently found Darby's insistence on predestination and the doctrine of the elect incompatible with his own slowly evolving views. It seems he could not resolve the tensions between God's sovereignty in salvation and man's ability to save himself alone.[17] Ultimately, the two preachers would strongly disagree, and Darby, whose formidable certitude that he and the Plymouth Brethren alone were on the right path, would say of Moody: "That active man at Chicago, lately in England, is deep in the mud" of this lack of understanding.[18] In the end, Moody condemned the Plymouth Brethren's divisive influence on the vast British evangelical community as he himself reached out to Low Church Anglicans, Nonconformists, and High Church Anglicans alike. Nevertheless, Moody had picked up enough of Darby's premillennialist expectations to incorporate some of them in his omnivorous heavenly view. It was Moody, therefore, who brought dispensational premillennialism back to America, where it took root, was assiduously fertilized by enthusiastic adherents, and today has so marvelously blossomed that old-line, traditional churches crouch in the shadow of the mega-churches that preach it to thousands of worshippers under one vast ceiling.

When Moody returned to Chicago, he was a national figure. He was toying with the idea of moving back to Northfield, Massachusetts, his birthplace. Reluctantly, the YMCA let him step down from its presidency in order to pursue the grand work of Christianizing the entire nation. "Mr. Moody is too valuable as an awakener to be shut up in one city . . . His gifts . . . are enough to put him in the very first rank. If he devotes himself to stimulating Christian laymen to work, and if he gives himself to the whole country, we doubt not he will work a revolution," wrote *Advance*, an evangelical publication, in 1870.[19]

CHAPTER FIVE

The Calamity of the Age

> *How doth the city sit solitary, that was full of*
> *people! How is she become a widow! She that*
> *was great among the nations . . . She weepeth*
> *sore in the night, and her tears are on her*
> *cheeks.*
>
> —Lamentations of Jeremiah

Between July and August 1871, Chicago was bone-dry. Only five inches of rain had fallen during the two summer months, and businessmen commented on dust-laden trees as ghostly as shrouds. It had been a busy year for the city's fire crews. More than six hundred fires were reported, many of which started in barns filled with hay and straw. Since 1858, Chicago's fire departments were made up of paid professionals, not volunteers, so vigilant was the city toward the danger represented by huge coal bins, lumberyards, wooden freight trains arriving on twenty-one-rail tracks, seventeen massive grain elevators along the river, stockyards, mills, wooden shops, wooden barges, boats, warehouses with flammable contents, breweries, wooden church steeples, and especially the wooden shanties whose occupants lit their stoves with sawdust leavings. Of the 530 miles of streets, only 70 were paved. The rest were made from pine blocks hewn from the surrounding forests, fitted like bricks into a roadway raised as high as four or five feet. One author likened them to "gigantic andirons supporting a load of well-laid firewood. Once ignited, they would draw like chimneys through the open spaces beneath."[1]

Horatio Spafford and two investment partners had purchased a large tract of land around Wright's Grove in Lincoln Park. For some time now, Horatio had been investing in real estate as well as practicing law. Although he was borrowing to do so, he felt himself in a strong financial position. Counting on the city's continued expansion, he had already acquired some land along the valuable lakeshore, and when the chance to buy this particularly choice parcel in Lincoln Park presented itself, he wished to seize it before anyone else could get his hands on it. Three days before the fire, he had measured off lots for a quick turnover. The next day he left for Indiana to discuss selling some of them to a prospective buyer. Anna was still very weak from the difficult birth of a fourth daughter, Tanetta, and it worried him to leave her. She had reassured him that she would be fine, and urged him to go. Therefore, she was alone with the children and servants at Lake View when the fire started in an impoverished area on Chicago's Southwest Side.

When Mrs. O'Leary's cow kicked over a kerosene lantern early on Sunday night, October 8, 1871, and ignited the hay in the barn, the fire crew was already exhausted from fighting a fire nearby in a small wood-burning factory all through Saturday night. Four blocks had been gutted before the crew, red-eyed and flayed by cinders, considered the fire under control at 3:30 on Sunday morning. They were in no shape to cope with another in the same area. This, combined with a series of calamitous mistakes on the part of signalmen who misread the new fire's direction, and a sixty-mile-an-hour wind blowing from the prairie in the southwest, resulted in a "red snow" of falling cinders north and east that could not be extinguished. Soon the roar was the sound of a thundering waterfall. Twin columns of flame advanced between Jefferson and Canal streets, glowing in rainbow colors. St. Paul's Church caught. "God will put it out," said an old Irish woman standing on the curb, even as moments later the roof collapsed.

Although the fire crews did their best, the searing heat scorched the legs of the horses drawing their mobile steamers close to the blaze. Sleep deprived, they watched their hoses melt. In the end, they were unable to fight the wind, which had become one with the conflagration. One by one, downtown's grand buildings were torched: Potter Palmer's palatial mansard-roofed Palmer House; Tremont House, where Lincoln and

Stephen Douglas had spoken from the balcony in 1858; Cyrus Mc-Cormick's Reaper Works, although the sixty-two-year-old tycoon himself organized the futile effort to save it. The Grand Pacific Hotel, with its beautiful glass dome and marble staircase, had tanks on its roof to release twelve thousand gallons of water at a moment's notice—but the tanks were empty. The post office and customhouse went with all their contents, as well as the handsome Presbyterian church where Horatio and Anna were married. A child, watching in his mother's arms, asked: "Mama, isn't this the Last Day?"[2]

By this time, a wall of flame, fanned by the steady wind, sent fledgling fires into the North Division, where Dwight Moody lived at 132 North State Street. His house was one of the first to go. Earlier, he had conducted a meeting for three thousand at Farwell Hall. Moody closed the meeting, and he and his wife, Emma, hurried home, recognizing that the fire was closing in. A friend took their two small children while Moody packed a baby carriage with household goods. Emma asked a passing stranger to take down a large portrait of her husband by a well-known painter. Moody expostulated: "Take down my picture? That would be a joke. Suppose I meet some friends in the same trouble as ourselves and they say, 'Hullo, Moody, glad you escaped; what's that you have saved and cling to so affectionately?' Wouldn't it be swell to reply, 'Oh, I've got my own portrait.' "[3]

The scene in the streets was a bedlam of lost children, dogs, cats, goats, pigs, and rats. Refugees were buffeted with cinders and debris, sometimes hurled against lampposts by the wind as they raced north and east to the lakeshore to take refuge among crowds standing at the water's edge. Posh houses and magnificent stores stood open. Looters, many of them drunk on whiskey from abandoned saloons, materialized. One thief calmly defied clerks defending a huge dry-goods store. As he loaded piles of silks into a store truck, a clerk drew his revolver. "Shoot and be damned," said the thief, and pulled the cart away.[4]

In the meantime, Anna Spafford stood on her porch in Lake View, staring at the orange inferno raging to the south. The noise of explosions had kept her awake all night. The new baby, Tanetta, had cried often to be fed, and she was exhausted as well as anxious. As the night progressed, she was grateful that she and her daughters were well beyond the trees of

Lincoln Park. They would be all right, she assured herself, but she missed Horatio and wondered if she could cope with the inevitable flow of refugees to Lake View.

The thought had no sooner occurred than an unknown woman was delivered to her door on a mattress laid across an express wagon. The semi-invalid, whom the family would call "Aunty Sims," had been abandoned by her husband and now looked imploringly at Anna. "Of course, you will stay with us," Anna said kindly, and sent the houseboy, Peter, off to hunt up as much food as he could while she and the servants made the stranger comfortable.[5]

Next, an elegant but soot-begrimed carriage arrived in the driveway. At first Anna assumed it was a party of fantastically attired Negroes, until she recognized her friend and former Dearborn classmate Mary Miller up in the coachman's seat wearing a dressing gown, her face pitch-black.

"My dears, my dears!" Anna hurried down the steps to welcome them. As she extended her hand to Mary's mother, they all laughed at the sight of the elderly lady scarcely able to move in six favorite dresses frantically donned before escaping. "Fit for an asylum, I am," Mary's mother said, giggling.[6]

Sadly, there was little else to amuse them. The eyes of Mary's husband, Halsey Miller, were badly seared and swollen shut, so Mary had driven the horses herself, and through the long and terrible day and night they had been without food or rest. Mary's bare feet were blistered. Her milk had dried up, and her baby was howling. While Anna sent for a farmer's wife nearby to be a wet nurse for the baby, Mary soaked her horses' burned hooves and poulticed them before she would attend to her own scorched feet. Anna comforted the Millers' three children, ordered food prepared, beds readied, and set about putting compresses of tea leaves on Halsey's burned eyes. Peter, the houseboy, had still not returned.

There was no time to tell of the awful things the Millers had witnessed. A neighbor came running to say that nearby trees were on fire, and they had better head northwest for the open prairie. Peter had taken the family horse, so there was nothing to be done but tie the Spaffords' buggy to the back of the Millers' carriage, re-harness the injured horses, hoist Aunty Sims and the children into the two conveyances, and leave.

Aimlessly, the little caravan plodded west, finding themselves in a river of refugees. Farming families took pity on the crowds, assembling what they could of meager food and drink, distributing blankets, providing water and rags to clean the soot from their hands and faces, and caring for hundreds of burn wounds. Hailed by a farmer she knew, Anna and her group were invited to join some twenty other refugees who had struggled there before them. They spent the night huddled together on prairie grass, and welcomed the cold drizzle of rain that began falling as early as 11:00 p.m. The next morning they returned to Lake View and discovered the fire had stopped at Fullerton Avenue just below Lincoln Park.

The house was safe. The fire had reduced fifteen blocks of the city's very heart and pride to smoldering ruins, killing as many as three hundred people and leaving a hundred thousand people homeless.[7] The YMCA's Farwell Hall would be one of many victims of the conflagration, as would Moody's own home, his church, his speculative land investments, and, soon, his commitment to Chicago. As for the Spaffords, to whose house in Lake View friends fled in search of food and safety, they, too, would see their lives altered.

Horatio returned from Indiana a ruined man. The city had to rebuild itself; it would be a long time before there could be expansion northward. But interest on the money Horatio and his associates had borrowed, as well as taxes on the property, would have to be paid. The fire was a misfortune for everyone, but Horatio feared that for his family it might lead to a calamity he would be helpless to avert.

News of the catastrophe was reported around the world. Aid poured in from every corner of America, and donations even came from Europe. Immediately, the rebuilding began. Those insurance companies that did not fail paid off what they could afford of their enormous obligations, while the thrusting energy of entrepreneurial Chicago asserted itself anew. Cyrus McCormick, the millionaire reaper king, met his wife at the train station in a half-burned hat and overcoat and took her to the ruined reaper works, where giant piles of pig iron had melted like taffy. She listened as he told the applauding employees that they would reopen as soon as possible. Potter Palmer promptly sailed for Europe to see how his next Palmer House Hotel could outclass anything on the Continent—and be fireproof to boot.[8]

Volunteers helped set up an improvised morgue. Only 120 bodies were recovered, but official guesses put the total between 200 and 300. Many victims had drowned in the river or been consumed without a trace. On Tuesday morning, awestruck citizens wandered the silent ruins. Block after devastated block of properties worth over $350 million revealed only excavations of cellars and layers of ashes. Nearly a hundred thousand homeless people had to be sheltered; seventy-three miles of streets and 17,500 buildings were obliterated. As Joseph Medill, renting a press to resume publication, observed in the *Chicago Tribune*: "There was more widespread soul-sickening desolation than mortal eye ever beheld since the destruction of Jerusalem."[9]

People were warned not to open the city's still-sizzling vaults and safes for a week lest the contents ignite. When they did, the banks discovered their cash and financial instruments had survived, which helped put the city's business back on track. Unfortunately, however, the U.S. Depository in the ruins of the post office was opened, and as federal troops and Treasury Department officials stood by gaping, the giant vault crashed into the smoldering basement, and everything inside—some $1.5 million in currency—burned. Ultimately a special act of Congress covered the depository's losses, and except for the Franklin Bank, which folded, the private banks opened for business a few days later. Although Horatio had already visited the remains of his law offices and found all his books and the law library he had lovingly put together destroyed, he had to wait as impatiently as everyone else for his safe to cool. When he opened it, he had not been lucky. Among the remnants of charred papers, only a small notebook, brittle from heat, was left to record the good years when they rode the tide of affluence.

Nevertheless, they were alive, their children safe, Lake View spared, and Horatio still had his practice. The property he and his partners had borrowed heavily to buy north of Lincoln Park belonged to them, and while the taxes on it were daunting, Horatio was sure that it would grow in value as the city recovered. Horatio and Anna told themselves that at least, with God's help, they had emerged in better shape than so many others. They volunteered to help restart the relief and aid committees formed during the Civil War. A new Presbyterian church on Fullerton Avenue that Horatio had helped found in 1862 had survived and became an aid center. Dwight Moody, whose investment in land had evaporated, told friends he had lost everything "but my reputation and my Bible."[10] Although he had decided to move back to Northfield, Massachusetts, Moody joined in the heroic effort to restore and rebuild the YMCA during a dreadful winter of poverty and suffering that followed the great fire.

Yet Anna was tired. Stunned by the terrible plight of friends and colleagues, their own newly straitened circumstances, and the increased mortgage Horatio was forced to take out on their house, she tried to pull herself together. Gamely, she reduced her staff, cut down on her well-known liberal table, and concentrated on her children, Annie, nine, Maggie, eight, Bessie, five, and the baby, Tanetta. But the continuing fatigue took its toll, while the addition of the semi-invalid Aunty Sims irritated her even as it became clear that the querulous old woman had no intention of leaving. Anna found that even short separations from members of her family made her feel extremely anxious—when Horatio left for work, or when the older girls were at school.

As it had never been possible to escape her husband's eschatological preoccupations, Anna decided to listen more attentively. Horatio had kept up his correspondence with Dr. Piazza Smith and his conviction of a fast-approaching millennium, and the notion that all "those who truly repent and unfeignedly believe His holy Gospel are saved" began to have a relentless appeal.[11] Dutifully, she attended Horatio's Fullerton church, and now, like so many others, she found herself attracted to Moody's energetic gospel preaching. At a time when she felt bereft, there was comfort in the good works of their evangelical friends, and in the idea that a soul could be redeemed through loving actions. Yet melancholy haunted her, and one afternoon, unable to shrug it off, she sharply reproved Aunty Sims for complaining incessantly. She was taken aback when her guest turned on her. "It's all very well for you to talk," Aunty Sims retorted. "It is easy to be grateful and good if you have everything." And when she pointed her finger, adding, "Look out that you are not a fair-weather friend to God!" Anna could not banish those words from her thoughts.[12]

Recently, the Spaffords had become fond of an earnest thirty-one-year-old graduate of a homeopathic medical college in Cleveland who was their family physician. When Horatio confided that he was in a bit of a jam and would appreciate it if Dr. Samuel Hedges could loan him $1,200, on which he promised to pay interest, the doctor was only too happy to oblige. At about this time a Mrs. J. P. Wills, who was getting a divorce, entrusted Horatio with $17,000, her only source of income, which she wanted him to manage. Horatio was also in charge of his recently deceased sister Eureka's estate that she had left to support his married niece Mary Murphy and his nephew Rob Lawrence. And then there was another estate for which he was responsible, that of a Miss Kopse, of an indeterminate value.[13] Incrementally, Horatio began to slide down the slippery slope, dipping into private funds in his charge, skipping interest payments, betraying the sacred trust of those dependent on him.

Like a gambler confident that a winning hand would enable him to make restitution, he persuaded himself that he was protecting his family. But Horatio was also facing a fearful new deadline. When he and Anna had signed their mortgage on the Lake View house in 1864, they had agreed to pay a certain John P. Crozer, who held their mortgage, $5,000 by July 1, 1873, or be penalized $10,000.[14] Horatio had no way of producing the money from his own funds. He did not consider selling the house, which over the years they had expanded and improved and which invariably prompted admiring comments from visitors. The house shone with fine polished furniture, books, handsome carpets, and cherished Spafford family portraits. It was the heart of Horatio and Anna's life together. And because Horatio was worried about his wife's health, he shared as little as possible of his financial problems.

Anna had never fully recovered from Tanetta's birth, nor could she forget the grim and heartbreaking days spent with refugees. She was losing weight, and Dr. Hedges suggested that a trip, perhaps, might be a tonic. Horatio sent her for a visit in Washington, D.C., to his sister Margaret Lee, but unfortunately Maggie was preoccupied with nursing her ailing husband, while Anna hated the separation from her family and longed to return. She came back to Lake View almost as soon as she had left.

Dr. Hedges and other friends continued to urge Horatio to get his wife away. Early one summer evening, Horatio asked Anna to join him under a shade tree in the garden, where they could enjoy their view of Lake Michigan. As the setting sun cast reflections over the water, he took her hand and announced he had booked passage on the French liner S.S. *Ville du Havre*, one of the most luxurious passenger ships afloat. The whole family, he said, would sail for Europe. They would put the two older girls in school in Lausanne, Switzerland, leave the two youngest in France in the care of their governess, Mademoiselle Nicolet, and depart themselves on an extended honeymoon. Anna's blue eyes shone as she searched her husband's animated face.

"But the expense?" she wondered, beginning to frown.

Horatio, laughing delightedly, responded that they would manage somehow. "God will provide," he said, in what would later become an often repeated refrain. Her health was what mattered now, and besides, they had never given themselves a proper honeymoon.

Together they began to plan. When Anna heard that a friend and neighbor in Lake View, Agnes Goodwin, and her three children, Goertner, Julia, and Lulu, had decided to change their reservations from another ship in order to share the voyage with them on the S.S. *Ville du Havre*, she was thrilled. The Goodwins and Spaffords had comforted each other after the fire, and become even closer friends. Daniel Goodwin had made a fortune in real estate law that had enabled them to keep their well-appointed house in the city, now destroyed by the fire. As Horatio practiced real estate law as well, the men often found themselves negotiating deals or verifying titles together. Daniel was detained from joining them on the voyage, but he assured them that he planned to come in a few weeks.[15]

There was a reason for Daniel to delay. On September 18, 1873, an event occurred in Philadelphia that affected almost every businessman in the country and many abroad. Jay Cooke, the high-flying financier who had raised millions in bond sales to finance much of the thirty-five thousand miles of track laid across the United States after the Civil War, abruptly closed his investment house and declared bankruptcy. The shock was enormous. Five thousand commercial houses fell into bankruptcy, and the New York Stock Exchange shut down for ten days. Cooke had been a leading promoter of what was to have been the Northern Pacific Railroad, a project that got under way with the completion of the transcontinental Union Pacific in 1869. For Cooke and the country, however, the railroad system at this time was overbuilt. Competition for freight traffic had become ferocious and finally ruinous. Cooke had recognized that it was impossible to raise the funds for a new system; President Ulysses S. Grant had tightened the money supply, and money was scarce. Cooke found himself overextended. When his bank folded, it took with it countless other banks and untold personal fortunes in a spiraling debacle that would shortly plunge the nation into the worst economic crisis of the nineteenth century. A total of eighteen thousand businesses failed between 1873 and 1876. The 1870s would see the country slide into a major depression. Of the country's 364 railroads, 89 went bankrupt.[16] The industry, which had been the country's largest employer outside of agriculture, contracted and left thousands out of work. Anyone who had borrowed to invest in railroad bonds was in deep trouble.

Horatio was one of many who either had bought the risky bonds or was caught in the financial turmoil that followed. Everything, including land values, plummeted, and Horatio had no margin to absorb the shock. Both lawyers had more business from unmet loans and land deals gone awry than they could handle, even as their wives, kept innocent of the mounting problems, chatted happily about their new dresses, their tender anxieties, their children's hopes, and the awful fact that they had too many things to fit in their trunks.

In November 1873, when they were packed and ready to leave for New York, Horatio at last admitted to Anna that he, too, would be detained. He and his partners, he told her, had suddenly received an offer from a man who proposed to buy part of the land in which they had invested so disastrously. If the sale went through, he said reassuringly, it would go far to relieve some debts he had incurred, and he could then join them later with a clearer conscience.

Horatio told Anna that she, the children, and Mademoiselle Nicolet must go on ahead. He would escort them as far as New York. The family, he explained, would continue as planned to France and stay at Bertry, a little village outside Paris where they had friends. Then he would join them. Anna resisted. Horatio was firm. Ten-year-old Maggie, the dreamy child of the family, was equally reluctant. Together with her younger sister Bessie, she slipped out to their favorite spot, a play post office in one of the big elm trees, and tucked notes into a corner, which were later found. "Goodbye, dear sweet Lake View," Maggie wrote in her childish scrawl. "I will never see you again."[17]

Then a telegram arrived and Horatio put it into his pocket. He had no intention of letting Anna know that the prospective buyer of the property had died suddenly of a heart attack.

CHAPTER SIX

Collision at Sea

Alas! the golden bowl is broken
Beneath the Deep,
And thou hast passed without a token
To thy last sleep.
Loosed is the silver cord asunder
In life's bright noon,
And thou lieth the deep sea under,
At rest so soon.

—Poem written by Daniel Goodwin Jr.
to his wife and children, 1873

Normally, the S.S. *Ville du Havre* took more passengers than it did on this voyage of Saturday, November 15, 1873. When it had crossed in September, there were 793, but now the enormous luxury ship was refreshingly uncrowded with 157 passengers, among whom were three French Protestant clergymen returning home, and 156 officers and crew.[1] One of the clergymen, Théophile Lorriaux, the Spaffords knew. His sister had been their governess for a time in Lake View. In fact, it was with the Lorriaux family in Bertry that the family planned to stay until Horatio arrived, presumably on the next boat. Horatio escorted Anna and his children on board, and at the last minute he changed their staterooms to two smaller ones toward the ship's bow from a more expensive pair mid-ship. Most likely he did so to save money, but later he said he had had a strange feeling that he must do this. Farewells were said, handkerchiefs waved to those onshore, the whistle blew, and the *Ville du Havre* moved slowly out of New York Harbor.

The first night was cold and clear. The liner's captain, Marius Surmont, had assured Anna and the Frenchmen sitting with her at dinner that he hoped for an easy voyage. It was still early in the season to worry about icebergs. Besides, he explained, his ship was very safe. Two years earlier it had been remodeled, a more powerful engine installed, its length extended by sixty-five feet, and a propeller now replaced the old-fashioned side wheels. Lorriaux and a second Frenchman, Nathaniel Weiss, told Anna that they were sharing a stateroom in the stern. Laughing, they said that when the screw turned, the racket was appalling, and their bunks were so narrow they were certain they would tumble out with a thump in the middle of the night. A third Frenchman, Émile Cook, a quiet Spaniard, and a Swiss were also at their table and equally friendly. Anna was delighted to have their companionship.

The second evening was also calm. Gentlemen and ladies took their coffee or cigars on deck, nodding pleasantly at one another. But that night the sea roughened, and the ship pitched and heaved through a howling storm. By breakfast, those few who appeared in the dining room retired quickly. Great waves washed the deck, passengers clung to whatever they could or lay miserably in the saloon. By mid-morning everyone had heard that a flange on one of the screws had broken. They were still off the Newfoundland Banks when the crew admitted that the trip would probably be delayed by another five days. Then for several days a heavy fog descended, blanketing the ship and requiring passengers to pass the time indoors, listening to the blaring foghorn.

On the morning of November 21, the sixth day out, the sun finally burst forth, scattering the cobalt waves with golden patches and restoring the atmosphere to almost giddy levels of relief. Even Captain Surmont beamed wanly, exhausted from forty-eight hours without sleep through both the storm and the fog. At meals, wineglasses were raised and toasts given, although, to the amusement of the Frenchmen, Anna took ice water. "We approach France, madam," Lorriaux announced gaily. "Capital Paris; Department of the Seine; Rue des Batignolles, Numero———." Anna laughed, and when Weiss invited her to stroll after dinner, she agreed.

It was a ravishing night. The stars were brilliant, and the sea calm. On the stern deck, they paused to admire the phosphorescence churning in the wake. Softly, Anna said: "I am contented."

"You were not before?"

"No. I've been sick. I find separation difficult. Sad. I feel the sea is dangerous."

"Mr. Spafford will join you soon."

"I know that," Anna replied. "I have struggled against these feelings. I know I did wrong. My children have borne it marvelously."

"Your children are gentle and charming. These feelings will pass."

"I hope they will," Anna said. "I believe they will." She bade him good night then. Later, he wrote that he heard her humming a hymn as she went down the stairs to bed.[2]

Weiss lingered awhile to enjoy the beautiful night some more, and finally retired himself. He was asleep perhaps two hours when he and Lorriaux heard what sounded like two explosions as the ship shuddered violently, followed by terrible screams. The noisy screw ceased grinding. Throwing on their clothes, the two men dashed into the corridor, bumping into the captain emerging from his cabin.

"It is nothing, nothing!" Captain Surmont said quickly. "A little vessel has struck us. That is all!"

They raced up to the deck, where half-dressed passengers and sailors were clawing at the ropes of boats and life preservers with axes, even with penknives. Aghast, they realized these were glued to the walls by dried paint. Leaning out over the stern railing, they could see the silhouette of a large sailing vessel whose bow was impaled in the *Ville du Havre*'s belly and attempting to draw free. A sailor dashed by, stopping briefly to declare that such a ship as theirs could not possibly sink. "It is too big, too safe, too many decks! You need not be troubled!"

Almost instantly they spotted Anna and her children huddled together in their nightclothes, Anna wearing a heavy wrapper and holding two-year-old Tanetta in her arms. "Please," called Anna. "You'll stay with us?"[3]

The little girl, Bessie, threw her arms around Weiss's knees. "You won't go? You'll take me with you?"

Weiss patted her head. "Yes, my child. Don't be frightened. But you are shivering. Stay here with Lorriaux. I'll get clothes." Weiss darted back down the staircase, shouldering his way through a panicked crowd. In his cabin, he grabbed his overcoat, blankets, and a shawl. As he reached the landing again, he found Émile Cook standing as if dazed, wearing nothing but a nightshirt. The ship's doctor ran up to them. Cook said that his stateroom was destroyed. "I can't understand why I'm alive. I helped a woman find her child under debris. Water is rising fast."

"You'll freeze, man!" shouted the doctor, tearing off his overcoat and thrusting it at Cook. Then the doctor turned for the stairway even as gusts of fire blazed from the ventilators. "I must help!" he called. "We've been struck athwart the mainmast to starboard!"

The center of the ship that took the blow was where Agnes Goodwin and her children had their staterooms. It was from here that Horatio had moved his family, their places taken by the quiet Spaniard and the Swiss. None of them appeared on deck.

Weiss found Anna and Lorriaux trying to approach one of two freed lifeboats but beaten back by the crazed throng. They saw a priest in striped underwear crying: "Are you a Catholic? Repent! I will give you absolution!" Then he elbowed his way to the boat and climbed in.

Several Americans wearing life preservers jumped overboard. Others grabbed deck chairs. A group of women sank to their knees, heads together, and began praying in a tableau of resignation. Just as some forty shouting occupants of the overloaded lifeboats demanded to be shoved off, the mainmast crashed down carrying the mizzen, and the two boats, crushed and fragmented, lurched into the sea bearing their loads of mangled bodies. Anna and Lorriaux, each slightly injured, listened to the sickening cries.

The huge ship careened dangerously to starboard. An awful silence descended before another loud crash resounded, the deck quivered, and the bow broke and sank. The last thing they remembered was little Annie saying, "Don't be afraid. The sea is His and He made it," as the ship made its final roll and they were swept into the swirling black vortex.[4] Only twelve minutes had elapsed since the collision, and the *Ville du Havre* sank carrying all aboard.

As Anna was sucked into the black funnel, she felt her baby torn violently from her arms. Desperately reaching out, she caught the tail of

Tanetta's nightgown. For a moment she held on, but it was wrenched from her grasp. When she reached again, she clutched corduroy trousers covering a man's leg. Years later in Jerusalem, when they were very poor, someone gave a child of hers a corduroy coat. The child never forgot the look of agony on her mother's face as she helped her put it on.[5]

The *Loch Earn's* lifeboats were launched somewhat late, but the British sailors were magnificent, picking up what survivors they could, taking off their own clothes to keep them warm, rowing them back to their ship, helping hoist them aboard, and shoving off to scout again. Sailors remaining on the *Loch Earn* let down ropes over the sides for people to hold until they could be brought aboard.

The sailors stroked on, as quickly as they dared. When a boat was filled, there was no alternative but to leave the remaining swimmers, who pleaded for rescue. All too often on the next run the supplicants had vanished. Early on, the sailors had seen a long beam to which some ten or fifteen people were attached, but when they returned, there was no sign of it.

Lorriaux, sputtering and coughing, rose to the surface. He did not know how to swim. Luckily, he saw a life preserver and then a bit of flooring to hold on to. Weiss managed to flounder apart from the confusion of thrashing arms and legs, but he had been struck by something, and his head and right hand were injured. He heard the sound of splashing oars and felt himself lifted. When he was deposited on the deck of the *Loch Earn*, he was bleeding profusely from a head wound.

They found Anna, unconscious, floating on a piece of shelving. She had probably been in the water for an hour. She was pulled into the lifeboat bruised and vomiting seawater. Her long hair was unpinned and her thick dressing gown shredded to ribbons.

On board the *Loch Earn*, frantic survivors rushed to the rail each time a rescue boat returned. They scanned the new faces, quietly embracing their loved ones as they were brought aboard or closing their eyes and turning away. Anna was always the first, shivering at the rail, waiting for her daughters. When a muscular young American was hauled up, he told of two little girls popping up beside him. He shouted to them to hold on to his coat while he swam. First the smallest one relaxed her grip and disappeared, and when he had nearly reached the *Loch Earn*, he felt the other child slip from him. Lorriaux was standing with Anna when she heard this. Uttering a groan, she tried to throw herself into the sea, and only by physical force was he able to restrain her until she quieted and gave way to racking sobs.

All that night, the crew scoured the icy water. By 4:00 a.m., as dawn broke and the sea roughed, the crews reported no more cries were heard; nothing but wreckage was sighted. The sea had swallowed 232 lives, including 6 stowaways. Only 87 people were saved: 6 officers and 54 crew members; 27 passengers, of which there was a twelve-year-old girl, 17 men, and 9 women. Everyone had lost someone; some families were totally wiped out.[6]

The *Loch Earn* was more than thirteen hundred miles from the French coast and badly damaged. The bowsprit was demolished, and there was a gaping hole in the prow. Leaks were developing, and the emergency pumps churned furiously. Captain William Robertson ordered the English flag to be raised upside down, the only distress signal available in the days before radio signals. However, as there was no cargo aboard, the ship rode high in the water. Encouraged that the damage was above the waterline, Captain Robertson sent the boats out one more time. As they searched, a ship was spotted coming toward them under full sail. A helmsman on the cargo ship *Trimountain*, headed for Bristol, had spotted the international distress signal.

Just as the collision and sinking of the *Ville du Havre* would remain the greatest marine disaster before the sinkings of the *Lusitania* and the *Titanic,* it is also extraordinary that in the space of a few hours, three ships should come together at the same spot mid-Atlantic. The captain of the *Trimountain* would later be given a handsome set of engraved silver by the grateful survivors, who among many others would consider his ship's appearance a miracle, even though, incredibly, the captain was censured for deviating from his route to Bristol in order to bring them safely to Cardiff on the Welsh coast.[7]

Captain Robertson himself would ponder the mystery for the rest of his life. He and the watch had seen the enormous liner from a long distance on that clear night, but he knew that the rules of the sea required that motor-propelled ships yield to sailing ships. Just before the collision, his helmsman had tried to swing clear, even as the helmsman of the *Ville du Havre* made the fatal decision to move in the same direction. It was speculated but never confirmed that due to Captain Surmont's exhaustion after days of storm and fog, proper vigilance had not been maintained.

When the *Trimountain* arrived and offered to take aboard all in need from the stricken *Loch Earn*, Captain Robertson was unwilling to let them leave. His ship, he insisted, could make it. The survivors were alarmed. Some believed he wanted the honor of saving them himself. Vehement, panicked at the prospect of another disaster, they insisted that Captain Surmont give the order for their release. Although some elected to stay on the *Loch Earn*, all who wished were transferred to the small cargo ship, which, by another miracle, had space to take them. A fortunate miscalculation had apparently been made by the charter company in New York, where a cargo of canned goods had been taken on, leaving a large portion of the middle deck empty. The *Trimountain*'s captain, William Urquhart, later reported the thought had actually occurred to him at the time that such a space would be useful should he happen on a sinking vessel.

The feeble and injured passengers on the *Trimountain* arrived at Cardiff on December 1. Those who had stayed with the increasingly disabled *Loch Earn* had weathered a second dramatic rescue after it, too, sank. They landed a week later at Plymouth. Mountainous waves from another winter storm had buffeted both ships badly, and many were ill. But Captain Urquhart and his crew had brought his survivors through safely and done what they could to make them comfortable. One survivor, Mary Adams Bulkley, wrote a letter to her mother while they were still days from Cardiff. Much later it was included in an anthology of shipwrecks:

> Eleven ladies and about twelve gentlemen [are] in two cabins, not a toothbrush among us and only such clothing as we had upon us when saved, which has been dried for us, and the flannel underclothing of the sailors. Only two ladies have shoes, the rest are in the woolen stockings the English sailors gave us. I have a pair of

gentleman's slippers and fortunately had my flannel wrapper on when I went overboard. All must use the captain's comb. But one of the young girls, a wonderful child of sixteen, Miss Mixter of Boston, combs our hair every morning. We have no hairpins, so we must wear it down our shoulders. This poor girl has lost her father, mother, and grandfather. She and her little sister of twelve were both miraculously saved, as I was.

I dare not think of my own future and only long for my return to you. It is mysterious to think why have I been saved, when with Lallie [her daughter who drowned] my life's work is done. I dare not say anything more about her lest I be overcome and not able to finish this letter.[8]

Anna Spafford was silent for most of the trip to Cardiff. Few others had much to say. They were extremely solicitous of one another, organized little duties for their mutual benefit, asked Lorriaux to hold a service, and endured. Lorriaux kept a close watch over Anna, fearing another suicide attempt. He was at her side when she finally spoke: "God gave me four daughters. They have been taken. One day I shall understand why. I *will* understand why."[9]

Nine days after the shipwreck, before daybreak, they disembarked in Cardiff. As soon as it was possible, Anna sent a telegram to her husband. "Saved alone."[10]

CHAPTER SEVEN

"You Must Give Yourself to My Work"

When peace like a river attendeth my way
When sorrows like sea-billows roll,
Whatever my lot, Thou hast taught me to say:
"It is well, it is well with my soul."

—Composed mid-Atlantic by
Horatio Spafford, 1874

Ten days after his family's departure for France, Horatio Spafford wrote Anna that he missed her sorely and longed to hear every detail of the children's activities.

"Annie and Maggie and Bessie and Tanetta—it is a sweet consolation to write their names. May the dear Lord keep and sustain and strengthen you." It was weeks before the letter could catch up with Anna and she would read those painful words.[1]

Horatio did not tell his wife about the failed land deal, but the depth of his concern was evident. "I feel more and more that the absorbing pursuit of anything earthly is not well for one's spiritual life," he wrote in the same letter. "I scarcely know what to do about the [Lincoln] Park matters. If I should withdraw altogether from taking an interest in things, it is very possible that great injury might be the result, not only to my own, but other interests. And yet I feel half-inclined to do so, so harassing, so vexatious, so even dangerous to one's spiritual peace do I esteem these selfish contests about money, money, money."[2] Horatio was close to the end of his tether. Everything he was admired for, how he appeared to others, and what he himself wished to be—responsible, honest, reliable, a devout and practicing Christian—had been jeopardized by his spiraling financial difficulties after the great fire. Now the Panic of 1873 had put him in further straits.

His wife and his children were Horatio's greatest comfort. Anna relied on him. Sometimes he had teased her for being "meek" and not standing up for her views, but actually he liked her deference to his positions. When he insisted, for example, that it was healthier and more convenient for the girls' hair to be worn in a short bob, she had accepted this eccentricity, even though he knew that she and his daughters preferred their hair fashionably long and adorned with pretty ribbons.[3] Horatio could hardly bear to contemplate what Anna would think if she knew the extent of his troubles.

Anna's telegram seemed like a mortal blow. When he saw that it came from Wales instead of France, he felt his heart stop. That night Horatio walked the floor in anguish. Moody's evangelical colleague Major D. W. Whittle, whom Horatio had been asked to help support, and Dr. Hedges, the family physician, stayed with him. As dawn broke, Horatio turned to Whittle.

"I am glad to trust the Lord when it will cost me something," he said finally.[4]

An answer was quickly cabled back to Anna. She should go on to Paris with Lorriaux and stay with his family at Bertry, and Horatio would leave immediately with Daniel Goodwin for New York to join her.

In the meantime, Anna and the other survivors, escorted by officials of the steamship company that owned the *Ville du Havre*, were brought to London. They were taken to the shops that had the finest mourning apparel and invited to select whatever they wished. As Anna confronted the racks of black silks, black veils, black bonnets, and black laces, she was overtaken by a powerful sense of rebellion. While the others outfitted themselves in the requisite and traditional black, Anna ordered a simple gown of black and white. Her companions stared in surprise, gently pointing out that it was not a suitable choice, but Anna ignored them. "I have not lost my children. We are only separated for a little time," she murmured as much to herself as to them.[5]

Reports of the shipwreck headlined every newspaper in the British Isles. Dwight Moody, enjoying unprecedented attention in Edinburgh, and carefully cutting out and sending on to supporters the many articles about his triumphant tour, read the news in disbelieving shock. "It will kill her," he said. He decided to go immediately to London.[6]

Always part of Moody's charisma was a ready access to his emotions. Finding Anna in her hotel, he simply looked at her and began sobbing uncontrollably. Self-contained, Anna responded quietly. She did not think of her girls as drowned in the ocean, she said softly, comforting him, instead of the opposite. "Christ permitted me to take them only that they be wafted up to Him. Christ saved my life so that I might come back and work a little longer for Him."

In a detached, gentle, and strangely remote tone, she recalled floating on her plank in the icy ocean. She had heard a voice saying: "You are spared for a purpose. You have work to do." Looking beyond Moody's tear-stained face, she said that she had resolved she would never be as Aunty Sims had warned, "a fair-weather friend to God." If privately the frightful demons of Norwegian folktales were pursuing her, outwardly Anna showed nothing but serenity. She turned her steady blue gaze back to Moody and repeated simply: "God gave me four little daughters. Now they have been taken from me. Someday I will understand why."[7]

Moody was overwhelmed, yet heartened to hear Anna volunteer the kind of Christian avowal that he invariably sought from his followers. Nevertheless, he was perceptive enough to wonder if Anna's declaration accepting God's will could be sustained. When the Spaffords returned home and the dreadful reality sank in, a disastrous reaction might follow. Searching her face, trying to read her enigmatic expression, he counseled Anna to go back to Chicago. "You must give yourself to my work," he urged, innocent of vanity. "You must be so busy helping others who have gone into the depths of despair that you will overcome your own affliction by bringing comfort and salvation to others."[8] Anna nodded, apparently listening. What Moody could not know was that his term "overcome" had already assumed a powerful and special meaning for Anna.

The captain of the transatlantic packet bearing Horatio and Daniel Goodwin to France invited them to his cabin. The position of the collision, he said, had been determined at 46°54′ north latitude and 35°6′ west longitude. He had calculated the exact spot, he told them gently, and his ship was passing over it now. He thought they might want to know where the *Ville du Havre* had gone down.

That night, on a piece of stationery taken from his New York hotel, Horatio composed a poem that remains to this day a much-loved hymn.[9]

When peace like a river attendeth my way
    When sorrows like sea-billows roll,
Whatever my lot, Thou has taught me to say:
    "It is well, it is well with my soul."

Tho' Satan should buffet, tho' trials should come,
    Let this blest assurance control,
That Christ hath regarded my helpless estate,
    And hath shed His own blood for my soul.

My sin—oh, the bliss of this glorious thought!
    My sin—not in part but the whole,
Is nailed to His Cross and I bear it no more;
    Praise the Lord, praise the Lord, oh, my soul!

And, Lord, haste the day when the faith shall be sight,
    The clouds be rolled back as a scroll,
The trump shall resound, and the Lord will descend—
    "Even so—it is well with my soul."

For me, be it Christ, be it Christ hence to live
    If Jordan above me shall roll,
No pang shall be mine, for in death as in life
    Thou wilt whisper Thy peace to my soul.

Profoundly, Horatio knew himself a sinner. He had been living with his guilty secret of financial malfeasance for several years, compounded recently by the financial panic. He despised himself. He could not be sure that the catastrophes befalling him were not the wages of his sins.

As a Christian, Horatio counted on Christ's sacrifice atoning for his lapses. But above all else, as he stared at bankruptcy and the emptiness of death, he heard the sound of Gabriel's trumpet heralding the Messiah.

Suddenly there was meaning and purpose. With the imminent Second Coming of the Redeemer, surely ecstasy, redemption from sin, and freedom from the madness of grief would follow. By embracing millennial expectations, Horatio could salvage hope. Without this hope, life in a cruel and unfeeling world was more than he could bear. Perhaps, he thought, there was no such thing as hell. Why should he be consigned to eternal damnation and not join his children in heaven? If God were love, why could not everyone be saved? Thus, gradually, Horatio rejected all remnants of Calvinist predestination and began his slow progress toward a religious system of his own.

Anna had been cared for in Bertry with great delicacy and kindness by Mrs. Lorriaux, who kept her own relief at her husband's safe return to herself. She encouraged him to escort Anna to Paris to stay with Bertha Johnson, an old schoolmate from Chicago. It was the height of the Christmas season, in the past a time for the Spafford family to trim the tree together and make each other little gifts. For Anna, no other time had been so pleasurable. Now she waited for her husband. When Horatio joined her at last, no record stands of their reunion. Nor did they attend services on Christmas Day, although Christmas parcels arrived at the doors of friends with notes that read, "From the children."

Numb with grief, the Spaffords, Daniel Goodwin, and other relatives of the lost who had converged on Paris or who waited at Le Havre tried to pry loose from the shipping companies involved all that was possible to learn of the disaster. Every remembered detail was exchanged as people attempted to re-create a picture of the twelve desperate minutes before the ship sank, and all that had occurred afterward. When Anna saw Daniel Goodwin, she told him that she had seen Agnes in the passageway. She had tried to reassure her, she told the distraught husband, but admitted she had not seen any of his family after that. There had been no time.[10] From Nathaniel Weiss, they heard that Émile Cook had died of pneumonia, leaving his widow and nine children.

A sense of finality eventually settled over those clinging to the frailest hope that their loved ones might have been found alive, or at least that their bodies might somehow have drifted to shore. But no further word was heard. After several weeks, most of the survivors, including Daniel Goodwin and the Spaffords, sadly booked their passage home.

CHAPTER EIGHT

Return to Chicago

*The European Sabbath is a simple holiday; the
American a holy day. The European idea is to
devote it to pleasure, the Anglo-American, to
piety and rest. In Europe it is the day on which
revelry and vice have full sway, in America it is
designed that virtue and religion should be promoted by it.*

　　—Philip Schaff, a first-generation American, 1869

The saga of the shipwreck had occupied the front pages of every
newspaper in the country for weeks but nowhere so intensely as
in Chicago, where the stunned citizenry grieved for their fellow Chicagoans from that first ghastly day. "The news received in this city yes-
terday afternoon," wrote the *Inter Ocean* on Tuesday, December 2, "passed
like a cold shudder. For hours it was the subject of half-frightened conversations upon the streets and in business places, everywhere the expression being one of pain at this vast calamity, and deep sympathy with the
bereaved among us." Businesses paused in their work; church pews
swelled with somber parishioners gathering to hear preachers intone on
the inexplicable. Friends, acquaintances, and business associates of the
Spafford and Goodwin families drew close to discuss how best to greet
them when they returned, and what to do for them in the future.

Yet when the Spaffords finally arrived back in Chicago, their friends
were astonished by their seemingly positive attitude. Their cheerfulness
struck some people as incredible, even weird. H. S. Beebee, who had

known them for nearly ten years, recalled that he had "naturally expected that they would be stricken with the greatest grief for the loss of their children, but Mr. Spafford smiled brightly and said that he was glad of what had happened; that the children were better off than they would be here. He did not give the slightest evidence of the grief he must have felt. Mrs. Spafford treated the matter in the same light and seemed to be perfectly happy."[1]

The *Chicago Daily Tribune* much later reported that Horatio's "faith was so strong [that] no event in life could move him and no disaster appall him. Everything was for the best to him and he had no question that every prayer was answered."[2]

Mary Miller, the school friend who had gone through the great fire with Anna, received a letter mailed from Paris. Anna spoke of the "joy to my dear children." Their "little lives," she wrote, "were so early dedicated to their Master. Now He has called them to Himself." She briefly described the prayers the little girls had offered, the resignation they had shown just before they were toppled into the sea, and told her friend: "If I never believed in religion before, I have had strong proof of it now . . . God has sent peace in our hearts. He has answered our prayers. His will is done. I would not have my children back again in this wicked world."[3] What she refused to say to anyone aloud, she instead confided to a scrap of paper: "How sad is my heart without my birds."[4]

Those left behind in the household at Lake View, however, were not so ready to put away their grief. When the Spaffords drove up the driveway, Aunty Sims was at the door to greet them, convulsed in tears. Weeping friends had hurried to place enlarged photographs of the children on easels in the living room. Despite Horatio's orders to put away the children's clothes, schoolwork, and playthings, the four little beds and the four dressers filled with their garments were still there, and the attic still contained four rows of rubber boots, skates, and sleds. Most wrenching of all was the discovery in the big elm tree of the two notes written by Maggie and Bessie. Anna could never bring herself to destroy them, and they were among the few things the Spaffords packed in their single trunk for Jerusalem.[5]

Their friends and fellow parishioners at the Fullerton Avenue Presbyterian Church postponed their Christmas fair and readied themselves instead to receive the bereaved couple.[6] And yet there were those who wondered about the Spaffords. What had they done for the Lord to treat them so harshly? These were only whispers, quietly uttered and at least for the time being ignored.[7] Mostly arms were opened wide and consolation offered, and Horatio resumed his role as "principal ruling elder." Friends accepted the Spaffords' remarkable stoicism, remembering that after the great fire, when their pastor had preached to a sobbing congregation, Horatio had left the church after the sermon saying: "This is a blessing in disguise; purified by fire, Chicago will be better for this calamity."[8] Now the Spaffords were once again victims, yet apparently they held to their unwavering faith.

It was accepted that Horatio had been financially hurt by the Panic. Anna realized that she had to mind her pennies carefully. There were days when she had barely enough money to put dinner on the table. But these were hard times when most people had to tighten their belts. As an elderly member of Fullerton remembered forty years later, "Those days as compared with the present were rugged ones . . . we had to work long hours . . . and every minute was a strenuous one with very little compensation in the line of pleasure."[9]

In the meantime, still in England, Dwight Moody planned his evangelical campaign in America with the same systematic care he had brought to Great Britain, where crowds had become so large that admission tickets were required. He intended to lead the mightiest religious revival that America had ever witnessed. He was in negotiation with the mayor of Brooklyn, an independent city until its consolidation with New York in 1898, as well as the mayors of New York, Philadelphia, and Boston. The business leaders of these cities all saw the benefit, both economic and spiritual, of bringing Moody to their towns and vied to be first on his list. But as far as the evangelist was concerned, the peak of satisfaction would be his appearance in Chicago, and Chicago was in enthusiastic agreement. Moneys for a vast tabernacle were being actively raised, and construction would soon be under way. Volunteers were already laying the groundwork for that supreme, climactic, and dazzling hour scheduled to occur in October 1876 and to extend into January 1877.

The city needed a revival, something to quiet the turmoil. In late December 1874, ten thousand angry workers had marched on Chicago's City Hall, demanding publicly sponsored work and the release of funds held by the Relief and Aid Society after the great fire. By now the Panic of 1873 had struck the nation with savage force, and the city was reeling. Thousands of eager immigrants, attracted to Chicago by the abundant employment opportunities in the city's rebuilding effort, were out of work. If they were not fired, their wages were abruptly reduced. Everyone was affected—most acutely the poor. A long, harsh winter following the crash had added to the general suffering, and with it came violence, suicides, and angry proletarian rhetoric. Rumors of a workers' revolution buzzed through factories, mills, slaughterhouses, shipyards, grain elevators, railroad depots, the McCormick works, Armour's meatpacking plant, Marshall Field's dry-goods business. The expanding gulf between rich and poor where "cash and caste are apt to be cause and effect," as the *Chicago Tribune* noted soberly, was creating alarming divisions. "A social stratification in which the lowest stratum is volcanic, is boiling over with hate of its condition and rage at those above it. When this is the case, look out for an explosion."[10]

The evangelical churches, nearly half of all the churches in Chicago, exerted a powerful influence on city life.[11] In the main, they were attended by both the very rich and the middle classes, who were overwhelmingly Republican in party choice and increasingly concerned about their slipping grasp on public affairs. The immigrants, especially the Roman Catholic Irish and the Lutheran Germans, were fervently Democratic. They burned with resentment at the harsh working conditions and unsanitary, ramshackle neighborhoods and had begun to bring pressure on the city council through an organized effort to elect their own representatives. Even before the Panic, their growing political clout was viewed with alarm. Effective action was imperative to calm the city, restore its faith, and secure the tottering authority of the comfortable classes.

"Chicago is an evil place," declared Annie Ballou, an intrepid Bostonian reformer who had come to rail against prostitution, Sabbath breaking, and especially the whiskey trade.[12] It was time to banish "King Alcohol" forever. In February 1874, thousands of well-dressed women had invaded the saloons and pubs of the city, destroying bottles and falling on their knees to pray and sing hymns as the pub owners cowered under their counters. In a movement eventually expanding throughout America, battalions of matrons brandishing umbrellas swarmed over Chicago, demanding signatures for the "Home Pledge," a promise not to drink intoxicants at home or even to cook with alcoholic beverages. Fourteen thousand signatures were gathered and presented to the city council urging the closure of saloons on Sunday. The city council, however, increasingly Irish Catholic in makeup, held the reformers at bay with an ingenious compromise: an ordinance was issued that merely required saloons to veil themselves; curtains on doors and windows fronting on the street were to be drawn. The ladies were outraged.[13]

Refusing to quit, they organized the Woman's Christian Temperance Union (WCTU), a national organization whose core was primarily evangelical. The majority of members were from evangelical churches and believed that by abolishing drinking, society could be redeemed. The way to begin was to reform every drunkard and lead him to God through personal conversion—the only cure for "crime, poverty, labor unrest, divorce, and the general disintegration of the American family."[14] Appointed to the important position of corresponding secretary of the WCTU was Frances Willard, the first dean of women at Northwestern University, a Moody associate, and a sometime guest of the Spaffords at Lake View.[15]

From England, an indefatigable Moody was firing off cannonades of correspondence to Miss Willard and another fellow toiler in the temperance movement, Miss Emma Dryer. Moody recognized the formidable potential of the gentler sex and solicited the help of these talented women in organizing a feminine network to carry the Word into the home of every man, woman, and child sunk in murky disbelief, and by 1886 the network had evolved into the Moody Bible Institute, headed by Miss Dryer and still influential today in evangelical circles. At this time, however, still concerned about Anna Spafford's state of mind, Moody begged them to sweep her into their movement. They were glad to oblige, as aware as everyone else of the Spaffords' tragedy.

Together, Miss Willard and Miss Dryer pressed Anna to help the WCTU prepare the way for the great Moody revival ahead.[16] Benumbed, still dazed by a sense of helplessness, Anna acquiesced to Moody's call. Her daughter's later claim that Anna had initially been put in charge of all women's activities in Chicago is unlikely.[17] She had neither the energy nor the will to serve as an administrator in either of his dynamic women friends' new organizations. At this point, she was still a follower of others, especially of her husband. But she did find consolation, a distraction from the intermittent depression she had suffered ever since the fire, and even an excitement, as she plunged into the private agonies of the struggling poor they hoped to reach.

As Anna entered Chicago's slums, it was as if she were catapulted back to her youth. Wandering through miserable tenements on stinking, unpaved streets, knocking on doors in crowded immigrant neighborhoods, she relived the frightening days when her mother and baby brother lay dying, when she heard the groans of the sick through thin walls, when a hearty meal, a pretty dress, and the attentions of a good doctor were rarities. Horatio had rescued her from this world, and now she wanted to rescue others. At "mothers" meetings, which she helped organize in threadbare parlors or humble church meeting rooms, she listened to the awful stories of women beaten by drunken husbands who had squandered their wages and left their families with nothing to buy food. The women's rage and helplessness echoed her own.

Her anger energized her. When a prostitute begged for some means of escape from her degrading trade, Anna tried to find a better place for the girl—but was refused. No one wanted to hire a "fallen woman."[18] Frustrated and indignant, Anna begged Horatio to intervene. She demanded that he make the authorities prosecute husbands who beat their wives, but when the men were dragged into court, she watched, furious again, as their wives refused to testify against them. There needed to be an institution for such people, she felt. They needed to be safe as well as saved. Anna tasted a new bitterness. Who dared to follow Matthew's injunction to leave all behind and follow Jesus? Was this Christ's gospel of love and forgiveness? And who, then, were the real sinners?

At home, Horatio meditated. In his Bible, he underscored the words "Behold, I am vile." With a blue pencil he drew a line beneath "Wherefore I abhor myself, and repent in dust and ashes."[19] He told his wife that she must avoid attachments. Acquiring possessions and making money were ephemeral goals, he said—a startling departure from his once dearly held conviction that God smiled on the prosperous. Everything vanishes, life is "transient," including friends, kin, and even one's dear children. The aim and goal should be heaven, he persisted, where they would be reunited. Faith alone had become his litany. To herself, Anna whispered over and over, "I will say God is love until I believe it."[20]

And then one day Anna looked at him with tears shimmering in her blue eyes. "I am pregnant, Horatio," she told him. Quietly, they knelt together and thanked God.

In Chicago, the drumbeat was quickening for Moody's arrival. Morning and afternoon, the Chicago papers reported the assault on America of the evangelist and his singing partner, Ira Sankey, whose fine voice added much to the revival's attraction. In Brooklyn, four times as many people were turned away from the gigantic Brooklyn Rink as were admitted. The *New York Herald* compared the crowds to "one large river of life" flowing to "a promised land," creating a scene "never before witnessed in any city on this continent." From October to November 1875, sidewalks and housetops were packed with fifteen thousand people pressing to hear the famous team. Hats were lost, shirts torn, women fainted, while desperate guards tried to hold the doors closed. Inside, Moody trumpeted the doctrinal points he had appropriated from Lord Shaftesbury and John Nelson Darby in England, including the necessity of returning the Jews to Palestine. "We will cross the Jordan . . . and possess the land!"[21] Hardly drawing breath, he gripped the audience with tales of errant sons or husbands converting at death's door. He was fluent, ungrammatical, and so richly sentimental that when he wept, the auditorium wept with him.

Philadelphia was next. Between November 1875 and January 1876, tirelessly promoted by the business and newspaper interests, Moody and Sankey were heard by more than a million people at the Grand Depot, a tabernacle the size of a city block, with a total of seventeen thousand staying afterward to discuss salvation in the inquiry rooms. The department store magnate John Wanamaker and Anthony J. Drexel, a leading banker, were among the evangelical elite who spent thousands of dollars to make the revival an unprecedented success, funding six hundred singers and three hundred ushers and spurring a fleet of volunteers to circulate 162,000 flyers. Even Jay Cooke, whose collapse had fueled the unrest that the revival was supposed to ameliorate, was there, piously passing the collection plate. Echoing the general sentiment, the *Public Ledger* called Moody "a great commander" and wrote in awestruck approval of his crusade's "moral grandeur."[22]

A $2 statuette of Moody sold out, a patent medicine maker linked the purifying nature of the revival to his elixir, an auction was arranged for Moody's personal towel, china toiletries, and shaving mirror, and on December 19 President Grant, his cabinet, and the justices of the Supreme Court arrived from Washington to join Moody and Sankey on the stage.[23]

Not all in the press were convinced of the revival's "moral grandeur," unflatteringly calling it "salvation of the slop-shop character" or pointing out Moody's "murder of syntax" and "sacrilegious absurdities." Others complained that any crusade that did not address underlying social problems brought on by recession would have no lasting effect. But these voices were in the minority and dismissed as Catholic if not hopelessly secular.

Sweeping on to New York in February 1876, Moody mounted a specially erected pulpit in the world's largest indoor arena, the Hippodrome, previously home to P. T. Barnum's elephants and acrobats, now commandeered by J. P. Morgan, Cornelius Vanderbilt, and the eager New York press anxious both to bring "a new Jerusalem" to Gotham and to not be outdone by any other metropolis. By now the marriage of business, press, and Moody's machine was complete, and Moody never failed to recognize his debt to "printer's ink."[24]

Every day through April, thirty thousand people "mad for Moody" crowded into the Hippodrome to hear him, while the papers cleaned up his syntax, edited his repetitions, and trusted him to "re-moralize" a city racked by the Tweed ring's corruption, a series of bribery scandals, and the brutal aftermath of the Panic of 1873.

Chicago would be next. The grand midtown tabernacle being built on property owned by John V. Farwell, at the corner of Monroe and Franklin streets, was almost finished and would seat nine thousand persons. After New York, Moody departed for his home in Northfield, Massachusetts, to take a well-deserved rest until October. All the while, the city girded for the onslaught.

Horatio's Fullerton Avenue Presbyterian Church was one of hundreds that "felt the mighty throbs of this great spiritual movement." The fourteen-year-old church, whose membership roll had previously not topped 150, now swelled to 300 parishioners. The Sunday school enrollment rose from 250 to 425, and the church's founder and leading pillar, Horatio Spafford, as its superintendent of the Sunday school, was credited with the increase.[25]

The Spaffords had given themselves unstintingly to the business of recruitment in preparation for the revival. Anna, in addition to her work in the slums, sat on the Fullerton ladies' auxiliary and endorsed an important new objective. After much discussion, the congregation had decided to join other evangelical brethren in sending missionaries abroad. Eventually Fullerton members would take up stations in China and the Middle East, and even the Spaffords' family doctor, Samuel Hedges, would go to Guatemala toward the end of his life.[26]

In the meantime, a new pastor had arrived several years earlier at Fullerton. The Reverend William C. Young, Doctor of Divinity, was youthful but experienced, having traveled extensively abroad. He was slender, elegantly dressed, spoke with a Southern accent, and stood solidly in the center of prevailing Presbyterian orthodoxy. At first Horatio had welcomed him enthusiastically, but they soon recognized that their doctrinal positions diverged. Young was a traditionalist who subscribed to the Presbyterians' Westminster Confession, which included the affirmation of biblical inerrancy: the Scriptures not only contained but *were* the Word of God, and were therefore errorless and binding. In addition, the confession forcibly advocated Calvin's doctrine of predestination and—fitting neatly with Protestant antipathy to Catholic Rome—asserted that the pope was the Antichrist. Horatio, on the other hand, was becoming obsessed by his Arminian views. God, he believed, loved all sinners, and all sinners might be saved, including Satan himself. He was even prepared to deny the existence of hell, and predicted a Savior arriving so suddenly that a man working at his business or a woman nursing her baby could be swept into heaven. As many of the parish's young men were drawn to Horatio's radical gospel, it was no surprise that a collision was in the offing.

With only three months to go before the revival was to begin, the *Chicago Daily Tribune* reported that a coup had occurred at the church on Fullerton Avenue.[27] While everyone knew that Horatio exerted a powerful influence, it came as a shock that he would use his position as head of the finance committee to unseat Fullerton's pastor, Reverend Young. At last, the hidden conflict was in the open, although matters did not go as Horatio planned.

On a Thursday night, he called a meeting to discuss what was alleged to be the minister's poor financial management. Evidently, he expected few members would find it convenient to attend. Instead, 150 parishioners were in their seats, listening intently. Horatio's committee failed to make its case. Embarrassingly, it even appeared that the church's finances were actually in better shape than they had been in some time. At this point, "a gentleman with more courage than the rest," the *Tribune* reported, rose to his feet. He had heard that Reverend Young "was disliked by some members." At that point, according to the *Tribune,* "the truth flashed on all at once. The Finance Committee had resorted to this way of ousting Mr. Young . . . supposing that there would be only a few present, but enough to carry out their designs."[28]

In an atmosphere of heated feeling, Horatio's "designs" were defeated by a vote of 126 in support of Dr. Young against 20 nays. It was a rout for Horatio. "The majority portion of the members are thoroughly disgusted with the instigators of this trouble, and expressed themselves verbally to that effect," concluded the reporter. Dr. Young and his mainstream Presbyterian views were vindicated. Fullerton kept their pastor and watched their "principal ruling elder" depart, leaving anger and indignation in his wake. Their resentment matched his own. Horatio felt that the church he had worked so hard to found had been snatched from his grasp. Anna, six months pregnant and shaken to the core by the debacle, followed her husband along with a handful of devotees.[29]

Back in Lake View, Horatio was white with anger. Immediately, he ordered that a chapel be built behind the house. He would have nothing to do with Fullerton ever again. Instead, he would bring a new church to life, and in this church—so he intended—he would regain his position as the undisputed pillar.

On October 1, 1876, at precisely 3:30 in the afternoon, Dwight Moody, buttoned into a slightly rumpled plum-colored Prince Albert frock coat, ascended the stage of the newly completed tabernacle, seated himself in a chair near the railing, and lowered his head in prayer. To his left, behind an organ, stood Ira Sankey, whiskered, erect, and, as ever, neatly tailored. Assembled before them were nine thousand men, women, and children of Chicago. Behind them on the stage, seated in crowded ranks, were three hundred local clergymen and dignitaries.[30] As longtime friends, the Spaffords were also in those ranks, as for the moment Horatio's welcome at the YMCA's Farewell Hall remained undiminished. Chicago's grand hour had arrived.

For nearly four extraordinary months the city burned again, this time aflame with religious zeal. Over a million residents and thousands from outlying districts felt the heat before the revival ended. Each day the tabernacle reverberated with the sound of gospel music issuing from nine thousand throats. Flogged by intense press coverage and supported by prominent business interests, Chicagoans gathered for prayer, personal testimony, and the sermons of Moody as he compared the world to a foundering ship ready to sink at any moment. God had anointed him, he told the vast audience, to save as many as possible if they would embrace true Christianity. Moody was bringing Darby's premillennialist gospel to the country, and it would linger among evangelicals ever afterward.

However well-intentioned the revival was, the majority of attendees were already churched.[31] Whether they were the virtuous or the backslidden in need of re-churching, this mixture of social levels, usually native-born and Anglo-American, believed like Moody that temperance and keeping the Sabbath were the answers to social unrest and the only means to secure Christian America's moral order.

Thanks to the publicity barrage, there were also plenty who came out of curiosity. But the poor were not among them. Moody had truly hoped to reach these "dangerous classes," yet despite earnest efforts by some churches to bring them in, Moody's rhetoric had little resonance for their personal struggles. Moody's sermons never questioned what might be wrong with a society that was ruthlessly acquisitive, and especially he never challenged the powerful men whose friendships were dear to him, who supported his revivals, and whose exploitative employment practices were largely responsible for the social unrest. The troubles that raged through Chicago and other American cities at this time and that had given impetus to revivalism were never addressed. Ethnic tensions, religious distrust, recession, chronic unemployment, decreasing wages, labor violence—all the factors contributing to social upheaval nowhere intruded into Moody's inspirational homilies. So when the great flame was finally extinguished without capturing the very souls whose cultural differences and economic plight threatened the social equilibrium, when Moody and Sankey, exhausted, at last bade the city goodbye, the citizens of Chicago returned to their lives and found that nothing much had changed.

Church attendance throughout the city did increase, at least briefly. But by 1877, when the city was again shaken by violent labor disputes, enrollments were back to where they had been, and the yawning chasm between the city's Protestant churches and the laboring poor had not been bridged.[32]

In the end, it was the evangelical churches that profited the most from the revival. Their recruits tended to stay permanently. The lower and middle classes especially—the clerks, bookkeepers, salesmen—for whom "maintenance of a stable social order was essential to their social and economic aspirations," had found in Moody's message "something new and clean and good." They now formed a solid and enduring community, subscribing to similar mores that celebrated honesty, hard work, temperance, Christian faith, and the reassuring knowledge that if people were poor, it was because they were lazy and had refused the gospel message. The world, they believed, was divided between saints and sinners. In the "cloudless morning" that followed the great American revival, the moral, economic, and even political views of the evangelicals came to seem not only fundamental but even inherent in the universe.[33]

Moody's movement represented the height of nineteenth-century revivalism. If his methodology—especially his attachment to the business community—undermined his message in the end, and people might be converts but not necessarily better Christians, it was an irony lost on the millions who remembered the mutual exultation, the feelings of spiritual transcendence he had brought them, as one of the most thrilling sensations they had ever had the privilege to share.

At Lake View, even as the revival was soaring to its apogee, the Spaffords received a gift from heaven. A baby boy, Horatio Goertner Goodwin Spafford, named for Daniel Goodwin's drowned child, was born on November 16, 1876. Anna was radiant. Horatio, still struggling to put aside his anger at Fullerton's betrayal, was determined to concentrate on their wee treasure. Holding the baby in his arms, Horatio welcomed splinter groups drifting in from his lost congregation to learn more about the discoveries he was making from his biblical studies. The freshly completed chapel was nearly full on Sundays these days, and the excitement generated was sufficient to call extra meetings on Thursdays as well.

When the revival finally ended and Moody and Sankey departed with appropriate fanfare, Chicagoans settled back into their normal lives, and the Spaffords looked to a new horizon. They knew they had heavy responsibilities now, and readied to marshal their energies and welcome a swelling crowd bent on hearing new truths from Horatio. He recognized that his developing doctrine needed to be properly articulated and began composing a treatise outlining views that he hoped would enjoy a wide circulation.

CHAPTER NINE

The Overcomers

> He that hath an ear let him hear what the
> Spirit said unto the churches: to him that over-
> cometh will I give to eat of the tree of life,
> which is in the midst of the paradise of God.
>
> Revelation 2:7

Under Horatio's tutelage, Bible study began in earnest. While Anna fretted about their deteriorating financial plight, she nevertheless felt pride in a husband who worked deep into the night on a pamphlet that, he told her, would change the world. He intended that his pamphlet explain the remarkable insights he had achieved. He revealed to his fascinated congregation that they were members of a church that had always existed. Abraham had founded it thousands of years ago, but it had "been buried away," suppressed by the institutionalized church. Now, with their help, it was "rising phoenix-like from the ruins" in this last of the dispensations before Christ's return. The Lake View congregation was the "Bride" of Christ and must "surrender themselves utterly to the Lord's will."[1] It was not enough to simply profess faith at an ecstatic moment during one of Moody's revivals; to be a true Christian, one must be "consecrated with the Bride," and together as the Bride they would "overcome" iniquity and apostasy on earth, just as the Book of Revelation had predicted. As they listened, he warned that the established church had failed in its mission. Only through their holy spirit would the world be led back to God.[2]

The arrival of Horatio's sister Margaret Lee was fortuitous. She and

Horatio had always been close, despite her living in Washington, D.C., after marriage. She admired her brother and now embraced Horatio's doctrines with boundless enthusiasm, adding some spice of her own. A year or two earlier, she had attended a religious camp meeting where she had asked for baptism in the Holy Spirit. She had been rewarded with "a thrill of delight" coursing "like an electric shock" through her body. She then asked for a tangible sign by which she might know God's will and was given, she believed, a sign that came with a loud crack of her teeth. "But as the cracking was very loud," wrote an observer, "it became unpleasant to her husband, especially as it would often take place in the middle of a meal, so she prayed the Lord that He would please give her a quieter sign, and her prayer was answered by the cracking of the jaw being stopped and the sign transferred to her eyes, which were drawn back into the head, as if by strings fastened behind and pulled by an invisible hand. From that time, everything was tested by the drawing in of her eyes. This was only an affirmative sign; when the answer was 'no,' there was no sign given."[3]

While Horatio concentrated on the intricacies of religious paradox, Maggie's jaw cracking and eye movements appealed to those in the Lake View crowd searching for a more dramatic form of worship than biblical exegesis. "A little community gathered round her," continued the observer, "who all brought everything in their lives to be tested by the cracking of her jaw. They engaged or dismissed servants, arranged their households, transacted their business, gave up old businesses, entered into new businesses, formed friendships, gave up friends, dressed, did everything in fact by the guidance of [Maggie's] sign."[4]

Soon, not just Maggie Lee, considered the group's "Moses," but other women in the fast-developing sect received messages, some so powerfully that they jerked and fainted to the floor. One had a "sign" indicating that oranges were to be used in their services, and for a time the congregation sanctified oranges as the presence of the Holy Ghost. Others simply opened their Bibles and whatever sentence their eyes fell on gave them direction. If, for example, a woman needed to purchase material for a frock, she had merely to ruffle the pages, put her finger randomly on a passage, and the Bible would lead her to the right yardage.[5] At one point a small party traveled to Boston with neither money nor purpose, guided solely by "a sniffle" from one of their "prophetesses." They were discovered sitting on a curbstone, waiting for further direction from the sniffle. While they all returned safely and quite enjoyed their excursion, the newspapers got wind of the escapade, and there was no end to the ridicule or the interest of reporters.[6]

At first Anna looked on silently as others received signs. Then slowly she, too, participated, although seldom with the frequency of Maggie Lee. Mostly she watched, and her dignity sobered some of the more radical women disposed to violent displays. It was her husband's insights to which she had given her trust and faith, and she was eager to share them with the new converts. Many who attended were troubled in heart and mind, and Anna's sensitive counsel brought them comfort and peace. In time she earned the respect of the congregation, who began to see Anna as possessing a quietly formidable power, different perhaps but equal in authority to that of her sister-in-law.

The congregation called themselves the Saints, subscribing to Horatio's teachings that all could be saved, including Satan, although sinners were to be cleansed by a rather nasty time in purgatory. At meetings, prayers were offered that they might all be transported to Jerusalem, where as the "Elect Bride" they would be "the only ones in the world who would be prepared for His coming," an event to be encouraged by the return of the Jews. They believed that "the day after they arrived in Jerusalem, the Star of Bethlehem was to . . . settle on the head of one of them, and this fact would go out to the world, and immediately all the people who were expecting the Lord's coming, and looking for it, would hasten as fast as possible to Jerusalem and gather round the Star, and then, when all the saints were gathered, the Lord would ascend, and His saints with Him, into the air above Jerusalem."[7]

The Overcomers, as people now called them, took care to keep from skeptical outsiders the innovative practices that often stimulated more excitable members to run noisily about during prayer meetings. Even so, and despite careful screening, the congregation grew apace, and by 1877 a twin church in nearby Valparaiso, Indiana, was also flourishing, with over two hundred members shuttling back and forth to Lake View to share revelations and trade sermons from their prophetesses. Seventy years later, writing about this critical period in her parents' lives, Bertha

Spafford Vester recalled: "I find it difficult to interpret to this modern generation Father's and Mother's attitude toward life at this time and throughout the following years without making them seem impractical, fanatical, narrow, and visionary." And yet, she insisted, "they were none of these things. The world has so changed in its outlook, its conceptions, its manners, and its vocabulary . . . that the problems which were important to them then seem almost unintelligible and meaningless now. Therefore it is hard to do them justice."[8]

The Spaffords and their followers were hardly unique in their strange views. At a time when large and small religious gatherings frequently took place in private homes, special camp meetings, or under great revival tents, seekers abounded who were eager to serve God and give themselves over to physical manifestations. Faith in the healing power of Jesus Christ was usually central, but many chose to interpret His message in ways quite removed from mainstream orthodoxy. Horatio's timely discovery that there was no such thing as hell was convenient, given his current difficulties. It was consoling to believe that his criminal abuse of trust funds did not consign him to eternal punishment. He had learned all too painfully that hell was life on earth. "He who commits sin here in this world receives his punishment at the same time" was his view, which he tried to explain to the numbers of reporters who were taking an interest in the goings-on at Lake View.[9]

Horatio had stopped practicing law entirely, despite the urging of friends to resume a reliable and respectable source of income. More than ever, Anna was watching every penny. She had only one servant to help her. Although the recent death of Aunty Sims had reduced the number of mouths to feed, members of the congregation often stayed for dinner. "God will provide," Horatio continued to assure her. They managed to get along because, unknown to Anna, Horatio was re-mortgaging property and borrowing heavily.

Their evangelical comrades had turned uneasily away, deeply disturbed by events. There was a general agreement that the Spaffords had been so crazed by grief that they had lost touch with reality. While Moody himself, conciliatory and forgiving by nature, never added his voice to those of Horatio's critics, he was distressed to learn that the pamphlet Horatio had written detailing the mission of the "Bride" of

Christ, and distributed by some of the more energetic Saints at the door of the YMCA, had brought down ridicule from some while scandalizing others. The YMCA's leaders were incensed about the pamphlet, and word went out in evangelical circles that it was "the work of an infidel."[10] The rift could not be healed, although one of Chicago's evangelical fraternity, William E. Blackstone, was extremely interested in Horatio's emphasis on the necessity of repatriating Jews to their ancestral land. An ardent millennialist himself, a Zionist before there was a Zionist political movement, Blackstone was single-mindedly dedicated to this theory, and would soon sponsor the famous Blackstone Memorial urging America and other nations to cooperate in helping Jews settle in Palestine. He conceded that the Lake View group was deviant, yet he could not resist periodic visits to learn if they had received any "tidings." Horatio had told him that he was in contact with Dr. Piazza Smith, the Scottish astronomer, and Blackstone was eager to know if the professor had pinpointed the cataclysmic date. To Chicago society in general, however, the Spaffords were no longer welcome. The break with Fullerton was complete, and now a new unpleasantness arose.

Horatio had begged his friend Major Whittle to intercede on his behalf with Moody, whose son, William, had married Whittle's daughter. Moody had published a collection of hymns that included songs by Whittle and the popular evangelical composer Philip P. Bliss. It also included Horatio's "It Is Well with My Soul," which Bliss had set to music. Enormously popular, the hymnal was a best seller, and Horatio wanted Moody to give him several thousand dollars from its proceeds. Whittle refused to ask Moody. He told Horatio it was wrong; the money was to go to Moody's work, which enraged Horatio.

But Whittle was angry, too. His family friend Mrs. J. P. Wills was in a desperate position. Divorced and dependent on the $17,000 she had entrusted to Spafford, she begged Whittle to remind Horatio that, at the very least, she needed some interest on her money. When Major Whittle approached Horatio about Mrs. Wills's "necessitous condition," Horatio confirmed that he was "probably bankrupt and that he had no means of raising money even to the extent of $5.00." At first Whittle agreed to pray with Horatio "that God might send him $100,000 which was what was needed to pay his pressing debts." But as the months passed and Whittle remained adamant about approaching Moody, the two men ceased to speak. Whittle was convinced that Horatio was leading his group into heresy and "warned my neighbors against them."[11]

Anna was still in the dark about the full extent of Horatio's business dealings, but on more than one occasion she panicked over their lack of an income. "Today the Lord brought us very low," she wrote in her diary. "We had our breakfast, but there was no prospect for dinner—We had milk but no bread or butter—We had also potatoes in our garden— We made up our minds we would eat milk and potatoes . . . I was a good deal cast down," she admitted. They prayed together and miraculously found that they had overlooked twenty cents. With some difficulty, Anna persuaded Horatio to let her sell newspapers, which provided another eighty cents to buy food.[12]

She was aware, however, that Horatio was more inclined toward borrowing than she felt morally justified. Their congregation had left them in charge of a cache of donated money. One desperate day, when they had nothing to eat, Horatio wanted to dip into it. "I felt a strong repulsion to it," Anna told her diary. "I thought it a temptation—and God was testing us—Horatio seemed quite clear it would be all right—and his opinion staggered me—and I thought perhaps I am wrong—I prayed and asked the Lord not to let us fall into sin but let us take the upper side of faith and trust Him to send us money."[13]

Mostly, however, during Horatio's fatal drift into quixotic heterodoxy, Anna supported him wholeheartedly. "One can hardly imagine what heartfelt praise is until one passes through hard trials," she confided resiliently to her diary.[14] With considerable good grace, she managed to accept their poverty and summon the strength to face ostracism from their former evangelical circle. She had persuaded herself of her husband's revelations and enjoyed the deference his disciples accorded her. Above all, she had been rewarded by her sweet baby Horatio, who had brightened her life, making it meaningful as nothing else could. Her husband, always reticent on business matters and still deluding himself that he could right his errors, was loath to tell her of the extent of his debts and of his legal infractions. He had watched her authority grow within their movement. How could he maintain her esteem and command her obedience if she knew? He had told Whittle of the debts only out of necessity.

Anna could not pretend that her husband was not anxious and preoccupied, closing his study door for hours or suddenly departing for a mysterious appointment downtown. Recently he had ordered that a fence be put up dividing their property into two halves. To Anna's questions, he merely said that it would create two lots and make the property more valuable. She was curious, but she was pregnant again, and when a girl was born on March 24, 1878, her hands were full. She told Horatio that she wanted to name the baby Bertha Hedges Spafford out of gratitude to their two friends who had been so kind through their trials: Dr. Hedges, who had delivered the baby, and Bertha Johnson, with whom she had stayed in Paris. Happiness at being a mother twice over had vanquished her depression completely, and she felt an inner confidence she had never known before.

Then, in February 1880, Anna took her babies on a trip, and after traveling a great distance by train from Chicago, she realized that three-year-old Horatio and nearly two-year-old Bertha were feverish. Desperate to get back home to Dr. Hedges, she left the train but had to sit in a drafty waiting room awaiting a train returning to Chicago. She telegraphed Peter, their houseboy, to meet her and to alert Dr. Hedges. When she finally got back to Chicago and boarded the narrow-gauge commuter train for Lake View, it was bitterly cold and snowing heavily. The buggy was open, and the huddled passengers were pelted with snow as Peter raced them home. The house was dark and frigid, and by the time Dr. Hedges arrived, little Horatio had slipped into a coma. Dr. Hedges diagnosed scarlet fever complicated by pneumonia. They telegraphed Horatio, who arrived in time to join Anna at their son's bedside, and together they watched him die on February 11, 1880.

Anna refused to accompany Horatio and the other mourners to the cemetery. Instead, she sat by the window. "I will say God is love until I believe it," she repeated tonelessly over and over.[15] How else could she survive? Still, she heard the whispers. She knew the Fullerton congregation, old friends, and even their own Saints wondered why God was punishing them so terribly.

When one of their group's leaders, a man they had relied on, offered to adopt her surviving baby, the proposal came like a mortal blow. Anna had fought crippling sadness—determined to believe and to overcome—but now she was gripped by a dreadful rage, even as it dawned on her that, once again, she was pregnant. No one would ever take away her child. In her grief, her thoughts turned to the promised descent of the Savior on Jerusalem. Previously an abstraction, the idea of going to Jerusalem, of being free forever from Chicago's sorrowful memories, from criticism and misunderstanding, now seemed like a blessed escape—even an imperative goal.

Shortly thereafter, Horatio called to her from his study. He was deathly pale. Suddenly afraid, Anna slipped into a chair as Horatio closed the door. "I must tell you something, Anna." He shut his eyes and put his head in his hands. "I am a ruined man," he said. And there it was, the truth she had avoided. "We are ruined," he repeated dully.

She listened with mounting dread as her husband explained the enormity of his difficulties. He had abused a number of trusts, including his niece's, he confessed wretchedly. Mrs. Wills was harassing him for money. The reason he had divided the property was to take out more mortgages—one with the Connecticut Mutual Life Insurance Company for $10,000 on the empty lot, and where their house stood, he had gone to Hetty Green, an enormously wealthy real estate developer, arranging for a loan of $30,000. He could no longer meet the payments. Mrs. Green's agents were threatening foreclosure on their house. "I did it all for you." He looked at her imploringly. "Values are sure to rise again, and I was trying to hold on to our properties for your sake, for our children—for the sake of the Saints."

Anna stared at him. "We will have to confess," she said coolly. "We will ask the Saints to pray for you."

The following Sunday when the congregation filed in and settled in their seats, Anna stood up and surveyed the room. Two hundred of the Bride of Christ looked back wonderingly. In a clear, low voice, Anna announced that their brother Horatio, her husband, was encumbered by debts. "We must pray now that Mr. Spafford is relieved by the Lord of these debts. We must pray that Mr. Spafford is delivered from those who are persecuting him. We must turn our thoughts to Jerusalem. To

Jerusalem we will go to await the Messiah, and when he has alighted, we, the Bride, shall return in great triumph and blessing to bring the Word to the world."[16]

The community was abuzz. Those with the sign were asked for guidance. Frequent prayer meetings were called. Talk abounded that Horatio owed more than $100,000—which in fact was the case. Yet he was the leader of their consecrated number. It was he who had told them this last dispensation was coming to its blazing finale. For the excited congregation, the prospect of Jerusalem had suddenly taken on the same reality it held for Anna.

On January 18, 1881, Anna went into her seventh labor. It was a difficult birth at a stressful time, leaving Anna weak and depleted and giving little Bertha a sister, Grace. During the month of May, the baby lost weight and would not suckle, and they feared they would lose her. Sleepless, walking the infant through the night, Anna prayed and dreamed of Jerusalem. Whatever it took, she would get there somehow. In her deepest being, she sensed that a long chapter had closed. All that she and Horatio had once shared with their evangelical friends, and particularly with Dwight Moody, she would cherish and look back on with the affection and gratitude that it deserved. But Moody, famous now, was the center of a faith that seemed as remote from theirs as the far and glittering Jerusalem that beckoned her. She and Horatio were moving on to another life, in which Dwight Moody and the others would recede like phantoms, to be occasionally remembered, as in a dream. Walking with her baby through the dark house, Anna silently bade her old friend farewell. Softly, she whispered goodbye to Chicago as well. In her heart, she was shutting the book on the past, yet she was not sorry. God had vouchsafed a better understanding than anything Moody could offer. Whether or not tiny Grace lived, Anna wearily resolved to enter a future with the Lord, and to be in Jerusalem to greet him when he came.

Mercifully, however, in June the baby showed signs of improvement, and Anna allowed herself to think Grace would live. When Dr. Hedges asked if he and his family could join the household, she was glad to have the doctor close by. Sympathetically, he told her that he realized she was exhausted, but that he was as well. He needed to get away from midtown, where patients called him at all hours of the night. Burdened with anxieties, Anna confided to Rachel Hedges that she lived in constant fear that she would come home one day and find a foreclosure sign on their door.[17] To make matters worse, reporters had been sniffing around, inquiring about the group and asking if it was true that the congregation planned to go to Jerusalem. Anna had read the scornful articles published about them and tried not to cringe. Horatio, fighting not to lose his grip, fearing that at any moment he would be served a subpoena from one of his creditors, reluctantly responded to their questions about his theology. But when a reporter from the *Daily Inter Ocean* asked him the dangerous question—what day did he intend to leave for Jerusalem?—Horatio showed him to the door.[18]

The previous week Anna had decided to approach William Rudy, a quiet businessman recovering from a serious illness who had joined the congregation at the suggestion of a well-to-do member, Amelia Gould, whose husband had recently died. Rudy was clearly fond of Mrs. Gould, helping her with her business affairs. He struck Anna as both kind and sensible, so in the strictest confidence she took him aside and asked his help. They agreed it was time to take action. Anna, Horatio, Maggie Lee, and Dr. Hedges stood talking on the lawn after dinner that signal evening of August 17, 1881. Mr. Rudy approached them, and when Horatio asked him where he had been, Rudy replied that he had just come from midtown and handed Horatio a telegram.[19] He had wired a steamship company in Canada and requested seventeen berths. The telegram was the affirmative answer. Horatio put it in his pocket and asked Dr. Hedges to join him in his office.

"Dr. Hedges," Horatio said, "we must leave in an hour and a half for Quebec. Will you stay in the house and do your best to hold it? And will you continue the meetings here and in Valparaiso?"[20]

Astonished, Hedges could only nod.

"Mrs. Spafford has had a supernatural visitation that calls us to Jerusalem. I am not sure how long we will be gone, but we hope to bring back a message of glory to the world," Horatio explained urgently. "I need you to help me with some business matters."

Horatio asked Hedges if he would consider $55 a month a fair rent. He went on to say that he wanted Hedges to send to a Mrs. Wills $25 a month and to his niece Mary Murphy $25. "I realize that I owe you

$1200, so I suggest that you put a value on the furniture remaining here and apply it to my debt."[21]

Still dumbfounded, Hedges agreed. They settled on $400 as a reasonable assessment of the house's contents. Although, as Hedges later testified, he knew that Horatio was straitened "because I could see it," it never dawned on him that Horatio was in danger of being arrested. Hedges, like everyone else, believed "their journey was necessitated by an imperative supernatural command."[22] He then took from Horatio a packet that contained instructions about his affairs.

Frantically throwing together what they could pack in an hour, the Spaffords and their two children, Maggie Lee, Amelia Gould, William Rudy and his foster mother, Caroline Merriman, two other couples with their daughters, Horatio's nephew Rob Lawrence, and fourteen-year-old Annie Aiken as baby nurse gathered again on the lawn to make their rapid adieus to the startled and marveling Saints, to whom the news came as a welcome and momentous shock. A bright August moon shone over the group as Anna announced that those departing were to be known as "the apostles." In all, there were twelve adults and four young ones, leaving one of the berths that Rudy had reserved apparently unclaimed. A whispered discussion of money took place, with Rudy, Mrs. Gould, and Mrs. Lee contributing what cash they could. Hedges, who had just sold a family farm, donated another $3,000, promising to cable more funds to them when they reached London.

And thus, in the greatest haste, did the group depart at nine o'clock that evening for Quebec, and thence to Jerusalem.

CHAPTER TEN

"Amelikans" in Yerushalayim

*As I looked before me, in all their glory and
majesty I beheld, magnificent in the light of
the setting sun, the walls of Jerusalem. I had
thought of that moment for years, in waking
and sleeping dreams. I had asked myself a hundred times, "What will you do when your weary
eyes rest on these holy walls?" Sometimes I
thought I should cry out aloud, as did pilgrims
of old; sometimes, that I should kneel down on
the road as did the valiant men who marched
with Godfrey and with Richard; but I did neither. My horse stopped on the road, as if he
knew that all our haste had been for this; and I
murmured to myself, "Deus vault"; and my eyes
filled with tears, and through them I gazed at
the battlements, and towers, and minarets of the
city.*

—Anonymous visitor, 1880

When the Overcomers landed in Ottoman Palestine in 1881,
the world they encountered was as different from America as
golden Byzantium had been to the followers of Mehmed II who captured Constantinople in 1453. These nomadic Turkish horsemen from
the eastern steppes, led by descendants of Osman, founder of the Ottoman dynasty, by the thirteenth century had abandoned their shaman-

ist beliefs in favor of Sunni Islam, and in due course controlled a vast polyglot empire composed of Turks, Slavs, Bulgars, Magyars, Greeks, Albanians, Kurds, Armenians, Berbers, and in particular millions of Arabs, all presided over by the Sublime Porte on the shores of the Golden Horn.

By the mid-sixteenth century, the Ottoman banner waved over much of southern Russia, Mesopotamia, the Christian Balkans, Anatolia, and the Arab east from Syria along the Red Sea coast to Yemen, as well as Egypt and the Barbary States of North Africa from the Nile Delta to the foothills of the Atlas Mountains in Morocco. Under the reign of Suleiman the Magnificent from 1520 to 1566, the empire had reached its zenith, and the sultan held the foot-long keys to the gates of Medina and Mecca. "The Shadow of Allah" to most of the Muslim world, the sultan was also their caliph, or spiritual leader, and ruled a theocratic state. In addition, he was protector of Jerusalem, a city as sacred to Muslims as it was to Christians and Jews. According to Muslim tradition, the Prophet traveled on his winged horse, Al-Buraq, to Jerusalem from Mecca and ascended from the summit of Mount Moriah into heaven on a mystical night journey.

The Ottomans took the holy city in 1516, ending a century of dreadful neglect under its previous Muslim rulers, the Egyptian Mamluks, and an earlier history of violence by Christian crusaders. The people welcomed the new conquerors and were rewarded with an efficient administration. The Ottomans improved the water supply, developed commerce, beautified the city with fine buildings and fountains, and protected it from bedouin brigandage by an encircling wall that towered forty feet high. Jews expelled from Spain in 1492 and Christians alike were encouraged to settle in the city by the farsighted Suleiman, who recognized the value of tolerance toward the *dhimmis*, or "people of the Book," to whom Islamic law offered special protections.

When the Ottomans were repulsed from the gates of Vienna in 1683, their hitherto irresistible advance finally halted, and subsequent centuries found them defending rather than acquiring territory. Even as a high culture flowered, producing some of the world's most exquisite art, architecture, literature, and mystical poetry, a slow decay began. In part it was fed by inept military leadership, fratricide, court favoritism, and rampant intrigue inside the seraglio. But also, the dangerous habit of incarcerating heirs in a so-called golden cage within the palace walls created Ottoman rulers too often deranged, degenerated, or untrained to rule such a huge and unwieldy state. No attempt was made to improve the quality of life for the empire's varied populations or to utilize the resources of its once fertile lands, which languished in neglect. Instead, a corrupt tax system exploited its increasingly unhappy subjects, victimized by the system in countless ways. Satisfied with their own splendor and unaware until too late of the unprecedented scientific discoveries of the West, the "Grand Turk" disdained modern industrial models and foundered in fatal ignorance. In 1853, Czar Nicholas called the sultanate "the sick man of Europe" and launched the Crimean War in a failed effort to seize the Dardanelles and obtain a warm-water port for Russia.

Periodically reformers tried to reverse the decline, but their efforts were sidelined by conservative interests, in particular by the Muslim clergy, or ulema. The Ottomans had borrowed a hierarchal ecclesiastical structure from the Christian Byzantines different from that seen in other Muslim countries. Although Islam was the state religion, and the empire guaranteed legal protection to other religions within its domain, jurisdiction over matters of law and life of the empire's Muslim subjects was in the hands of local muftis, or bishops, whose supreme head was the grand mufti of Constantinople, or *sheikh al-Islam*, who in turn was the ultimate authority on the Sharia, the Islamic code of law. Only Europeans living in the empire enjoyed the special rights of extraterritoriality that accorded them tariff concessions, tax exemptions, and adjudication of their legal disputes by their consular representatives. This tradition of "capitulations," dating from the sixteenth century, did much to strengthen the hand of foreigners who, by the middle of the nineteenth century, had penetrated far into the economic and political life of Ottoman Turkey.

By 1881, Sultan Abdul Hamid II had occupied the throne for five years. A reclusive autocrat, but a surprisingly deft manipulator of European ambitions, the sultan was determined to reverse Turkey's decline. Almost immediately he was plunged into a second war with Russia, which he lost and which put Turkey into even greater debt to European financiers. The empire having earlier lost Greece, Abdul Hamid was then forced to relinquish Romania, Serbia, and Montenegro, and reluctantly cede autonomy to Bulgaria as well as parts of Armenia to Russia.

Cunning, cautious, and often underestimated, Abdul Hamid had dissolved parliament, was doing his best to stem the advance of Western ideas, and was trying to hold on to his remaining territories even as they burned with secessionist fevers. Suspicion and intrigue reigned in the capital while the sultan's spies lurked everywhere, including in Jerusalem. While the holy city—Al-Quds Al-Sharif to his Arab subjects—was as neglected as other parts of the ailing empire, its sacred places ensured continual attention from the international community. Indeed, it had been an argument over who was properly the protector of the Christian sites that had caused the brutal Crimean War. The deeply religious sultan Abdul Hamid took his responsibility seriously as the city's guardian, and although he did little for his Arab subjects in Palestine, he had no intention of allowing another religious conflict to arise. So while the Overcomers would find the resident Arabs inured to poverty and indifference, deprived of modern techniques to till their fields or create industries, a firm Turkish presence was evident. There were few amenities in shabby Jerusalem otherwise, but a large garrison of soldiers stood ready to preserve peace between an astonishing variety of different faiths not always well disposed toward one another.

The pilgrims arose before dawn on their first morning. From their bedroom windows in the Mediterranean Hotel, they could make out the Mount of Olives shrouded in long streamers of gray vapor, a ridge of steel-colored mountains running behind it to the east. A mist had settled over the silent, darkened city below, washing its rooftops with dew. As the gentle light of early morning pulled aside the veil, they could see the glittering outline of the Dome of the Rock crowning the vast pavilion that was to the Muslims their "Noble Sanctuary," or Haram al-Sharif, as it was the "Temple Mount" to the Jews. Listening, entranced, the pilgrims heard the city find its voice: shopkeepers chattering under them in the cobbled street, a donkey's bray, a semi-naked dervish ringing his bell and crying for alms, the pillowed feet of camels shuffling toward the souk, their drivers shouting their way through the gathering crowds. As quickly as they could relish a breakfast of hot flatbread and strong coffee, the pilgrims sallied forth from their dirty caravanserai into the stream of varied humanity that was Jerusalem in 1881.

Jostled by porters bent double beneath staggering loads, picking their way between pushcarts, animals, beggars, blind men or cripples, uniformed Turkish soldiers, swarthy bedouin from the desert followed by their tattooed wives, tall, fierce-looking Kurds armed with swords, water carriers, veiled women, Armenian and Russian peasants, richly robed clerics wearing the strange headgear of their orders, the little group of Overcomers made their way along David Street, turning into the Christian Quarter toward the Church of the Holy Sepulchre. Formally dressed, the ladies in lacy shirtwaists with muttonchop sleeves, the gentlemen in city tweeds and bowlers, the Chicago pilgrims themselves received scarcely a second glance as they gaped at the outlandish scene.

Anna and Horatio, anxious to know if the flow of Jews to the Holy Land was increasing as quickly as they hoped, were reassured by Elias, their dragoman, or interpreter, whose inclination anyway was to inform this fresh group of "Amelikans" about everything they cared to know. Yes, Jews were coming, he said. He didn't mention that recent appalling pogroms in Russia had spurred a Jewish flight to the Holy Land, but he waved his hand toward the city outskirts and said that several decades before a British Jew, Moses Montefiore, and later Baron Rothschild, had begun financing scattered agricultural training farms in order to free Jerusalem's Jews from dependence on foreign charity. For centuries, he told them, the city's Jews had lived off the *haluka*, a stipend raised by international Jewry to fund study of the Talmud and Torah and to keep a Jewish presence in the city. With a laugh, he said that Jews didn't like to work. They didn't mind being money changers, he said. They didn't mind being shoemakers or even tailors, but few engaged in other trades. For instance, there were no Jewish coffin makers: the Jews of Jerusalem did not bury their dead in coffins, as he understood Jews elsewhere did. Instead, they wrapped them in shrouds to expedite their return to the Temple Mount on the Day of Judgment.[1] If they wished, he would take them to the Temple Mount, and then to the famous Wailing Wall, where they could see for themselves how it was that Jews were coming to Jerusalem.

The Overcomers liked Elias Habib. He was an Arab who wore a red fez, but he was not Muslim. He came from a Greek Orthodox family of artisans, builders, and especially silversmiths in the Old City. Elias associated his name with that of the biblical prophet and was attracted to the group's interest in biblical prophecies. In due course he even became a member, volunteering as a market man, cook, and overseer of native help.

The group's first stop was at the most venerated church in Christendom, the omphalos, or "navel of the universe." As they neared the Holy Sepulchre, the Overcomers wondered about the rags hung about on trees. Elias patiently explained these were scraps of clothing left by pilgrims. The group's surprise was even greater when they entered the arched portal of the vast, musty high-domed building and saw armed Turkish gendarmes stationed at attention. Again, Elias filled them in. From the time of the Fourth Crusade, he said, when the Latin crusaders had pillaged the Byzantine Greek capital of Constantinople, the relationship between these Christian orders had been poisonous. Bloody fights in the church between Latins and Greeks were common. Ottoman sultans had long seen the need to keep soldiers at all the major sites to prevent Christian sects from tearing each other to pieces. Long before, the sultanate had entrusted the keys to the Holy Sepulchre to two of Jerusalem's notable Arab families. It was a Muslim, therefore, who opened the door in the morning as an anxious Christian priest looked over his shoulder. And it was another Muslim who locked it at night.

The Byzantine emperor Constantine's mother, Empress Helena, touring the Holy Land in search of the True Cross and the places of Christ's birth, crucifixion, and burial, had identified the spot in 326 and built the first church. Ever since, it had been the focus of vicious and continuous struggles among Christianity's rival sects that had endured unabated until the present. Possession had been fought over not only by Greeks and Latins but also with equal intensity by Armenians, Syrian Jacobites, Nestorians, Romanian Orthodox, Melkites, Copts, Ethiopians, Monophysites, and other Christian orders, convinced of the rightness of their creeds and anxious to have their designated area of the precious ground. The most recent bloody fracas, Elias told them, had occurred just a few years before over Roman Catholic dust swept from a staircase landing in the Greek Orthodox area. Priests had fallen on one another with murderous abandon and were separated by Turkish soldiers who themselves suffered serious injury.

Like others before them, the Overcomers were shocked to learn of such discord in a holy place. But for Anna, remembering the misery caused by ugly doctrinal differences in Chicago, and their injury to her husband and to her own life, the revelation only confirmed her growing contempt for establishment churches.

Even so, the majesty of the great, dimly lit edifice touched them all. In awed silence, they smelled the incense, heard the chanting, and watched as weeping pilgrims crawled on their knees to kiss the stone slab covering the rock where the Son of God had been anointed with oil before burial. Called the Stone of Unction—but actually put in place in 1810 at the time that the Greeks forced the removal of the bodies of the Crusade's leaders, Baldwin I and Godfrey of Bouillon—it would have been hacked to pieces by souvenir-greedy pilgrims had the authorities not given it a protective covering.

Outside once more in the brilliant sunlight, blinking and bemused as they digested their first encounter with the stunning realities of their new home, the Overcomers now made their way through narrow crooked streets to the Via Dolorosa. Perhaps because he felt Anna's eyes on him, Elias was encouraged to tell his group what few visitors heard: the presumed route of Christ's Passion had been invented in the seventeenth century by Franciscan friars. That it might not have been the true path of the Passion would have spoiled things for most travelers unfamiliar with the story of the city's multiple destructions over the millennia. The truth, however, was that the Franciscans had enjoyed a taste for martyrdom in emulation of Christ's sacrifice. Unlike the Greek Orthodox, who emphasized the Resurrection, the Roman Catholic Franciscans came to Jerusalem to do battle with Islam. They encouraged each other to storm the Haram al-Sharif, or Noble Sanctuary, brandishing crosses and cursing the Prophet. For this violation of Muslim sacred ground, two monks were executed. The order then sought a less dangerous and more symbolic method of celebrating the Crucifixion, leading processions of barefoot pilgrims down what they termed the "Via Dolorosa" on Friday evenings and stopping to pray at eight "stations" delegated to be those of

Christ's last journey. They capped it off with a stop at the Golgotha rock inside the Holy Sepulchre. In due course, the route acquired fourteen stations observed by European Christians, and in the nineteenth century another six were added.[2] Anna listened carefully to this account, and again was struck by the plethora of nimble inventions proffered, she felt, in the name of religious truths.

But she was also hungry. The group admitted they all were, although they had noticed no restaurants on their walk. Elias suggested getting a simple bite from one of the many tiny cook shops. The gentlemen agreed. The ladies, however, exchanged glances, their faces blushing. "Where," Anna courageously asked for them all, "might there be a lavatory?"

Suddenly they realized why the city stank. Jerusalem, they soon understood, sat on four thousand years of refuse, which had filled in the valleys between what in ancient times were the clearly defined hills of Acre, Bezetha, and Moriah. The Tyropean Valley, or Valley of the Cheesemongers, as Flavius Josephus called it, ran from outside the low-lying Damascus Gate at the north to the aptly named Dung Gate at the southeast. Over centuries, as one generation built on top of another, the valley had filled in. Some forty feet below the piles of construction, the Tyropean had become one vast sewer, a drain for the winter spates rushing from north to south. The curious might look down through an occasional iron grille to the pungent abyss below and imagine a grand Herodian mosaic floor or long-vanished frescoed wall. Although under the Romans the city had enjoyed a sophisticated water supply and drainage system, the city's infrastructure had been left to decay under such subsequent conquerors as the Persians, crusaders, Ayyubids, Mongols, Tartars, Mamluks, and the indifferent Ottoman successors of Suleiman the Magnificent, despite improvements made by him.

Not long after the Overcomers arrived, they would see British archaeologists attempting to trace the remains of the old water system. In the meantime, a city dweller building a new house simply sank his pottery pipe down into the infinite muck and placed a squatting latrine over it. As for the visitor wandering the city, the only recourse was to follow whatever odor most viciously assaulted his nose until he located a half-folded piece of shoulder-high sheet iron propped like a shield in some fetid corner, and stood behind it.[3] As for the Overcomers, they hastened back to the dirty and foul-smelling but marginally more bearable comforts of the Mediterranean Hotel.

Clearly, they needed a house of their own. Fortunately, a few days later, when they finally visited the Haram al-Sharif, they had an important encounter. The entire group had been eager to see this mysterious place. From their first afternoon, when they had hiked up to the rocky summit of the Mount of Olives and gazed down from its height over the city, they had marveled at the beauty of the golden dome covering an exquisite mosque inlaid with mosaics, the famous Dome of the Rock, Jerusalem's most majestic structure. It glowed like a jewel in the midst of an immense platform shaded with cypress trees and dotted with enchanting Oriental shrines.

The Haram, Elias told them, was the leveled peak of Mount Moriah, where Abraham offered his son Isaac—"and God," he declared with a flourish, "stayed his hand!" It was also here that Solomon had his temple before the Babylonian captivity and a later temple built by Herod was destroyed by the Roman general Titus in A.D. 70. The Prophet Muhammad, guided by the angel Gabriel, had ascended from this spot on his mystical night journey to heaven. Then, when the Prophet's armies exploded out of Arabia to create an Islamic empire larger than Rome's, the fifth Umayyad caliph, Abd al-Malik, had restored the platform in 691. To honor the sanctity of Jerusalem, he gathered the best of Syrian and Byzantine architects and built the Dome of the Rock. When one of the Overcomers inquired about a huge gate walled up with stones leading into the Haram, Elias told him that it was the Golden Gate, adding that Christ was said to have entered the city on Palm Sunday through this gate and at the Second Coming was expected to appear through it again.

The city, as the Overcomers soon discovered, belonged equally to Jews, Christians, and Muslims and was sacred to all alike. Yet of all its treasures, rising loftily on its great platform, with its elegant buildings and aura of quiet sanctity, the Haram was unquestionably Jerusalem's most beautiful and compelling focus. But the group was troubled by something Horatio had told them earlier. In the eyes of Orthodox Jews, Horatio had said, the Haram and its Dome of the Rock would have to be destroyed so that a third temple could be built in its place. Until this occurred, the Messiah would not return. Once more, Anna's thoughts lingered on what seemed to her savage and unnecessary contradictions between different confessions. When Elias offered to take them to the Haram, she and the others accompanied him eagerly on a sunny morning a few days later.

Innocent of Muslim religious prejudices that prohibited Christians and Jews from entering the Haram—an Arabic word meaning "forbidden"—without express permission from Jerusalem's Turkish *mutasarrif,* or governor, the Overcomers strolled along David Street toward the Haram's entrance. As soon as they entered, they felt its extraordinary serenity. In a body they mounted the marble steps, walking directly up to the door of the Dome of the Rock.[4] An attendant in long robes confronted them and requested their papers. Clearly agitated but polite, he begged them to wait and hurried off. As they milled about, suddenly "a whirling apparition crowned by a monumental green turban approached like a diminutive jinn ejected from an uncorked bottle."[5] It was the sheikh custodian himself. Instead of protesting their presence, the tiny sheikh invited their story, and when it was told through Elias, he inquired where they were staying. When they told him, the sheikh spat on the ground. "Tell these good people," he directed Elias, "that in my quarter near the Damascus Gate there is a very large house which can contain them all. It belongs to my cousin, and can be had for a very low rent." Tomorrow, he said, he would call at the Mediterranean Hotel and take them to see it.[6]

The house was on the crest of Mount Bezetha, the highest point in the Old City in the Arab Quarter between the Damascus Gate and Herod's Gate. The Overcomers trudged up a tortuous network of cobbled streets and through a tunnel-like entrance, and were greeted by a lovely fragrance. Elated, they found themselves in a walled courtyard covered with sweet-smelling white jasmine vines and bright red geraniums. A fountain burbled peacefully at its center. When they climbed an angled staircase to the flat roof, a spectacular view left them collectively ravished. Beyond the domes, spires, and minarets of the Old City, they saw fields and rocky expanses far to the west and the Mount of Olives, Mount Scopus, and the distant Judaean hills to the east.

The house was built against the city wall itself, and the group gazed down over a precipitous drop of over seventy feet. "Below you are the quarries of Solomon." They turned to see an enormous soldier in uniform bearing down on them. As Elias interpreted and the sheikh al-Haram made the introductions, the Overcomers met Ali Bey Juzdar, commander of the Turkish gendarmerie and the owner of the house. Even the grown-ups felt some anxiety at the sight of this powerful figure surveying them with one good eye. In the other eye, beneath a hideously scarred eyebrow, a poorly made glass lens swam on mucus tears in its vacant socket. Ali Bey, they later learned, had been blinded in a melee at the Holy Sepulchre when he had taken the blow intended for a Franciscan by an ax-wielding Greek monk, and had waited to see a doctor until his men had restored order in the church.[7]

Alarming as this huge Ottoman official initially seemed, it was quickly apparent from his rumbling laugh that he meant only friendship. His house, the group chorused, was just what they wanted. It was even better when they heard they could also rent two smaller adjacent buildings. Horatio could have a study in one, they said. They forbore to mention that the height of the house made it particularly desirable, a little above the dreadful smells that so offended them in the surrounding Arab and Armenia quarters, and especially the stench from the wretchedly poor Jewish neighborhood to the south.

Soon there was a flurry of activity. A fellow American working as a dragoman volunteered to negotiate an exceedingly reasonable rent of forty French napoleons. Next, they located workmen to cut windows in the dark downstairs rooms and install a guardrail around the rooftop. They also put in ventilating pipes, an innovation that fascinated the workmen and that visitors sometimes remarked on.[8] Beds, chairs, and tables were ordered, while Anna and the ladies searched the souk for pots, pans, rush mats for the floors, and bolts of Turkey red cloth to sew into curtains. When the renovation was finished and servants had been engaged for cooking and laundering at agreeably low wages, the pilgrims were ready to move in. Anna gathered dried grasses and arranged them in vases, adding collages of postcards from friends back home to adorn the simply furnished but light-filled parlor. At last, the Overcomers were residents of the Old City within the walls, close by the Damascus Gate.

From the start, it was apparent that William Rudy, who had counseled Anna and obtained the tickets for the voyage, should handle their finances. Invariably nattily dressed, the former owner of Pennsylvania flour mills had a natural bent for numbers. A serious illness had sent him into early retirement, and he had been introduced to Horatio's church by Amelia Gould. Out of concern for the tall, willowy, and aristocratic widow, he had followed the group to Jerusalem, bringing with him his elderly foster mother, Caroline Merriman. Now thirty-six, with a high forehead and brown beard and hair, Mr. Rudy was usually silent during the services. Indeed, his religious views remained something of a mystery, although his protective and affectionate regard for Mrs. Gould seemed clear. Six years older and childless, Amelia was a prominent member of Chicago society, and her family wealth from a large wholesale grocery business had helped the Spaffords during the troubled days in Chicago. During her husband's terminal struggle with tuberculosis, Amelia had sought consolation with the Lake View community. She was an emotional woman, and in joining the Spaffords on their journey to Jerusalem, she was apparently under the impression that a fantastic event would reunite her with her deceased husband. Her capital had been left in trust with her husband's brother, who sent interest payments monthly. In fact, it was on these funds that the group now relied.

Despite Amelia's rather excitable nature, she never purported to be given the "sign" that often came to Anna and Maggie Lee, nor did Mrs. Merriman possess the gift. Mary Sylvester, however, the English wife of the couple who had joined the group in London, frequently experienced energetic displays of "the Spirit," while the two other women, Mary Whiting and Lizzie Page, both thirty-one years old, were mostly docile participants. Lizzie and her husband, Otis Page, a former employee in the Goulds' wholesale enterprise, had jumped at the chance to come to Jerusalem. As they had no money to buy their tickets, their passage had come out of the group's funds. With them was their daughter, Flora, ten, the age that Anna's lost Tanetta would have been had she lived. Flora was a vibrant, charming child whose laughter often cheered the group, but Anna tended to look the other way when Flora was petted or praised. Anna was also inclined to ignore Flora's parents, who were not well-educated people, nor were they able to make even a small contribution to the group's upkeep, as the others had. They sometimes found this hurtful, but Otis Page was sweet and willing like his daughter, and his carpentry skills had been useful during the renovation of the house.

To Mary Whiting and her husband, John, on the other hand, Anna was quite attentive. Like Amelia, the Whitings were well-off. They had left the Fullerton fold with the Spaffords and joined the Lake View congregation over the vociferous opposition of both their mothers. Quiet and a trifle otherwordly, the Whitings could be counted on to do as the Spaffords directed. They had a year-old baby, Ruth, and Mary had recently discovered that she was pregnant again.

By now Anna had decided that her companions should take new names. They were novitiates, she said, in a new life as if they were entering a cloister. She was to be called "Sister Anna," and Amelia should be "Sister Elizabeth." Otis Page was assigned "Brother Samuel," Mary Whiting became "Sister Mary John," and Mary Sylvester became "Mary Cephas," doubtless because the early Christians believed that Jesus' spirit dwelled in this devoted follower. Mary's severely crippled husband, "Captain" William Sylvester, had fought in the Civil War and emerged with broken kneecaps. Despite constant pain, he had nonetheless toured England in a specially outfitted carriage, preaching the gospel. Some years earlier in Chicago, he had met Horatio, soon revering him as a brilliant and innovative thinker. Horatio liked to call him "Captain," so "Captain" he remained. The others were given special names as well, although Horatio continued to answer to "Mr. Spafford." And for a long time, Mr. Rudy was simply "Mr. Rudy."

Central to the group's life together were their morning and evening prayer meetings. To their astonishment, almost as soon as they were settled, Arab neighbors began attending. Strange as it seemed that Muslims would share a Christian religious service, Horatio was delighted and welcomed them. His personal doctrine had been incorporative from the start. "There is no longer male nor female, bond nor free, Jew nor Gentile, for we are all equal in Jesus Christ," he would say cheerfully, quoting Galatians 3:28. Although he was never to learn Arabic, he was beginning to understand enough about Islam to realize that there was nothing to offend their Muslim guests in their simple gatherings. They had no idolatrous icons, no mysterious celebrations of the Eucharist, no liturgical chantings, and above all no cross bearing the dead and naked figure of a tortured Christ—a scandalous image to Muslims, who found incomprehensible the "notion of a God who would lower Himself to become a man and then allow His own son to be killed."[9]

As far as these kindly Arabs were concerned, they shared the respect that the Prophet Muhammad had taught for "the people of the Book," the Jews and Christians who were the *dhimmis* and who were legally protected minorities under Ottoman rule. After all, just as Abraham was for them the first Muslim, "a good soldier of God," they accepted the revelations of the Old Testament prophets. Indeed, they revered the miraculously born and sinless Jesus, who had ascended to heaven with Moses and Muhammad. They were happy to take out their prayer beads and pray silently with their Christian friends, and they listened, entranced, as the Americans sang their beautiful hymns.

Above all, these new friends respected the freshly arrived "Amelikans" because they made no attempt to proselytize—unlike the various Protestant missionary groups who had come intent on converting as many as possible, apparently ignorant of, or simply indifferent to, the fact that it was a capital offense for a Muslim to convert. Mostly their guests understood very little English. One, a fine old man, Sheikh Abu Yusuf, whose clan were hereditary custodians of King David's Tomb, always arrived promptly for the eight o'clock meeting. Stone-deaf, he would remove his heavy turban, wipe his shiny skull, take out his ninety-nine-bead prayer string, wrap his legs around the chair that was especially reserved for him, bend forward in deep concentration, and begin counting his beads. His only English words were "one, not three!" which he would shout loudly at intervals.[10] Startled at first, the Overcomers came to understand that while the old sheikh enjoyed an opportunity to pray harmoniously with Christians, he felt the need to assert the profoundest tenet of Islam, that there were no gods but God—in Arabic, "La ilaha illa Allah!"—rejecting the complicated Christian doctrine of a tripartite Father, Son, and Holy Ghost.

No one seemed to mind these creedal differences in the pleasure of mutual prayer and singing. There were some halting exchanges in the beginning over a few doctrinal points, but language remained an obstacle for any serious discussion. Simply, the Americans and the Arabs became friends, and the Americans quickly became dependent on the Arabs' generosity as their funds dwindled. As for the Overcomers' preoccupation with an imminent Second Coming, the Arabs accepted this eccentricity with good grace. In their view, it was not for mankind "to calculate the time for the Day of Judgment. They believed that Allah still ruled the universe and when He wished to bring it to an end, He would do so without the calculations or prognostications of His creatures."[11]

In one important respect, however, the Overcomers were not fully open with their new friends. The singular practices initiated in Lake View had resumed immediately when they arrived in Jerusalem, but were carefully concealed from outsiders. Maggie Lee and Mary Sylvester continued to "have the sign" rather vigorously, but it was Anna who had received the stupendous revelation that they were to go to Jerusalem. Imperceptibly, she was emerging as the strongest prophet of the three women, and like the others, Horatio accepted her messages. Originally it had been the group itself that had been the "Bride." Lately, however, Anna had started to lay claim to the title for herself, while she called on the group to regard her husband as the "Branch," invoking the Gospel of Saint John: "I am the vine, ye are the branches."[12] While Maggie Lee and Mrs. Sylvester continued to be seized by visions, it was Anna's "manifestations" and especially her messages that had the greatest force, despite attempts by Maggie Lee to reassert her role as the group's "Moses." John Whiting, assigned the task of secretary, wrote in his diary: "The old life is to be laid aside and the prophetess is to share her power with the Branch—he to have the same supernatural power but may not have the sign."[13]

At first, tense expectation gripped them all. Talk of the "great event" was constant. Their daily visits and prayerful anticipation on the rocky slope of the Mount of Olives had excited the children as well. Before they moved from the Mediterranean Hotel, they had been surprised and amused one evening at dinner when little Bertha Spafford suddenly dashed into the dining room in her nightgown, crying: "The Lord has come!" The sleeping child had been awakened by the light of an enormous and brilliant moon flooding her bedroom.[14]

Now that they were settled, the daily visits continued, but with something of a holiday air and accompanied by hampers of pastries and a teapot and brazier to brew tea. On one such afternoon, the simmering competition between Anna and her sister-in-law spilled over. A newspaper article later ridiculed the incident: "The appointed time found the Overcomers' assembled in ascension robes on Mount Olivet. But while waiting for the heavens to part Mrs. Spafford happened to refer to herself as the bell-weather of the flock, and Mrs. Lee immediately claimed the honor for herself. From good-natured argument they advanced to a vitriolic spat. Of course there was no second advent, and the party returned to the city in anything but an amiable mood."[15]

As Anna continued to insist on primacy in interpreting the signs that appeared in their secret séances, she began to put her husband to tests. At one meeting, John Whiting recorded, "concerning the Branch, we laid hands on him."[16] The group gathered around Horatio, touching his head, shoulders, back, and legs. Then Anna, impelled by a powerful manifestation, commanded that the "Branch" lift Captain Sylvester. As the Overcomers watched in silence, the old veteran obediently struggled to lower his broken legs to the floor, and with difficulty Horatio managed to pick him up. The group did not need to be told they were reenacting the moment when Saint Paul caused a cripple to walk and told the amazed spectators "to turn from the vanities" of paganism to belief in "the living God."[17] They were, however, puzzled by the strangeness of another message that Anna received: "Seven years in the land" had been the enigmatic revelation. Anna said simply that God had sent it to Horatio—through her.

On another occasion, Maggie Lee, who was devoted to her elder brother and one of his most attentive disciples, "had a vision of the Lord." According to John Whiting, "she had been praising Him that he was a living God. The face, which had been indistinct, became that of the Branch."[18] Perhaps unwilling to grant that her husband was "a living

God," as his admiring sister seemed to see him, Anna countered with a vision of her own. "The prophetess," John Whiting recorded, "had a manifestation, looking up and blinking as if the light was too strong."

As the months went on, Maggie Lee acquiesced with the others to the dominance of their beautiful Norwegian leader, however strange her manifestations. Even though one day, in the grip of a trance, she repeatedly stuck out her tongue, they took what she did as thrilling, natural, and sacred. John Whiting carefully noted her words: "When my tongue went out, it meant that the Lord was speaking."[19]

CHAPTER ELEVEN

The Gadites

Perhaps, sometime, the day may come when all together will be agreed that there is no spot in the world more holy than another, in spite of associations, because the whole earth is the Lord's. Then the tender interest which those who read the Scriptures will always have for [Jerusalem's holy] places . . . may have a fuller and freer play—apart from lying traditions, monkish legends, and superstitious impostures. For, to use the words which Cicero applied to Athens, there is not one spot in all this city, no single place where the foot may tread, which does not possess its history.

—Walter Besant and Edward Henry Palmer,
Jerusalem, the City of Herod and Saladin (1871)

The presence of the Americans had not gone unremarked. "There has recently been an arrival at Jerusalem of eighteen persons for permanent residence, from Chicago and vicinity, under the influence of some strong religious impulse, sustained by their interpretation of the unfulfilled prophecies," wrote the American consul in his dispatch to the State Department in Washington on November 16, 1881. "They are praying, watching, waiting for, the grand events soon to transpire in this land, as they suppose. They appear to be people of culture and wealth:

they have taken a large house in the Mohammedan quarter of the city, and are living as one religious household."

The consuls in Palestine had their hands full, given the variety of tourists, missionaries, pilgrims, archaeologists, and most especially the cranks attracted in ever rising numbers as obstacles to visiting the Holy Land receded. The American consuls, who were badly underpaid relative to their European colleagues, invariably felt deluged by countrymen who had been robbed by bedouin, had been fleeced by their dragomans, needed desperate medical intervention, or exhibited some sort of religious pathology that often required the consul to scramble for funds to get them back home. In addition, extraterritoriality, the long-standing privilege wrested from the Ottoman Empire by the European powers, exempted aliens from Ottoman law and empowered the consuls to adjudicate the civil and criminal affairs of their nationals according to their home country's laws.[1] All too often new arrivals wound up dumping their problems in the consul's lap. Thus the appearance of a new group of American "innocents" who kept to themselves in what the papers reported was some sort of "communist" arrangement had the U.S. consul on the alert.

The U.S. consul was not alone. The missionaries were also struck by the new arrivals, especially by the attractive Mr. and Mrs. Spafford. The Reverend A. Hastings Kelk, the minister of Christ Church and head of the London Jews Society, a formidable British Protestant organization presided over by Lord Shaftesbury and dedicated to converting Jews to Christianity, immediately invited them to his house and "was much pleased with their conversation and their singing of hymns which was very sweet."[2] In short order, his fellow missionaries did the same, "believing them to be earnest Christians" whose views should be shared and discussed. Enthusiasm for "the Spaffordites" waned, however, as the missionaries learned more of their "peculiar notions," most distressingly of Horatio's view that "even the Devil could be saved," and their tendency to take "one word out of one passage of Scripture, two out of another, and so on, stringing them together so as to make the sense they wished . . . to be the Word of God."[3] For them it was also odd for unmarried men and women to commingle under one roof. Stories circulated about their daily picnics on the Mount of Olives, Arabs freely entering the Bezetha house, and the interest the Spaffordites seemed to take in Jews.

Indeed, the Overcomers were very interested in Jews. Repeatedly they visited the Wailing Wall. For centuries, this segment of the Haram's southwestern wall had been chosen by religious Jews as a place of lamentation. Most believed that its massive stone blocks were the remains of Solomon's Temple, although recent work by British and American archaeologists had proved that the oldest stones were Greco-Roman from the Herodian period. To Muslims, this wall was sacred as well, known as Al-Buraq, after the Prophet's horse, and beneath its stones lay a subterranean mosque of that name. So powerful to international Jewry, however, was the wall's sacred nature—the holy place of the *Shechinah*, where God was present on earth—that if they were unable to go there themselves on the Day of Atonement, or the Day of the Destruction of the Temple, they sent money to Jerusalem's Jews to do their praying for them.[4]

The Wailing Wall had always struck Christian visitors as extraordinary. As one Christian tourist wrote home: "It was a most strange and indescribable sight that burst upon us as we entered the wailing place. The nearly one hundred men, women and children were either sitting and intoning in sad, monotonous voices scriptural references to the city's downfall and defilement, or clamorously lamenting their predicament by throwing themselves on the pavement or burying their faces deep within the joints and cavities of the wall while real tears stream down their cheeks. It is the most touching ceremony to be met with in all the strange and melancholy things to be seen in or about Jerusalem."[5]

For the Overcomers, propelled by messianic urgency, it was of the first order of importance to connect with Jerusalem's Jews. It took a while before they adjusted to the different Jewish communities or understood how much acrimony existed between the ultraorthodox and Reform Jews, who wished to fuse traditional religious practices with science and modern techniques. At first they had no idea which were the Sephardim—Jews principally from Spain who became Ottoman subjects after their expulsion in 1492—and which were the Ashkenazim, who were from Eastern Europe and Russia. Instead, they marveled at the enormous variety of this mix of races all calling themselves Jews: turbaned Jews from the Maghreb, black-skinned Ethiopian Jews, Polish Jews with long curling sideburns beneath huge black velvet hats rimmed in fur, and hulking red-haired, blue-eyed Russian Jews in pointed black lamb's wool hats.[6]

It was certainly apparent that the numbers of Jews were increasing. When the Overcomers landed, there were about thirty-one thousand persons living in the Ottoman *sanjak*, or district of Jerusalem: six thousand Christians, eight thousand Muslims, and probably seventeen thousand Jews. This was more than double the number of Jews since the turn of the century.[7] The Overcomers had no idea then that secret, highly illegal groups were forming abroad, desperate to save their co-religionists from vicious pogroms and brutal military service, and were funding an exodus. In Russia especially, where the czarist government condemned all national movements, clandestine committees quietly mushroomed. As time went on and more Jews arrived with news of a movement to return them to Zion, the Ottoman government, responding to the apprehension of Arabs fearful of losing their land, periodically forbade further Jewish immigration. Horatio and Anna were always alarmed when they read of some new prohibition, but their worries were inconsequential. The Ottoman government was far too weak to enforce containment, and the European powers, particularly Protestant Britain, which had come to Turkey's aid in the Crimean War of 1853, were opposed to any interference with their Jewish clients, of whom Britain, still in the grip of millennialism, and whose leaders saw a political advantage to having friendly Jews settle in Palestine, claimed to be protector.

Horatio and Anna did not wish to evangelize the Jews they met anymore than they hoped to convert their Arab friends. The time was not ripe, they acknowledged to themselves, although one day the Lord would surely summon the world to the truths He had vouchsafed their little fellowship. Still, Horatio was anxious to discuss teleological questions with the very people who were key to the Messiah's arrival. The missionaries could not fathom why Horatio wandered through the Jewish Quarter, engaging ragged rabbis in conversation. So many of their own had been driven out under a hail of stones, flung trash, and once a dead cat.[8] Even the well-funded London Jews Society, despite a fair number of young Jews converting through the influence of their evangelical teachers at the society's Mission School, had not met with the measure of success deemed necessary to fulfill the prophecies, the purpose for which the society had been founded.[9]

Horatio's efforts did not go unrewarded. One day a large contingent of Jews, evidently prepared for a discussion, called at the Bezetha house, accompanied by three learned religious scholars. "Do you keep the law?" was their chief concern. Horatio, anxious to avoid an argument but determined to state his credo, replied: "Only love will conquer the world." To Anna the exchange was biblical, like the conversations between Christ and the Sanhedrin. She wrote her sister, "They are exceedingly polite to us, which they are not to everyone. They have invited us to their synagogues and to their Feast of Tabernacles."[10]

That next spring, in 1882, an event occurred that confirmed Horatio's most fervent expectations. The previous winter had been exceptionally harsh; Christmas had been meager and cold; homeward thoughts intruded, needing banishment by earnest prayer. When spring finally came, carpeting the rocky hills and cemeteries in green, and wild asphodel and bitter hyssop poked up from the nooks and crannies of masonry, the Spaffords and some others departed through the Damascus Gate and up Nablus Road, bound for a picnic.

Almost immediately they saw the miserable tents. Arrayed in a meadow near the Tomb of Simon the Just were scores of men, women, and children, so pitiful in their tattered clothing that the Spaffords wondered if they might be gypsies. They sent Elias to investigate, and he came back with the news that they claimed to be Jews, recently arrived from Yemen, but he could barely understand their Arabic. Much affected by the sight of such a strange assembly, the Spaffords asked to talk to the rabbi in charge. When they learned that the group had no money and had been spurned by the Jewish community, Horatio invited him to call at the house.

Hurrying home to gather what clothes they could spare, and charging the kitchen staff to prepare food, they were ready the next morning when the rabbi and six other men knocked at the door and were ushered into the living room. The Overcomers watched as a frail, dark-skinned spokesman, identifying himself as Rabbi Shuni, draped over his shoulders a striped prayer shawl and solemnly tied first to his forehead and then around his left arm a pair of small square leather boxes, attaching them by leather straps. Rabbi Shuni was treating their living room as a place of worship, and accordingly he had applied his phylacteries before saying a brief prayer.[11]

"Is it not remarkable," he began quietly, "that our own kith and kin, the Jews living here in Jerusalem, should refuse to help us, saying that we were not Jews but Arabs? We have told them our history, but they will neither believe us nor, and this is the most important matter to us, will they help us to find the man, a Jew like themselves, who stole and carried off our ancient Pentateuch."[12]

Was this, the group asked, the reason for coming to Jerusalem?

"Yes! In fact the theft of our Torah was what decided us to come," answered Rabbi Shuni. "We felt strongly that through this unfortunate incident the Lord was beckoning to us to return to our Promised Land."

Surrounded by sympathetic faces, the old rabbi described a long, grim, and dangerous journey from Sanaa, the old Shiite capital of Yemen, where most of them had worked as jewelers for untold generations. Nearly five hundred had left with them, but, simple, uneducated, and easily misled, many ended up in India, while others had died of starvation, disease, or exposure. Still others had given up and returned to Sanaa. The rabbi's group had managed to find a steamer, which ultimately brought them up the Red Sea. They were deposited at Aqaba and began an overland march by foot and by donkey over the wadis and mountains of Transjordan. When the rabbi described how they stood on Mount Nebo looking across the Dead Sea to the land of Canaan, a deep murmur, almost a sob, arose from the Overcomers. They realized that these impoverished Jews had trod in the very footsteps of Moses when he led his people out of Egypt.

Horatio stared at his guests, noting their slight bodies, Arab dress, and graceful movements. They reminded him of lithe bedouin. "The classical purity" of their faces was unlike anything he had seen in Jews from the United States or here in Palestine. Could these men—the thought struck him like a thunderclap—be one of Israel's lost tribes? Barely able to contain his excitement, he was suddenly positive that his visitors were none other than the ancient Gadites, a tribe that had fought with Joshua, settled in Moab and Ammon, escaped the Babylonian captivity, and disappeared—perhaps to southern Arabia?

Elated, Horatio listened as the rabbi finished his story of the Jewish visitor to Sanaa who had tricked them and gone off with their ancient scroll. "Blessed be he that enlargeth Gad," Horatio quoted, springing to his feet. He would personally see to it that they were fed, clothed, and sheltered. To his fellow Overcomers, many of them in tears, Horatio announced that this tattered band's arrival was irrefutable proof that the End Times were at hand.

The Overcomers immediately scrambled to rent rooms. Every day representatives of the "Gadites" came to take back meals of kosher meat, bread, and even hard-to-find milk for the babies and invalids. Horatio wanted to plead their case with their co-religionists, convinced that they had been rejected because their people were unwilling to share the *haluka*. He also wondered if the scroll's thief might not have turned up in Jerusalem. There was a brisk trade in antiquities in the city, and a lot of chicanery as well. Someone in the Jewish community might have heard something. Horatio decided to take the problem to a new friend, Eliezer Ben-Yehuda.

Ben-Yehuda, tiny and sporting a goatee, was one of several scholars who had recently come to teach Hebrew at the Alliance Israélite Universelle, yet another of the newly opened institutions cropping up around Jerusalem to teach agriculture and other skills to Jewish immigrants. This young Lithuanian visionary believed passionately that the only way to unify Palestine's diverse Jewish population was to pry the people away from their separate Yiddish, Spanish, Arabic, and Russian languages. Everyone must learn Hebrew, Ben-Yehuda argued, if there were ever to be a Jewish nation.[13] Horatio, who had recently volunteered to teach English at the Alliance and greatly admired Ben-Yehuda, offered to help promote this idea. Ben-Yehuda in turn was willing to intervene for the Gadites.

Some months later, the Bezetha house received a surprise visit from a Gadite delegation. Their people, they said, were being accused of "eating Christian food." Moreover, it was bandied about that the Spaffordite group was out to convert them. Could the Overcomers give them gold instead?

While it cut into their remaining funds, it was agreed that this must be done. In due course Horatio and Ben-Yehuda's efforts on behalf of the Yemenites were successful, although their scroll was never restored to them despite their finally identifying the culprit.[14] Mostly, the Jewish community's fears and suspicions were allayed, and gradually the Yemeni Jews found a place among their people, enrolled their children in one of the new Jewish schools, and began to pay their way by fashioning exquisite jewelry in the tradition of their fathers. In gratitude for his help, the Gadites presented Horatio a Hebrew prayer elegantly composed on parchment by their scribe, who held his reed quill between his toes because his arms were paralyzed.

The arrival of the Gadites had confirmed to Horatio the validity of his predictions. At the daily prayer meetings Anna and the others agreed that the End Times loomed thrillingly near. But their generosity had cost the Overcomers dearly. The only money now coming from Chicago was a small check from Amelia Gould's brother-in-law, the income of a trust she had left in his charge. While Anna and William Rudy urged her to demand the entire fund, frustratingly, her brother-in-law refused. The household felt they had no recourse but to take on credit the meat and greengroceries, fuel for heat and cooking, and baskets of eggs that their Arab friends regularly delivered. They would pay, they promised, as soon as they could sort out the problems with the families of Mrs. Gould and the gentle, retiring Whiting couple, who also had funds, and they were confident that it would be soon. Their towering landlord smiled forgivingly; two brothers of the greengrocers' clan said they could also wait; and the Arab vendor who brought eggs seemed unperturbed. Horatio, gazing into the far distance, reassured his wife and his flock as he had so many times in the past. "God will provide," he said. But Anna worried.

CHAPTER TWELVE

Bad News and Good Works

*Jerusalem is full of cranks. This sounds a little
coarse, perhaps, but it is the only expression
which I know adequate to convey the precise
thought. The Holy City, while it is the object of
the most solemn and tender regard by all Christians, is at the same time an attraction for all
the religious driftwood in this great world . . .
Each clique lives in a certain rut of thought,
and never gets out of that particular rut, even so
much as to crawl up to a point where they can
look over it into the rut immediately next to
them. By thus living in a rut the members are
able to harmonize everything in the Bible with
their strange theories and wonder at the stupid-
ity of the world in not seeing as they do . . . The
majority of these religious cranks hail from the
United States, which has produced so many and
such strange religions.*

—Ichabod, *Daily Inter Ocean,* July 6, 1884

Despite his optimism, Horatio was preoccupied. The Ottoman
mail service was hopelessly erratic. If the seas were too rough at
Jaffa, ships simply sailed on to Beirut, and sometimes there were quar-
antines during which no mail at all could be off-loaded. Even so, Horatio had received a letter from Dr. Hedges in October 1881, and the

report had been reassuring. Hedges had sent, as instructed, the first two monthly payments due Mrs. Wills and Mary Murphy. He also wrote that exciting events were still taking place at Lake View and Valparaiso. The remaining Saints had witnessed an "anointed" sick member delivered from her illness through "the laying on of hands." The Chicago group, Hedges assured Horatio, was prepared "to stand for you all" and continued to believe "that God will manifest himself to you gloriously."[1]

A letter received in early December was more troubling. According to Hedges, mail was arriving opened. Regularly, visitors came to inquire what had happened with the Spaffords. A representative of a Boston law firm was pressing him for some deeds. "I do not know what they may do, by law, to compel me," he wrote, "but I shall take good advice and find out my duty as to you & perform it." The two women had received third and fourth payments, some money from another source had come in, but an office space that Horatio had charged him to lease out was still vacant, and the doctor had had no luck selling its furniture. As for the Saints, there had been "a change of leaders." Members were growing impatient for the Event. A sick baby whose parents had refused medicine in favor of prayer had died. Another had refused to allow the body to be buried, claiming she would raise it from the dead, and Horatio was being blamed.[2] "Everything seems dark and many are shaken out of the sign, and some out of the truths," Hedges concluded anxiously. "We do not hear anything from you but we shall keep our eyes on God & be ready with our loins girded."[3]

And then it happened. The letter from Dr. Hedges finally arrived to say that an agent of the real estate magnate Hetty Green had come to Lake View to foreclose on the house to which she had obtained title on December 30, 1881. Knowing nothing of this deal, Hedges had been flabbergasted. However, Mrs. Green was willing to sell him the house, and Hedges wrote that he had bought it. His letter to Horatio offered "out of a spirit of friendship" to let Horatio buy it back at the same price, plus expenses. He wrote that when he let Mrs. Wills and Mrs. Murphy know of the foreclosure and sale, and that they should expect no further payments, Mrs. Wills informed Hedges that Horatio owed her $17,000. Again Dr. Hedges admitted amazement.[4]

Horatio did not reply to Dr. Hedges's letter. He showed it to Anna, who showed it to William Rudy and Mrs. Gould, but it was not some-thing he cared to discuss. Instead, he ordered seeds with which he in-tended to reforest Jerusalem and "remove the curse from the land." Often he meditated, or wandered out for long walks. And then he began to borrow money. The largest bank at that time, impressed by Horatio's respectability, gave him a considerable loan. From a fellow American, a veteran of the Civil War whom he had recently met, Horatio borrowed $1,200 with a promissory note.[5] It was clear to everyone that if the Over-comers did not see the need to work, it was because they had money in Chicago. For the time being at least, borrowing was not difficult.

Horatio's meditations were fruitful as well. As he wrote a friend, God was making things clear to him at last. It was critical "to be emp-tied of self." This was his grandest insight. "It is not the physical life that is meant," he continued, "but one's selfishness, one's natural selfish hu-man nature . . . one's pride and self-love, all of which, as the Word tells us, is so wholly opposed to God. It has to be brought to the block, to the cross, *to death*."[6] Horatio planned to tell Anna this—with all its impli-cations—as soon as the moment was ripe.

Anna called her husband's excursions through the countryside his "rambles." He ranged far afield, looking into the surrounding villages and appreciating the biblical stories attached to them. He encouraged the group to help the odd, even deranged characters that frequently turned up at their door. They were "to live like the ancient apostles," he reminded them, to donate their worldly possessions to serve the poor and needy. Helping the Yemenis had only been the beginning. When they learned that an American who claimed to have discovered perpet-ual motion had abandoned his sick wife and son, the group took the family in. They were nursed and recovered, although, according to be-liefs that had evolved during the Lake View period, the Overcomers re-fused to call a proper doctor, substituting faith healing through prayer and the anointment of oil. Others arrived claiming to be Elijah, or John the Baptist, or the Messiah. The Overcomers aided them all, even the inebriates, as well as one whose temper was so violent he terrified the children. Several Jewish boys ostracized by the Jewish community because they had been converted by the London Jews Society found their way to the Bezetha house and were helped to get on their feet. On a number of occasions Mary Whiting, Lizzie Page, or Mrs. Merriman volunteered to be quarantined with a poor family caught in the throes of smallpox, and stayed until they were well. Not always were their beneficiaries grateful. Having nursed some sick Americans who believed their father to be the "Prophet Daniel," the house was surprised when the wife turned her head away on meeting an Overcomer in the street. They had rejected her husband's theological claims, and she was angry.[7] Anna, whose cleverness never ceased to amuse her friends, called these characters "simples in the garden of Allah."

As Horatio increasingly absented himself, the daily affairs of the house fell to Anna. She now assigned chores as well as new names. Amelia, or Sister Elizabeth, was responsible for the laundry. Sister Mary John Whiting looked after the garden. Brother Samuel Page taught joinery to nineteen-year-old Cousin Rob Lawrence, who proved an apt pupil not just at furniture making but at almost any needed chore he tried his hand at. He learned Arabic well enough to be his uncle's interpreter; he made shoes for Anna; he became a talented landscape painter and was fascinated by the digs being undertaken by European and American archaeologists streaming to Jerusalem to document biblical history. Flora Page, Bertha, and the other children adored Cousin Rob. He always found time for them and made some of the very few toys they had to play with. It was Rob, the orphaned nephew, who supplied gaiety to a mostly somber household. Rob made friends easily, including with the U.S. vice-consul, who plied him with books, several dealing with Christian faith. Both the consul and the vice-consul thought it strange when Horatio appeared the following morning and gave them back the books. "We have no need of these histories. Our true education is about to come."[8]

For her part, Anna was strict with the children, and they were spanked if naughty. But she was always more lenient with her little girl Bertha, an exceptionally pretty child on whom she kept a watchful and doting eye. She forbade the group to wear the marvelously colorful, beautifully embroidered dresses or Arab robes that looked so comfortable and unconfining. "Standards must be kept. We must not lapse in an alien land as others have," she said to anyone who showed an inclination to "go native." Only the soft red leather shoes sold in the souk were acceptable—and these only inside the house.[9]

Anna's growing responsibilities were not without cost. The group relied heavily on her "manifestations" to point the way and to assuage doubts about the delay of "the Coming." She knew how important it was not to lose control, lest the awful doubts that had afflicted the Overcomers back in Chicago visit her Saints in Jerusalem. As her husband "rambled" and she steeled herself to her leadership role, the flow of milk from her breasts dried up and she could not nurse her baby, little Grace. She had no choice but to buy expensive cans of Nestlé's condensed milk, the only tinned milk available, and bottle-feed her.

One day, deciding that it would be pleasant to take the baby for some air, she relieved Mrs. Gould and some others of their household duties to accompany her on a picnic. They trooped to the Wadi al Joz, a peaceful walnut grove that they did not know was the property of a family belonging to the aristocratic Husseini clan, notables who had long played an important role in Jerusalem's history. The eldest boy in the family approached, curious. Through Elias, Anna learned that his mother had just given birth to twin baby girls whom she could not feed. He invited them to his house, and soon the boy's mother and other Arab mothers were coming to Anna for instruction on baby care. They were from the effendi class, not peasants, and their friendship would be valuable.

It was not long before they asked Anna to arrange tutoring for their sons in English. Horatio said it was a good idea, despite his belief that education was unneccessary, as the only learning that counted would come with the Messiah's arrival. Soon the Overcomers had a little school of sorts, with Arab neighbors sending their boys. Since the Ottoman conquest, the Arabs had yearned to be free from their Turkish masters, and clearly education was essential if freedom was to be their future. Since the United States enjoyed a reputation for impartiality and stayed clear of the colonial machinations of the Great Powers, it was natural for upper-class Arabs to trust these well-meaning "Amelikan unbelievers."

It was not just Arabs, however, who brought their children to Mount Bezetha. Several Jewish families did as well, and Horatio liked the thought of Jews and Muslims together. None of this was without controversy in such a center of confessional discord. There were articles in Protestant mission publications charging that it was impossible to "know what [the Overcomers'] religious beliefs are, for their members never reveal them," or that "one of their beliefs is that none of them will die before the Lord's coming."[10] This had been one of the group's core beliefs since the Lake View days, yet the missionaries' antagonism hurt the Overcomers' children deeply. They even developed a favorite game, dressing up as missionaries and showering contemptuous remarks on the younger ones assigned to play their parents. "Their unfriendly attitude toward us," Bertha wrote years later, "embittered my early years with a feeling that we were different, marked and strange."[11]

The Reverend A. Hastings Kelk, who had initially welcomed them, was by now a vocal antagonist, particularly after he heard that Horatio was repeating, "God has showed us that 'the Church' in all its parts— Protestant, Catholic, Greek—is destitute of spiritual power . . . Theirs are false teachings,"[12] and Anna had called Kelk's church and that of his fellow missionaries "Babylon."[13] Kelk headed the London Jews Society's Mission School, to which the Spaffords had briefly sent Bertha. They removed her now, telling the disappointed child it was because some of the little boys had kissed her.[14] The school's headmistress was a small, birdlike English spinster, Clara Johanna Brooke, who became interested in the conflicting stories about the Overcomers. When she heard that Horatio had started a Bible study class, Miss Brooke thought she might like to join, but Kelk warned her strongly against it. Clever and spirited, Miss Brooke visited the Bezetha house anyway and was moved to witness the baptism of the new Whiting baby, John, and his two-and-a-half-year-old sister, Ruth. Miss Brooke confided to Mrs. Gould: "The Lord is very near to you all here. I want the Lord to take the same tender care of me."[15]

After some discussion with Horatio and Anna, Miss Brooke was invited to join the household and asked to teach. Eventually she was also put in charge of the education of Bertha and Grace, as well as Ruth and John Whiting. After 1886, when an Arab woman added two children to the household, and an American father arrived with four more in 1890, there were enough to keep her busy. Initially Miss Brooke had difficulty adjusting to some of the stranger practices of her new home. She was accustomed to being "very strict in keeping the exact letter. She is learning now that 'the letter killeth but the spirit makes alive.' "[16] In any case, Miss Brooke stayed for decades, whether out of conviction or because she had no other place to go, or perhaps because of the real affection she developed for her expanding classes of young charges, as well as sheer fascination with the adventure in which she found herself.

At about this same time, the Overcomers took in an attractive, sparkling-eyed, and strapping seventeen-year-old boy whom Cousin Rob had met. Jacob Eliahu's parents were Sephardic Jews who had come from Turkey and been among the first converts made by the London Jews Society. Since such a decision was crass betrayal for purely economic benefit in the eyes of Orthodox Jews, his parents most likely left Jerusalem to avoid the unpleasantness of ostracism. Jacob, who was extremely intelligent and multilingual, remained in the city as a student-teacher at the Mission School and was as fascinated by archaeology as Rob. In fact, the year before the Overcomers arrived, Jacob had stumbled upon an important Hebrew inscription while exploring an ancient tunnel, a discovery that sparked tremendous excitement in archaeological circles and was the start of a long career of working with archaeologists in the city.[17]

The gifted boy enjoyed the respect that his discovery brought him, but his decision to leave the Mission School distressed Reverend Kelk, who was upset at losing such a promising student. Jacob's allegiance to the Overcomers was instantaneous and complete; the house became his home and his life. He followed Anna like a faithful dog, ready to do anything she asked. She began to rely on him as no one else, while Horatio drafted him to teach English to the assorted schoolboys they attracted. They even decided to give him the Spafford name, "adopting" both Jacob and Cousin Rob as their sons in a special ceremony.

There were few books, as the group had brought none with them, and were any ordered, the Turkish censors often "lost them" or held them for months at Jaffa, returning them with whole passages cut out for no apparent reason. From the start, Jacob showed himself something of a martinet, insisting that his students memorize "not only the books of the Bible, but recite endless lists of names, such as the Judges of Israel,

the twelve tribes, the plagues of Egypt, the Commandments, the Beati-
tudes, the twelve disciples," as one student remembered, uncertain how
useful such disciplines were in the end.[18] They did acquire an old encyclopedia as time passed and some volumes of Shakespeare as well as
Plutarch's Lives, but their teachers knew best the stories of the Bible, and
the children grew up knowing it by heart, always fascinated by its imme-
diacy in the stones around them.

Still, for the children of the original Overcomers, it was a lonely
childhood with few outside friends, for they seldom played with the children attending the little school. Flora Page, older than the others, was
sent to an eccentric Englishwoman and given lessons for a time. In her
hoopskirt and lace cap, Mrs. Poole, who lived in a tenement suffocat-
ingly crowded with odd curiosities of every imaginable description, was
a true intellectual, versed in astronomy and a wide range of other subjects. Horatio was captivated by her stimulating conversation, admired
her visits to the poor in the worst parts of the city, and enjoyed her company. Unfortunately, Anna thought Mrs. Poole talked too much, and her
arrival for tea too often merged into her staying for dinner, and then, because it was so late, staying the night. Mrs. Poole eventually sensed this
dissatisfaction, and when the lessons for Flora were stopped, she quietly
slipped from life on Mount Bezetha.

If Horatio missed Mrs. Poole's company, he, the household, and the
rest of Jerusalem were electrified by the arrival of a famous military hero,
"Chinese" Gordon, in January 1883, on leave and prepared to "elucidate
a number of biblical issues, in particular the true site of the Crucifixion."[19] An intense and deeply pious bachelor, Charles George Gordon
was accompanied by a handsome young minister, Herbert Drake, and
together they rented a house in the nearby village of Ain Karim. Through
the winter and spring, Anna and Horatio welcomed the two Englishmen
and frequently dined with them. While Horatio's doctrines caused Gordon's eyebrows to lift and his mouth to purse, his companion found
them exciting. Young Drake began spending nights at the Spaffords' and
became so charmed by Anna that he decided to stay with the Overcomers. Gordon wrote a friend resentfully: "The Americans do not care for
me to see Drake alone much."[20]

Nevertheless, Gordon found the Spaffords' stunning rooftop view just the place he needed for reflection, so Anna put a chair out for him, and he sat for hours immersed in thought. During one of these vigils, staring out at a rocky cliff known as Jeremiah's Grotto, Gordon spotted what appeared to him as the image of a giant skull, the cave opening making eyes, the rock strata a nose and gaping mouth. Mindful that a "place of the skull" was mentioned in three of the Gospels, the general was positive that he had located the "real" Golgotha, which in Hebrew meant "skull," a discovery that in a city such as Jerusalem provoked immediate and rancorous controversy. Had General Gordon been less eminent, his claim might have been easier to dismiss. When he next pronounced a recently discovered rock-hewn tomb as that of Joseph of Arimathea, another brouhaha ensued. A prominent archaeologist, Dr. Conrad Schick, was called in, but by 1901, when he published his carefully considered rejection of Gordon's theories, devout adherents had gathered, maintenance funds had been raised, and the Place of the Skull and the Garden Tomb had joined the infinity of other sites attracting ever-increasing crowds of pilgrims.

The Overcomers accepted Gordon's claims and remained proud of their association with a man who went on to even greater fame. Summoned by his government in 1884, Gordon was sent to the Sudan to suppress a revolt by Muslim fanatics, led by a self-declared Mahdi, or messiah. In January 1885, stubborn and defiant inside a starving British garrison in Khartoum, Gordon was hacked to death by the Mahdi's dancing, shrieking zealots, and his head "fixed between the branches of a tree in the public highway, and all who passed threw stones at it."[21]

A member of the Overcomers by this time, young, blond Reverend Drake was teaching at their little school, and the valuable silver Communion plate that General Gordon had left with Horatio was sold for a tidy sum.[22]

CHAPTER THIRTEEN

Friends and a Foe

Muslims are stumbling, Christians all astray
Jews bewildered, Zoroastrians in error's way.
We mortals are composed of two great schools—
Enlightened knaves, and religious fools.

—al-Maarri (973–1057)

The Overcomers had met the American Rolla Floyd during their first weeks in Jerusalem, and from the start he befriended them. Tall, barrel-chested, and irreverent, Floyd was a survivor of a group of millennialists from Maine who had followed the "Reverend" George J. Adams to "the land of milk and honey" in 1865, only to meet disease and disillusionment that killed thirty-three of their number and bankrupted the rest.[1] Floyd, not fooled by the amiable charlatan who led them, nor convinced by his millennial rantings, had really come in search of a kinder life than that offered by impoverished post–Civil War Maine. He found employment in Jerusalem as a dragoman for Thomas Cook & Son and soon gained the respect of the natives with whom he worked and learned some Arabic.

It was Floyd who brought General Gordon and Reverend Drake, together with thirty-five of their large iron boxes and several trunks, to shore in 1883. It had been quite a struggle, not because of the baggage, but because the year before Rolla had quit Cook & Son, realizing that the agency was exploiting him with overwork and low pay. Now Cook's was out to ruin him; but he was a formidable rival. Cook's had bribed boatmen not to row him to the steamers arriving with passengers in Jaffa harbor; the agency had cheated him of more than $7,000 and had set thugs to harm him. But Rolla Floyd was not a man to be broken easily. He continued his work despite the obstacles Cook & Son threw in his path.

When the Chicago Saints first arrived, Rolla had attended some of their meetings. He negotiated their rent, and when he discovered that the U.S. consul's dragoman had cheated them, he urged Spafford to complain to the consul, and was greatly impressed when Horatio replied: "Oh, we will pray that God will make a better man of him." Rolla commented, "This is the kind of people they are."[2]

Rolla and his wife, Docia, had seen their four boys die, one after the other, from Palestine's plagues, and thus felt a deep sympathy for the Spaffords' loss. Although Horatio and Anna viewed them as simple and uneducated people, they respected the Floyds for persevering in Jerusalem and were grateful for their kindness to their group. In turn, the Floyds were touched by the benevolence the Overcomers showed to the homeless deluded so frequently found wandering penniless about Jerusalem. Now and then Rolla steered another one of "the crazies" to Mount Bezetha, but he also sent them prosperous tourists with no place to stay, and these deep-pocketed visitors were able to compensate the Overcomers handsomely. Often they were journalists, or clergy, or important politicians who mentioned the goodness of the group in travel reports back home.

Rolla and Docia helped the needy themselves. In April 1883, Rolla brought to shore an American named P. H. Winterstein, his wife, and his young son. "He says he was sent here by the Lord," Rolla said with a sigh, adding, "One more crazy." The Floyds kept them without charge until a kindly Englishwoman gave them money to travel to Jerusalem, where they claimed they intended to live.[3] Rolla told Winterstein to look up the Overcomers. As he anticipated, they took the family in and kept them for several weeks, renting two rooms for them in a cheap boardinghouse and even sending over food.

Unfortunately, it happened that Winterstein was a correspondent for *Our Rest and Signs of the Times*, a widely read evangelical periodical that kept a close watch on events in Jerusalem. His account of his stay at the Bezetha house appeared in the July 1883 issue—and it was devastating. "Satan," the article began, has "looked to America for his agents . . . from America's Sodom, Chicago."[4]

Their ungrateful guest went on to reveal the innermost secrets of their meetings. "One Mr. S. claims to be the Branch; his wife claims to talk with God, and if any one of their members is in doubt as to whether the Lord would have them speak on what is in their minds, they refer the matter to her, she communes with God, and He tells her yes or no. She is the prophetess Anna, while a Mrs. L. has claimed to be John the Baptist, Elijah, Moses and Aaron. Others in the company have received or taken to themselves very high and exalted positions." These "poor souls," he concluded, were "filled with pride and self-love and can not see it."

The group's cherished doctrines were brutally laid out for ridicule and condemnation. Preposterously, Winterstein told his readers, the group insisted that they alone were "the body of Christ" and had been so since the beginning of time. They imagined themselves singularly anointed to "convert the world." While Winterstein marveled that they were "men and women without question of sound minds . . . and nearly all highly educated," he railed at their claims to heal the sick without medicine, their refusal to work, and their willingness to borrow. He described in detail a session when Captain William Sylvester was visited by "the Holy Ghost." Describing the mystical encounter, Winterstein said derisively it "comes with such force that it shakes them up . . . like a very bad case of swamp ague." Sylvester was led over to his chair, told to lay hands on Winterstein's head, and began demanding loudly that Winterstein receive "the Truth." Noting that he had withstood "a pretty lively shaking but sat perfectly quiet," Winterstein concluded scornfully: "I, a lump of perishable clay, had the power to resist the power of God." Disclaiming any "personal difficulty" he might have had with them, he warned that the Overcomers were the very personification of the "anti-Christ" predicted in the Book of Revelation, spreading false gospels and "lying wonders" to the gullible.

Rolla read the article, as well as another the journalist had written praising Rolla as a superb guide through the Holy Land. He liked the last, but was troubled by the first. "I am not a religious man," he mused, admitting, however, that he did wish to believe that he and his lost boys would be reunited in heaven.[5] He continued to admire Horatio, but after a while became watchful of Anna, for it seemed to him that things were not quite right; the youngsters did not seem as happy as children ought to be. Nonetheless, the Floyds continued to welcome the Overcomers in Jaffa and deliver guests into their care.

Two years earlier, President Garfield had succumbed to an assassin's bullet, and when his vice president, Chester Arthur, became president, he appointed the forty-five-year-old Reverend Selah Merrill to be U.S. consul in Jerusalem. Bespectacled, short, slightly stooped, impatient, and confident of his own considerable abilities, Merrill was a Congregationalist minister but preferred to be viewed as an archaeologist, historian, and scholar. He and Mrs. Merrill had arrived on July 1, 1882, just a few months after the Overcomers. His qualifications for his job as consul—a commission he had been keen to obtain and had lobbied hard for in Washington circles—were impeccable. Educated at Yale and the New Haven Theological Seminary, an infantry chaplain with a Negro unit in the Civil War, Merrill was a respected lecturer in Hebrew studies at Andover Theological School and the author of many articles as well as a much-praised and readable book, *East of the Jordan.* In fact, Merrill "could legitimately be considered the first Middle Eastern professional ever to hold the Jerusalem post" for the United States.[6]

During the 1870s, Merrill and his fellow American biblical scholars had watched enviously as British teams were the first to explore and scientifically map the Holy Land under the auspices of the British Palestine Exploration Fund in an effort to verify biblical sites. Finally, funds had been mobilized for establishing a similar American undertaking, and in 1875 Merrill was a member of the first expedition launched by the newly created American Palestine Exploration Society to survey the Jordan valley. For two years, Merrill avidly collected rocks, plants, pottery shards, coins, and fragments of ancient inscriptions and statuary. He was also a crack shot, adding thousands of specimen birds and animals to a peerless collection that he brought home in dozens of crates in 1877, the first such compilation of Palestinian artifacts of its kind in America.[7]

Merrill, much annoyed to discover just how small and underequipped his office was in the U.S. Consulate building just outside the Jaffa Gate—unbecoming, he thought, to the prestige of his country—

nevertheless settled in. He was surprised at the immensity of his duties, and particularly at the extraordinary powers accorded him by Ottoman law. Merrill resolved to perform his duties with exactitude. At the same time, he had no intention of missing any opportunity to amplify his remarkable collection. As soon as he was able, he was charging through the hinterlands in search of new trophies. He thought nothing of commandeering his *kavass,* or consular guard, his dragoman, or even his vice-consul for help. To the locals, his office became known as "the butcher shop." Anyone who chanced to interrupt as he plied his taxidermy skills to a dead bird, a gazelle, or a Palestinian fox saw his eyes flash in annoyance.

Merrill's tenure coincided with the first of many great waves of Jews to the Holy Land, and his reports were to have considerable impact at the State Department in developing policy on Zionism. He would be returned to Jerusalem by three Republican administrations over a period of twenty-five years, the longest-serving consul in American history. He believed the best interest of America lay in preserving Palestinian society, including the traditional Ottoman segregation of religions into strict, protected groups. The influx of Jews worried him as potentially destabilizing, and as a conservative, anticommunist, and anti-millennialist, with a deep belief in the value of frugality and hard work, he viewed the American Colony as apparently defying all that was civilized. When critics came to complain about them, he began keeping a careful record. It did not take long for the supreme American authority in Jerusalem to become the Overcomers' most implacable foe.

Merrill's first encounter with Horatio, however, was perfectly ordinary. Horatio called on him a month or so after his July arrival, as did many of the 202-odd native or naturalized Americans living under consular protection in Jerusalem, the European consuls, the various missionaries, and a constant stream of sundry others. So if Merrill barely remembered the occasion, he was to be forgiven. He was busy with his duties, his archaeological investigations, and especially his collecting. He wrote learned articles, yet found time to swamp the State Department with careful and perceptive reports. "I trust the Department will not consider that I am going outside my sphere when I venture to suggest certain modifications in the Consular service in Palestine which our interests seem to require" was a refrain Washington, D.C., learned to expect.[8]

Merrill wanted the underpaid staff at Jaffa, where the big ships arrived, to be better compensated for important custom and interview duties, especially as Jews were pouring into Palestine no matter what efforts the Ottoman government made to control immigration. Many of these sought American passports under one pretext or another, so he noted that he was keeping an eye out for fraudulent claims. He was pressed as well by the four hundred to six hundred Americans visiting Jerusalem annually, all wanting to see the Mosque of Omar, which required him to obtain official permission as well as a consular guard lest "they be insulted and stoned." Repeatedly, he sought expense money. "Princes, generals, and many people of high rank visit Jerusalem every year," he complained, chiding the department for a salary too meager to cover the obligatory receptions he and his wife constantly held.[9]

However, when local vendors to whom the Spaffords owed money converged on his office, Merrill started to pay attention. In particular, he was disturbed by a complaint from his own vice-consul, Samuel Bergheim, whose father was the banker who had loaned Horatio a considerable sum on assurances that the prosperous-looking group, and particularly their Mrs. Gould, had funds in Chicago. Nothing had been paid back, not even the interest, and now Horatio was returning to the bank to borrow more. Bergheim asked Merrill if he would mind making inquiries in Chicago to find out if Mrs. Gould was rich.

It happened that the former lieutenant governor of Illinois, William Bross, was a longtime family friend, so Merrill wrote him. In a letter dated July 7, 1883, Bross wrote back. "H. G. Spafford was for several years a prominent and successful lawyer . . . For some years past, they, Mr. Spafford and his wife, have been a little off, cranky if not crazy. Their old friends lament the state into which they have fallen and pity them sincerely. Warped at first in their minds, they have gone from bad to worse; from having a beautiful house, and a large prosperous business, Spafford neglected everything, got into debt all he could, of course paid nothing, and by his pretended revelations got one of his followers to furnish him $3,000 or more by which he made his way to your city. Thus in all charity he became not only a crank but an unmitigated rascal. 'Facilis descensus,' etc."[10]

Bross enclosed the address of Amelia Gould's brother-in-law, noting that Mr. John S. Gould was "one of our leading merchants" and it was his understanding that "he was sending her interest payments regularly but the money had been so placed in his hands that she cannot get at the principal." He could not tell Merrill about the other members of the Spafford party, but "so far as the Chicago members are concerned, your banker will be anxious for a long time."[11]

If not exactly surprising, the news was disturbing. Merrill next wrote John Gould, who replied:

> Some months after the death of Mrs. Gould's husband (my brother), Mrs. Gould, in response to my intimation that the Spafford party would get all her little property away from her and spend it, said to me in the presence of family friends: "No they will not, for I now put all my securities into your hands to keep and take care of for me and in no event pay me anything but the interest." This charge was made several times and has been faithfully kept by me.
>
> About two years ago she wrote me that "the Lord directed" her . . . to have all her securities converted into money and sent to her. This, by advice of our mutual friends and my attorney, I declined to do, and the matter was dropped.

Mr. Gould then went on to say that in 1883, Amelia again asked for her principal and again he had refused, advised by his attorney that if Amelia ever came to her senses and shook off her "delusion," she could easily return and accuse him of not protecting her at a time when her friends and he all knew she was "incompetent."

Writing yet again, Mr. Gould stated that Amelia had asked him to

> collect her wedding presents and dispose of them and send her the money. Previous to her going to Jerusalem, she gave many of these away to relatives and they were loath to give them up to be spent in the way she intends. I wrote her for more specific instructions

and that she sign her proper and legal name, and not "Sister Eliza-beth" . . . We do not think her competent to transact any financial matters while she is under the will and direction of the Spaffords. She has but little money anyway, and to have it wasted by the Spaf-ford crowd would be shameful.

Mrs. Gould has an impulsive temperament and she has been deluded by Mr. and Mrs. Spafford, and this delusion was the more captivating at the time of, and subsequent to, her husband's sick-ness and death when they claimed the power to cure his disease (consumption), and then after his death, to restore him to life so that he would meet her in Jerusalem.

You will do the bankers a favor to advise them not to advance these people, Mr. Spafford and Mr. Rudy, any money on the strength of Mrs. Gould's agreeing to make it good. As to Mr. Spafford, his debts for trust funds and borrowed money amount to between $100,000 and $200,000, and from what is reported, I do not think he would dare face his creditors. Some of his followers declare that he kept secret the hour and depot of his departure for fear of being detained by officers of the law.[12]

This was all very unsavory. Further, Merrill heard that Horatio had given legal advice on several occasions, an incredible thing to do in Merrill's view, as Spafford not only had a tainted reputation but knew nothing of Ottoman law. Merrill found it particularly maddening that prominent visitors kept giving him glowing accounts of beautiful eve-nings of music and conversation at the Bezetha house. Yet, critical of Horatio as he was, Merrill was invariably arrested by a certain quality the man had—a gentleness, a dignity, an aura of saintliness. Surely it was this that so impressed others as well.

Earlier, when Mrs. Gould had come to Merrill for a consular signa-ture on a document, Merrill had urged her to return to Chicago to re-trieve the money she was supposed to have. She flatly refused. Now he thought he knew why. For the rest of his first tenure in Jerusalem, on those rare occasions when he encountered Horatio, Merrill never forbore to remonstrate about his debts, or point out the injury he was doing to the poor vendors who could ill afford subsidizing a houseful of able-bodied men who refused to work. Horatio would look wounded, and reply simply, "The Lord has better things for us to do than work."

But Merrill had been in the Holy Land long enough to know its lunacies, and as the Spaffordites apparently did not have any money, nor any property that could be seized for debt payment, he could only sympathize with their creditors and advise them to wait, hope, and avoid lending anything more. For himself, he had no intention of having any social intercourse whatsoever with the house on Mount Bezetha. He left Jerusalem in 1886, deeply satisfied to take back many more crates of specimens to the collection in Andover, and would not return to the holy city until 1891, again commissioned by a Republican president, Benjamin Harrison.

In the interim, while Merrill was absent, staggering challenges were to occur in the house on Mount Bezetha. The wounding article by Mr. Winterstein would fade in importance as the Overcomers' house was shaken to its foundations and the very existence of its special fellowship was threatened by a nearly ruinous turn of events.

CHAPTER FOURTEEN

Overcoming Temptation and the Dangers of Attachment

This secretiveness also meant that what was known about [the early] Christians by contemporaries was both limited and vulnerable to distortion. The "eating of Christ's body" and "drinking of his blood" at the Eucharist could easily be presented as some kind of cannibalism, and the stress on Christian love could be mistaken for free sexual love, always a concern to traditionalists because it threatened the breakdown of social order.

—Charles Freeman, *The Closing of the Western Mind*

The house on Mount Bezetha was apparently exempt from illness. While periodic epidemics of smallpox, cholera, scarlet fever, and influenza raged through the city, it was said in Jerusalem that the Overcomers were always spared. Tuberculosis and malaria, known as "Assyrian fever," assaulted others, but miraculously left the group unscathed. It was reported that these "holy people," who believed they would never die, nursed all who asked, even the lepers who clustered by the holy sites, baring their hideous sores and crying, "Bakseesh!" as they thrust out fingerless hands for alms. When visitors arrived to enjoy the refinement of the high-ceilinged salon with its charming flower arrangements, splendid piano, caged songbirds, and delicious homemade bread and stewed *mishmish*, they asked if it was true that they nursed the sick yet did not become sick themselves. Anna nodded modestly. Their care and prayers were for everyone, she said, but they did boil their water and wash their vegetables carefully. True, several of their household—including her own two girls, Bertha and Grace, and the Whitings' little boy, John—had been infected with smallpox by an Arab goatherd bringing milk. They had welcomed him, not noticing the sores until his kaffiyeh slipped from his face. Yet they had recovered, and a visitor could see for himself that little Grace and John were in fine shape, although their faces were left pocked. Grace's older sister, Bertha, had been luckier; only one tiny scar, as dainty as a beauty spot, marred her plump cheek.

However, in September 1885, death made an appearance. Rob, the adored cousin, weakened by a congenital heart defect, stayed too long on a scorching September day to help Arab friends plant a field. He was brought home unconscious and died that evening. Anna assured a weeping Bertha, "What a wonderful awakening; now he sees Him." A week later, old Mrs. Merriman, Mr. Rudy's foster mother, had a heart attack and also died. Both were buried in the German cemetery, as the group had no burial plot of its own. Anna did not attend, so Maggie Lee held little Bertha's hand.

The deaths shook the group, and some Saints admitted dreading their risky acts of mercy. Horatio reminded them that no one would die as long as "they believed in God and overcame all worldly temptations."[1] Anna herself never nursed the sick. Her girls needed her, she said. Besides, Grace was still underweight and sickly, taking much of her attention and strength. Moreover, with Horatio continuing to wander off, someone needed to maintain order in the house. Her responsibilities vexed her, as well as the constant anxiety over money. She tried to restrain her irritation but more than once caught herself speaking sharply to one of the group. And recently she had had a particularly unfortunate encounter.

A missionary lady, a Mrs. Dunn, was invited to stay in accordance with the group's custom of welcoming visitors. Like so many others, Mrs. Dunn was curious about their beliefs and peppered Anna with questions. At dinner on the second night, as Anna was extolling the love and perfect accord of their household, Mrs. Dunn had stared hard at her, asking: "But what if love would in some instances fail of this object?"[2]

Anna, thrown off guard, had snapped back: "Then force would compel obedience." Looking appalled, Mrs. Dunn had risen from her chair, collected her things, and departed. Anna knew that Mrs. Dunn would repeat her words to the missionaries.

In the meantime, an increasingly distracted Horatio returned from long saunters to sermonize his flock on "avoiding temptation" as the only guarantee of immortality. The subject seemed to energize him, and soon discussions of "temptation" became the Overcomers' dominating theme. One day, after a particularly long absence, Horatio reappeared with an armful of cyclamen, wild pea, blood drops, and clover blooms that he presented to Anna. Taking her aside, he said he had something important to say. He wished her to know the Lord's latest command.

"A truly consecrated man is one whose will is broken," Horatio began haltingly, looking intently at his wife. "Everything—reputation, time, money, life, everything—must be wholly on the altar."[3] Anna waited uncertainly as Horatio reminded her that Saint Paul had demanded sacrifices. "The apostle preached that the old Paul had to die for the new Paul to live." His voice steadying, Horatio continued: "Paul looked the terms of discipleship squarely in the face. He counted the cost." Horatio paused, drew a breath, and then delivered the message over which he had long been deliberating: "And there be eunuchs which have made themselves eunuchs for the kingdom of heaven's sake."[4]

"St. Matthew, nineteen, twelve." Anna recognized the reference to the Savior's enigmatic message that for some, celibacy was necessary. All at once, she understood what had been preoccupying her husband. Unbidden, a tiny, angry flame flickered in her breast. They both were aware of the seepage of authority from him to her. Did Horatio resent her power? Perhaps he had cooled to her, as she had not felt well for some time. Suddenly Anna saw only joyless burdens. Her ascendancy in their group had been an assignment from God, which she had accepted, but Horatio's cavalier borrowing, his vagueness, his leaving everything up to her—was it fair, should she be punished more? She tried to listen to him as she had always done, to make herself understand and accept. But she needed a message from God.

Some days later, she spoke to Mary Whiting. Mary confided that she and John had ceased to sleep together. Anna thought about it. John had been suffering "congestion of the liver" for months, so surely their sexual estrangement was the result of his illness. She reported this development to Horatio, and again he repeated that for "the kingdom of heaven's sake" he could no longer sleep with her. For the moment, Anna said nothing.

John Whiting died in December 1886, adding the expense of his wife, Mary, and two small children to Anna's cares.

Then, one morning not long after John's funeral, Anna and Horatio strode together into the closed meeting. They had a new revelation to announce. Henceforth, the household would be celibate. All bodily as well as spiritual temptations were to be fought. "We will overcome the sins of the flesh," Horatio began. The Saints' surprise was evident. All sat erect and attentive as Anna warmed to her husband's new theme with a ferocity that made it seem as if it were her own. "We will destroy our wedding rings!" she cried, yanking off her own gold band and thrusting it at her young protégé, Jacob Eliahu, standing, as always, close by.[5] "We have to guard against attachment!" Her glorious blue eyes probed every face. "Attachment is the danger. Attachment is the sin. Remember! God forms a Trinity between brother and sister—and God is *first*."[6]

Finally, Lizzie Page spoke up. She did not believe it was a true message, and she would not destroy the wedding ring that symbolized a sacred vow. Her husband looked on, torn and confused. Anna turned on Lizzie vehemently, declaring that "the devil" was in her. For days afterward, in meeting after meeting, in the halls, on the stairs, the struggle went on. It had become the custom at their sessions to confess all shortcomings—especially salacious thoughts, no matter how painful—after which Anna usually forgave the sinner. But Lizzie Page refused to confess. She would not let Anna separate her from her husband. The strain became unendurable. Lizzie developed a cough and was feverish. "Sickness is the fruit of sin!" Anna shouted. She directed that Lizzie be carried, protesting, to a small rented room at Ain Karim, six miles away.

Otis Page went with her. It was cold and they had no money for fuel or food; what little they had had vanished into the communal purse. Only infrequently did the group send out supplies. Lizzie developed tuberculosis, and her husband was helpless, unable to find work.[7] When she died, the "brothers" came to bury her in an unmarked grave, and Otis Page begged to return. Anna was reluctant to receive Brother Samuel, but ultimately relented, although she turned down his request that he be paid for the chairs, cots, tables, benches, bureaus, and shoes he made for the household. Afterward, he never received the wonderful hugs and kisses Anna gave the other men. He wore "the mark of Cain" on his forehead, she said.[8]

To Horatio, these measures seemed harsh. His gospel of love, of forgiveness, of sacrifice, was becoming distorted. Yet, it was true, temptation had to be wrestled with, "individual will had to be broken," and all ambition and desire had to be placed "on the altar." He had even tried to explain his theory to Dr. Merrill, despite the look of disbelief in the consul's eyes.[9] Most distressing, however, was Anna's interpretation of what they had discussed. The group, she announced one morning, must begin putting itself to tests. For "the spiritual training" of herself and her husband, she told the group, she would become "one" with another man. The blood drained from Horatio's face.[10] When Anna named the Reverend Herbert Drake as her "tempter," the colonists, embarrassed and electrified, looked down at their hands clasped tightly in their laps.[11]

For days at a time now, Anna shut her door and stayed alone with the handsome blond English cleric. Lurid stories circulated in the small English-speaking community of Jerusalem. Alice E. Davis, who had arrived in the city in 1881 just two weeks before the Overcomers, represented a millennialist group from Boston that published a paper, the *Age to Come.*[12] As its correspondent, she had been interested for some time in finding the truth of the Bezetha house. When Horatio came down with "chills" and asked if he might enjoy her lovely, breezy garden high over the stink and filth of the city, she was happy to oblige. Mrs. Davis often offered it to "those in poor health," who would then camp in tents near a cistern of pure water, hoping to heal themselves. Time and again,

Mrs. Davis sat with Horatio between bouts of fever in his tent, "offering him such little comforts as might be of benefit." An excellent listener, she found Horatio much more communicative than Anna or the others who came up the hill to visit him. They were "shy or reticent" about discussing their beliefs, Mrs. Davis later wrote, while Horatio struck her as "more fearful than unwilling . . . and it leaked out little by little that he was not in harmony with the house in which he lived as a member, and unhappy to a degree of sad dejection and heart misery." As Horatio worsened, she was touched by "his extreme unhappiness" and incredulous that he appeared to be dying even as his community strenuously disavowed the possibility of death and never called for a doctor. Eventually, after Horatio's transferal back to the house, she went for a visit and found him alone in the parlor in "great trouble of mind." She sat beside him on the divan and listened as he talked distractedly about his group's future. His face was waxen and yellow; she could not imagine how he could recover. She leaned forward as he rested "his elbow upon his knee and his head upon his hand, seemingly forgetful . . . of any human presence," and began a barely audible monologue. "What does it mean?" Horatio mumbled. "What is it all coming to? Is it a phase of Spiritism or what? What will come of it all? I cannot believe that this is the work of Spiritism . . . What does it mean?"[13]

Troubled and saddened by his misery, Mrs. Davis was shocked to hear a few days later that Horatio had been "condemned for unfaithfulness and tabooed from the notice or speech of the inmates for forty-four days." On top of this, he had been "shamefully abused and contemptuously treated—even to personal indignities—by the one he had taken up from a helpless orphan, educated, and married." To Alice Davis, who lost no time reporting the tragedy to friends in Jerusalem, Horatio had been "martyred" by his wife. She and others agreed that something should be done "to save the innocent and unsuspecting from that fearful snare, the Spaffordite community."[14]

In the Bezetha house, Horatio lay emaciated, close to death. Anna stood with ten-year-old Bertha at her husband's side, listening to his labored breathing, then quietly left the room. Outside she listened to the stillness of the night, where not a leaf stirred. Slowly, dreamily, then more wildly, Anna began to dance. "I will dance before the Lord," she cried, invoking the psalm. Her arms thrown wide, her skirts swinging about her, Anna whirled and skipped and danced until perspiration drenched her blouse. Finally, exhausted, she returned to the house. As she entered the sickroom, Horatio opened his eyes. "Annie," he muttered, "I have experienced a great joy; I have seen wonderful things," and then he fell silent. Anna turned to her daughter. "Bertha, stay with Father. I must go away," she said, and stepped from the room, leaving Bertha alone with her father and Annie Aiken. A short time later, Horatio stopped breathing, and Bertha went to tell her mother. "He knows it all now," Anna said quietly. "He has seen Him face to face. We must not sorrow like those who have no hope."[15]

They had been married twenty-seven years. Anna did not cry, not then, not ever. Bertha crept off to a niche in the rampart wall and wept. Anna retired to her bed, getting up only to cover the rough pine planks of the casket with branches of pepper tree. She stayed home as the funeral cortege moved through the Damascus Gate along the long, dusty route to the little American cemetery on Mount Zion, offered as a resting place by the Presbyterian missionaries. Jews and Muslims helped to carry the casket, taking turns with several orphan boys who had left the London Jews Society school for lessons at the Bezetha house; pupils and teachers from the Alliance Israélite Universelle laid wreaths across the casket; and the Overcomers followed behind. A Russian cantor from the Russian Orthodox cathedral who had loved evenings singing hymns with the group asked if he might pay tribute "to a father to the fatherless."[16] Selah Merrill's Democratic replacement, Henry Gillman, had become fascinated by Horatio during the previous year and a half, and later wrote a novel about a gentle, visionary clergyman.[17] He never mentioned the group in his consular reports, and now directed that the American flag at the consulate be lowered to half-mast. Gillman, emotional and romantically inclined, unlike his predecessor, gushed to a newspaper reporter: "No one but Mrs. Spafford will miss him more than I will. It has been a great blessing to have such a man in Jerusalem."[18]

That afternoon the Turkish governor of Jerusalem called at the house to express his condolences. No one seemed to have noticed that there was no headstone to mark Horatio's grave.

Anna Lawson was noted for her
remarkable blue eyes, musical
voice, and keen intelligence that
attracted friends to her—and
very soon as well a prosperous
and well-regarded suitor, the
handsome lawyer Horatio
Spafford.

Horatio Gates Spafford, a Republican lawyer
from Troy, New York, arrived in Chicago
determined to reform a troubled society
turning from an agrarian way of life to
industrialism.

Dwight Lyman Moody was only nineteen when he came to Chicago from Northfield, Massachusetts, but already he showed extraordinary talent as a preacher, and while many initially criticized his methods, he soon assumed leadership of Chicago's evangelical movement.

The Great Chicago Fire of October 8, 1871, claimed an unknown number of lives and cost an estimated $350 million. Horatio Spafford would soon find it nearly impossible to make up his own stunning financial losses.

The disaster that would alter the Spaffords' lives forever occurred at 2:00 a.m. on November 22, 1873, in the middle of the Atlantic when the grand luxury liner *Ville du Havre* was rammed by an iron sailing ship. Anna, who had been traveling with her four daughters, sent a telegram to her husband: "Saved alone."

When the Overcomers first arrived in Palestine in 1881, they were not aware that infidels needed permission to visit the Dome of the Rock. They plunged uninvited into the sanctuary and met its astonished Muslim guardian, who helped them find a house to live in.

From Damascus Gate the road north to Nablus leads to the Overcomers' "Big House," now the five-star American Colony Hotel, just a short walk outside the city.

Settled at last in the "Big House," Anna shows two unidentified male guests its flower-filled courtyard. At her left is Mr. Rudy, and to his left is the tall inventor Elijah Meyers, who recorded Anna's messages in a book. Brother Jacob, wearing a fez, is fourth from Anna's right, standing beside her ardent Swedish follower Sister Tilda. On the edge of the apparently dry fountain, Mary Whiting sits with Otis Page.

Sickly as a baby, Grace Spafford (*left*) was never as strong as her sister Bertha, on whom her mother particularly doted.

The Spaffords' friendship with the powerful Adwan tribe continued through subsequent generations with visits back and forth. Here Ruth Whiting stands in front of Mr. Rudy on the steps; Bertha kneels between warriors; and Grace, wearing a white cap, sits on the ground with Furman Baldwin standing beside her.

Jacob Eliahu, the son of Sephardic Jews, was a brilliant student at the London Jews Society school, which he left to join the Overcomers. He adored Anna, and she trusted him as no other.

John Whiting and his sister, Ruth, the objects of a fierce custody fight when their grandmother left them a fortune in her will, were always treated with special care by Anna. When John married Grace Spafford, he gave the bulk of his inheritance to the colony.

Almost immediately upon his arrival in Jerusalem, Horatio, anxious to see proof that Jews were arriving in large enough numbers to ensure that the biblical prophecies would be fulfilled, often wandered off to talk with rabbis at the Wailing Wall.

The Overcomers concluded that the band of impoverished Yemeni Jews encamped outside the city walls must be the lost tribe of Gad, and dipped deeply into their scarce financial reserves to feed the Gadites and find them rooms.

Olof Henrik Larsson founded the Swedish Evangelical Church at 5487 Madison Avenue, Chicago.

After encountering Anna's charm and her assertion of possessing "a higher light," Olof's congregation saw their pastor pushed aside and Anna mounting the steps to his pulpit. When Anna revealed special messages, the congregation agreed to follow her to Jerusalem.

The industrious Swedes had brought to Jerusalem their own looms from Nås and lost no time setting up a weaving room, where they made pillows, rugs, and bedspreads as well as clothes for themselves and others, which helped swell the colony's exchequer.

Edith Larsson, the daughter of Olof Henrik and Mathilda Larsson, was initially separated from her parents when they joined the colony in 1896. She grew up to marry Lewis Larsson, who ran the American Colony Photo Department.

Tipers Lars Larsson, a prosperous Nås farmer whom Olof urged to hurry to Jerusalem, sold his properties at a terrible loss. His wife died in Jerusalem soon after they arrived, and his daughter could not marry the man she loved because of Anna's celibacy requirement. Their tragic relationship was the focus of Selma Lagerlöf's epic novel *Jerusalem*.

Lewis Larsson (*left*) developing film with an assistant in the American Colony photo laboratory, the colony's most lucrative business.

Amelia Gould, or "Sister Elizabeth," was a well-to-do widow from Chicago whom the Overcomers depended on financially. She accompanied the Spaffords to Jerusalem, persuaded by Anna that she would meet her resurrected dead husband there.

William Rudy also joined the Overcomers in Chicago. A quiet businessman and former mill owner who retired after a serious illness, he was appointed by Anna as the group's bursar, and Amelia later drafted a will leaving her estate to him.

General Charles George Gordon, or "Chinese Gordon," claimed to have found the true place of Christ's crucifixion and tomb while staying with the Overcomers.

"Sister" Johanna Brooke left the London Jews Society school to join the Overcomers. Her religious zeal cooled, but her love of the young and interest in stimulating their minds never waned.

Kansas was no less affected by millenarian angst than the rest of the country, so it was no surprise that Brother Jacob found ready converts among its farmers. This grain elevator was covered with warnings to get one's soul right with Jesus before it was too late.

From left: Grace Spafford, Ruth Whiting, an unknown (possibly Swedish) companion, and Bertha Spafford, after they moved in with Olof Larsson's Swedish group.

Finally, in 1904, after years of waiting, Anna announced the "new dispensation" that allowed the Overcomers to marry. Shown here, Flora Page, the sweet-tempered daughter of Otis Page, was assigned to wed Farid Naseef, nearly ten years younger than she. It was destined to be an unhappy union.

Anna's girls were growing up and considered extremely attractive by the young Turkish officers and Arab officials who attended Anna's evening salons.

There was unprecedented
excitement as the Holy Land
prepared for the much-heralded
visit of Kaiser Wilhelm II and
Augusta Victoria in 1898.

All along the royal route from Haifa to Jerusalem, the kaiser and his
kaiserin were cheered by tumultuous crowds while a German orchestra
played the German national anthem.

The kaiser immediately embarked on an exhausting round of ceremonial visits to all of Jerusalem's varied sects and communities. Here he is escorted over the Haram al-Sharif, accompanied by Turkish officials and Muslim dignitaries who guided the royal presence.

Sultan Abdul Hamid II, the last Ottoman autocrat, promised the German emperor a large site on Mount Zion to build a Catholic church, an ambitious plan that would entangle a U.S. consul, the Presbyterian Board of Missions, and the American Colony in a dispute of extraordinary bitterness.

Theodor Herzl, an Austrian journalist, was appalled by the anti-Semitism aroused by the Dreyfus affair in France. Eager to persuade the kaiser of the importance of his Zionist dream, he journeyed to Jerusalem in 1898, hoping for a meeting.

The specter of war became more real with every passing month. Here, in Jerusalem, a man performs the war dance in front of the American Colony Store as a crowd looks on.

Djemal Pasha, the third member of the triumvirate running the Young Turk government, spared the colony from the harsh measures imposed on others and made frequent use of the Photo Department to document critical events, such as the locust plague, and places of potential military significance, including the area around the Dead Sea, where he is shown here in 1915.

First plague and then famine took their toll on the people of Palestine, and supplicants soon gathered at the door of the American Colony, pleading for a bit of food and shelter.

A fallen camel, devoured by locusts. The desert was littered by the carcasses of animals during the plague and terrible famine.

The Red Crescent staff, including, standing center, back row, John Whiting, and, seated just to the left of center, wearing glasses (next to man in uniform), Grace Spafford Whiting, 1917.

Animals were requisitioned for transport, and as the supply of coal ran out, the Turkish army was reduced to cutting down trees to run the railroad, decimating the forests of Palestine. Here a camel train carries grain to Jerusalem in 1917.

The Turks had decided to make their stand against Allenby's army at Beersheba, inland and presumably safe from the guns of Allied warships. Here brave Turkish Lancers rallied west of Beersheba in 1917, but they could not escape the British planes, which owned the skies.

Probably the most famous image to emerge from Palestine in World War I, this picture was taken by Lewis Larsson. It captures the mayor of Jerusalem trying vainly to formally surrender the city to two very surprised British sergeants as an interested crowd of Turks and Arabs gathers. The surrender flag was merely a bedsheet attached to a broom handle. It is now in the Imperial War Museum.

General John S. M. Shea (standing center with walking stick), commander of the Sixtieth Division, designated by Field Marshal Allenby to accept the surrender of Jerusalem, was late for the historic moment. He was extremely unhappy to find that two officers, Watson and Bailey, had arrived ahead of him and that the mayor had tendered the surrender to them. He demanded that the American Colony photographers destroy all their negatives of these important moments.

By 1920, when Sir Herbert Samuel established the High Commissioner's Office, the British had their hands full trying to keep the peace. Here a police officer searches a Jewish rabbi as the rabbi's furious son jumps into the fray.

Bertha embraced British officialdom, and those administering the mandate heavily relied on her. In turn, she was a frequent visitor to Britain's Government House. When Winston Churchill and his wife, Clementine, visited Jerusalem in 1921, Frederick and Bertha Vester were among the elite invited to the reception.

It was often said that the great salon of the "Big House" was the most beautiful room in Jerusalem. Today, journalists and diplomats continue to favor the American Colony Hotel when they visit the holy city.

CHAPTER FIFTEEN

Struggling On

To each is given the manifestation of the Spirit
for the common good. To one is given through
the Spirit the utterance of wisdom, and to an-
other the utterance of knowledge . . . to another
faith . . . to another gifts of healing . . . to an-
other the working of miracles . . . to another
prophecy, to another the ability to distinguish
between spirits, to another various kinds of
tongues, to another the interpretation of tongues.
All these are inspired by one and the same
Spirit, who apportions to each one individually
as he wills.

—1 Corinthians 12:4–11

For weeks, Anna stayed in her room with the door closed. Members of the household crept in and out. They murmured together of the strange message that "Mother Anna" had received the year they arrived. "Seven years in the land," Anna had declared in 1881, adding bafflingly that the message had been "for Horatio." Now it was 1888, seven years since the original Overcomers had disembarked at Jaffa. And now, whispered the members, marveling, Horatio was dead.

Forlorn, trying to be unobtrusive, Anna's daughters waited to see their mother, but she would not permit them to come into her room. Finally, she assented to being brought to Rolla and Docia Floyd in Jaffa, carried in a large carriage outfitted with a bed. The Floyds looked after her for a time, tiptoeing by her bedroom, respecting her desire for silence. Another Jaffa couple who had met the Spaffords when they first came, Baron and Baroness von Ustinov, then took her in to their spacious house.[1] Here she sat for hours in their garden, listening to the splashing fountain and the cry of birds. During the long months she was away, Captain William Sylvester succumbed to angina pectoris and was buried in the American cemetery beside his friend Horatio. When at last Anna returned, terribly weak, thin, and pale, she seemed still unable or unwilling to resume command. The Overcomers had carried on as well as they knew how during her absence, trying not to mourn as they had been instructed. But apprehension filled the silent rooms, and those who had followed the Spaffords from America felt far from home. They all wondered what would become of their leaderless community, whether they could continue to carry on their work—even how they might find means to survive.

At this difficult time, two figures from Chicago's past materialized in Jerusalem. Dwight Moody and his partner, Ira Sankey, had arrived in the Holy Land on a last major tour. Although evangelicals coming to Jerusalem often called at the house, there had been no correspondence between the Spaffords and their former Chicago colleagues. For Anna and Horatio, the break with Moody and his friends had been complete. However, hearing of Horatio's death, Moody decided to call on Anna as soon as he had completed his duties.

Times had changed since the grand days when Moody's performances captured the hearts of two nations and extraordinary crowds attended him. By 1888, the year of Horatio's death, the verities upon which both men had depended were under sustained attack. Archaeologists, researchers, and evolutionary theologians, influenced by Darwinism, now employed scientific methods to analyze biblical texts. Old creedal assumptions were being challenged on many fronts. Increasingly, liberal Protestants embraced a new social gospel, dismissing as myths the seven-day Creation, Noah's Flood, and the Garden of Eden. Even the YMCA, the springboard of Moody's early success, was packed with young men harboring secular notions and querying the nature of the Trinity. By the last decade of the nineteenth century, the evangelicals' efforts to spread the Word through revivalism and ecstatic conversion seemed increasingly questionable, archaic, and ineffective as a means for healing society's problems.

Hoping Moody and Sankey could wrap up their tour with a spectacular finale in Jerusalem, their scouts had arranged for an open-air service on top of a cliff that was an old, if rather neglected, Muslim cemetery, a fact apparently unknown to the organizers. When Moody mounted a grave in order for his audience to see him better, the scandal rocked the Muslim community, and afterward the Turkish governor forbade Christians to enter the cemetery without a permit. Probably the good-natured Bible-thumper, who hated controversy and loved people more than ideas, was unconscious of his cultural transgression. He made his way up to Mount Bezetha, his thoughts given to all he had once shared with Spafford, the Sunday schools they had built together, and the once thrilling discussions.

Anna stayed in her room when Moody knocked at Bezetha's door. She did not intend to mourn Horatio. He was with her drowned daughters in heaven. Moody had comforted her once, and she had been grateful. She did not need him now. Therefore Moody found himself alone in the parlor with Horatio's daughters. The evangelist put his arm around Bertha and pulled Grace onto his knee, shedding such copious tears, Bertha remembered, that they formed a pool at his feet.[2]

Slowly Anna recovered. The months of seclusion had been a time for healing, for meditation, and, as she grew stronger, for difficult decisions. But finally she felt able to reenter the life of the house once more. The relief of the Overcomers was palpable, and the never-ending stream of visitors resumed. Anna understood that many enjoying the American Colony's hospitality left "smirking up their sleeves." She knew some regarded them as naive at best, and deluded at worst. However, visiting American evangelicals were different, more serious and intent, usually querying her at length on prophetic signs. They would sit for hours sipping tea, nibbling on the colony's scarce supply of bread and jam, pondering whether the Mosque of Omar should be destroyed in order to build a new temple on the Holy Mount, or if there really were enough returning Jews to presage the Second Coming. So when William E.

Blackstone, whom the Spaffords had known slightly in Chicago, showed up, Anna was not surprised.

Blackstone called himself "God's little errand boy." As an energetic lay minister in the Chicago Hebrew Mission, and a firm believer in pre-millennialism and a seven-year tribulation by the Antichrist, he was bent on ensuring that God's promise to His chosen people be expedited in anticipation of an imminent Rapture. His small tract *Jesus Is Coming* was selling briskly in religious circles. Although Blackstone had always said that he had "labored hard" to convince his friend Spafford to abandon "his vagaries," for months after the group left for Jerusalem, he paid regular calls on Dr. Hedges to see what news Horatio might have sent of a glorious event. In the summer of 1888 he took his daughter with him to attend the General Missionary Convention in London, and now they were in Jerusalem with an invitation to stay with the Overcomers.

He had many conversations with Anna and confided to her his grandest ambition: to organize the first world conference between Jews and Christians. In fact, Blackstone's conference, "The Past, Present, and Future of Israel," in November 1890 gave birth to the famous Blackstone Memorial signed by 413 prominent Christian and Jewish leaders, and was presented to President Benjamin Harrison. It urged the United States to use its influence with the world's governments to facilitate the immigration of Jews to "Palestine as their ancient home" and became a milestone in the history of Zionism. The first Jewish Supreme Court justice, Louis D. Brandeis, in 1916, wrote that he was "infatuated" with Blackstone's work and considered him "the father of Zionism," even before Theodor Herzl.[3]

When Blackstone returned to Chicago, where reporters never failed to pounce on any new tidbit about the bizarre American Colony in Jerusalem, he gave a positive report. "The singing at those meetings is the nearest to the music of Heaven of any I have ever heard." He was a little puzzled, he admitted, about how they paid for themselves: "I think they are sometimes short. But when they are, a wonderful spirit of self-denial prevails among them, and each one strives to be the only sufferer. I think they would divide their last crust with each other, or with any worthy person who was in want."[4]

Anna clipped every article and put it in her scrapbook, whether it was favorable or not. She was very pleased when such a luminary as Bishop John Heyl Vincent wrote in the *Independent* about how struck he had been by the colony's "utter surrender to the Lord . . . self-sacrifice . . . practical philanthropy . . . and secrecy in almsgiving." Bishop Vincent approved, he said, of a sensibility that "kept no record" of good works "and published nothing to the world." Anna knew how vital the good opinion of such an influential figure was. Bishop Vincent was the much-admired Methodist Episcopal founder of the Chautauqua movement, already a powerful educational force in America, advocating rationalism and science in biblical study. While the bishop was appalled by the "hatred and malice" he found among "warring sects" in the holy city, he had been touched by the dedication of the colonists. Although he admitted that they had many detractors, and that he himself did "not fully understand them," Anna nevertheless could feel the sting less when he praised "their unselfish works" and regretted that "bitter misrepresentations" were causing a drying up of donations.[5]

Indeed, the future seemed ominously opaque. In August 1890, young Herbert Drake died of malaria; when he went into convulsions, no doctor had been called, even though quinine had become a proved and available antidote. Anna sat stony-faced as the mourners escorted his casket to the cemetery. The next year Aunt Maggie Lee dropped dead of a heart attack. Debts continued to mount. They collected their jewelry, including wedding rings, and sold them in the souk.[6] Rolla and Docia Floyd tried to help, once delivering twenty loaves of bread and a large quarter of mutton from Jaffa. Another day, sixty more loaves of fresh white bread arrived unexpectedly, apparently a gift arranged by someone in Chicago, and the egg man continued to bring eggs and an occasional chicken. Despite this generosity, Anna felt her throat constricting with anxiety.

No bank, she knew, would lend anything to her, a penniless widow. Nor was it an option to send Mrs. Gould back to Chicago to demand her securities, since Anna could not be certain that her emotional friend would not fall under a negative influence. She ached to know just how much Amelia really had, which might be as much as $20,000. More promising, news had come that Mary Whiting's mother-in-law had died in Springfield, leaving a fortune. Old Mrs. Whiting and Mary's mother,

Regina Lingle, had always fought the colony, and Anna was well aware they accused her of exerting an evil influence over their families. Mrs. Lingle had actually come to Jerusalem after John Whiting died, to try to detach her daughter and grandchildren and, at the request of his friends, to put up a headstone on John's grave. When the colony members told her they could not do that, because they expected John to rise soon and meet them walking in the street, Mrs. Lingle had been livid. Naturally, they had let her talk to her grandchildren, in the company of colony members of course, but the children had said what they had been told: that they would see their father soon in the streets.[7] Still, Anna thought, if she could just raise enough to send both Mary and Amelia to Chicago, with either Brother Jacob or Mr. Rudy to keep watch, their problems might be solved.

Visitors never stopped. Some days as many as six parties arrived, one group coming in as another left. An American, charmed by Anna in a navy blue frock with a bunch of fresh violets tucked at her waist, noted that she seemed "exhausted." Nevertheless, she insisted on taking him for a tour of the house. "These good people get little credit for what they do," he concluded in a sympathetic report home.[8] Altogether, it was repetitive and even grueling work. Anna, by now a polished spokeswoman for the house, always began with the story of the shipwreck, followed by an entertaining litany of endearing tales about their pure life, including the varied personalities they had helped.

Article after article cited familiar stories of visits to bedouin camps in the desert where the nomad women took off Anna's stockings and admired her white uncalloused feet, or the bedouin men's visits to the house, hanging up their guns and spears and rolling themselves in blankets for a night or two on the drawing room floor. Anna would amuse listeners with the tale of an Arab milkman falsely arrested for murder, describing how the group intervened for him with the authorities and prayed for his release; when he was finally free, the rejoicing "brothers [had] lifted him on their shoulders and carried him up the stairs."[9] Then, to laughter, she would conclude with a description of the Arab charcoal dealer who witnessed their kindness and exclaimed, "All this for an Arab? You *are* good people," and thenceforth delivered free charcoal to the house. Enthralled, appreciative visitors usually left donations.

Although she could not deny that her "influence" was "far-reaching and powerful," Anna worked hard to counter all the "misrepresentations." Sometimes she failed completely. An English visitor left deeply perturbed, then published an article that decried the group's "knowledge" that they alone "were illuminated" and were "able to recognize others who enjoy the same illumination." It was unpleasant to read the man's screed: "Nothing could lay the foundation of a more intolerant sectarianism than such an assumption . . . or be more calculated to foster spiritual pride."[10]

Anna simply shrugged it off. She knew they were special—and when another saw similar truths, they welcomed him or her as a member. "You must become it before you can understand it," she said.[11] And as long as Anna told her fellowship what to do and where to go, they obeyed. Besides, how could they have "spiritual pride" when at every private meeting she forced them to self-criticize, to cast out sin for the good to enter, to annihilate their very selfhood?

In 1891 a six-foot-four-inch Presbyterian missionary, the Reverend Edward F. Baldwin, arrived in a flowing burnoose with four children. He and his wife had been running a hospital mission in Morocco when Baldwin decided that faith superseded the need for medicine; the established churches were "drunk with the wine of tradition"; and Anna's house offered pentecostal fraternity.[12] Alarmed, his wife and their remaining five older children sharply disagreed and stayed away, but were unable to prevent him from giving Anna what money he had—and some of his wife's—and joining the Overcomers. There were now ten children under the age of fifteen to feed, house, and clothe, so when two single gentlemen moved into the house—George A. Fuller and John A. Miller—and died within the year, their savings remained with the colony, and Anna could breathe a little more easily.

In May of that same year, 1891, Amelia Gould wrote a will, declaring that she was leaving all she had to "Brother" William Rudy.[13] Anna had strenuously encouraged Amelia to do this, supported by Rudy himself, and they agreed that Rudy should get off a letter to Amelia's brother-in-law as quickly as possible. "Remit to me without delay any funds in your hands [belonging to Mrs. Gould]," Rudy wrote, but John Gould demurred, reminding Amelia that it was she who had asked him to guard her money in trust.[14] The means to collect Amelia's principal now obsessed Anna, but she still dared not risk sending her wealthy friend back to America.

Private morning meetings were different from the informal services attended by visitors, where prayers were offered standing, a lesson was read and thoughtfully commented on by the members, and the service closed with tea and cakes. When the group was alone, it was time for soul-searching, confession, and Anna's latest messages from God. Usually she asked Jacob to offer a concluding prayer, which he intoned with a rabbinical bobbing of his head. Often Reverend Baldwin was also invited to read a lesson, and the newest recruit, a slightly mad, multilingual Indian Jew from Bombay with a knack for machinery, Elijah Meyers, who had arrived wearing a green silk turban so voluminous that the ladies were able to cut it into dresses, earnestly scribbled every message of Anna's into a plain brown notebook, which he treasured as the utterances of God.[15]

If there were doubts about immortality among members, a revived Anna reminded them that as long as sinful thoughts were not excised with the ruthlessness of a surgical blade, people would die. As the adults tearfully ripped themselves apart, or lit into the failings of the others, the assembled children sat quietly, absorbing it all with obedient, unblinking attention. The youngsters accepted that Bertha and Grace Spafford got the piano lessons, the French and German tutoring, and the good meals when there was little to eat. John and Ruth Whiting had fuller plates of food as well, but they, too, had to walk behind with the others when Bertha and Grace rode the big black donkey to their lessons. With Horatio gone, it was now Jacob who took them out to the barn and thrashed them when they were naughty. Bertha and Grace were spared, but the others found it humiliating as well as painful when he made them strip, even the girls, as he meted out their punishments.[16]

During this difficult post-Horatio period Anna concentrated on her theme, "attachment" and its "dangers." During her long seclusion in Jaffa, she had understood things she determined never to forget. When she married she had expected to be safe. She had been too self-satisfied

with her rise from an immigrant's status, too dependent on her husband
and her love of hearth and home. But God alone can protect against disaster. For too long in her marriage, she had been subservient to her husband's influence, his opinions, his ineptitude. His refusal to work,
forcing their dependence on the charity of others, had always grated; it
had shamed her. As a girl, she had seen the hypocrisy of the church, but
allowed Horatio to lead her back into the fold, until he, too, had seen
the light. She had cared too much for her dead children; such attachments were wrong. Love not devoted to God was a sin, and sorrow mere
egotism. During those solitary ruminations, she had come to realize that
she was alone with God, and alone at last she was powerful, free to do
what she knew was right for herself, and for these people who depended
on her. As she had painfully freed herself, she must free them as well
from insidious personal attachment.

At a meeting, Anna revealed a message. Her followers were to be
tested by having "affinities."[17] There were no longer any married couples.
Instead, each man was to have an "affinity" with one of the younger
women. Anna set about designating couples, commanding them to
spend the night in bed together. They were to abjure sexual attraction as
a vehicle to "overcome" temptation, and to report to her any details of
their relationships.[18] "We are to be like Adam and Eve before the fall,"
she warned, and frequently invited Jacob Eliahu to her room alone.[19]
The members noted that when he was not actually at her side, his ador-
ing gaze followed her every move.

In the evenings Anna played the piano, Jacob joining his rich tenor
voice to her exquisite soprano; Amelia sang alto, and Elias Habib rang in
with a rumbling bass while the others either sang along or listened with
contented smiles. Usually there was an assortment of Arab men and
Turkish officials in the softly lit salon, enjoying a tête-à-tête in a darkened corner with one of the younger women. The Muslim men found it
novel to chat with unveiled women by the glow of a gaslight lamp. A
young effendi from one of Jerusalem's noble families, Mahmoud, became attracted to Annie Aiken, now a pert young woman of twenty-four
of whom most of the group was fond. He "spoke soft words" to her, and
before long she was in love.

"It is between me and God," Annie wrote Anna in a note, disclosing that she had gone to the Kaminitz Hotel. Anna rushed there immediately, demanding the truth and reminding the love-besotted girl that "all sexual feeling is merely a remnant of your fallen state."[20] When Anna returned and rang the house bell for members to assemble, she sensed their sympathy for the lovers and a rebellion brewing that would require quelling. She insisted that a delegation attend the hotel day and night to keep Annie's movements under surveillance while she paid a call to Mahmoud's family. In front of his frowning parents, exceedingly unhappy to learn of the affair, the blushing suitor was obliged to say that he loved Miss Aiken only "as a sister" and could not marry her, as his family had already promised him to a Muslim lady.

Distraught, furious, and ashamed, Miss Aiken retaliated, going to the U.S. Consulate. Selah Merrill had returned to his desk in 1891 and was delighted to hear Miss Aiken's flood of accusations against colony practices, and especially her indictment of Mrs. Spafford's psychological tyranny. With his help, Annie made her way back to Chicago and looked up Mary Whiting's mother, Regina Lingle. While Anna dealt with her rebel members and brought them back under control, the Lingles celebrated with friends. At last they had the longed-for ammunition to blast their bewitched Mary free from the iron grip of the American Colony in Jerusalem.

CHAPTER SIXTEEN

The Whiting Affair

*I am certain that her notions—wild and vague
as they appear to be—center in sexual relations.
On this subject she is actually morbid . . . The
body and all that pertains to it—passions, appetites, etc.—can be spiritualized and become
absolutely pure. In that case, or state, there is no
more law human or divine; there is no Bible; no
Christ; no sin; no sacraments; no marriage, no
offspring. These all belong to the flesh which is
vile. One must rise above them. But once thus
risen, sublimated, etherialized, spiritualized,
unhumanized, Anna Spaffordized, all appetites
and passions are pure, holy, heavenly. Then two
"pure affinities" can sleep together in one bed.
There is no sin in it whatever—provided they
do not happen to have a baby . . . Her household is a mixture of sensuality, selfishness, slavery, disloyalty—and all the while she is
sheltering herself and all that she does or teaches
under the name "American."*

—Dr. Selah Merrill[1]

It was August 1893, the dry season. Limestone dust coated the
roads and rooftops. When the west wind blew in the afternoon,
every living thing was smothered in powdery flakes as if from a snow-

storm. Selah Merrill, diligent and precise, sat in his office and composed comprehensive reports to the State Department. He had been back at his post for two years now and, as before, was concerned over the impact that a steady influx of Jews, heavier than ever, would have on the Ottoman administration in Palestine. Merrill, who had Jewish colleagues in academia and was not ill disposed to Jews personally, nonetheless found the anxious and often poor Jewish immigrants he was dealing with in Jerusalem obstinate and "quarrelsome." Unlike the other consuls who could close their doors at noon, he felt the necessity of keeping the U.S. Consulate open all day in order to deal with Jews claiming American protection. Their purchases of property in contravention of Turkish laws, and the subsequent friction with the Turkish authorities, he had noted irritably in his first term, were "well-nigh interminable." Either he or his dragoman was forced to "spend many hours every week in the Serai," or local Turkish court. "Very seldom," he reported, "is a Jew satisfied or does he allow a case to remain decided when a decision is adverse to himself."[2]

Now, in his second term, he informed the department that all the talk of Jews as " 'the Chosen People,' descended from Abraham and 'destined to be reestablished as a Kingdom in the land of their fathers,' " was making for trouble as "the Turks have no intention of allowing such a Kingdom, at least not in Palestine." Further, it was Merrill's considered opinion that until Jerusalem's Jews learned to rely on themselves and not on "the bounty which is almost lavishly bestowed," until they abandoned this pernicious *haluka* as well as such practices as child marriages, until they gained an "education of a higher order" and not merely instruction in the Talmud, they would never be fit to govern themselves. A far sounder and more rational solution to the general Jewish problem, he suggested almost wishfully to Washington, was "assimilation" in their countries of origin.[3] If these views were not welcomed by the evangelical community eager to witness a Jewish return, they found a sympathetic hearing among State Department diplomats attempting to grapple with the realities of the Middle East.

Then, in July 1893, a note from a professor at the University of Chicago distracted him. "I have a sister living with a fanatical company in the house of a Mrs. Spafford," David Lingle began, explaining that he was in Jerusalem to see his sister Mary E. Whiting. He had recently learned from a former member of that house that "some of the people there were living immoral lives. This has made me most anxious for my sister and her children . . . and I have come to investigate the matter and if possible remove my sister from such dangerous surroundings."[4] He believed the group was deeply in debt. Could Consul Merrill tell him what he knew about their finances?

Merrill was only too happy to oblige. He invited the professor in for a chat, and then laid out a catalog of the Spaffordite offenses: their occult preachments, slander of the established churches, and bizarre omission of tombstones to mark the graves of their dead; their refusal to work; and the audacity of their calling themselves "the American Colony" when they included Turkish, English, and other nationals. And finally, the most troubling allegation, unmarried men and women lived in an atmosphere suggesting sexual "imprudencies." Looking Professor Lingle sternly in the eye, Merrill emphasized that he had *never* set foot in the house on Mount Bezetha. He was therefore unable to confirm personally all these rumors of immorality. However, as to their debts, the colony's landlord, Ali Bey Juzdar, commander of the Turkish gendarmerie, had recently been in his office to complain that the colony had not paid rent for over two years. All Ali Bey needed to do was ask the Turkish governor for an eviction order and he, Merrill, would be obligated to execute it.

This complaint came on the heels of another from Merrill's colleague the German consul, concerned about several of his nationals who were owed a substantial debt by the so-called American Colony. He wanted to know if Merrill was in a position to compel Mrs. Gould to get her money from America so that they could be reimbursed. All told, Merrill concluded to Lingle, he was aware of forty-one creditors demanding payments of some 36,377 francs, worth about $8,000. "You will see that my position is embarrassing," he expostulated. "How the Spafford people justify their course of life in living along year after year on the money of other people, I do not understand."[5]

Shortly afterward, in great agitation, Professor Lingle returned to Merrill's office with the news that members of the house had prevented him from having a private conversation with his sister, that Mary was always surrounded when he visited. "My sister is a prisoner . . . unable to act freely. I believe the coercion consists in threats and so-called judgments of so terrible a nature that a timid woman would be completely overcome." He added: "They have a motive for retaining her since Mrs. Whiting's minor children have some money left them and the Spafford people hope to secure it. They have already made two abortive attempts to do this."[6]

This news fit with all the consul had already darkly concluded. It was clear he needed to intervene. He asked Mary to come to his office, but she refused. Outraged, invoking Section 47 of Regulations for Consular Courts in Turkey, the consul sent his *kavass* with a summons for her to appear before him at three o'clock that afternoon, accompanied by her children, or "be liable to the penalties of the law." Again, Mary refused to come. Five days later, on August 10, after Merrill had deputized four rather surprised but willing Americans visiting Jerusalem from the Syrian Protestant College in Beirut, explaining that a fellow American believed his sister "detained against her will," the deputation arrived at the house with a warrant for Mary's arrest.

With Merrill's *kavass* and dragoman at his side, Franklin T. Moore knocked on the door while the other three kept watch outside. "We were treated with apparent cordiality," Mr. Moore later wrote in an affidavit for the State Department, "until our purpose was announced. Mrs. Whiting happened to be in the first room we were shown into. On pretense of preparing her wraps, she was pushed gently into a side room by Mr. Baldwin . . . the door was immediately locked by three men . . . one of whom announced that the woman should never leave the house except by force.

"The woman was already escaping by means of a back stair; immediate chase was given and she was caught in another part of the house. A large number of the 'community' gathered around her and, after a loud discussion, engaged in a religious ceremony that appeared to my mind fanatical and irreverent."

Captured, Mary and her children were ushered into a carriage that made its slow way to the Grand New Hotel, the newest and most comfortable that Jerusalem offered, where Merrill and his wife lived and where he had booked rooms for them. One of the colony men had

jumped on the carriage's steps, while two other colonists walked immediately in front. "At all times," Moore's report noted, "the men belonging
to the 'community' endeavored to deprive the woman of the opportunity to express herself or to act freely."[7]

Now it was the colony's turn. Pawning Jacob Eliahu's watch to pay
for it, they telegraphed the Department of State, which promptly wired
an inquiry to Merrill: "What is going on there?"

"Woman is in care of her brother. Matter legal and simple," he wired
back.[8]

Mary was told that she had the freedom of the hotel, even the freedom of the city, but for a few days she was to be in the care of her
brother, who wanted to know her actual wishes. Merrill sent a notice to
Mount Bezetha. "Mrs. Whiting is not your servant, nor a relative. As
you have no jurisdiction over her, you are to leave her alone while she is
with Professor Lingle."

As news of the drama spread rapidly through the city, for three successive days and nights colony guards stood beneath Mary's window,
calling up to her; others crowded in the Grand New Hotel's corridor,
knocking on her door, or rushed in and out, shouting at guests that she
had been kidnapped. On the third day, after many vain attempts by Lingle to hold his agitated sister's attention, the door of his room opened
and Johanna Brooke appeared. He rose and approached her, but she
screamed: "Don't touch me! I am a British citizen!" Realizing that she
was in the wrong room, Miss Brooke jumped onto a balcony that connected to Mary's suite and disappeared into it, locking the door behind
her. The British consul, who had already refused the colony's request that
he give them British protection, was called to eject her.

But by now Lingle felt beaten. "I have not been able to have as free
a talk with my sister as I desired and hoped for," he said dejectedly. "I
have seen and heard enough to convince me that she is completely under the control of Mrs. Spafford and hence does not wish to return with
me to America . . . I do not believe it is her real wish." Before he left, he
added, "These people have exercised such espionage over her as to convince me that the community is perfectly jesuitical in its methods."[9]

Mary was returned to Mount Bezetha. The colonists had won the
first round. Merrill wrote his account for the State Department, which

read the dispatches and felt as much bemusement as the Jerusalemites. The colonists, he said, have "threatened me with terrible vengeance, but they do not frighten me."[10] Still, he was somewhat unnerved. So it was consoling to hear from a number of prominent Muslim families, in particular Mahmoud's parents and relatives, that they had "ceased altogether" associating with Mrs. Spafford on "the ground that the house is not a proper place and the influence of its members is dangerous."[11] An even greater relief, of course, was State's message of November 23, 1893: "You acted within your jurisdiction."

CHAPTER SEVENTEEN

The Trial

"He that overcometh shall not be hurt of the
second death."
"To him that overcometh to him will I give of
the hidden manna."
"He that overcometh, and he that keepeth my
works unto the end, to him will I give
authority over the nations."
"He that overcometh shall thus be arrayed in
white garments; and I will in nowise blot
his name out of the book of life."
"He that overcometh, I will make him a pillar
in the temple of my God."
"He that overcometh, I will give to him, to sit
down with me in my throne, as I also
overcame, and sat down with my Father in
his throne."

—Biblical reference cited by W. H. Wilson,
after a visit to the American Colony, 1895

"As unexpectedly as if they were the sheeted dead, Mrs. Amelia Gould and Mrs. Mary E. Whiting have reappeared in Chicago," exclaimed the *Chicago Daily News* when the two arrived in March 1894. They had come, the ladies announced, "to look after certain property interests."[1]

Actually, Mary's mother, Regina Lingle, had made the painful deci-

sion to petition the probate court to remove her grandchildren unless
Mary quit the colony. So Mary was obliged to appear. However, Anna
decided it was best to keep the Whiting children with her in Jerusalem
and asked Mary to leave Mr. Rudy with a power of attorney to speak for
them while she was absent. As an escort for the ladies Anna appointed
the ever-reliable Brother Jacob.

Rooms were rented and interviews arranged with newspaper reporters eager to revisit a story that always sparked avid interest. While
Jacob listened silently, Amelia stated her conviction that her brother-in-
law, John S. Gould, was withholding from her as much as $20,000,
while Mary Whiting said that her children were being denied an inheritance of $60,000 as a result of "religious persecution." The ladies did
not tell reporters that they had already visited Springfield, Massachusetts, to take up the matter with the Whiting estate's executor, H. H.
Bowman, the dignified president of the Springfield National Bank. The
conversation had been unsatisfactory. Mr. Bowman had stated flatly that
he would "pay not one cent" as he had no assurance that the money
rightly belonging to the children would not be squandered settling
colony debts. When, prodded by Brother Jacob, Mary threatened to take
the matter to the Massachusetts Supreme Court, Mr. Bowman suggested
they go right ahead. On consideration, they decided not to, and came to
Chicago instead to challenge Mrs. Lingle's custody assertions.

With statements from all parties concerned, the reporters had a field
day going over old stories of Horatio's angry creditors, Anna's prophecies, and such tidbits as the trip some of the Overcomers had taken
to Boston directed by a series of "sniffles." John Whiting's old mother,
quoted as being "a cordial hater of the 'Overcomers,' " had been in touch
with the Lingle family before she died. She had hoped to make them
guardians of her grandchildren, but was prevented from doing so by
Massachusetts law. Regina Lingle, a social figure of consequence, and her
son David, a professor of biology at the University of Chicago, were described as regarding "the 'Overcomers' with abhorrence . . . a set of lunatics . . . They speak slightingly of the charities of the colony, saying
they were done with money borrowed from the natives, and never re-
paid."[2]

The newspapers even spelled out the terms of Mrs. Whiting's will, which provided that no payment be made to the children "until such time as my trustee shall be satisfied that the sums so paid will be applied to the sole maintenance, use, education, and advancement of said children, *and for no other purpose whatsoever.*" Further, in case the children died before their mother, "my trustee shall provide a comfortable maintenance for the said Mary E. Whiting so long as she shall live . . . and *provided that she shall reside in the United States of America.*" Otherwise, the estate was to be equally divided between the American Baptist Home Mission Society and the Woman's American Baptist Foreign Mission Society.[3]

Amelia and Mary both engaged lawyers. Amelia's warned her that bringing her brother-in-law to court would be "tantamount to a trial of Mrs. Gould and the 'Overcomers' for insanity," so she might do better to agree to an out-of-court settlement. John Gould was apparently relieved to be free from his burden and agreed to settle the matter for $7,000, which was accepted when he proved that Amelia's expectations had been greatly inflated.

Much of the money was used for transportation, as Mary's lawyer insisted the children, Ruth, fourteen, and John, twelve, be brought to Chicago. They arrived in mid-October, accompanied by Anna, her two daughters, and William Rudy. Anna was ready to testify and would be an effective witness, as they all knew. But she had other pressing reasons to return to Chicago, not least her desire to separate her daughter Bertha, a well-endowed beauty of sixteen, from a dashing young man of German-Swiss parentage with whom she had fallen in love. Frederick Vester was nine years older, and Anna was intent on introducing Bertha to more eligible American men, hopefully with better financial prospects. Finally, she wanted to get her Lake View house back.

It was rumored that Anna's return heralded the collapse of the Jerusalem group and that all the Overcomers would have returned had there been sufficient funds. Mrs. Gould, according to one story, was now writing letters to her relatives "offering for sale even the burial lot in which her late husband's remains are interred." One reporter ringing the bell at their rented house at 1084 West Monroe Street waited for hours outside, but no one answered. He noted that there were heavy shutters on the windows and the Spafford group was "extremely sensitive over their vagaries, and there are not a half dozen people in the city who can get access to them."[4]

The publicity barrage was ceaseless. Were these gentle widows being deprived of their rights? Was a male trustee interfering between a mother and her children? Was this religious persecution in the land of free speech and creed? And, supremely interesting, how could a grandmother wish to deprive her daughter of her children? Anna allowed herself to be interviewed and, not surprisingly, was brilliant. In a deep, animated, mellifluous voice, with sweetly self-deprecating smiles, she enchanted her listeners, describing the dramatic signs portending fulfillment of Jeremiah's prophecies—the wondrous increase of rainfall in the Holy Land, the new roads, the new buildings, and particularly the arriving Jews. "This fact alone," said Anna, blue eyes sparkling, "seems prophetical." When she said, "we instruct the Mohammedans and the Jews in the cultural arts, music, painting, languages . . . we go on, assisting all in need, trusting and confident, living entirely on faith," a captivated reporter returned to his city desk. The admiring story he filed for the morning paper compared her to Jane Addams, founder of Chicago's Hull House, whose pioneering work educating the underprivileged was soon to set international standards for which Addams would receive the Nobel Prize.[5]

Anna could not have asked for better. Supportive inquiries began arriving in the mailbox of the heavily shuttered two-story brick house on West Monroe. One such letter from a wealthy Kansas farmer in the small corn-belt hamlet of Salem, adjacent to the equally small town of Lebanon, invited the group to pay a visit and discuss their beliefs. Anna sent Jacob, who stepped down from the train onto the dusty station platform in a silk top hat and frock coat. Many years later, Lew Felton, a young farmer, remembered him as "the greatest slicker and talker I ever saw. Cunning, above average height, dark hair, piercing eyes, he had all but put a hypnotic control over people."[6] Jacob stayed a number of weeks, casting his spell, returning several times to talk with as many farmers as he could in the area. His influence proved extraordinary. Soon a number of families were putting their farms on the market and packing for Jerusalem.

Anna was less successful in retrieving her house. With Amelia, she called on Dr. Hedges at his office in April 1895. It was a distasteful exchange. When Anna insisted that her former friend and erstwhile Saint had pledged to return to Horatio the Lake View house when the Spaffords found the funds to reimburse him, he vigorously denied making any such promise. "Your teachings were false," he told her. Angrily he accused Horatio of leaving Chicago stealthily at night. He added bitterly: "I have learned now of Mr. Spafford's business affairs."[7]

Even unhappier was William Rudy's visit a day or so later.

"I have come to correct you," said Mr. Rudy.

"Don't tell me what I said," objected Dr. Hedges. Strong words followed, until Dr. Hedges declared: "You had better leave."[8]

Mr. Rudy did leave, and some months later there was a hearing on the matter before the master in chancery of Cook County involving testimony by a number of former Saints, as well as allegations and counter-allegations that much confused the master. However, he eventually opined in his final report: "After carefully considering all the competent testimony and evidence, much of which is vague and conflicting . . . I find the said Hedges . . . the rightful owner of the premises."[9]

The time was at hand for the dreaded custody battle in the probate court. "If [my daughter] were only away from Mrs. Spafford she would soon be herself again," a sorrowful Mrs. Lingle told the press.[10]

The proceedings began at 2:30 in the afternoon of April 17, 1895, in a packed courtroom. Mrs. Lingle, Mary Whiting, and the estate trustee, H. H. Bowman, hurrying in from Springfield, all testified, but it was Annie Aiken, twenty-eight, who created the sensation. "Small of stature and what lawyers call a good witness, she was modest and not over eager to speak, and her testimony was clear, consistent, and unshaken to the close. A great stillness settled over the courtroom while she was testifying," reported the *Chicago Daily Tribune*.[11]

All that Annie Aiken had rebelled against, all that had hurt her, was laid bare. Calmly, her eyes carefully avoiding Anna's, she described how "Mrs. Spafford" had completely taken over after her husband's death. "The colony was absolutely subject to her. What she said was spoken of as 'what the Lord said.'" She said that Anna had despised marriage, forbidding them to marry and forcing "those who were . . . to live as if they were not." Confessing that she had felt uncomfortable about "their bathing customs," she said that "Mrs. Spafford told me they were all right, that the feelings of the sexes toward each other were a remnant of their fallen state, that we should return to a state of innocency in which we were indifferent to sex, and Mrs. Spafford told me that she herself had attained this state."[12]

The crowd buzzed as the hearing was adjourned to the following week. Anna rose from her seat and walked out, erect and confident, surrounded by her friends.

Anna had reason to feel confident. All the attention had won her a handful of new converts who were quietly moving in with the group at West Monroe. All had donated their savings, and the house was becoming somewhat crowded. Plans were afoot, organized by Brother Jacob, for more to come from Kansas as soon as they could sell their properties. While funds were still tight, Anna had every expectation that the Kansas delegation would ease the situation, particularly the wealth of its leader, Joseph Meyers, one of Salem's largest landholders. Meyers, a well-regarded, churchgoing mainstay of the little farming community, had persuaded several of his sons that there was a pressing need to get to Jerusalem in time for the Messiah's arrival. His wife and daughter were convinced as well—indeed his entire family was packing. Only his oldest son and married daughter vehemently resisted Jacob's blandishments.

The Overcomers' lawyer, Luther Laflin Mills, had been sick, so it was not until May 14 that the trial resumed, and again Annie Aiken was called to the witness box. "I was tired of everyone always telling me his faults. It was such a ridiculous custom," she said, responding to a question.[13] Then the young woman turned and looked full in the face of Anna Spafford sitting below her. Miss Aiken's cheeks burned a deep scarlet. She half-rose from her chair, visibly trembling, her eyes fixed on Anna. "I had a terrible experience. She wielded a horrible influence over me." The young woman caught her breath. "But she doesn't now. I don't have to stand before her now to be forgiven. I want *God* to do that! She *must not think that I want her to forgive me.*"

The courtroom watched in frozen silence as Annie's lips worked; she seemed to be fighting off a strange influence. The blue eyes of her former mistress and mentor were locked on hers.

Finally, Edmund Palmer, Mrs. Lingle's lawyer, stepped in, rescuing

Annie and breaking the painful moment. "What is your motive in testifying?" he asked.

"Because of the many homes broken up." Annie wrenched free from the blue eyes. She turned to face the lawyer. "To save the children from what must come to them in future. What 'the sign' tells them to do they will have to obey—in spite of heaven or earth—they dare not resist."

It was Luther Laflin Mills's turn. "And what, Miss Aiken, is 'the sign'?"

"Mrs. Spafford tells us what to do; she says she has a sign from God, and should heaven and earth move, we would not dare disobey," Annie repeated. She went on to tell how others in the group might have a sign, but only Mrs. Spafford, who called herself a "prophetess," could determine whether it was authentic. She described signs that came as "twitching" or "heavy breathing" or sometimes "grew so noisy" that a person "would run all over the house." She described the fate of Lizzie Page, who had rebelled against the celibacy rule. She said that Mrs. Spafford's children were treated differently from the others and "forced to learn," but Mrs. Spafford had neglected the education of the other young ones—including her own, she added with obvious resentment. They did not need education, because, when the millennium came, "they would be educated in a moment."

An edge of sarcasm in his voice, Mills asked: "Can you say anything good about the Colony?"

Annie paused. There were people who had been good to her during those twelve long years she had been part of their community—people whose gentle sweetness she had admired. "Yes. They took care of the sick, and were kind to the poor."

"Thank you. That is all I need to know," said Mills.

When Edmund Palmer submitted an affidavit from Selah Merrill, reciting the consul's usual criticisms, Mills came back with an impressive stack of affidavits of his own—unanimous in praise of Mrs. Spafford and the colony's pure life and extraordinary good works.

Then finally, as Mrs. Spafford herself was called, the courtroom fell quiet once more. Modestly yet fashionably dressed in a black frock and bonnet, Anna gazed serenely over the crowd of spectators. Turning to the judge and interrogating lawyer, she began several hours of uninterrupted testimony, once more spinning the familiar stories. Her voice was low, musical, and so deliberately soothing that, according to one rather skeptical reporter, "it disturbed neither Mr. Palmer's nap nor that of the judge . . . Mrs. Spafford would have had all of the prophecies fulfilled had she been given time."[14] But finally Mills interrupted the soporific flow, asking about her quarrel with Annie Aiken.

"We were all deeply grieved and I decided that this was a case where we must try to overcome—that is, Annie must overcome . . . I tried to protect her." Anna shifted to an earnest tone, giving her own version of the love affair with the young Muslim. As she reached her conclusion, her voice rose dramatically: "Then Annie swore she would throw mud at me and bring my gray hairs with sorrow to the grave. She would kill me with grief, then have my children sent . . ."

At this point, according to the *Chicago Daily News*, the court clerk "rapped loudly on the desk with his gavel, the judge yawned, the counsel woke up." Court was recessed.

The following day an unwelcome surprise awaited Anna. Somehow, the diary of Mary Whiting's deceased husband had found its way into Edmund Palmer's hands. Not only did it describe the secret séances in detail, but it directly contradicted many of Anna's previous assertions, including her denial that she had ever claimed to be a "prophetess," that she exercised any authority over others, or that she was the "Bride" and her husband the "Branch." In the midst of strenuous objections by Mills that Palmer's reading of the diary was inadmissible and irrelevant, Anna said, as pleasantly as she could manage, that it was impossible for her to explain "these things to the uninitiated."

In the end, as the hearing wound to a close, the little band of Overcomers were left uncertain what the judge might decide. Both young Ruth and her brother, John, had behaved well on the stand, insisting that they wanted to stay in Jerusalem with their mother. Many had been moved by their poignant avowals. Bertha Spafford, by now seventeen and possessed of her mother's charm, had also been an effective witness. Obviously well educated and poised, she told the court that the colony's school had thirteen children. They were given instruction, she offered sincerely, in German, French, mathematics, drawing, history, geography, and music. Although this was false, and only she and her sister and the Whiting children had benefited, there was no one to contradict her, especially not the neglected youngsters back in Jerusalem who dearly wished—as Annie Aiken had—to have been offered such advantages.

More than a month of anxious waiting passed before Judge Kohlsaat recovered from persistent illnesses and rendered his decision. At last, to a hushed courtroom, he announced: "I might not agree with this Colony's religious beliefs. Indeed I have my own opinions of them that I shall keep to myself." Nonetheless, the judge did not feel the evidence warranted taking the children from their mother. Looking down over his glasses at Mary Whiting, he allowed that it would be better if the children were given a higher education. "I hope that some future arrangement will be possible so that John and Ruth can benefit from their grandmother's fortune."[15]

So there it was. Mary could keep her children, even if they had failed to obtain their inheritance from the Springfield banker. Headlines trumpeted: "Colony Is a Winner."[16] The house on West Monroe rang with hymns and hosannas. Soon it was packed. The Kansas delegation arrived with nearly thirty more excited millennialists. One, Johnny Dixon, had almost missed the train. His wife had done her best to keep him back, but when he heard the departing whistle, Johnny had raced to the station in his nightshirt, dropped a shoe in his haste, and rode fifty miles clutching a handlebar outside in the cold. When he duly surrendered his money, Mr. Rudy sent him out with just enough to buy a new pair of shoes.[17]

As for Anna, she seemed continually to be smiling. Even though the Chicago health authorities had arrived with warnings of an imminent eviction due to overcrowding, she smiled. Perhaps something even better for her group was in the wind—and she had absolutely no doubt that if she worked it well, if God remained at her side, it would bear excellent fruit.

The Chicago Swedes

May you be in no doubt that the end is now in sight . . . rub the sleep from your eyes, light the lamp, examine the clock, look it up in your own Bible and underline the passages to which I refer, and you shall soon understand the Heavenly Clock and realize that the time has come to rise up!

—Frederick Franson, Swedish eschatologist

A small parish of Swedes belonging to the Swedish Evangelical Church at 5487 Madison Avenue, on Chicago's South Side, had followed the news stories with keen interest. What had particularly caught their eye was Mrs. Spafford's repeated assertions that Jesus was on the brink of returning. To them, this concept was spoken of in elegiac terms as the "Parousia of Christ," and increasingly it had taken hold among them, as it had for many friends back in Sweden.[1] Fifteen years earlier, Dwight Moody had organized a conference devoted to the Parousia prophecies. He had invited a passionate Swedish missionary, Frederick Franson, to speak about his theories of predestination, millennialism, and especially his "Heavenly Clock," which was inexorably ticking toward the awesome and inevitable moment. Earlier, when Horatio Spafford had tried to persuade Moody of Dr. Piazza Smith's pyramid predictions, Moody had preferred to stay neutral. He elected to maintain the same position when Franson offered his own careful calculations that

souls must be put in order by Easter 1897 or else burn in the eternal fires. However, many Scandinavians, both in Chicago and back home, embraced Franson's Heavenly Clock, particularly after they felt the savage impact of another major financial disaster that had devastated the country—the Panic of 1893. Many Swedish ears had begun to hear an ominous ticking, and many anxious Swedish hearts yearned to find "a higher light."

It was a fateful day in the fall of 1895 when members of the Swedish Evangelical Church came to call at the crowded residence on West Monroe. They listened approvingly as Anna read aloud a chapter from the Scriptures. They enjoyed lunch. They heard Anna's stories. They were charmed by her attractive and well-dressed friends and the well-behaved youngsters. They felt a rush of sympathy that such agreeable people should be crammed into such tight quarters. Enthusiastically, anxious to return such fine hospitality, and especially to further explore various theological issues on which they seemed in almost miraculous accord, they urged Anna and her companions to come to their church on Sunday. On their way home, the Swedes agreed that "they had never set eyes on a more delightful and charming woman."[2]

The leader of the Swedes, and founder of their church, was a gruff, bulky former freighter captain, Olof Henrik Larsson, who was the same age as Anna, fifty-three, and looked at the world through similar blue Scandinavian eyes. Some twenty-five years before, enticed like so many of his countrymen by America's radiant possibilities, and uplifted by encounters with Boston evangelicals, Larsson had quit smoking, tossed his comforting pipe into the sea, and dedicated himself to the Lord's work. For him the clock was ticking loudly, and he desired to save both his own soul and the souls of others. Settling in Chicago, he had benefited from the real estate boom, earned enough to purchase a house and a building for his church, and survived the recent economic depression. Some thirty of his Swedish followers, mainly housemaids and handymen, moved into the house, shared their earnings, and quaked before his warnings. "You are on your way to Hell," he would rail from his pulpit. Those who did not see the light "will spend eternity swimming in the sulfurous rivers of Hell!"[3] While fearsome as their leader, Larsson was genuine in his faith and despite his brusque manner had a kindly heart. He wished his little community to be democratic, sincerely encouraged discussion, and allowed disagreement within its ranks.

The following Sunday Anna arrived with several other Overcomers. Larsson's much younger wife, Mathilda, showed them around the spacious rooms, dappled with sunlight pouring through large windows. Anna remarked admiringly on the flower-filled vases, pretty children, and the pleasant orchard outside. Upstairs, in an adjacent house, a large room served as the church, where Larsson was already stationed at his raised pulpit, waiting to preach a sermon. Anna climbed the stairs, cast her eyes over the assembled Swedes, then closed them in a look of ecstasy.

"This is the room," she ejaculated so that all could hear. *"This was the message I received."* She opened her eyes and gazed at the men and women staring at her in fascination. A divine message had come before she left Jerusalem, she cried joyously: she was to meet brothers and sisters in Chicago. And then, after she arrived, a second message had come: "I will show you an upper room."[4] The assembly expelled a collective breath. Steeped in Scriptures, they instantly understood the reference: Jesus and his disciples celebrated the Last Supper in an "upper room."

In his pulpit, Olof Larsson stood bewildered. His followers clustered around Anna, ignoring him. Immediately, she launched into her tragic story of shipwreck and the message she had received that she was spared to fulfill a calling to the holy city, where harmony would reign.[5] Her words, it was later said, "fell like summer rain on dry hearts."[6]

It did not take long for Larsson's followers to offer shelter to Anna's cramped congregation. By the end of November, thirty Overcomers were on their way south to Madison Avenue, women and children on the streetcar, the men trudging through the snowy streets, laden with boxes and suitcases, as there was not enough money to pay for all to ride. That very evening, after beds had somehow been found for the multitude and all were assembled downstairs, Anna drew from her reticule a "book of messages." Lifting her eyes to the ceiling, she read: "God has predestined that we should meet. Now it is complete." In the reverent silence, heads nodded. It was as if all heard the ticking together and assented to the inevitable.

Suddenly it was Anna who conducted the morning prayers; Anna to whom the concerned brought their fears; Anna who strode to Larsson's pulpit one morning to declare, as she would many times again in the future: "John the Baptist came first. But he had to withdraw to make way for the clearer light."[7]

Olof Henrik Larsson had been set aside. When more messages came that the two groups were to merge, even that Larsson must sell his properties and use the money to voyage to Jerusalem, the abandoned leader was in agony. Was he to relinquish all that he had built in Chicago? Unable to match Anna's adroit maneuvers, he attempted to challenge the decision, but his agitated followers had seen their leader falter. They told him that he had been harsh, that his preachings were too violent, that he must accept that Mrs. Spafford possessed a "higher" or "clearer" light."

It was a particularly bitter pill when his own wife agreed with his critics. There was a reason for this: she had never forgiven him for refusing to let her call a doctor for their sick baby several years earlier when she and Larsson had been in Sweden, and the infant had died. Shy and deeply religious, Mathilda Helgsten had come to Chicago from the little parish of Nås, in Dalarna, the dales and valleys of southwestern Sweden. Her homesickness had been relieved on joining Larsson's flock, although she had been rather surprised and a little intimidated the day he announced that she was to marry him. Always in awe of her muscular, blunt-spoken husband, whom she could never bring herself to call by his Christian name, she nevertheless respected his earnest efforts to be fair-minded. Some years earlier he had even allowed her to return to Nås when a friend and sister congregant, Lisslasses Karin, had received a "calling" that the two women were to spread the word in Nås of the Chicago group's Swedish Evangelical Church.

The women had been in Nås only a short time when Larsson himself had appeared in the autumn of 1889, and almost immediately stirred up an enormous excitement within this remote and sheltered parish of peasant farmers burning with the same religious desire that had long affected the United States. He also created great controversy. Larsson's raw brand of revivalism won some, but antagonized others so much that stones were thrown against his window. Many condemned him for the anxiety and dissent he provoked with his "burning eyes" and terrible judgments. Starved for novelty, however, and thrilled by his dreadful preachments and the concept of "the ticking clock," a significant group of followers pledged themselves to him. When he and Mathilda returned with several converts to Chicago in 1891, leaving their Swedish affiliate in the charge of a well-to-do farmer, Nås was in angry turmoil; family ties were frayed; the Swedish national church dissociated itself from the Larssonite gospel; the parish priest of Nås declared himself a sworn enemy. That Larsson had let his baby die was neither forgotten nor forgiven. The 1890 official bureau of deaths and births recorded: "The parents, who claim to belong to an unfamiliar religious denomination, refused to let the child be buried in the legal manner. They dug it down in its own grave after the child had been inspected by a public authority."[8]

In Chicago, as Anna skillfully pressed her vision among the Larssonites, tensions sprang up. "We have been warned to look out for frauds to come in these final days," some whispered, wondering if the predicted Antichrist might not be behind these recent events. Mathilda felt wrenched between the enthusiasm welling around her and concern for her distraught husband. Observing her conflict, Anna took her aside. "You are acting in your own interest," she said severely, her blue eyes boring into Mathilda's. "Was it not said that we must hate our father and mother, wife and children, for the sake of God's kingdom?"[9]

When the question of selling was put to the Swedish Evangelical Church's congregation, the final vote went decisively against its founder. Mathilda did not even look at her husband as she raised her hand. His followers were surprised and touched when he made a strangled apology for having been too hard on them. Anna smiled. A departure date was set for March 5, 1896. With no time to advertise, Larsson accepted a low offer of $20,000 for his property. The buyers, a Methodist group, promised to pay part in cash and send the remainder on to Jerusalem as soon as they could raise it.

As the excitement in the little parish mounted, Larsson remained troubled and sleepless. He demanded that both he and Mathilda have all their teeth extracted. As an old seaman, he insisted, he knew how bad things could get when one found oneself far from a dentist.[10] Resentfully, his wife complied. Then, one month before they were to leave, Larsson secretly sent a letter to his followers in Nås, addressing it to

Tipers Lars Larsson, a prosperous farmer, and Gastgifvar Mats Matsson, an innkeeper, who headed the Swedish affiliate and with whom he had stayed in fairly constant touch. He had already apprised them of the developments back in Chicago, without, of course, revealing his humiliating marginalization. Now, his gums aching, almost feverish with despair, he urged on them an impossibility: sell everything immediately and come to Jerusalem. You can catch our ship when it lands in England, he insisted unreasonably, in a desperate hope that a preponderance of Swedes would right the balance between Anna and himself. Sadly, however, a mere three weeks was not enough time for the Nås contingent to dispose of their holdings. But when the letter was read and discussed in the kitchen of a Swedish farmhouse, a shock of mutual understanding thrilled the listening peasants. It was agreed that preparation for the noblest experience possible in this mortal vale of tears was to commence instantly, and departure scheduled as soon as practicable.

On March 6, 1896, the *Chicago Daily Tribune* headlined an extraordinary exodus from the city:

> There was no clash of cymbals, but there were plenty of songs of praise and rejoicing to mark the departure of the "Overcomers" for Jerusalem last night. Two cars full of them—men, women, and children—left for Philadelphia over the Grand Trunk road at 8:15 pm. The pilgrims had another carload of baggage and lunch baskets piled on the seats and in the aisles. They bore almost as much baggage as did the crusaders in whose footsteps they will go and they were provisioned as though for an arctic journey.
>
> No solitary "Overcomer" was left behind. Indeed, so strong was the fear of missing this train the earliest arrivals were nearly taken to San Francisco on the 5:30 train.
>
> One half would sing "I Hunger for the Palm Groves in the Land of Galilee" while the other half attacked the lunch baskets. Finally as the train pulled out they drowned the whistle with "Before We Reach the Jordan We've One More River to Cross."

Fifty-six adults, nineteen children, and one infant crossed the Atlantic to Liverpool on the S.S. *Waesland.* The preferred port of entry to the Ottoman east was Alexandria, but they learned it was quarantined against the plague and changed their plans and accepted berths on a small, dirty, poorly equipped ship that would take them directly to Jaffa from Liverpool. The weather turned violent. Most of the pilgrims were seasick, and Mathilda's brother, an uneasy believer who had come along reluctantly, became so ill that he lost consciousness. As they neared Jaffa, Anna entered his bunk room and stayed a while. When she reemerged, she informed Mathilda that a vision revealed her brother would die, and he did—the day after their ship anchored. The pilgrims marveled at Anna's mystical insight. Through her grief, Mathilda also marveled. Had her husband, who had angered her, yet whose drooping shoulders worried her, brought down a punishment? Was it on her as well? She listened carefully now to everything that Anna said.

As the group waited to be carried to shore by Arab boatmen, the pilgrims had also marveled at the sight of an athletic-looking young German swinging his leg over the ship's rail and shouting, "Bertha! Bertha!" Even more astonishing was the sight of Mrs. Spafford's daughter, petticoats flying, racing over the deck and into his arms. He kissed her, and she kissed him back. While Anna had avoided raising the incendiary issue of celibacy with her new recruits, and the younger, newly married Swedes were ignorant of what lay in store, at least some of the older pilgrims had an inkling of what those views might be. No one, however, said a word. Nor, when the weary travelers, hauling their suitcases, finally sweated through the Damascus Gate and up the steep cobblestones to find a house much smaller than their old one on Madison Avenue—with no beds for them—was any note of disappointment uttered. That night the men moved to the smaller adjacent house. In the main house, mattresses were laid on the floor, even on tables, for the women and children. All agreed the house was lovely and its view stupendous. Tomorrow they would wake up refreshed—and be truly in Jerusalem.

Perhaps it was written that night, or perhaps somewhat later, as the letter was undated. But soon Miss Annie Aiken in Chicago received a note from the holy city. "The words which God gave to us have been fulfilled because we were betrayed by one of our own. I feel that I must say from the bottom of my heart that *I have forgiven you.* As always, your friend, Anna Spafford."[11]

CHAPTER NINETEEN

The Swedes from Nås

Come you who rejoice in God and
  make your joy known
Strike up the merry sound of song.
Let the Heavens ring
We are going to Zion, blessed heavenly Zion
We are going to Zion, God's wondrous
  heavenly city.

—Swedish folk hymn

Mercifully, they had already moved into the huge mansion when the letter from Nås came. It was addressed to Olof Henrik Larsson, but of course Anna read it. She read all the mail now—what came in, and what went out. It was one of many new customs to which the Chicago Swedes were adjusting. They were all to call her "Mother." They were not to speak Swedish together, but to learn English, for Anna would not tolerate any "narrow nationalism" in her house. For the older Swedes in particular this was a hardship. But when Anna announced that "all natural drives and worldly ties must be sacrificed . . . nothing must stand between full submission to God," the Swedes were dumbstruck, not sure they had understood.[1] When Anna made it clear that this startling new caveat meant celibacy, it caused some difficulties with the virile young Swedish husbands. But for the moment at least, all energies were absorbed by the great task of repairing and outfitting the fine old stone building.

Anna did not welcome the news that the peasants from Nås were going to join them. It had been difficult enough to negotiate the rent for the house, start the renovations, and arrange the move without a new infusion of Swedes to add further confusion—possibly even an insurrection. Correctly, she suspected that Larsson would try to use this development to reassert his old authority. There was only one solution: send Larsson back to Nås under the supervision of Brother Jacob with instructions to dissuade as many as possible. Resigning herself to the probability that it might be too late to arrest their momentum, Anna told Jacob and Larsson to make sure that only those with means, and who could pay their own way, were accepted. The two men had not been in Jerusalem a month before they set off again to Sweden.

The remaining members worked, the men erecting a carpenter's shed and filling the urgent need for beds, sofas, bureaus, chairs, and the like. Thriftily they broke up their packing cases for wood. The women sewed curtains of unbleached cloth and made mattresses from tenting materials that could be rolled under high beds during the day. Oil barrels, covered with thin muslin, became dressing tables.

The house had been rented from the Husseini family, one of Jerusalem's most prominent, whose patriarch, the late Rabbah Daoud Amin Effendi al-Husseini, built it near an old mosque named for Sheikh Jarrah, a general who had helped Saladin wrest Jerusalem from the crusaders. A mere ten-minute walk north from the Damascus Gate along Nablus Road, it was in an area that had become fashionable for other rich and notable Arab clans after Rabbah Effendi pioneered living outside the walls in 1860. The old patriarch had installed his three wives in three grand rooms, carefully identical in refinements according to the Prophet's injunction that men treat their wives with equal favor. When his harem failed to produce an heir, he took a fourth bride and built her a separate wing, making a total of twenty-five rooms and fourteen bedrooms to accommodate his relatives and servants. By any measure it was a magnificent house, despite much of the space now being partitioned by the colonists into barracks-like sleeping quarters to house the younger men, women, and children separately. Some of the older couples, including Olof and Mathilda Larsson, would be allowed to room together, but were to address each other as "Brother" and "Sister" and live accordingly. For herself, Anna had taken the spacious bedroom of the old effendi.

It was even hotter than usual that summer, and they all appreciated the thick stone walls, high ceilings, and marble floors that kept the interior cool. A spring-fed fountain gurgled in the middle of a large garden courtyard bordered with flowers. A balcony large enough to hold a hundred people ran along one side of the house and eventually proved a fine background for photographing some of the many famous visitors to come. But it was the glorious sitting room on the second floor that was considered the most beautiful room in Jerusalem. Visitors would always remark on the inlaid floor of Italian stone and marble, the high arched windows, and especially the golden stars that studded the painted blue ceiling. If, in fact, Anna had dreamed of an "upper room," this far outshone the simple upstairs at the Swedish Evangelical Church in Chicago.

Before Larsson and Jacob left for Sweden, Anna had made Larsson write to his followers in Nås, telling them not to come. It proved a shrewd move. When Larsson and Jacob arrived in the little hamlet, the earnest peasants of the Swedish vales who had been loyally abiding by his fundamentalist warnings were upset by his sudden contradictions. They had believed him when he promised the imminent return of the Messiah and the need to choose between heaven and hell. Now he and Jacob were warning them of the unhealthy Jerusalem climate, the value of their ancient way of life, the beauty of Dalarna. Also, their leader seemed a changed man. He was quiet and less forceful; the burning eyes that had read their souls seemed irresolute and skittish. His mouth was strange, fitted with clumsy dentures. Instead, it was Jacob who did most of the talking. Since Chicago, Anna's clever adopted son had been learning Swedish and was almost fluent, adding this language to five others. The Nås peasants listened in bewilderment. In haste and for a pittance, they had sold ancestral lands farmed for generations by their families, braving the anger of relatives. How could they turn back? While some did, thirty-seven others overcame their suspicions of the Jew who collected their money and arranged for transportation—fourteen adults between thirty-five and fifty-six years of age, fifteen children under the age of fifteen, and eight young adults between seventeen and twenty-six—packed their spinning wheels and looms, plow blades and wagon wheels, fur-lined coats and hats, and on July 23, 1896, assembled with crates and suitcases in twelve horse-drawn wagons to be driven to the village of

Vansbro to catch the train to Göteborg.[2] It was a sight the Dala folk would never cease to talk about. Farmers working in their fields dropped their pitchforks as the wagon train passed and rushed to the road to wave goodbye. With a mix of traditional peasant suspicion, sadness, and dread, they watched their neighbors depart. Many wept, others prayed. As the last wagon disappeared around a bed in the road, a sudden storm turned the sky black. Hailstones the size of pigeon eggs rained down on the rye fields, bloodying the farmers' faces, pulverizing their fields, and throwing "new shoots of grain onto the roads so that it looked like the aisle of a church strewn with rice," according to an account by one witness.[3] Those in the wagons, however, only experienced a pleasant shower of light rain as they bounced over the rutted road. They did not know that the stunned friends left behind now wondered if the leader they themselves had rejected was, after all, truly a prophet.

Energized and purposeful, the pilgrims sang as they boarded the ship that Jacob had chartered for Antwerp; they sang on another that brought them three weeks later to anchor outside Jaffa. For most, the voyage had been the first time they had seen the sea, or sat on silk and velvet lounge chairs, or been waited on by servants. The experience was thrilling. As they entered their new life in Jerusalem, they would have occasion to remember this brief encounter with luxury.

A blast of searing summer heat wilted the newcomers in their woolen coats and dresses; they coughed in the choking dust. On the newly established rail line from Jaffa to Jerusalem, they ate unfamiliar fruit that doubled them over with stomach cramps. But twenty fellow Swedes were on the platform waving and singing to them when they alighted, riding with them in wagons to the Big House on Nablus Road. There, an erect blue-eyed woman greeted them. Her soft white hair was fashionably upswept and threaded with palest gold. She was plump, but her waist was tightly corseted and her breasts rode high and youthful under her ribboned blouse. "I would like you to call me Mother," she said warmly, her eyes sparkling with vitality and intelligence. Yet when the smile left her lips, her mouth closed in a thin, uncompromising line.

The new order was immediate and efficient. Chores were assigned and duties delegated. A bell rang for breakfast, commencing the day in the communal dining room. Food was set out on the long tables with fresh brown bread, but none of the milk or eggs or butter that had been the Dala folks' daily fare at home. They would have to wait for spring before they could drink boiled, watered-down goat's milk "with thick black hairs in it, along with other, suspiciously dark objects," as Lars Lind remembered when he arrived with his large family as a boy of five.[4] Six of them would shortly be dead, victims of malaria, smallpox, or other diseases, including Lind's powerfully strong and fearless father, his mother, grandmother, and three siblings. Anna did not stray from her strict ban on medicine and doctors, leaving Lars and his brothers as orphans to be raised by the colony. Sixteen in all, mostly Swedes, died in those hard first two years.[5] Yet in their letters home, they wrote that death brought "a feeling of life and resurrection."[6] Back in Nås, these letters were read and puzzled over for their lack of any real information. The recipients had no way of knowing that all letters leaving the colony were read aloud at the meetings before they were sent off. One, typically declaring "everyone is so kind to us," nevertheless did note that "the people here are so strange and serious."[7] Not a letter ever mentioned the weird and fascinating stories they were hearing: Mrs. Spafford had been "literally lifted between the floor and ceiling in her fight with the Devil whom she conquered," or she had been "transported bodily to the Mount of Transfiguration."[8]

Bertha, always her mother's adored daughter, who sat apart at mealtime with Anna, her sister, Grace, Brother Jacob, William Rudy, Amelia Gould, the three Whitings, and whoever else might be currently in Anna's favor, professed herself touched by "the courage of these people." Removed by thousands of miles from the traditional life of their forebears, the dark green forests and clear streams of their homeland, the horses and cattle, fields, farms, and freedoms they had known, they "must have been lonely and homesick," Bertha wrote, "but they never made us conscious of it."[9] Yet she surely saw the tears, especially of the little ones, forcibly taken away from their parents to be supervised and to sleep in rooms with unmarried women.

"I remember that I used to go down one flight of stairs, and stand on my tiptoes to reach the keyhole in the door, just to get a glimpse of [my parents]," Olof Henrik Larsson's daughter Edith remembered years later.[10] "Mamma heard me and opened the door, and I rushed into her arms which held me so tight, as if she never wanted to let me go. But I could not stay long—I was afraid of being punished." One of Larsson's most ardent former followers, Sister Tilda, a prudish and grimly strict spinster, was now one of Anna's most devoted disciples. She had embraced Anna's vision that family ties must be systematically destroyed and took charge of little Edith, who was only four. Either because the child was so miserable or because someone had a change of heart, Edith was finally allowed to go back to her parents. "I was so joyful to be able to put my arms around Mamma's neck, kiss her goodnight, and know that she would tuck me in and make me comfortable. 'I missed you so, Mamma,' I said. 'Don't let me be moved again.' "[11] The child nevertheless remained in deathly fear of Sister Tilda. Later, one Christmas, she received a porcelain doll that she treasured and made clothes for. The colony had succeeded in making Christmas a major event in a city otherwise lacking such communal gatherings, and guests of many faiths flocked to see the huge Christmas tree, watch colorful pageants, and hear the Christmas hymns beautifully sung by the colony chorus. When a little Muslim girl came a year or so later with her family to share the Christmas celebrations, Sister Tilda took the doll away from Edith to wrap for the little girl. "Love thy neighbor as thy self," she admonished. Except for the Spafford and Whiting children, most of the colony children did not have toys, and this was the last doll Edith ever had to call her own.[12]

The practical-minded Swedes were exceptionally industrious. Idleness was unknown to them, and soon the colony became a paying concern. Looms were set up. Tablecloths, napkins, rugs, and endless bolts of cloth were woven from which to make clothes for the colonists—and even to sell to appreciative locals. A Norwegian from the Chicago group proved a talented tailor; those in the city who could afford his suits began coming for fittings; the frocks created by his seamstress wife were sought after by the fashion-minded. A blacksmith built a forge, and the colony even found itself shoeing the horses of the Turkish police. Land was leased from Arab property owners, and the Swedish farmers harvested corn, grapes, olives, and wheat. They acquired farm animals to supply the longed-for milk, butter, and eggs—soon selling them to the city at a considerable profit. Scythes, plows, and a threshing machine were ordered. Orthodox Jews were some of their best customers for grain, and the children were sent to harvest it, told by the supervising rabbis not to drink any water all day lest a drop of moisture soil the kernels and make them unfit for kosher standards. For the children this job was arduous, especially as they were also forbidden to sing for the same reason, but the colony did well with the haying contracts.[13] When a steam mill was built to produce high-quality white flour, the colony initiated such a successful bakery that its cakes, pies, and pastries sold out to clamoring tourists as well as locals. Anna encouraged these endeavors. She intended to move far from the troubled years of debt and felt a profound satisfaction that at last neither Consul Merrill nor any of the missionaries could criticize her or her fellowship for indolence.

Mathilda Larsson was given the task of sewing caps, and then umbrellas. Eventually she worked in the bakery, for years getting up well before dawn to allow the bread to rise. By lamplight she would see the younger women plodding downstairs to heat the heavy irons in the laundry. Her silent husband was ignored by most colonists, who were afraid to speak to him and incur a reprimand. Although he had never done tinsmith work before, Olof was assigned to solder the colony's big soup cauldrons and other broken cookware. During the tourist season, when the colony rented out its big rooms and routinely moved members "like playing musical chairs" to sleep in drafty hallways, cellars, or attics, the Larssons had to change rooms more than any of the others. For the colony this was lucrative, but it was also one of the ways that Anna maintained her hold. She told her followers that it was "overcoming," and the members understood that having no place to call their own was a forcible reminder of their powerlessness. Despite the exhaustion of these endless shiftings, Larsson refused to complain. He spent his days in a small shed on the colony grounds, which became a refuge for Mathilda, too, when she was at last free to sink into a chair beside him at night. Here, he worked and prayed, and while they were still allowed to stay with their parents, before they were permanently assigned to a large room with other women, Edith and her younger sister, Hannah, would sit on his lap and listen to his stories of the sea.

With over forty children in the colony, Anna had recognized the need for a disciplined way to organize them. She still believed education was superfluous—excepting her own children's of course—but something had to be done. Thus, every day a bell rang, the children were lined up and marched two by two down Nablus Road, threading their way past camels, donkeys, and flocks of goats being herded to market, through the Damascus Gate, and up the steep cobbled path to school in the Old House on Mount Bezetha. As a result of the newly filled colony coffers, William Rudy had paid off a number of their outstanding debts, enabling the colony to keep renting the original home, although, due to its tangle of family owners, it would be a long time before they could buy and actually own it. The youngest children were taught English and played nursery school games with some of the younger "sisters." The oldest were given the education the colony's first youngsters had longed for, especially when two experienced teachers, John Dinsmore, former dean of Lincoln Academy, Newcastle, Maine, and his wife, Mary, arrived in 1898 with their small daughter, Ruth. Like many others in the colony's eclectic collection of eccentrics, John Dinsmore was a gifted scholar able to bring a degree of intellectual rigor to his pupils, and, as a botanist, later to make substantial contributions to the study of Palestinian flora.

It was the only coeducational school at the time. Although never accredited by the Turkish educational system, it was soon so respected for its ecumenical mix that children of prominent Muslim families as well as Greek Orthodox, Armenians, Ethiopians, French, Russians, German Templar Colony offspring, and young Sephardic and Ashkenazic Jews began tramping up Mount Bezetha. Even Rolla Floyd sent his adopted son, despite his reservations about the colony's theology. Many parents had become eager for their children to profit from an English education, and as the students were not required to attend the morning prayer meeting that preceded classes, parents had no fear the colony would try to convert their children to its beliefs. In time there were actually more "outsiders" than "insiders." Even a banker named Mr. Behar, a Sephardic Jew, was willing to sit in on class with students half his age in order to work on his English. Classes were free, although students had to pay for their textbooks, while the colony children shared a single text among five. They were always delighted when the Muslim or Jewish students

shared their tasty lunches, for their own fare was exceedingly plain, usually a thin, lukewarm stew of indefinable vegetables hauled up the steps
by some of the older colony boys.[14]

As the school grew, it was moved to the Big House. After that, the
colonists' children found their studies frequently interrupted as any
adult needing a chore to be done could summon their help, particularly
the older youths who were constantly called out of class to carry sacks,
move furniture, beat carpets, fetch water, or make a delivery somewhere
in the city. When he was a grown man, Lars Lind would write that the
youngsters were Anna's "slaves"—and he would not be alone in his resentment. Yet using fear as a blunt instrument was effective. Anna would
quote Matthew in meetings: "One will be raised up, and the others will
be left behind." It became the litany of supervising adults, terrifying the
children. Dread of being "left behind," as Edith Larsson remembered
bitterly, "created a fear of death in us, as a judgment for our sins, directly
from God. I think it is impossible for anyone who has not lived under
such religious fear to understand the impression this leaves in the consciousness of children."[15]

Curiously, "Sister" Johanna Brooke, who had once played an active
part in Anna's utopia, apparently had cooled somewhat toward "overcoming." At some point she had ceased teaching her Bible courses—indeed, she now seldom spoke of religion at all, devoting herself instead to
piano or painting lessons and, in particular, sharing the wonders of reading with her pupils. This wisp of a teacher occupied a small closet on the
staircase landing of the Big House in which, somehow, a cot had been
shoehorned along with bookshelves brimming with newspaper and magazine articles and what few books she had managed to collect. Miss
Brooke alone was free from the peripatetic indignities suffered by the
others; her room was simply too small to commandeer. As a bright lad
who yearned to read, Lars recalled the gratitude he felt for her surrepti-
tious loans, which needed to remain carefully hidden from "Mother," as
all knew Anna "frowned upon this zeal to teach. Knowledge should
come only from above."[16]

"Walking up or down that staircase," Lars wrote of his boyhood
years, "to or from those interminable meetings or hastily called assemblies, the little green door would open and I would be beckoned into

that tiny larder of information. From her shelf, she would take down a wrapper saying this contained some valuable instruction in literature, history, art, geography, poetry—which I would return when I was through."[17] Lars recounted hiding the book under his peasant-style blouson shirt, a uniform all the boys wore. Then, checking that the stairway was empty and creeping back to work, he would wait for a chance to read it. "Somehow, while chopping up wood, or cutting the sugar cane, or turning the wringer for the Monday wash, the precious text could be furtively extracted." The best place was the men's outhouse, safely distant from inspection by Anna's spies. One day, however, Lars was caught. The book he was trying to read was *Vanity Fair*. At the following morning confessional Anna hissed, *"He* spends his time reading *Thackeray,"* pointing her finger as all heads turned in his direction. Lars never forgot his terror and humiliation, and even as a grown man he could not bring himself to finish the novel. Worse, at subsequent meetings, Anna often repeated the accusation. Eventually, Lars came to pity older "sinners" like Otis Page, who continued to wear "the mark of Cain" and remained a target of "hurled" denunciations. Mary Whiting, too, her usefulness apparently over, was frequently rebuked for her delight in gardening. "She," Anna would say, fixing Mary with an icy stare, "loves *flowers* more than *God*."[18]

"What agonized looks," Lars wrote, "came from these poor frightened creatures who had never harmed a soul in their lives." He admired Johanna Brooke because "she never broke, never confessed or 'uncovered' anything right to the end. To her, knowledge was irreversible and continuous." For Lars Lind and many others among the colony's children, Miss Brooke became a model "for escape from the loss of personality in a self-deluded religious group such as ours." For most of those, however, who remained in the house that Anna built, it was always "safer not to think at all."[19]

CHAPTER TWENTY

A Cemetery War Begins

Vengeance is mine; I will repay, saith the Lord.
—Romans 12:19

It was September 1897. With prosperity in sight at last and a quiescent household—she was fond of remarking on the marvelous harmony around her—Anna was annoyed that some old problems still lingered. As if she had not had enough trouble with the fortuitously recalled Selah Merrill, for the past four years she had had to deal with another Presbyterian cleric serving as U.S. consul, Edwin S. Wallace, installed by the Democratic president, Grover Cleveland. From the moment Wallace arrived, it was clear that Merrill had influenced him. Anna had sent Mr. Rudy and the Reverend Edward Baldwin to pay a welcoming call on him when he was staying at the Grand New Hotel. They had found him prematurely balding, clean-shaven, and far too self-confident for a twenty-nine-year-old newcomer. He had greeted them in an overbearing and insulting manner, declaring that when he assumed his duties, they would find that his "word was law."[1] Like Merrill, he began slandering them to visitors. He had even written an article calling them "the worst cranks in Jerusalem."[2]

While it pleased Anna greatly to have so many attractive guests crowding the colony's seasonal parties—the *tableaux vivants* at Christmas, the children's fife and drum parades on the Fourth of July, the Easter cakes and tea—and while it really was no surprise that some new recruits had seen fit to leave, she wished that Wallace could respect the contribution that her house was making to Jerusalem. If he shamelessly refused to appreciate their help to the poor and the sick, there was the school, the bakery, the carpentry shop, the forge—all making life better for so many. Entirely thanks to the American Colony, there were now marvelous handmade goods, dairy products, wheat, and clean white flour available for purchase. Nonetheless, Wallace was close to the Anglican bishop of Jerusalem, the Very Reverend George Francis Popham Blyth of Christ Church, an important figure who presided over the city's social center. It distressed her that Wallace spoke so negatively of her, and she was fairly certain that the bishop was no fan himself, although he was invariably polite when they encountered each other at receptions. The thought that prominent British visitors could be unfairly turned against her gnawed incessantly.

Everyone knew how powerful the British were at the time, which mattered a great deal as the Ottoman Empire was tottering. Queen Victoria, who at seventy-eight ruled a quarter of the earth, had recently enjoyed a grand jubilee. In 1882, her armies had invaded Egypt to crush Arabi Pasha's peasant rebellion at Tel el Kebir, so now the khedive was also under the British thumb. People called Egypt the "Veiled Protectorate." Britain controlled the Suez Canal, and there was constant speculation over what role it might take should the sultanate founder. Of course, the French were doing their best to maintain their long-standing relationship with the Sublime Porte in Constantinople despite having seized the Ottoman province of Algiers in 1830 and later Tunis in 1881, the year that Anna and Horatio had come to Jerusalem. French merchants were active in Syria, particularly in the Lebanon, where Napoleon III had secured special privileges after sending in French troops during the terrifying massacre of Christians in 1860. The Italians were talking of establishing a counter-sphere of influence in Ottoman Tripoli, while the Russian czar's eyes were on northern Anatolia and he had long desired to control the Dardanelles—something evident to everyone for half a century.

The Germans, on the other hand, had been late in the influence game, although under "Iron Chancellor" Bismarck that had changed. The arrogant and ambitious young Prussian kaiser had fired Bismarck, and everyone knew Wilhelm II harbored colonial ambitions. He was looking eastward and was cultivating the goodwill of the sultan. In fact,

Wilhelm and his kaiserin, Augusta Victoria, were planning a visit to Constantinople and the Holy Land. It had energized the Turks to build roads and furiously scrub Jerusalem in preparation for a much-heralded royal visit scheduled for next year. It would be interesting to meet them when they were here, although, Anna reflected, there had been that bad patch with the former German consul over a few old debts incurred when Horatio was alive. If Wallace didn't spoil things, she could hope for better relations with the new German consul.[3]

Anna sighed. Bertha was still enamored of the young German Frederick Vester. His father had arrived as a missionary, and later started a small antiques store outside the Jaffa Gate. He was not a particularly successful manager, and Anna was toying with the idea of purchasing his store. She had hoped for better for her beautiful daughter. Frederick was nine years older than Bertha, and while he was tall, good-looking, athletic, and decently schooled in Switzerland, his was not a prominent family with money, nor one to help her smooth the way in a promising new chapter she anticipated for herself and her girls. Thus far, Anna had held firm when Bertha brought up the subject of marriage. Frederick was persistent—she had to give him that—and ever present, attending meetings, staying late after dinner to sit with Bertha in the big salon upstairs, chatting with the Arab men and Turkish officers who seemed to regard the room as their clubhouse. Now that she had a houseful of rosy-cheeked young blond Swedish girls, she told them to make themselves "attractive to the men" in the evenings.[4] Any personal presents they received, of course, she confiscated, as she could not allow invidious feelings among her women.

In March an important member of the Husseini clan, Ismail Bey Husseini, who had once been a student of Horatio's and was now the director of public education, had asked nineteen-year-old Bertha to head a school for Muslim girls. Ismail Bey was an Arab modernist. When he was a young man, he and his friends were always in the salon in the evening, fascinated by their intimate exposure to American women and English conversation. Anna knew that his grandfather, who, as far as she knew, did nothing but smoke his hookah with a jasmine blossom stuffed up one nostril, did not approve of his grandson's friendship. But for the colony, the young man's current prominence in the Turkish government was useful. After agreeing to the proposal, Anna had sent Johanna Brooke along with Bertha, and already the school, attached to the Haram al-Sharif in an ancient building erected in Saladin's era, was well attended.[5]

But she worried about Bertha. As she had her congregation, in private talks she had warned her daughter about "attachment." She had seen Bertha mature into someone who could dress down, indeed flatten, an upstart member. But if she became too attached to Frederick, it could hurt her, and she wanted Bertha to remain strong. She was confident that her daughters recognized her to be singular, that she was truly the "Bride," and that by following her lead, recognizing the powers with which God had endowed her, Bertha and Grace would triumph at her side. Moreover, although Anna had come to believe her own preachments that she was immortal, should the Lord see otherwise, the colony would need a leader. Bertha had to be the one. Grace lacked force.

Bertha had immediately grasped the gravity of two unfortunate recent events. In April, an elderly couple from Harvey, Illinois, had left the colony after staying with them eighteen months. They had gone to Wallace, who probably had engineered their departure. Bertha, Jacob, and Mr. Rudy had all guessed what vicious things John and Amelia Adamson undoubtedly told Wallace. Neither Anna nor Bertha had ever trusted Adamson, formerly a publisher of a minor religious journal in Chicago called the *Voice of the Reaper*, although they thought he was under control when Anna assigned him an affinity. Usually men were easier; it was their wives who were always the problem—and Mrs. Adamson had proved one of the worst. She had been reluctant to come from the outset, and continued to be defiant. She had felt herself too good for the menial jobs she had been given to subdue her and was enraged when Anna separated her from her sixty-year-old husband. They had sent him out to the vineyard with a hoe, arduous work he dared to complain about. Unlike the Swedes, the Adamsons simply could not grasp what it meant to "overcome." When they slipped away, Anna sent a delegation to the consulate, headed by Bertha, to demand a copy of what they told Wallace. "This is not a public record," the consul had huffed, though he admitted it had been dispatched to the State Department. Anna was frantic, sending another delegation with Rudy back again and again, insisting they had a right to see the testimony. Mr. Rudy was patient and entirely reasonable. He told Wallace it was all just "hearsay," that Wallace was wronging them by not allowing "the two parties" to talk it out together. Wallace had refused to listen.[6]

Then, just a month later, in August, their clever Norwegian tailor, Axel Strand, whose beautiful tailoring drew many customers, had also gone to Wallace. Strand and his wife, Alvilde, who had become dressmaker to Jerusalem's fashionable, had lost their three-year-old baby the year before.[7] The child, conceived in Chicago but born in Jerusalem, had been buried in the old American cemetery on Mount Zion, but Strand could not put aside his grief, and for his own good they had separated him from Alvilde. They knew him to be "weak and excitable," but it was a shock when he crept off to Wallace, telling the consul that he "was not allowed to see his wife." Apparently Wallace had shouted, "If it were my wife there would be some shooting!" He wrote down what Strand had said. Fortunately, Strand refused to swear to it, and then Alvilde went to the consulate to show that her movements were completely free. When Strand finally returned after a bad week, he had overflowed with repentance. Naturally, and after a time, Anna forgave him.[8]

After these incidents, Anna resolved to send Mr. Rudy to Washington. This persecution by American consuls must be stopped. The colony now had friends in Washington, important congressmen who had visited in Jerusalem, and she intended to use that influence. Twice, she had dispatched Rudy to the consulate, first for a travel certificate, as neither he nor the rest of the fellowship had passports, and again on a second matter. To their astonishment, Rudy reported back that Wallace had been cooperative, giving Rudy the paper without a fuss and even asking nicely how the colony's search for a cemetery was going, a search recently launched in a hurry because they had been told that the Presbyterian Board of Missions soon planned to sell the old American cemetery on Mount Zion due to overcrowding. But on Rudy's second visit, the consul declared the cemetery would not be sold after all; they could call off their search for another place to transfer their buried dead. This news had been a relief, and five days after Rudy's visit to the consul's office he had left for Washington.[9] Still, it had all been rather peculiar, this back-and-forth about the cemetery—first yes, then no—and Anna had reason to believe that Wallace was up to something.

A knock on her sitting room door interrupted Anna's reverie. Jacob stood glaring at her, accompanied by Brother Baldwin, with Olof Larsson staring dolefully over his shoulder. They were perspiring, looking winded. She thought Baldwin and Larsson had gone to Wallace asking for the cemetery key because Mats Matsson, another of those supposedly robust Swedes, had died that morning. In this heat, bodies had to be interred immediately.

"The cemetery has been sold," Jacob burst out. "Wallace was curt with us. All the bodies have been removed."[10]

Anna sprang to her feet. "Mr. Spafford? You say my husband's body is gone?" Anna shook her head. "All are gone? Rev. Drake? Mrs. Lee? Where are they? This is Satan's doing," she cried. Larsson, with his usual defeated look, mumbled that Wallace would not tell them where the bodies had been taken.

"Go to the Greek Patriarch," Anna commanded. "Ask him if we may use the Greek cemetery to bury Brother Matsson," she said as the men retreated. "We must find out where the bodies are."[11]

Over the years, eight of her community had been buried in the little American cemetery on Mount Zion whose key reposed with the U.S. Consulate: John Whiting, Horatio, Captain Sylvester, Reverend Drake, and, in 1891, Maggie Lee. In the past year, three more colony dead had been added, including the Strand baby.[12] But the colonists had always disliked having to go to the consulate for a key. Merrill never lost an opportunity to say that if the colony would allow medicine and doctors, there would not be so many dead. It was the same with Wallace. And both consuls demanded to know why their graves had no headstones. It was none of the consuls' business, Anna believed, but when John Whiting died, and then Horatio, she had insisted that headstones prevented the dead from rising, and besides, headstones were expensive. To Anna, it became far preferable for the "brothers" to take their dead, especially if they were not Americans, to the gardens of Muslim friends in Ain Karim or the valley of Jehoshaphat and bury them secretly. Secrecy was important as under Ottoman law a burial place automatically became a *waqf*, or inalienable religious foundation.[13]

Anna was not sure herself where her followers had been interred. She never went to burials. Personally, death did not interest her. She had mastered death and cauterized her heart against grief. The process had been painful, leaving old assumptions behind and contempt for the church's sacraments, including that of the burial service. As for her followers, they believed her when she said, "Death is the punishment for sin."

Yet, six years ago, after Maggie Lee's funeral, she had been much troubled to hear the mourners return, reporting they had found a number of trenches dug through the little graveyard. At the time, she assumed this was Consul Merrill's doing; the tireless archaeologist was probably looking for remains of a buried crusader church said to be in the area. Anna had been indignant and sent a colony delegation to confront him, but, infuriatingly, Merrill merely retorted that they should identify their graves with headstones. Now Wallace was insulting their dead anew. She was confident Wallace was behind this. She would force him to admit it and find out what he had done with Horatio.

A sudden marvelous thought gave her new strength: God had delivered a means to punish these consuls for their cruelty to her house. This was desecration, done clandestinely, clumsily, and insultingly. Pleased and decisive, Anna realized she must cable Mr. Rudy immediately. He could now tell those important men in Washington of a new terrible persecution. In the meantime, she would get to the bottom of it and discover just how Wallace had conspired with the Presbyterian Board of Missions to ruthlessly disturb the remains of their dearly departed—and heartlessly keep their whereabouts a secret.

Early in the nineteenth century, American missionaries had decided to leave Palestine's souls to the British and moved operations to Lebanon, in Ottoman Syria.[14] They left their cemetery in the charge of the U.S. consul for the burial of American citizens. Small and now overcrowded, the cemetery was close by the Mosque of the Tomb of David, built after the expulsion of the crusaders in 1523. Just as Muslims revered the Old Testament prophets, they held in high regard the king of Israel whose settlement was assumed to have been outside the present city walls on Mount Zion.[15] The hardscrabble 2,536-foot hill was layered with as many legends as it was scattered with tombs, graves, and bones. Where it was believed that the apostles had met for the Last Supper, Saint

Stephen had been martyred, and the Virgin Mary was said to have died, Christians had worshipped. On the ruins of a very early church dating well before Constantine, the crusaders had built an enormous cathedral in the twelfth century, long fallen into ruin. Like any of his eager archaeological colleagues, Merrill had wanted to ascertain the existence of the old crusader church, and guessed that one of its walls lay under the little cemetery. He undertook his probes at night, willing to risk the ire of the despised American Colony.

Anna had an inkling of what was behind this recent and far more disturbing cemetery matter, but there was something else she could not have guessed. In anticipation of Kaiser Wilhelm's upcoming visit, Sultan Abdul Hamid had promised the German emperor a large site on Mount Zion in order to build the Church of the Dormition for his Catholic subjects, as there was already the new Church of the Redeemer for German Protestants inside the city. This undertaking would be, as Selah Merrill was to write the State Department, "a blow to French supremacy," as previously the French had claimed sole right as protector of the Catholics.[16] The kaiser was nothing if not ambitious, and the preparations for his arrival were growing more splendid by the day. The erection of a Catholic church would solidify his imperial role as sovereign to Christians of all persuasions.

It made sense for the Board of Missions to quietly arrange to sell its overcrowded cemetery to the Catholics and develop a larger one elsewhere. Moreover, it was in the interest of the United States to aid the kaiser in his grand project and reap the goodwill of the sultan in the bargain. But as cemeteries were permanently hallowed by Ottoman law, it would need to be cleared of the dead, inspected by the Turkish authorities, and desanctified before it could be sold and built upon. To avoid stirring up the emotions typically attending such a transaction, a Presbyterian missionary from Syria, the Reverend William K. Eddy, sometime earlier had visited Jerusalem to alert relatives of the dead, calling on Anna as well as others, all of whom expected to be notified. Eddy had assured Anna that if she were unable to locate a cemetery for her colony in time, he would temporarily transfer her dead to the English cemetery. But Wallace had no confidence that Anna would cooperate when the moment arrived, and he advised Eddy that the removals should be made at night, and without giving notice.

Wallace and the American consul general in Constantinople understood perfectly the importance of facilitating the kaiser's project. Indeed, Wallace had offered his office to draw up the sale agreement, for which service he was to be reimbursed. The date for the signing was September 10. Anxious that nothing should leak out, he had deliberately misled Rudy, telling him that the cemetery sale was off. Two days later, Rudy left for Washington. On September 18, when the colonists came for the key to bury Mats Matsson, the agreement had been signed, but not all of its clauses fulfilled, as the cemetery was not yet cleared, and Wallace, still fearing the deal might get out, acted rudely. Eddy consulted with Wallace, and arrangements were made with workmen to come after dark, remove all headstones, and smooth over the earth so that the Turkish inspector would be satisfied. While they felt uneasy about these decisions, they were extremely pressed, and the importance of their covert mission overcame their compunctions. Unfortunately, Wallace's dislike of the Overcomers was so intense that he deliberately withheld any information, including that the bodies had been taken to the English cemetery. In part, the consul correctly expected a storm of protest from the Spaffordites and wished to head it off as long as possible, but he could never have anticipated that Anna would seize on it as a means to ruin him.

In the meantime, the thought of Rudy complaining about him in Washington was worrisome. Wallace, a graduate of the Princeton Theological Seminary, was now thirty-three. He was eager to perform his duties well in the Holy Land, hoping to stay long enough to publish a book and enhance his career. "Because I have refused to associate with them on terms of intimacy and thus give an outward sanction to their, at least, suspicious practices, they choose to regard me as their personal and official enemy. If I have made any mistake in my official treatment of them, it has been in exercising too great leniency towards them," he had nervously written State.[17]

Thus, as a new and perilous war began between the colony and the consulate, Wallace committed another folly. He acquiesced to the offer of a printer, T. J. Alley, who had assisted in the capture of Mary Whiting five years earlier, to distribute a printed circular accusing Anna of "dark machinations" and practicing "free love." Purporting to expose "the Spaffordite Fraud" to the authorities in Washington, it was addressed to the U.S. president and bore the signatures of twenty-seven Jerusalemites. The circular concluded with a recommendation that Wallace be retained for his "unprecedented promptness and equity . . . in conducting the business of the Consulate in all particulars."[18]

When the circular came to Anna's attention, she read it with cold rage. She knew Wallace was behind it, but the description of herself was intolerable: "A small, blue-eyed, cramped-featured woman of Norwegian birth and determined bearing, [who] in a measured, rather trembling voice, promulgates her 'messages.' " From that moment, Anna was prepared to give Wallace no quarter. She would bide her time, but she would destroy him. Again she cabled Rudy in Washington.

Rudy's trip to the nation's capital coincided with Mr. and Mrs. Adamson's arrival back in Chicago and a new blast of titillating publicity. "A household of 175 persons, of whom 100 are women, many others girls of marriageable age, and only 40 men, has its secrets," began the *Chicago Journal*'s account of Amelia and John Adamson's scandalous treatment at the hands of the infamous American Colony.[19] They had only wished to spend their declining years in a quiet Christian brotherhood, helping to tend to the sick and the poor. Instead, the unfortunate couple found themselves in a hotbed of sexuality. Members "kissed indiscriminately." Husbands were encouraged to "find an affinity among the younger women," where they held hands together and whispered in dark corridors. Shocking confessions were solicited at morning meetings—in the presence of children. They were spied upon constantly. They were virtually starved, given food so bad they threw it up. Old as they were, and unused to manual labor, Mrs. Adamson was forced to be a servant, and Mr. Adamson sent to the fields under a brutal sun. Although Mrs. Adamson had fought to stay with her husband, she was "put into a common chamber with the women" where she overheard "very strange things." She and another wife were not allowed to remain in the great, dimly lit dining room after dinner with the young women, the men, and the male Arab and Turkish guests, because they "were not 'Overcomers.' " If they approached, their entrance was barred. Their savings of $700 had been taken; they were now destitute, and Mr. Adamson was forced to sell Holy Land literature to survive. He confided to the reporter that he was looking into a legal suit; however, his burning purpose was to prevent yet another group of Spaffordite recruits, who had been waiting for two years at 6003 Throop Street, from going to Jerusalem and suffering as they had.

In Washington, Mr. Rudy made his case. The colony was "persecuted." Mrs. Whiting had been roughly "imprisoned." They were the victims of hearsay from critics who disapproved of a "communistic community." Most arrestingly, Rudy claimed that their dead had been violated and spirited away under cover of darkness, an outrage that required investigation in the name of Christian decency. While the colony's influential friends were appalled, the State Department met Rudy's accusations without comment. The slanderous printed circular calling Anna "cramped-featured" was making its rounds. Rudy was requested to supply a statement of his colony's character and methods, but Anna cabled him not to draft such a document as she could not be sure to what or to whose legal ends it might be put.[20]

Over sixteen years, the department's file on the Spaffordites had grown fat, and officials felt sympathetic to the trials endured by their consuls. What action, it was wondered internally, should be taken? As F. Van Dyne, the department counsel, pointed out: "While the acts and practices of Mrs. Spafford and her lieutenants are immoral, it would probably be difficult to obtain evidence of actual crime."[21] There was always a writ of habeas corpus to invoke should a consul receive a sworn statement that an American was being held against his will. The trouble was, as both Merrill and Wallace had frequently noted, no one actually held in the Spafford house had ever formally requested help. The consuls had dealt only with those who had broken free. State agreed to protect Wallace in refusing to hand over the Adamson testimony through Article 479 of the 1896 Consular Regulations. It also sent a copy of the testimony to the governor of Illinois, with a suggestion that someone look up Miss Annie Aiken.[22] As to Merrill's and Wallace's oft-reiterated complaint that the colony had no right to call itself the "American Colony" as it was composed of Swedes, British, Norwegians, Danes, Serbians, Indians, Jews, and Turks, among others, State felt at a loss. If the colony would only incorporate as an American entity, then perhaps something could be done. But since no American official had actually witnessed these alleged behaviors, appropriate action was hard to determine.

Still, the colony's claim that its dead had been violated was a serious charge. Wallace had gathered letters from ranking personages in Jerusalem—including Lord Bishop Blyth and the head of the London Jews Society, as well as the British consul—all of whom emphatically denied that the dead had been irreverently treated. Nevertheless, reluctant as the department was, the matter needed looking into.

While Mr. Rudy did not leave Washington completely empty-handed, he had hoped for greater satisfaction. He journeyed on to Chicago to meet with the Throop Street group. These were the rest of the farmers from Lebanon and Salem, Kansas, as well as several others from Ohio and Illinois who had used up most of their funds during their long wait. Rudy needed to see what might be done about them. He also held a power of attorney signed by Ruth Whiting. At seventeen, the girl was close to reaching her majority. Rudy was charged with dislodging her inheritance. Finally, Anna had asked him to collect the rest of the money owed for Olaf Henrik Larsson's house.

His mission was becoming more complicated by the minute. The press had now discovered a Miss Katrina Hanson, also recently escaped from the colony's "clutches." She was impecunious and telling all who listened that they must save the Throop Street group "from bondage." To "retain a penny is treachery," Miss Hanson was wailing, "yet the leaders seem to prosper."[23]

At home, Anna clipped articles for her scrapbook and seethed. A letter that Wallace had written to John Adamson calling her "the Devil in the Valley of Jehoshaphat" had made its way into the papers.[24] And while she instantly telegraphed the politest of protest letters to publishers—written by her, but signed by her followers—whose tone was one of noble forbearance, the ridicule continued. She was referred to as "once a Norwegian servant girl."[25]

Rudy gave his best effort. "We want Wallace to go . . . He denounces us to tourists as if we were a lot of American hoboes . . . We are not free lovers." The signers of the dreadful circular were "jealous."[26] He dismissed them scathingly: "He is an inebriate . . . She paints postcards for travelers . . . He *claims* to be a missionary and peddles tracts."[27] Curiously, it seems that Rudy made no mention of the cemetery imbroglio to the papers, perhaps because Anna was not yet certain what the circumstances were behind Wallace's actions, still did not know where the bodies were, and had not finished consolidating her plans.

Finally Rudy could leave. America and its relentless press had left him weary, feeling oddly vulnerable, and eager to return to the familiar surroundings of the colony. He had accomplished quite a lot. Mr. Bowman had allowed Ruth Whiting $2,000 from the estate's income, which Anna would use to purchase the Vesters' store, and from the Methodists he received the remaining installment of Olaf Larsson's money, using a small portion to purchase tickets for the Throop Street group. Amounting to nearly $10,000, Olaf's gold weighed heavily in its sturdy leather suitcase as his ship set sail. One night in his tiny cabin, he opened the bag and studied the shining coins. Wearily, he thought about it. This small fortune could spell freedom—if he chose. He was fifty-two. He had endured much, including humiliating descriptions that called him "an extremely cautious person with a long beard and a small, round head, almost bald."[28] Rather vain, Rudy was stung. Yet Mother Anna trusted him as few others. Only he and Anna knew that when he was finally back in his own pleasant bedroom—from which, fortunately, he never had to move—every night a young Swede came to him in her nightgown. She was married and the mother of two children. They spent the night together and did their best to resist the temptations of the flesh. But should on occasion they fail, they knew they had only to confess quietly to Anna, and she would forgive them.[29] Still, he could not put the thought of the gold from his mind.

When Rudy returned, Anna congratulated him and gave him her most ardent kisses in gratitude. No one was around the night he went to the colony's garden and buried half of the gold.[30] To what and from whom, he occasionally wondered as the colony absorbed the new members and he resumed his duties as its bursar, should he seek forgiveness? The colony seemed to be making a good income now, but one could never be sure what the future might hold.

Yet within the colony leadership a feeling of security quietly blossomed. From their many profitable enterprises, money rolled in. There was no question these days that the Big House had become the favorite place to stay in Jerusalem, and tour directors vied for its spotlessly clean rooms. Few guests were aware that the members squeezed themselves into temporary sleeping quarters in hallways or attics, or that the young were called from class—the boys to haul mattresses and rearrange furniture, the pretty Swedish girls to wait on guests delighted by ice cream and American pies.

In the grand salon, Anna presided with renewed graciousness. A fortunate guest would find himself beckoned to sit beside her, where she would adjust her skirt to move a little closer, lower her voice, and have a confidential chat. To those who seemed particularly interested, Anna always mentioned the atrocious actions of the American consuls. She confided softly that from the day they had arrived in 1881, the dreadful Selah Merrill had made their lives miserable, and, incredibly, both he and Edwin Wallace had disturbed the sanctity of their beloved dead. Merrill was gone now, she would remark thankfully. As for Wallace—that terrible man from the State Department—he was to be replaced momentarily.

And this was true. With the election of a Republican, William McKinley, Grover Cleveland's Democratic administration ended. It took a while for the Republicans to sort themselves out, but when they finally selected Selah Merrill for a third term in Jerusalem, Anna was stunned. She did not allow herself to be discouraged. She knew she would overcome eventually. And the good Lord's retributory justice could be meted out just as well on two enemies as on one.

The Sultan, the Emperor, the Zionist—and Buried Bodies

If Jerusalem is ever ours, and if I were still able to do anything about it, I would begin by cleaning it up. I would clear out everything that is not sacred, set up workers' houses beyond the city, empty and tear down the filthy ratholes, burn all the non-sacred ruins, and put the bazaars elsewhere. Then, retaining as much of the old architectural style as possible, I would build an airy, comfortable, properly sewered, brand new city around the Holy Places.

—Theodor Herzl

The neglected, shabby, odoriferous town into which Selah Merrill had moved in 1882 was becoming a lively metropolis. Modern hospitals, hotels, schools, and philanthropic and scientific institutions built under the auspices of the various European powers jostled for space to the echo of hammer and pickax blows. Much was new— new suburbs spilling outside the walls, new roads, new hospitals, even new consulates opened by Western governments recognizing Jerusalem's growing importance. There were now ten thousand Muslims, the same number of Christians, and thirty-five thousand Jews living in Jerusalem.[1] The traditional peace between these "enclaves of difference" saw increasing friction. Skirmishes were occurring more frequently since the officially sanctioned Russian persecutions of 1881 to 1884 had sparked an exodus to Palestine of as many as thirty thousand Jews seeking a return to the land of their forefathers. To Jews, Arabs were a motley, illiterate collection of feudal clans or ignorant bedouin, and as far as they were concerned, Palestine, as it later came to be said, "was a land without a people for a people without a land."

For their part, Arabs laughed at the efforts of Jewish farmers attempting to harness camels to horse carts, but they did not laugh when Jews violated the traditional sharing of the fields or drove off the Arab goatherds, beating them and sometimes even seizing their herds.[2] There was a good deal of resentment among Arab peasants when Jewish farmers refused to hire Arab workers in the agricultural settlements funded by wealthy Western Jews or put barbed wire around their villages to keep the Arabs out. These enclaves were exclusively Jewish, and the Arabs feared and envied their use of sophisticated techniques to produce crops more efficiently, and they paid their workers higher wages than Arabs received. Alarmed by the rapid increase in land purchases, and seeing no end to the stream of new arrivals, a number of prominent Palestinians had recently petitioned Constantinople, demanding enforcement of laws against foreign Jews buying land or staying longer than three months, but these regulations were circumvented with astonishing ingenuity and determination. The Turkish police did their best to stem the tide of small boats bringing emigrants in by night along the coast, or by the new railroad, or by lone wagons arriving from the north and the east. But Ottoman officials had long been susceptible to bribes, and absentee Arab landlords, living luxuriously in Beirut or Damascus or Constantinople, were happy to take Jewish gold for pieces of their vast holdings. They never heard the piteous keening of their tenant farmers forced to leave their homes and fields.

Resuming his desk on January 28, 1898, Merrill concentrated on "the Jewish Question." His immediate predecessor had been sympathetic to Jewish aspirations and a national future. "Once the Turk gets over his animosity toward his elder brother, the Jew," Edwin Wallace had written, "there will be nothing in the way of the increase of the new city. The Jew wants to come. He is anxious to buy a plot of ground and build him a home in or near the city of his fathers. He simply asks to be let alone, freed from oppression and permitted to enjoy his religion. The land of the new city is ready for him."[3]

Merrill, however, saw the situation as more complex and potentially disturbing to U.S. interests. "The Zionist movement is filling the air in England, and to some extent in the United States," he wrote the State Department, explaining that U.S. policy on the matter was disastrously vague. Indeed, he felt it critical that a new treaty with Turkey be negotiated to clarify the position of both countries.[4] He was besieged by Jews, principally Russians, clamoring for American passports, which not only gave them protection but shielded them from certain taxes and other duties—notably military service. By the hundreds, they resorted to "bribes, tearful pleadings, fraudulent certificates, false swearing to parentage, place of birth, residence in the U.S." He found them using passports of deceased people or purchasing passports of living people. While Merrill did his best to be fair, and went to considerable trouble to authenticate these demands, he was in a difficult position. On the one hand, he felt obliged to offer American protection to those who qualified—and many Jews, especially Russians, had obtained passports merely for staying a short time in the United States, often in Chicago or New York, demonstrating themselves as qualified residents and then traveling on to their real goal, Jerusalem. Yet Merrill felt a duty to enforce Turkish law. As the vast majority of passport claimants were not "bona fide tourists" but intended to stay and colonize, he could not "compel the Turks to ignore their own laws against immigration."[5] In the past he had simply given his word about a visitor, but now the authorities were suspicious of all arriving Jews, asking pointed questions and throwing up obstacles to their entrance. The Zionist movement was causing "overwhelming changes" in Palestine, Merrill wrote State. As matters stood, without further clarification, the "United States Government is aiding and abetting the Zionist Movement and Jewish colonial schemes." Was this the policy the U.S. government intended to pursue—a policy, Merrill pointed out, that was "a menace to our friendly relations with Turkey"? In March 1899, the State Department responded to its concerned representative. The situation was to be studied and a report issued "on the status of persons, chiefly Jews, claiming the protection of this Consulate as 'naturalized American citizens.' "[6]

Although acutely aware of the consequences of Zionism "stirring in the air" in Britain and America, Merrill may not yet have heard the name of a thirty-eight-year-old Viennese journalist named Theodor Herzl, nor known that he was behind a dynamic secular vision of Zionism. In Paris, in 1895, as correspondent for an influential liberal newspaper, Herzl had been appalled by the trial and wrongful conviction of Alfred Dreyfus, a French officer who was Jewish—as was Herzl—and who was sent to Devil's Island for a treason he did not commit. Suddenly, in the cradle of "liberty, fraternity, equality," a violent anti-Semitism ignited screams of "Death to Jews!" Herzl decided that only a state of their own would protect his people against anti-Semitism. He was not a religious man. He had once even toyed with converting to Christianity. As far as he was concerned, Uganda or Argentina could be the Jewish homeland, but a homeland was essential, and toward this goal he was literally working himself to death.[7] "We must," he wrote in his diary in 1895, "expropriate gently the private property on the state assigned to us. We shall try to spirit the penniless population across the border by procuring employment for it in the transit countries, while denying it employment in our country. The property owners will come over to our side. Both the process of expropriation and the removal of the poor must be carried out discreetly and circumspectly. Let the owners of the immovable property believe that they are cheating us, selling us things for more than they are worth. But we are not going to sell them anything back."[8]

In 1896 he wrote *Der Judenstaat*, or *The Jewish State*. In 1897 he headed the first Zionist Congress in Basel, Switzerland, which launched this irresistible movement, ultimately supported by politicians in Europe and America who believed it the solution to "the Jewish Question." Handsome, bearded, persuasive, Herzl was bent on meeting the sultan in Constantinople, and when the kaiser came to Jerusalem in the fall of 1898, he was determined to meet him as well. Both, he hoped, could be convinced that Jewish money and enterprise would benefit two empires, Ottoman and German.

These days, everyone was seeing advantages in the offing. In his Yildiz palace in Constantinople, the wily sultan Abdul Hamid, always clever at manipulating tensions between the European powers, had surprised those who thought him on the brink of collapse when his German-trained army had invaded Greece to snuff out a rebellion in Crete by Greek nationalists in 1897. It had fortunately distracted attention from the recent massacres in Armenia that had earned him odium as "the monster of Yildiz" and "Abdul the Damned."[9] Justly afraid of assassination, reliant on his secret police, cowering in Yildiz, and hanging on to what was left of his still-vast empire after uprisings in the Balkans and other provinces, the sultan needed the kaiser. With the loss of Christian populations in the Balkans, three-quarters of the remaining imperial territories were Islamic, and the sultan wished to corral the intense Pan-Islamic sentiment raging among Muslims as a reaction to imperialism.[10] He was their caliph. He needed to unify his empire, and what better than a railroad system reaching to Baghdad and the Persian Gulf in the east, as well as the holy cities in Turkish-controlled western Arabia? A railroad system would facilitate the transportation of pilgrims on their annual hajj to Mecca, as well as convey troops to repress secessionist tendencies or foreign interventions. And who better to build it than the efficient Germans?[11]

For the kaiser, this was also a splendid idea. Not only would German industry benefit from the enormous price such a railroad would cost, but he intended to gain rights to the rich oil and mineral deposits on either side of its path. His military advisers had won the confidence of the sultan, boosting German trade, investment, and influence. German experts had overhauled the Ottoman army. Delivery of thousands of Mauser rifles, ordnance, and heavy field artillery was keeping German factories humming. The kaiser was aware that neither France, which had established itself as protector of Lebanon in 1860, nor Britain, anxious to protect the route to India and eager for Persian Gulf oil, relished a German-made railroad system for the Ottomans. But the Great Powers had long been engaged in a jousting game, ever seeking advantage, constantly studying the infirmities of the Ottoman Empire, and waiting for a ripe moment to pluck from it what they could. Furthermore, like the sultan, the kaiser believed it was his divine right to rule. Both monarchs were absolutist anachronisms, frequently interfering in the affairs of state. Like Napoleon a hundred years earlier launching his invasions of Egypt and Palestine, Wilhelm was convinced that fame as well as fortune lay to the east. With that in mind, he looked forward to the fall of 1898 with pleasure. He would have the honor of being the first reigning Christian monarch to enter the holy city since the emperor Frederick II captured Jerusalem during the Sixth Crusade.[12]

As representatives of the sultan and the kaiser organized the extraordinary fanfare that would accompany this mutually advantageous and much-heralded royal visit to Jerusalem, the American Colony was in its own fever of activity. It took the form of a letter-writing campaign. After the British consul informed Miss Johanna Brooke that the remains of the missing colony dead had been "numbered and [were] lying separately in the British Cemetery," letters from colonists flew around Jerusalem and across the Atlantic.[13] Asserting their right to their own dead, the colonists bombarded the Presbyterian Board of Missions, various departments of the U.S. government, representatives of assorted governments in Constantinople, all of the resident consuls in Jerusalem, Consul Wallace, Reverend Eddy, Bishop Blyth, and as many others as they could think of. For a time they were shunted back and forth between Wallace and the bishop, each of whom told them that they should speak to the other. But it was the letter to the British consul John Dickson from Mrs. Sylvester, insisting on her right to her husband's body as an English subject, forwarded to the British minister in Constantinople, forwarded again to Whitehall, and finally landing on the desk of the British prime minister, Lord Salisbury himself, that produced results. An order came to Consul Dickson to ask Bishop Blyth to ask his workers to open the British cemetery and allow Mrs. Sylvester the contents of coffin "No. 13."

On February 7, 1898, a crowd gathered on Mount Zion. Mrs. Sylvester was there, accompanied by others from the colony: Amelia Gould; Elias Habib, the interpreter; Otis Page, whose wife had been disposed of in Ain Karim; Axel Strand, whose baby's body was missing; Eric Lind, whose sister's remains were as well; Jacob Eliahu, ready with pen and notebook; the Reverend Edward Baldwin and his young son, Furman, who was in love with Grace Spafford; Bertha Spafford; her patient lover, Frederick Vester; and assorted others, including a workforce of sturdy young Swedes holding shovels. The Catholics, purchasers of the old American cemetery, were represented by Dr. Savignoni of the Mission of Terra Santa.[14] The British dragoman was there, too, as well as the custodian of the cemetery, but neither Consul Dickson nor Bishop Blyth—both deeply annoyed by all the fuss—had seen the necessity to attend. Neither had Anna.

The young Swedes dug in, watched by forty-some eyes under the broiling sun. As the shovelfuls of earth were displaced, a large pit was revealed, big enough to accommodate thirty coffins. But there were no coffins—only a chaotic tumble of seemingly ordinary packing boxes, some on their sides as if dumped casually, or worse, in a hurry. Some were marked with numbers; some were unmarked; some were marked with several sets of numbers. They were flimsy, cracked, and the lid of one box was open, plainly disclosing two skulls and a jumble of broken bones. Whoever had done the transfer had violently smashed the skeletons with a sharp instrument, dismembering them and cramming together odd bones, locks of hair, and clothing scraps. Exclamations of horror arose from the colonists peering over the edge. The Swedes toiled on in the pit as Furman Baldwin supervised the lifting of the boxes to the surface and Jacob Eliahu scribbled with his pencil. Mary Sylvester was looking in vain for box No. 13, when Bertha cried, "There's father!" One of the skulls was missing two front teeth, and everyone remembered that Horatio had a bridge in the front of his mouth.[15]

This harrowing revelation complete, the boxes were replaced, covered again with earth, and the colonists hurried back to tell Anna the gruesome news. Anna's mouth twitched with concealed pleasure, and again when she learned that they could expect a visit from the American consul general from Constantinople in April. "God will use the bones of our members as a means to uncover the rottenness and wickedness of the American Government and the Christian Church," she predicted triumphantly at the morning assembly.[16] More letters went out, considerably more colorful now that they could include a description of "violently dismembered bodies, the sinews of limbs torn apart . . . boxed like rubbish and dumped."[17]

The same young effendi who had asked Bertha to head the Muslim girls' school, Ismail Bey Husseini, was so incensed on behalf of his friends that he wrote a protest to the president of the United States: "All my sense of propriety and decency was scandalized; for, assuming that the customs of your country may be different from ours, where public sentiment and law would never permit of a cemetery being sold, yet such acts, in which inhumanity and barbarism appear, made me doubt whether the boasted justice and humanity, which I failed to be able to perceive, were to be actually found in your honorable Government . . . A howl of condemnation was heard from Europe and America when it was said that the Turks had desecrated Armenian cemeteries. But what shall we say of this in which the Christian American consul digs up the dead of his own nation?"[18]

One of Axel Strand's repeated requests to various wearied consuls who had heard rather more than they wished from the colonists produced an agreement that Strand could continue to dig for his baby if he insisted, but only if he promised "to cease giving Mr. Eddy trouble."[19]

The State Department's investigation was disappointing, at least from the colonists' perspective, although they were initially pleased to see a reluctant Reverend Eddy summoned back from Syria.[20] Consul General Charles M. Dickinson arrived from Constantinople full of brisk purposefulness and asked the colonists pointed questions about themselves and their mode of living. These were answered earnestly, if not necessarily fully. But to the colonists' frustration, Dickinson seemed more interested in the colony's practices than in the scandal of the cemetery. Mr. Rudy and Reverend Baldwin, acting as the colony's counsels, attempted to interrogate Eddy, demanding if he had "seen any dead people dug out of this plot."

"Yes, I have," Eddy replied. But when Brother Rudy stepped in and tried to pursue the subject, Eddy declined to testify further, and the consul general sustained him. It was the same with Consul Wallace.

"How much money did you receive in the cemetery sale?"

"Need I answer?" Wallace asked.

"No," replied the consul general.[21]

Maddeningly, Dickinson ultimately decided that the old American cemetery was, legally speaking, not a cemetery. At that point, the colonists had not located the original deeds or other proofs from the sale sixty years earlier, nor any of the other documents that they later acquired in their tireless pursuit of redress. Except to show that no taxes had been paid on it, there was little they could do to prove the cemetery had been secretly and unlawfully sold. They rightly suspected that it was in the interest of the United States to help the kaiser obtain his land. To their enormous annoyance, they had to endure advice from Consul Dickinson that they register as Turkish subjects, which, he averred, would make them all "better off." Their single satisfaction was hearing the consul general reprimand Consul Wallace for refusing to give Axel Strand a copy of his testimony after he had recanted it. They also managed to suggest to Dickinson that his Jerusalem representative was a mercenary minister who had engaged in suspicious deals and took financial advantage when he settled estates. This kept the State Department busy for some time trying to straighten out Wallace's rather confusing bookkeeping. In the end, however, State found him innocent of the charges.[22] It did not result in Wallace's dismissal for incompetence or venality, as Anna and her advisers had hoped. Still, Anna had no intention of letting go the "cemetery war." She could bide her time until God revealed a more effective course of action.

It was a relief to all parties when Dickinson left rather abruptly, called back to Constantinople for, apparently, more pressing duties. Before departing, he observed bemusedly that while "one would think it would be a pleasure to visit Jerusalem," the atmosphere was rather "overburdened with crucifixion."[23]

Now Jerusalem's atmosphere was charged with excitement. Whole Arab families, including children, were set to work by the authorities on a new road to a northern spur of the Mount of Olives, where the kaiser intended to build a vast hospice named after his empress, Augusta Victoria. Other workers tore down picturesque old buildings and painted many ancient monuments a garish yellow and black, the imperial colors. The Jaffa Gate was widened and heightened so that the kaiser could ride through on his mount without risking damage to the peak of his helmet. Two hundred cooks, ninety carriages, five hundred horses, two infantry regiments, an orchestra, and twelve detectives were sent from Germany, as well as three steamers bearing mostly German guests. Thomas Cook

& Son, responsible for the arrangements, managed to beg, borrow, and steal enough water to sustain the expected crowds through the inevitable suffocating heat.[24]

When one hundred tents and prefabricated rooms arrived to house the imperial couple and their retinue of courtiers, the Turkish authorities asked twenty-year-old Bertha Spafford to help. She had always been the colony's diplomat with "the outside," and while a few prominent Muslims frowned on the mixed gatherings in the great salon, many other Muslims continued to savor its good conversation and rare ecumenical atmosphere. In the process the colony's Muslim guests had acquired a considerable respect for Bertha's beauty and grace, as well as for her obvious competence. The tents, she was told, needed to be furnished with appropriately "Oriental" carpets and furniture, so Bertha was given blanket permission to take anything she deemed necessary from any Turkish house. She was also asked, as the head of the Muslim school for girls, to oversee a gift to present the empress. Since sewing and embroidery constituted the main portion of the girls' curriculum, it was to be an example of the students' handiwork. She selected a piece of fine tapestry with the Turkish coat of arms that someone had ordered earlier, had it handsomely boxed in olive wood, and then discovered that none of the students' parents were willing to allow one of their daughters to present the gift. They declared themselves fearful that their daughters might suffer the "evil eye" of envy. Ismail Bey Husseini stepped in to help. As an eager modernist, he wished to disprove such silly superstitions and volunteered his eight-year-old daughter to make the important presentation.[25]

At last the great day arrived. The imperial white and gold yacht *Hohenzollern*, escorted by two warships, brought their majesties to Haifa. There followed an extraordinary parade through triumphal arches, waving banners, gaily tossed garlands, and cheering spectators as the royal couple made their way to Jerusalem. On Friday, October 28, 1898, the kaiser, robed in a gold and white burnoose of his own design, his spiked helmet sparkling in the sunshine, rode a prancing black stallion through the Jaffa Gate to the roar of guns while a full band played the German anthem.[26]

The kaiser then embarked on a whirlwind round of entertainments embracing each of Jerusalem's warring denominations. He and his kaiserin visited the holy places; Wilhelm consecrated the new Church of the Redeemer on Luther's Day, and both royals attended a service on the Mount of Olives. Bertha and Frederick, wandering close by, were surprised to find themselves invited to join the worshippers and even more surprised to be shown to seats right behind their majesties. The imperial entourage then gathered on Mount Zion to dedicate the spot for the future Catholic Church of the Dormition, including the plot that the Reverends Wallace and Eddy had labored to obtain for that purpose. When the royal carriage drove up Nablus Road past the American Colony, the children gathered on a stone wall and threw their caps in the air with a ringing "Huzzah!" They saw the carriage pause at a narrow bend, and later learned that the kaiser had wished the road widened at that point in order to facilitate the passage of cannons.[27]

In the meantime, Theodor Herzl was staying at a hotel near the Jaffa Gate. His interpreter was Horatio's old friend the diminutive scholar Eliezer Ben-Yehuda, still dedicated to making Hebrew the language of a resplendent Jewish state.[28] Herzl had already seen the kaiser briefly in Constantinople, where he had been offended by the German emperor's contemptuous reference to Jews as "usurers." Herzl did not look on Jerusalem "with delight," he wrote in his diary. He was disgusted by "the musty deposits of two thousand years of inhumanity, intolerance and foulness" lying in its "reeking alleys." He was equally offended by the Wailing Wall. "Any emotion is rendered impossible by the hideous, miserable, scrambling beggary pervading the place."[29] Instead, like Ben-Yehuda, inspired by the dream of a gleaming, modern city outside the city walls, Herzl and four comrades donned frock coats and starched bibs to call on the kaiser, who met them in his luxurious tent, wearing a gray colonial uniform and a veiled helmet and clasping a riding crop in one gloved hand. As the group's leader, Herzl outlined a vision of a cleaned-up city supplied with ample water. It might cost millions, he conceded, "but will produce millions."

"Well," responded the kaiser, tapping his boot with the crop, "you have plenty of money—more than all the rest of us."[30]

Like many European leaders, the kaiser believed the myth of the bottomless wealth of international Jewry and its potential usefulness, but he had seen the sultan's hostility to Jewish immigration and concluded the better policy was to return a disappointed Herzl to Europe without his backing. Having achieved a soon-to-be-fatal alliance with Turkey, the kaiser departed with his kaiserin on November 4, 1898, for Damascus. There he took the occasion to stand beside the tomb of Saladin and announce, "Tell the three hundred million Moslems of the world that I am their friend," prompting a rumor that the kaiser was a secret Muslim convert.[31]

As for the American Colony, Elijah Meyers, the Indian Jew from Bombay, had obtained a camera and documented this singular moment in the story of Zionism. Together with Frederick Vester, Elijah had been commissioned by Herzl to photograph Jewish settlements in Palestine so he could show the pictures to the kaiser. The two men followed the royal party on their rounds, then dashed back to their studio, developed the plates, and sent colony boys to take them to the Austrian post office, the only truly reliable mail service in Jerusalem. All during the kaiser's historic visit newspapers from London to Berlin competed for American Colony photographs. In no time the American Colony Photo Department gained an international reputation as the place to turn to to satisfy readers' ever-growing interest in Middle Eastern events.

Anna, now a vigorous fifty-six, had every reason to look approvingly at her "flock of evenly sheared sheep."[32] Under her tutelage, after the Swedes arrived, the colony became a smoothly working, self-sustaining, and ever more prosperous cooperative village. Her unpaid labor force had made a booming success of the Vesters' antiques shop that she purchased. Conveniently—and doubtless prodded by Bertha—Anna had received a "message" that Frederick Vester was to manage the shop. "Him your guard" were the curious words wafting from the great beyond, and none dared criticize when Mr. Rudy was replaced and the colony's deeds and funds were put in the name of "Vester & Co., American Colony Stores."[33] Now it was Frederick who rode with bulging saddlebags every day to the Deutsche Palastina Bank by the Jaffa Gate. Tourists flocked to buy Holy Land photographs, stereopticon slides, ancient pottery and iridescent glass, silks, rugs and inlaid brassware, bedouin jewelry and costumes, the products of the bakery and confectionery, Palestine's flowers or butterflies pressed and framed, and olive-wood mementos crafted by artful colony members.

Besides one hundred adults, Anna had some fifty young people in service. They were disciplined, willing, and impeccably polite in their clean hand-me-down clothes. Anna was confident that they took pride in being members of a group dedicated to selflessness on behalf of the needy. One had only to walk out of the colony door to see the daily cluster of the destitute lined up in the courtyard, waiting for soup or shoes. At a moment's notice Anna's people were ready to nurse the sick, even those with virulently contagious diseases, in the true spirit of Christ—something one could not always say for the sanctimonious missionaries. Dissatisfaction in her ranks was unacceptable, but should any arise, she knew she could deal with it.

The Novelist

Strange, when you ask anyone's advice you see
yourself what is right.

—Selma Lagerlöf

More often now the ululation of Arab women sounding their piercing "death cry" filled the streets. The Turks were rounding up husbands, sons, and brothers for military service as new threats to the empire erupted and the Arabs of Yemen persisted in their revolt. Wives, mothers, and sisters knew they would never see their menfolk again after they were marched away to defend the empire's farthest corners. Cutting off a trigger finger, or otherwise maiming themselves, made no difference; the ravening maw of the military consumed them by the thousands.

Personally, Anna did not care for politics. She was committed to the return of the Jews, but otherwise uninterested in the complicated issues worrying the sultan, the Great Powers, or Herzl. But she was used to guests who asked questions. In March 1899, therefore, when a small upper-class forty-year-old Swedish novelist with a pronounced limp called on her, Anna was hospitable. While Anna thought little of most women, there was something in the direct gaze of her visitor that was worthy of respect. Not until later did she learn that Selma Lagerlöf had already acquired a reputation for rendering the darker side of the Swedish spirit through eerie tales of night creatures and folk demons.[1]

Anna saw no danger in introducing her to the Swedes, since she had only to cast a steely glance for them to know how to behave. But she could not ask them to suppress their joy at hearing their forbidden native tongue as they crowded around the visitor. They clapped their hands when Miss Lagerlöf showed them an introductory letter from Nås and listened raptly to her reports of events back home.

Miss Lagerlöf was traveling with her secret lover, Sophie Elkan, a writer herself, and they had booked rooms at the Grand New Hotel near the Jaffa Gate. Encouraged by Sophie, Miss Lagerlöf had already begun a fictionalized version of the much-publicized migration in Swedish papers of the Dala folk who had abandoned farms and families to greet the Messiah in Jerusalem. Possessed of a powerful and probing intellect, Miss Lagerlöf hoped to draw out stories from the colony's Swedes. She was intrigued when Selah Merrill, who lived at the same hotel with his wife, approached her. The consul told her firmly that the Swedish-American home was "no place for a lady." His vehement assertions that the group was "immoral" whetted her curiosity. He informed her that just a few days earlier another couple had left the colony and urged her to talk with them. Constantine Antoszewsky had given Merrill a sworn statement that was even more explicit about the colony's inner workings than that of the Adamsons. Naturally, Merrill had forwarded it instantly to the Department of State and was now quivering with renewed indignation over more revelations of the beating and oppression of children.[2] Miss Lagerlöf looked forward to her interview with Mr. Antoszewsky, but when they talked, it proved disappointing. He seemed unwilling to offer much, as if he were afraid to tell what he knew to a stranger.

Disturbed yet fascinated, Miss Lagerlöf spent several weeks interviewing the Swedes but was unable to learn anything that confirmed the worst of Merrill's allegations. She had sensed that somehow the Swedes were suppressing their Swedishness, and she queried Anna on this topic. Anna's rationale interested her. Nationalism, Anna said, made for "disunity" and disunity for "war." Only "unity" would save mankind. The author made a note of this and later would use it in a famous speech.[3] But at the same time she tried to get a sense of the Swedes' true conditions. The men seemed vigorous and fairly happy, but she noted that most of the women were pale, quiet, and docile. Curious to understand how Anna had seized control from Larsson, she attempted to talk to the old man, but Olaf had long since withdrawn into his own uncommunicative shell. She then turned her attention to a young couple, Jon Jonsson and Karin Tipers, who she had learned had been in love before the migration but by colony rules were prohibited from marrying. It struck her as particularly poignant that the lovers had to arise in the middle of the night to work side by side for long hours in the bakery. To Miss Lagerlöf, the suffering caused by this unnatural renunciation was folly. She decided to use them as central characters. Anna, who would appear as "Mrs. Gordon," was given a fairly sympathetic treatment as a strong leader, but embedded in her characterization was a warning against adopting the views and regulations of more powerful others.[4]

Before Miss Lagerlöf and her companion left Jerusalem for Constantinople, Anna had extracted a promise that she would mention to the Swedish plenipotentiary that Anna and her house were being systematically denigrated by the U.S. consul. By the time she was ready to leave, the author had grasped a lot, if not everything, about the inner workings of the colony. She gave Anna a long searching look and remarked pleasantly: "Mrs. Spafford, you are the best-looking woman I ever saw to be so wicked."[5]

The Swedes came to their hotel with gifts to see the ladies off and were standing by the city gate singing wonderful Swedish songs as they passed through. Pity misted the travelers' eyes as they waved goodbye. Later they would visit Nås, bringing the Dala folk gifts from their friends in Jerusalem. "I wish a painter could have captured those simple people while we were speaking . . . To watch them listen and ponder, falling silent to try and reconcile our account with what their relatives had written to them. They had been expecting us. We were the first people who had seen the Colony in Jerusalem to arrive with greetings to Nås, and their gratitude was very moving," Sophie Elkan recorded in her diary.[6]

In the sweeping two-part novel *Jerusalem* that resulted, it was clear that Miss Lagerlöf believed the Swedes' sacrifice had been in vain, that commitment to God was best reflected in loyalty to country, land, and the traditional values that she concluded the Nås pilgrims had abandoned in their quest for salvation elsewhere. It was seen by reviewers worldwide as the quintessential statement of Swedish identity, alive with personal tensions and philosophical conflict. *Jerusalem* was an instant literary sensation, translated into many languages, and in 1909 Selma Lagerlöf became the first woman to win the Nobel Prize for Literature, for the body of her work, but principally for this magnificent book.

Apparently unfazed by its implicit criticisms, surprised to find herself the central figure in such a prestigious epic, Anna was delighted to claim the famous writer as a friend. But she did not tell her people about *Jerusalem* and refused to let them see it. It remained on Anna's "index" until well past her death, and for many years the Swedes were ignorant of its existence.[7] Much later, an annual pageant based on Miss Lagerlöf's novel was initiated in Nås, attended by thousands celebrating the haunting story of the migration to the American Colony in Jerusalem. Afterward, Scandinavians of every class made a point of stopping in at the colony when visiting the holy city. Anna received them with dignity, and later her daughter and successor, Bertha, welcomed them. Finally, in one of history's ironic twists, there would come a day when the memory of the famous novelist had faded, while the fame of the American Colony soared as one of the most beautiful and historic hotels in the Middle East.

The New Dispensation

*And they became of one heart and one soul; and
no one spoke of anything they had as theirs, only
everything they had in common.*
                                        —The Apostolic Faith

Anna was a woman uncommonly blessed. Raised by an authoritarian father, groomed in the violence and poverty of the slums, exposed to abuse and fear—her childish imagination stimulated by the twisted fantasies of her ignorant Norwegian caretaker—she was a survivor extraordinaire. Now she held dominion over a small universe that many in the outside world were calling "an idealistic Apostolic commune."[1] With her uncanny knack for organization and sharp nose for human weakness, Anna intuitively understood the importance of instilling loyalty to the colony above family or country of origin. She did her best to break any interfering bonds, building control in many ways, especially through her tight grip on the colony's purse strings. A young man never kept a tip, nor a girl a gift. Even children could not keep butterflies or flowers plucked at a picnic—they were required to hand these in to be pressed and framed for sale at the store. Like the superb despot she was, Anna did her best to crush individual spirit and enhance submission through fear and awe. Only the members ever heard the terrifying gutter language she unfurled, pink with fury and shaking her fists, especially at her womenfolk. "These wicked women," she could rage, "these wives, these mothers, these devils, are no better than street sluts with puppies!" Mothers who showed too much affection for their children were condemned as "idolaters" and a delegation was sent to their room to announce they were to be indefinitely separated.[2]

Her "theology" was vague and contradictory, but agile opportunist that she was, Anna was able to wave away such disappointments as the tardy Messiah. The Advent was delayed because her followers had been "iniquitous." Credulous and pious, most members did not want to think they had subscribed to a faith that led nowhere. They persisted in believing that Anna was in direct contact with God—something she, too, apparently genuinely believed. As Edith Larsson wrote years later: "This gave her limitless faith in herself . . . she spoke with authority, and no one dared to doubt her words, and they came ever more under her influence."[3]

Yet of her many skills, perhaps her sense of timing helped her most. So far, she had managed to control the combustible force of sexual attraction. But now children were growing up and becoming teenagers. A soft glance here, hands brushing accidentally there, created all-too-natural tensions. No matter how vehemently Anna declared that "marriage was license to sin," or preached "overcoming the flesh," there were consequences to this proximity as well as to their exposure through school or work with the outside world. For some time, Anna had instituted a system of "watchmen" who reported on their activities and grilled them on their thoughts. One day in the morning assembly, a girl who had shown an unacceptable level of interest in the opposite sex suddenly shouted, "What is man without a woman?" Her mother and sister promptly hustled her out and stood by as her hair was shorn. The girl, who had attempted to rouge her cheeks and pretended to be in high heels by walking on tiptoes, was confined in a nearby medieval tower rented by the colony. For months the young listened to her cries as they went about their work and learned a hard lesson. When she was finally brought back and reinstated with the other girls, they saw her cast her eyes to the ground whenever a man passed by.[4]

Naturally, these incidents were kept from the outside. But Anna, ever the realist, decided it was time to countenance young men and women "going together," and accordingly received a "message." She alone decided who was to be "engaged" and to whom. While this did not always mesh with the wishes of those involved, it suited Bertha and Frederick perfectly and gave legitimacy to a relationship that everyone inside the colony and outside in Jerusalem had already recognized. Still, Anna continued to withhold permission for her daughter to marry Frederick, and for the time being at least, Bertha impatiently acquiesced.

In the meantime, Grace Spafford, as second daughter, was enjoying the competition between young men in the colony for her favor and with it a possibility of belonging to the reigning "Family." For a time Grace anointed Reverend Baldwin's son, Furman, as her escort. Furman, a talented and energetic twenty-five-year-old in the Photo Department, was given leeway to join Grace for buggy rides or solitary canters on horseback in the hills. But when she suddenly spurned him, and Furman put a borrowed gun to his head and pulled the trigger, the blast shook the colony and caused ugly gossip in the city.[5]

The entire colony was in an uproar. Mercifully, Furman had survived the suicide attempt, although in bad shape. In haste, a meeting was called of the agitated members, where it was decided that prayer, applications of oil, and the usual laying on of hands might not be sufficient to guarantee Furman's recovery. For the first time, it was agreed that a doctor should be called. Anna hurried across the road to the room where Furman lay in a house shared with other men. She stood at his bedside, demanding he write a statement exonerating the colony. Two hours passed, therefore, before Frederick Vester was sent to the U.S. Consulate to report the incident and try to explain how it could have happened. Dr. Merrill heard Frederick out in cool silence, then commented acerbically on the time gap before directing his vice-consul and his *kavass* to hurry to the colony. The men were relieved to find Furman conscious and able to summon the strength to speak. In a fairly clear voice the young man offered to dictate a statement, which the vice-consul wrote down: "I F. O. Baldwin, July 14, 1901, living at the American Colony, whose principles are to overcome everything natural such as wishing to be first, jealousy—in a moment of desperation left the dinner table came over here and shot myself, no one being in the house at the time. I only hope God will forgive me and the holy and pure inhabitants of the American Colony for the disgrace I have brought them."[6]

At this point, Merrill had not laid eyes on any of the colonists for almost two years. In turn, they had avoided all contact with the consulate, though the colony's efforts to blacken his name had never flagged, nor had Merrill's reports about their activities to the State Department. In fact, just five days earlier he had written State that a newly arrived Turkish governor had received one of their endless petitions impugning him. The governor had torn it up in Merrill's presence and dropped it into the wastebasket. Merrill had also reported that the Turkish authorities had no objection to burials resuming in a newly purchased American cemetery, despite violent protests from the colony. "The shameful falsehoods which these people retail wholesale about the U.S. Government, the Consul General in Constantinople, the Consulate in Jerusalem, and first, last, midst, and without end the poor Consul myself, are enough to make the very stones in the streets cry out," his dispatch had concluded wearily. "But Mr. Merrill still lives," he added in an attempt at bravado. "And I have not heard that the United States Government was likely to fall."[7]

Considering the alarming nature of this new colony scandal, Merrill's notification to State of the suicide attempt was laconic. But he and the department had long shared accord on matters pertaining to the Spaffordites, so he merely enclosed Furman's statement to the vice-consul with the bare facts unadorned with further commentary.

Within the colony, the tragedy cast a gloom over the young for several years, and Anna no longer felt the necessity of further "messages" appointing "going together" between couples. When she finally resumed this practice, she made sure that her daughter Grace chose John Whiting, since he was due a very large inheritance. That he loved another woman was not viewed as an impediment.

At last, however, a moment arrived that was propitious. In March 1904, a luxury liner brought eight hundred delegates to Jerusalem for the World's Sunday School Convention. To contain the delegation meetings, a tremendous tent, taller than any building in the city, was erected and filled with a thousand folding chairs specially imported from New York for the occasion. The colony piano and harmonium, and even the colony's by-now famous choir, were lent for the huge prayer meetings. Anna had known about this religious gathering for months ahead, having been requested to provide rooms for delegates. It was the perfect moment, she now decided, to announce a "special dispensation." The morning assembly was electrified when she looked fondly over her gathered flock. Everyone sensed that something important was afoot and listened expectantly. "The time has come," Anna began solemnly, "when marriage may occur in the right way." There was not a sound from those in the room as she went on to praise their sacrifices, their faith, and their efforts to abandon sin and to rid themselves of fleshly desires. Finally they had won their battle for purity, she announced. And she was bringing them a new and powerful message: "Now we may give to Caesar what belongs to Caesar!"[8] It was time for the biggest and most spectacular wedding ever held in Jerusalem.

Earlier, Anna had exchanged letters with two rich Americans who had underwritten the convention.[9] They were staying as her guests, and their prominent friends were paying well for the privilege of filling every room at the colony. The grand salon and other public spaces were festooned by excited members in a fever of creativity. Garlands made from flowers picked the day before by the colony children were hung from the rafters, and bouquets were everywhere, turning the mansion into a fragrant bower. On March 24, with the pastor of the German Church of the Redeemer officiating in a Lutheran ceremony, Bertha Spafford, twenty-six, and Frederick Vester, thirty-four, were pronounced man and wife.[10] Forgotten at last, it seemed, was the church as "Babylon." The house buzzed with hundreds of guests from all sectors of Jerusalem society, and the wedding was followed by a reception under the convention's vast tent. In attendance were the same Turkish governor who had torn up the colony's petition three years before, many of the resident consuls, even a very reluctant Dr. Merrill, bowing to social necessity. Rubbing cordial shoulders were Arab sheikhs in turbans and robes, Arab gentry, merchants, and grocers in tasseled red fezzes, veiled Muslim women, bedouin chieftains with curved swords and daggers, Sephardic and Ashkenazic Jews, and as many of the dazzled conventioneers as could squeeze themselves in.

The stunning couple—Bertha in an elegant wedding dress lovingly designed and sewn by colonists, Frederick bristling with a mustache like the kaiser's—had waited ten long years for this moment. Their reward was gifts without end. The Old House on Mount Bezetha was put at the bridal pair's disposal, and now spilled over with carved tables, chairs, cupboards, a handsome sideboard, panels of sweet-smelling cedar, and porcelain and silver sets—all hauled up the steep steps by colony menfolk. They were even given a piano, although that challenge could be met only by Jerusalem's strongest *hamal*, a muscular midget who carried it on his back secured by a strap tied around his forehead and clamped between his teeth. Visitors gasped at the abundance and remarked the house looked like a well-stocked museum. After the World's Sunday School Convention closed, after the wedding of the century, after the delegates and wedding guests bade each other goodbye, the great convention ship sailed away. Comfortably settled in a flower-filled suite, Bertha and Frederick began the first of at least two honeymoon trips as guests of Anna's friends the two American millionaires.

The American Colony was changed forever. It had taken its dignified place in the center of Jerusalem society, but this "new dispensation" brought with it challenges for Anna. She would not be able to control all that would flow from the change in her teachings. At the same time, Anna was beginning to feel her age. She adored her daughter and increasingly needed her support to run the colony. She had conceded the impossibility of continuing to resist Bertha's desire to marry the man she loved, and now would have to countenance future weddings. Once the colonists adjusted to their mixed feelings toward a message that put previous values into strange dislocation, Anna allowed weddings to commence almost immediately. Most were between the young, but a number of aging members, even some sixty years old or older, began plighting their troths. These were simple affairs, spare, yet quietly joyous nonetheless. Anna did her best to caution the couples. She reminded them "that intercourse, other than for procreation, is sin."[11] When confessions were forced in the morning assembly, and flush-faced couples subjected to Anna's rebukes, it spurred some to leave, departing without compensation after years of labor.

The rescinding of the marriage ban came too late for one pair. The baker Jon Jonsson, whose love for Karin Tipers had so touched Selma Lagerlöf, had already abandoned hope that he could win Karin from her faith or, more probably, from her dread of sex acquired in the previous eight years. Secretly, Jon wrote his family for money, and his parents, who had always opposed the colony, let his letter be published. Anna happened to read the Swedish newspaper story and discovered the betrayal. She compelled eighteen of the remaining Swedes, most hurtfully including Karin, to sign a protest letter to the paper accusing Jon of being "a person of the flesh." Jon was then subjected to a campaign of "shunning." When he refused to ask Anna's forgiveness, an ugly encounter followed with Anna attacking him physically with her fists.[12] He left, somehow making his way to America, and in May 1904 received a letter from one of Lars Lind's brothers. Eric Lind, shortly to be expelled himself with a total of $10 from the colony treasury, wrote:

> I believe you have heard that they are getting married now. It seems so idiotic when I see them chasing after each other. I laugh by myself since I cannot laugh with anyone else. And this thing that we now may marry is God's divine plan which has been revealed to one and one only, Mrs. Spafford . . . The speeches at the meetings are the same, day in and day out. I put a little "French" book into the Bible so I can amuse myself. You better believe that I have become a very God-fearing man since you left . . . No, I think I will soon change my way of life. I can't sit here and read the rest of my life. I have still not seen anything godly here. And if I haven't found it now, I will never find it.[13]

As for Furman Baldwin, the bullet remained in his temple, marked forever by a telltale blue circle left by the gunpowder. He married one of the girls who had come from Chicago, and when she died, after they had settled in America, he married an orphan from the colony who had escaped herself and wrote a generous memoir revealing some of the cruelty she had experienced, but emphasizing her affection for many of the colonists during a fascinating and tumultuous time in the history of Palestine.[14]

Triumph

Mother Spafford was a wonderful woman, a
mother to us all. She loved us with a holy love.
She held us in fear and trembling.

—Mathilda Larsson

Anna's orderly machine rolled into a twentieth century that was changing rapidly. On the whole it was a good period for most of the hundred-odd remaining colonists. Not only did the members take pleasure in the settled feeling resulting from the marriages, but the older members at least continued to be unified in the conviction that "our religion was unique, and that we were in the process of developing a plan through which the world would learn to understand and be brought back to God," as Edith Larsson later wrote, struggling to explain an ethos that had held them together for so long.[1]

Bertha, on the other hand, was determined to put behind the old ways and join the city's social cream. As she and her husband were charming, intelligent, energetic, and now rich, her efforts were paying off. The company as well as the advice of the attractive Vesters was sought by newly arriving merchants, scientists, artists, diplomats, military officials, and every prominent visitor seeking to understand the ways of Jerusalem. A tennis court was added and became a center of attraction. Jerusalem's first bicycles were ridden with much hilarity by the colony's more daring members. Ever-larger crowds attended the annual Fourth of July celebration, where hundreds of guests munched home-made donuts, drank lemonade, and watched colony girls dance quadrilles costumed in star-spangled blue bodices and striped red skirts, while colony boys outdid themselves in gymnastic competitions, in a grand festival of intercity mingling.

There was great excitement when the colony won the bid to install the first telephone system in Jerusalem. The chief of police had decided his headquarters by the Jaffa Gate should be connected to stations elsewhere in the Old City as well as the *serai*, or government offices, by the Tower of Antonia. Abandoning their classes, the colony boys clambered for months over rooftops, taking care not to alarm the harems within or damage any ancient monuments as they used ingenuity and agility to wire the city. The colony wrested a concession to allow the first private connection linking the Big House on Nablus Road to the Vester store at the Jaffa Gate, which caused their bedouin friends to say it was amazing that one could "step on the tail of this long dog and hear it bark a mile away."[2]

The colony youth often served as guides to the learned men come to dig out Palestine's past, connections that helped turn them into knowledgeable amateur archaeologists. Alone among infidels, they were allowed to visit the Haram's sacred precincts without official permission. As they lived in a community that frowned on demonstrations of affection, lightness and laughter came from kindly Arab friends, as well as from Rolla Floyd, who had long made clear the benefits of irreverence. Now elderly and hugely fat, he teased the boys who had spent years attending Bertha on her donkey. Just days before her wedding, he had told them that when she became Mrs. Vester, they no longer needed to help her mount her ass. "Those whom God hath joined together," opined Rolla, rolling his eyes mischievously, "let no man put ass-under." The boys loved it.[3]

When a baby girl, Anna Grace, was born to Bertha in 1905, no one was surprised that a doctor attended. Dutiful to her mother, however, Bertha gave the baby to be baptized not in the Lutheran church but in a special ceremony at the colony conducted by Brother Jacob. The baby was spoiled and doted on by Swedish spinsters, and the younger girls loved being asked to babysit. The grand salon now witnessed parties and dancing attended by Jerusalem's attractive younger set. One day old Olaf Larsson happened to see this shocking innovation. After he protested at the morning assembly and Anna told him that he would no longer be welcome at the meetings, he was seldom seen again. A few years later his wife found him in his shed, unconscious and dying from a stroke, his forehead resting on his Bible opened to Corinthians: "Love is patient and mild."[4]

"It was most pitiful about Mr. Larsson because [Mother Spafford] gave him the hardest messages," remembered his wife, Mathilda, in an interview years later. "She thought he had not spared others, and now she would not spare him . . . Poor Mr. Larsson! Poor Mr. Larsson." Mathilda's grief and guilt were severe. Anna told her to "be joyful at God's will" and reminded her that when Horatio Spafford died, she had danced.[5]

Consul Merrill's antipathy had not waned, but his was a lone voice now, and the city had learned to turn a deaf ear to his complaints at dinner gatherings. His unsalaried vice-consul, Herbert Clark, whose real business was the tourist industry, had been a great help in expanding the colony's hostelry, sending far more guests than either Cook & Son or Rolla Floyd.[6] But Clark did not attempt to remonstrate with Merrill. His consular position was useful, so he kept his appreciation to himself. When the colony store ran up the American flag, he simply sighed when Merrill made them take it down, sharing amusement with others among what were now twelve consulates in the ever-expanding city. These days, it was evident that the colony's undertakings were beneficial, however peculiar their religious views. What was past was past, was the general feeling.

During Holy Week 1906, an American journalist visited Jerusalem. It was the time when the Christian Easter coincided with the Jewish Passover and the Muslims' riotous festival of Nebi Musa.[7] These were taxing times for the Turkish gendarmerie as multitudes from all faiths converged on every square and corner of the city. But it was the struggle between Christian sects to light their candles during the "holy fire" ceremony in the Church of the Holy Sepulchre that the beefed-up garrison most dreaded. Invariably it turned into an appalling melee as Orthodox and Latin bodies jammed together, and all too often some were crushed to death, even as the Muslim guards tried to protect the frantic infidels from spilling their blood on the ancient stones.

This was also the time for thousands of Orthodox Russian pilgrims to dip shrouds in the blessed waters of the Jordan and take them home to be wrapped in when they were buried. Herded by *kavasses* holding whips, marching four or five abreast, and clutching their crucifixes, samovars, and crusts of bread, the ragged army topped the last hill, saw the holy city for the first time, and burst into song for which the whole city paused to listen. A thousand voices old and young filled the air like music from a heavenly organ. The colony, hearing the gorgeous sound from afar, always looked forward to the sight of the long columns of ragged muzhiks plodding and singing along the road past their gate.

Alexander Hume Ford had wished to see this extraordinary sight as well as the holy places and other spectacles enlivening Jerusalem at Eastertide. With a companion from Texas, Ford had been one of the first tourists to ride the nearly completed Hejaz Railway. The two men entered the city from Transjordan and immediately went to the U.S. consul to pay their respects. Ford had heard of the American Colony back in Chicago and, like all his scribbling brethren looking for local color, asked Dr. Merrill what he knew about them. Little could Ford have anticipated the journalistic bombshell that suddenly fell into his lap.

"I have since seen Vesuvius in eruption, her most magnificent display in thirty-four years, but the memory palls before the recollection of that half-hour with the American consul in Jerusalem," he wrote in a devastating story published at the end of the year.[8]

As few in the city were ignorant of Merrill's abiding bête noire, neither did many know that a persistent sore throat and cough had been bothering the consul. It had become increasingly difficult just to speak. Acutely, he felt the press of time and strove in the evenings to complete a grand work on Palestine's archaeology. This and the fatigue he felt as he helped organize what would become one of America's most distinguished overseas scholarly institutions, the American Schools of Oriental Research, had the consul in a state of near collapse.[9] To have to listen to this traveling newspaper fellow's frivolous questions seemed a final straw.

"Are you friends of these people?" Merrill's strained voice grated as he leaned ominously over his desk. "If you are, I shall not receive you!"

The men were taken aback. "In a bitter storm of vituperation," as Ford described it, Merrill venomously dismissed the colony. "It does not exist," he declared. It could not be considered "American," and "the stench of their 'goings on' was the most putrid odor in the nostrils of Jerusalem," recorded the fascinated journalist. Unable to check himself, Merrill went too far. The women were immoral and "trained" their children to be immoral; the products sold in the colony's store were fraudulent—they had not been made by the colonists. As for Mrs. Spafford, he all but strangled on his ire. Ford tried to pursue it calmly. How could Merrill know—since he claimed never to have crossed the colony's threshold? What specific charge could the consul make?

Suddenly Merrill was overwhelmed by the years of contending with the colony. He had spent precious hours writing reports to the State Department on their debts, treatment of children, escapees' testimonies. As a patriotic American, he had endured the shame he felt that this mixed rabble of deluded vagabonds brought his country; as a churchman, he had suffered for their hatred for his church. Urgently, he wished to be free from them forever—and free from further visits from the idly curious, like this reporter. He rose from his chair, sputtering. He told Ford and his companion that if they visited the colony, he should not wish to see them again.[10]

Naturally, Ford was delighted. He could already feel the story writing itself as he made his way to the American Colony. Having been "carried off" his feet by the "molten" flow, the journalist was disposed to lend Anna's community a sympathetic ear. When Anna descended to meet him and offer tea and cakes, she recognized her opportunity immediately. The wished-for hour, she realized, had come at last. In her possession, waiting for just such a heaven-sent opportunity, were some incriminating photographs she had acquired when the colony surprised the Reverend William Eddy sneaking back to Jerusalem the year before on a mission to exhume buried bodies.

Eddy had returned in 1905 at the request of the Presbyterian Board of Missions with instructions to reopen the English cemetery as quietly as possible and transfer buried Americans to a recently purchased and much larger American cemetery. Alerted by Arab workmen, the colonists converged on the open pit at dusk armed with cameras, catching Eddy in the midst of sorting out the impossible mess of broken remains from the debacle eight years before. When the unfortunate cleric attempted to escape, the cameras clicked as he put up his hand, as he ducked, as he tried to shield his face. The grotesque collection of boxes and bones was also recorded, and some members fanned out through the city to alert anyone of importance of this latest disgrace by the Presbyterian board.

Professor Gustav Dalman, director of the German Archaeological Institute, was summoned to the site. Since becoming Sweden's consul, the professor had taken an interest in the Swedish members and given them Swedish passports, something the Americans refused to ask of Merrill. Dalman studied the chaos of broken boxes and concluded that Eddy could not possibly discern which body was which, and therefore was making an arbitrary choice.[11] Triumphant, the colonists insisted that Eddy stay until they finished a careful examination of each box and supervised its tender reburial. Finally, as night fell, Eddy was allowed to depart with what were clearly random bones but which he hoped would nonetheless satisfy the families who had wished their dead reinterred in the new cemetery.[12] The colonists returned home to develop the pictures in the photo laboratory.

Now a journalist had arrived most fortuitously, innocent of the role he would be assigned by Anna, or of the bitter history of skirmishes between herself and the consuls. Ford believed that he was conducting his interview with laudable delicacy, taking care to avoid undue pain to this regal, white-haired matron beside him whose face was "kindly but firm." Nor was he the only one that afternoon sipping tea and listening to Anna's tales of shipwreck, loss, survival, and utopian hopes so heartlessly ridiculed and degraded by the U.S. government. A number of American ladies from two cruising ships were also gathered around Anna and "were in tears over the cruel charges they had heard."[13]

Appleton's Magazine featured Ford's story in its December issue, accompanied by photographs of children in Fourth of July costumes, decorously dressed ladies, and handsome young men at leisure or at work, topped off with a photo of the radiant bride and groom surrounded by their elegant attendants. Apparently, either the editors or their lawyers had thought it best to pass up photographs of Eddy cowering in the cemetery. The State Department, for twenty-five years on the receiving end of reports on the American Colony, surely must have shuddered when *Appleton's Magazine* went on the stands, as it enjoyed a wide readership. The Presbyterian Board of Foreign Missions, Consul General Dickinson, and the U.S. consuls Wallace and Merrill could only have been apoplectic. The Reverend William K. Eddy, however, was spared the furor. On November 4, one month before the issue came out, he collapsed and died of a heart attack hunting bear in the mountains behind Sidon.[14]

Truths, half-truths, and out-and-out falsehoods were mixed, twisted, and manipulated for maximum effect in the article. Neither the representatives of the church nor the U.S. government came off well. Wallace, "a Christian clergyman," had it hard enough, accused of personally removing and dumping bodies into a pit in "the dead of night." But Merrill was blamed for seriatim savagery so shocking and so capricious that were *Appleton's* not such a respected publication, it would have been difficult for a reader to credit.

The standard story of the little band—which "carried absolute unselfishness to its extreme," according to Ford—was retold affectingly. It claimed Mr. and Mrs. Spafford were the "only wealthy ones to give their all"; that Horatio's "genius" was such that when he died "the Colony was well organized and had begun to prosper"; that Merrill searched "for relics" and broke up "freshly interred bodies," engendering "the most bitter religious warfare Jerusalem has known in a century"; that on seeing the broken body of her father, his daughter Bertha had been "taken home in a fainting condition"; and that only "the skilled generalship" of Mrs. Spafford had sheltered her friends and husband from a "War of the Graveyard" until after her beloved's death.

Ford's article glowed with admiration for the colony's accomplishments. "The education of Syrian womanhood fell into the hands of Yankee citizens . . . with more than one thousand children under the charge of the Americans," while "the Turkish Government . . . and Turkish governors, majors, ministers of education and chiefs of police vied with each other as to who could do most for the Colony that was uplifting the youth of Turkey." All the while, the fiendish Dr. Merrill was contriving with the colonists' relatives to "stop the funds" to which they were rightfully entitled. Merrill had put Mary Whiting "in prison" when her brother came to see her until "friends cabled to the Department of State . . . and Mrs. Whiting's release was ordered and Mr. Merrill removed from office until another administration replaced him."

The distortions and inaccuracies were endless. Merrill's efforts to separate Mary from her children resulted in a case where Mary "was absolutely vindicated" and the case "thrown out of court . . . on the ground that the evidence in favor of the community was so clear and convincing, and the absence of any evidence against it so conspicuous." Further, Merrill collected his trove of scandalous allegations "in the form of affidavits from native Mohammedans who have since stated that they gave false testimony for a consideration." The plaudits in letters from Selma Lagerlöf and Ismail Bey Husseini were quoted. The sheer preposterousness, the article continued, of suggesting that the dignified sixty-four-year-old Mrs. Spafford, or any other of the white-haired men and women sitting with the reporter in the parlor—especially the much-abused Mrs. Whiting, whom Mr. Merrill had caused such terrible suffering—could engage in "midnight orgies" was utterly laughable.

Mrs. Whiting, Ford noted sympathetically, "sat with lowered head, for she is very old." Mary Whiting was then fifty-six, eight years younger than Anna. Doubtless, her head did hang low, and probably it was true that the experiences she had endured since she came to Jerusalem had aged her greatly, but she was not to be the only one to suffer now. The defamatory article ended with a treacly salute to the Christmas spirit—it being the Christmas issue—with Merrill as the villain persecuting the "little group of struggling Christians." With a brutal coup de grâce, the article concluded: "He, alone, in all Jerusalem, stands aloof at the anniversary of the time when Christ came to make one brotherhood of mankind."

When Merrill saw the article, he was struggling to resume life after an operation on his larynx that left him unable to speak. In May, after his Easter interview with the journalist, his good friend George Wheeler, head of the English Mission Hospital, had been concerned. "I was very sorry to find you looking depressed and specially noticed that your voice was no better—and if anything worse," said Dr. Wheeler, who like Merrill was saddened by the recent death of their friend John Dickson, the English consul who had also had his tussles with the colony. "As your physician and friend, I have warned you . . . you must have change at once and for a time absolute rest and quiet. It is imperative also that you should see a London specialist and that without delay. One cannot trifle with such symptoms."[15]

Merrill, driving himself to finish his projects, delayed for months. Finally he and Mrs. Merrill journeyed to London, where a specialist confirmed that he had cancer. "The trouble," as Mrs. Merrill wrote State, "proved to be more serious than was anticipated."[16] An operation was followed by an extended rest in a private nursing home, before Merrill, equipped with a pad and pencil, could return to the holy city just in time to receive the full impact of Ford's article in *Appleton's*.

Back in the United States, the Reverend and Mrs. Edwin Wallace were living in Greensburg, Pennsylvania, where they had moved in 1899. After relinquishing the consular post to Merrill, Wallace had presided at the First Presbyterian Church over a large and prosperous congregation in a parish that dated from the Revolution. In the eight years of his tenure, Wallace had pushed for a number of reforms and had made clear his view that clergy—notably himself—were underpaid for the duties expected. This had riled some on the vestry, but on the whole he was well liked and his management considered "somewhat turbulent but in many ways constructive."[17]

Everyone in Greensburg, it seemed, read *Appleton's Magazine.* Those with whom Wallace had differed now seized on it. Profoundly shaken, his honor as a man of the cloth besmirched, Wallace tendered his resignation. Despite the reluctance of most of the parish to accept it, Wallace insisted. Proud and decisive, he said: "In my judgment, for the best interests of this church, which I have always tried to put first, and for my own good which I must also consider, this pastorate should come to an end . . . Let me further assure you that the decision is final and the resignation irrevocable."[18]

On Sunday, September 29, 1907, Wallace preached a farewell sermon to a packed church. According to a Greensburg daily paper, "He said that he bore no ill will toward any person. He referred very feelingly to the friendships he had formed here and said that it was no easy thing to break the ties . . . There were not many dry eyes in the congregation."[19] Now Wallace was ready to sue Appleton & Company.

Merrill, humiliated and mortally ill, wanted to bring suit as well, but the State Department refused to give him permission, as it would have been "inappropriate" and against policy for State to open its records to the public. Without those records of twenty-five years' service, Merrill would have been left without the necessary evidence he needed to demonstrate that he had been libeled. After the shocking assassination of President William McKinley in 1901, the succeeding president, Theodore Roosevelt, had installed new officers at State who now agreed that it would be better for all concerned if Merrill were removed from the controversies in Jerusalem. Accordingly, the aging scholar was summoned home. State soon reassigned their expert on Palestinian archaeology to head a consulate in Guiana. One can only imagine what Merrill thought when he learned he was to head a mission in an obscure French colony on the northeast coast of South America, flanked by Suriname and Brazil and known principally for the notorious penal colony Devil's Island.[20]

Merrill let his wife do most of the talking when they arrived in Boston and were interviewed by the *Boston Sunday Herald* on August 18, 1907. But he did manage to convey that his new position was a "promotion." After conferring with Washington, he scribbled on his pad to the reporter, he expected to transfer as soon as possible.[21] His tenure was to be short, as on January 22, 1909, Merrill died at the age of seventy-two. He was buried in Mountain View Cemetery, Oakland, California, where the stone cross over his grave can be seen to this day.

Reverend Wallace spent two years in a costly litigation with Appleton & Company that, as an underpaid clergyman, he could ill afford. Depositions were taken from many of the colonists and colony friends in Jerusalem, but not from Anna. To at least one of the charges in Ford's article, Wallace was vulnerable: he had not let the colonists see the testimony of Mr. and Mrs. Adamson, yet had shown it, or at least quoted parts of it, to "religious journals antagonistic to the American Colony . . . or used by them to create prejudice."[22] Nevertheless, he won his defamation suit and was cleared of wrongdoing in the cemetery controversy— too late to bring any satisfaction to his deceased predecessor in

Jerusalem. In April 1909, a jury in the U.S. Circuit Court for the Southern District of New York decided in his favor, but the jury must have found the nocturnal removal and breakup of bodies distasteful, as they awarded him only $250, not the $50,000 in damages that he had sought. Wallace finished his book on Jerusalem and worked in private business in the Pittsburgh area before serving again as a respected pastor of two other churches—the second position lasting until he reached the ripe age of eighty-five. He died at ninety-six in Florida, on August 15, 1960.

Possibly he read the book that Bertha wrote, *Our Jerusalem*, published in 1950 after the city had survived two world wars. By then a white-haired social queen of Jerusalem and legend in her own right, she mentioned nothing about his winning his case. Indeed, she left the impression that he had not. Instead, she averred that "Mr. Wallace had to resign his church" after Ford's story in *Appleton's* and that he had sued the magazine, concluding with barely contained relish that "the trial had undoubtedly cost Rev. Edwin Wallace several thousand dollars," while her mother's other opponent, Dr. Merrill, underwent an operation "that removed his power of speech." Although she writes that "the Arabs were convinced that God had punished Dr. Merrill for his persecution of the American Colony," it is difficult not to assume that actually Anna, her followers, and Bertha herself were the ones who believed God had stricken down a man reckless enough to oppose a "clearer light."

"It must be remembered," Bertha cautioned in concluding her chapter on the cemetery wars, "that the case brought by the Rev. E. Wallace was against Appleton's Magazine and not against the American Colony. For us, there was no redress other than having been vindicated. But a persecution that had lasted twenty-five years was ended."[23] And so it was that through her daughter, Anna had the final triumphant word.

In Jerusalem, as 1907 came to its dramatic close and a new year opened, triumphalism seemed in the very wind. By then, the colony had purchased a cemetery of its own on Mount Scopus, where henceforth the colony dead would rest. The colony had also seen a new U.S. consul choose John Whiting, engaged to Grace Spafford, as his vice-consul, giving him an unpaid but important role that lasted on and off until 1917 to the great benefit of the membership. It was not just Anna and the colonists who had seen their enemies brought low. In Constantinople the Young Turks had staged a revolution. A dashing twenty-seven-year-old Turkish officer, Ismail Enver, fleeing from arrest, had been joined by mutinous troops in a revolt that rocked the empire and put Enver's name on all lips. Troops marched against the capital, and Sultan Abdul Hamid was forced to restore a constitution suspended since 1876, although he was allowed to stay on his throne.

Plans for a coup had simmered for years in clandestine cells scattered throughout the empire. Now a disciplined group composed mainly of officers emerged to lead the reform movement. It called itself the Committee of Union and Progress, or the CUP. There was euphoria everywhere, as people were ecstatic at the prospect of reform. At last, they believed, there would be some kind of autonomy for the different peoples and, even better, freedom from usurious taxes and a broken system that enslaved its people and kept them in ignorance and poverty. In Jerusalem, Arabs ran through the streets, crying, "Hurriya!" or "Freedom!" To Anna, looking over her colony with pride, and unaware of the upheaval these events would precipitate in the near future, it seemed a truly golden moment indeed.

War

Henceforth, we are all brothers. There are no
longer Bulgars, Greeks, Roumans, Jews, Mo-
hammedans; under the same blue sky we are all
equal; we glory being Ottomans.

—Enver Bey

At best, in any society, freedom is a relative condition. This was as true for colony members as it was for the peoples of the Ottoman Empire despite the triumph of the Young Turks and the promise of better things to come. To be sure, after the revolution of 1908, it seemed that the old bonds preventing freedom of expression and movement were breaking down, but the delirium was not destined to last— neither for the peoples of the empire nor for Anna's diminutive domain. Through difficult times Anna had held her colony together by fealty to her and faith in the millennium. Similarly, as the Latin and Orthodox Christians of Ottoman Europe bolted from his empire, the Ottoman sultan had attempted to bind the vast majority remaining, the Muslims, through their attachment to Islam—whether they were Sunni, Shia, Sufi, Alawi, Kharijite, Ismaili, Yazidi, Druze, Ash'ari, Zikri, Kalam, or any of the seventy or so other sects drawing inspiration from the angel Gabriel's messages to the Prophet—despite their many doctrinal differences.

Now a new regime was in place. Initially the reformers were as optimistic as the population at large. Their plans were grand: to push the empire into the twentieth century under an all-inclusive Ottomanism, to secularize its institutions, to banish corruption, to revise family law, to emancipate women, and to put aside old taboos. But confronting irresistible forces pulling the empire asunder, they acknowledged a need to retain the caliphate. Suddenly reduced to a figurehead, the sultan no longer ruled, but as the Prophet's successor he still reigned as the Shadow of Allah and Leader of the Faithful. In the eyes of the restive Arabs, this was as it should be. Full of hope and great excitement, prominent Arab friends of the colony packed their bags and headed for the capital to take their places as delegates to the Ottoman parliament, where, among other things, they could raise the issue of Zionism and its impact on Palestine. At this point, still glad to call themselves Ottoman subjects, they departed to participate in the longed-for elections that, they hoped, would give their fellow Arabs the autonomy for which they had been yearning.

In the American Colony in Jerusalem, the "new dispensation" sanctioning marriages in 1904 had stirred its own hopes and expectations. Parents could raise their own babies now—something observed rather wistfully by orphaned youngsters who had grown up under the harsh discipline of men and women who had never had children, who had never allowed them to have anything exclusively their own, not even a longed-for pet.[1] By now, a number of families were living in houses. But they could be arbitrarily moved, as these were the property of the management and registered in the name of Anna's son-in-law, Frederick Vester. Anna and Bertha had not relinquished control over the details of the members' lives, maintaining it through the simple expedient of summary expulsion. Any person showing a tendency to question the status quo was sent packing. There was never a hearing. The deed was done quickly and efficiently before support for the erring members could be mustered. Bertha, increasingly sharing the reins with her aging mother, was able to say, and frequently did, that she and her mother were providing the "necessities."[2] However, as the buttress of the early faith in the Second Coming eroded, and a father was still not allowed a bank account of his own, members began to feel more and more acutely the humiliation of asking for money to buy a suit or even a pair of shoes.[3]

Outsiders who knew the colony well were often baffled that so many grown men and women continued to cede control over their everyday decisions without insisting on a communal council. Yet what recourse did they have? The capitulations, shielding foreigners from Ottoman law, were still in place, removing the opportunity for legal redress in Turkish courts, while the consular courts lacked jurisdiction in such matters. Moreover, lacking personal funds with which to sue for a fair share of communal property, members were helpless. From the outset, their now-aging or deceased parents had laid their wealth at Anna's feet. Believing themselves like the early Christians who placed all at the feet of the apostles, and trusting in Anna's leadership, no one had dreamed of asking for a receipt. The faith of the older members remained unshaken, while the younger ones had been so deeply indoctrinated that they found it difficult to question or think about their circumstances objectively. Only recently were quiet whispers heard among younger members that things might be unfair. The boys especially worried about their future and envied their well-to-do Arab friends heading off to the excellent Syrian Protestant College in Lebanon, later known as the American University of Beirut. But neither Anna nor Bertha had attended college themselves and saw no reason to pay for higher education. The colony boys had received a fairly good grounding in history and literature from in-house teachers like Johanna Brooke and Professor Dinsmore as well as a variety of useful skills taught by Brother Elijah and other talented members. This might suit them for work in a trade, perhaps, but not a profession.

Nonetheless, since the "new dispensation" had considerably relaxed the puritanical atmosphere, the large number of young truly "enjoyed a rare fellowship, and there was plenty of fun and laughter."[4] Time was found for picnics in the hills, swimming in rock pools in summer, fruit picking, and community excursions that bound them in a special camaraderie. The American Colony Store was doing well, and access to small comforts had eased under Frederick Vester's administration of colony funds. Even if they had to apply for cash to buy what they needed, they generally liked Bertha's husband and considered him fair, more so than Bertha, whose inclination was to treat them like servants as she pursued her ambitious personal social agenda. On the whole, therefore, even if they read in the news sheets that the Great Powers were circling each other and growling, for themselves there seemed reason to hope for an ever brighter future.

———

As the tumultuous year passed, dissatisfaction was replacing optimism among the Arab delegates in Constantinople. A hidden competition for leadership in the new government had intensified, but the chief players all were Turks and showed a preference for authoritarian rule almost as pronounced as Sultan Abdul Hamid's—but unlike the deposed sultan's, their pronouncements simmered with contempt for Arabs.[5] When a wave of strikes across the empire was bloodily suppressed and the workers punished, it appeared that the new administration was not serious about listening to the voice of the people. Promised reforms were slow in materializing, although there were some improvements such as new schools and efforts at better urban sewage and tax collection and discussions had begun to revise family law.

In 1909 a countercoup by Abdul Hamid was foiled, the weeping sultan exiled to Salonika, and his ineffectual brother recalled from thirty years' confinement among the ladies of the seraglio. Sultan Mehmed V, who now strapped on the sword of Othman, was a drooling imbecile in the eyes of many. He composed graceful Persian poems, but was otherwise unfit for office, a puppet doing the bidding of the Committee of Union and Progress, which ordered eighty dissidents hanged, including the publisher of a liberal newspaper. Martial law was imposed as angry troops continued to mutiny. Another massacre in Armenia by Kurdish militias went unpunished, while parliament saw its powers severely curtailed. For the first time, and despite the capitulation agreements, Christians and Jews who were Turkish subjects were no longer exempt from the army, an alarming development that prompted those colony members who had not already done so to scramble to obtain foreign passports. The kaiser had given citizenship to German residents during his 1898 visit—so Frederick Vester was safe. The Swedish consul, Dalman, issued passports to the Swedes from Nås, who had arrived holding only a church permit. It was a bit more problematic for the American members, whether born in Sweden or America. Few had thought to bring birth certificates. Fortunately, however, Edwin Wallace had been followed by consuls friendly to the colony. Two had even taken rooms at the Big House, and both were glad to issue temporary U.S. passports, which Selah Merrill had foreseen would eventually become important for foreign nationals.

In Constantinople three members of the Committee of Union and Progress finally emerged from the power struggle as the leaders to be reckoned with: the handsome but brash young officer Enver Bey, whose act of defiance had sparked the revolution; the triumvirate's real brains, a former postal clerk named Mehmed Talat; and Colonel Ahmed Djemal, soon to be governor of Syria and Palestine, where he would reveal himself a man of exceptional ruthlessness. They exhibited little respect for Arab sensibilities and showed no tolerance for dissent.

These men faced a superhuman task. The empire's deficits were staggering; foreigners owned many important parts of the infrastructure, like the railroads, post offices, steamship lines, and banks. Determined to create a modern, secularized, and centralized nation, the triumvirate had first to save it from outside threats. Bulgaria and Crete had rebelled, and Austria had annexed Bosnia-Herzegovina in 1908. In 1911, as Turkish troops put down violent protests by Arabs from Albania to Syria and crushed a revolt in Yemen, Italy invaded Libya and seized the last of the empire's African provinces. Arabs who had previously danced in the streets now wondered if the new government was capable of protecting fellow Arabs. They were further insulted at contemptuous new regulations requiring Turkish in law courts and secondary schools in place of Arabic, the language of the holy Koran. Through 1912 and 1913 two Balkan wars raged, adding Macedonia, Albania, Thrace, and most of the Aegean Islands to the list of lost territories. By 1913, over a third of the empire had passed out of Ottoman hands.[6] Although the Turkish army won back Edirne in Thrace, Turkey's last redoubt in Europe, every day more Muslim refugees driven from their ancestral homes poured into Constantinople to add crowding to food shortages. Arab leaders quietly plotted a new course to freedom in Lebanon, Syria, and the Hejaz.

At the colony in 1912, Olof and Mathilda Larsson's daughter Edith had accepted the diploma presented her and other graduates by Professor Dinsmore. She was now informed that she might pin up her long hair, don a long skirt, and take her place among the womenfolk. She was eighteen and in love with Lewis Larsson, the thirty-one-year-old photographer who had taken over the Photo Department. When the group came from Nås in 1896, Lewis at fifteen had been the protector of his widowed mother and sisters, despite his unwillingness to subscribe wholeheartedly to his mother's new faith. Edith admired such filial loyalty, especially when Lewis told her that he had refused to accept his rich uncle's offer to stay in Nås and become his heir. As time passed, however, Lewis had acquiesced in the colony's belief that "all things are shared in common" and had given over a small inheritance received on his twenty-first birthday.[7] Now the lead photographer, Lewis had taken such superb pictures of Syria, Jordan, and Palestine that newspapers, universities, religious organizations, and publishers were ordering them by the thousands, making it the colony's most lucrative business.

Growing up, Edith had frequently been told by Mrs. Spafford that she was "too much like her father," that she "always wanted to take the lead." Like everyone else, she feared and respected "Mother" but tried to resist the criticisms, which "made me depressed and scared." Although she remained silent, "I knew that I had no such thoughts, but I loved life and had the strength to enjoy it."[8] Lewis had always been kind to her, and now engaged, she missed him when he went off on prolonged photographic expeditions.

Shortly before they were to be married, Edith was readying a room on the top floor that she and Lewis had been assigned. She glanced up to see Anna at the door. "I wish to remind you of the serious step you are taking," Anna began, her expression severe. "Marriage is intended as a spiritual union." Edith's delight in her task evaporated. "I was so young and ignorant of all that marriage entailed that I could not understand what this was all about," she remembered later, trying to explain the impact of Anna's words. "But I felt nervous and unhappy, and was afraid that I would make a mistake—and in some way displease God." Edith hung her head as Anna persisted. "Recognize that you both are called to become a part of God's kingdom, and that all worldly desires must be subordinated to this ideal." Anna turned and left the room, but her warning had its effect. Edith and Lewis "began our married life in fear." Theirs would be one of only two weddings during the difficult years that

lay ahead for the colony, yet in their own way these two fortunate innocents were able to overcome—if in a rather different way from what
Anna had intended. Eventually, more successfully than some others, they
learned how to put aside Anna's injunctions, and, as Edith later recorded, "our love and our trust grew stronger in time."[9]

In Constantinople, on January 23, 1913, with a Koran tucked under
his tunic, Enver Bey led troops in a putsch. He stormed the precincts of
the Sublime Porte and forced the resignation of the pro-British grand
vizier. With the assassination of the war minister five months later, Enver became the new war minister, the commander in chief, and the husband of the sultan's fifteen-year-old niece. Unsympathetic army officers
were purged, leaving the triumvirate in complete control. Recognizing
that they would need a strong ally if their infant government was to survive, Enver and Djemal made quiet approaches to both the British and
the French but were rebuffed.[10] Thus they turned to Germany. The
kaiser graciously responded by sending his brilliant general Otto Liman
von Sanders to " 'work unobtrusively . . . steadfastly and harmoniously'
for 'the Germanization of the Turkish army.' "[11]

At this point, the new leaders were not yet resigned to their dependence on Germany or its growing influence. Turkish pride in a long Ottoman tradition of superb soldiering was frequently offended by German
disdain, and many were reluctant to lose the help that British and French
investments offered the stumbling economy. All saw the clouds of war
gathering between the Great Powers, yet if the system were to be re-
formed, Turkey freed from foreign indebtedness and made safe from
further encroachments by the Great Powers, time was needed. Clearly,
neutrality was the better option. No one could have known that the
British ambassador in Constantinople was writing the foreign secretary,
Sir Edward Grey, in 1913 that "all the powers including ourselves are
trying hard to get what they can out of Turkey. They all profess to the
maintenance of Turkey's integrity but no one ever thinks this in practice."[12]

Ahmed Djemal, now naval minister, was keen to upgrade the Turkish fleet. Accordingly, two battleships were ordered from a British ship-

yard, a decision so enthusiastically approved that across the empire school-children offered small coins in a burst of patriotism, reminiscent of the contributions raised earlier for the Baghdad Railway. Over 3.5 million pounds poured in from both rich and poor to finance the purchase.

And then it happened. In Sarajevo on June 28, 1914, a young Bosnian revolutionary acting for Serbia's clandestine Black Hand gunned down the Austrian archduke. Suddenly Europe, hopelessly entangled in alliances, was plunged into the dreaded but long-anticipated conflict. The British first lord of the admiralty, an ambitious young politician named Winston Churchill, abruptly seized the just-completed Turkish ships, leaving four hundred Turkish naval personnel who had arrived to collect them stranded at Tyneside, England, empty-handed, helpless, and outraged.[13] The strong anti-British feeling this aroused among Turks and Arabs alike was only slightly mitigated by the kaiser's loan of 200 million in gold bullion and two German cruisers, albeit commanded by German officers.[14]

On July 28, Austria declared war on Serbia, and by August 4, Germany was at war with Russia, France, and Britain. While the great armies of Europe readied for battle, a secret alliance between Germany and Turkey was concluded, irrevocably committing a reluctant Turkey to the German side. On September 9, the capitulations that had exempted Europeans from Turkish laws were unilaterally abolished by the CUP, alarming foreigners who could no longer enjoy the protection of their consuls and who feared the capricious justice of Turkish courts. Finally, in November, Djemal Pasha allowed the newly acquired German cruiser *Goeben* to shell Russian installations along the Black Sea. The die was cast. Turkey, too, was now at war. On November 11, the sultan issued a call to jihad, and while the CUP was far from well liked, the population generally shared its devotion to the defense of the Ottoman-Islamic order.[15] Parliamentary delegates from Jerusalem who had not already departed the capital now made haste to return to the holy city.

Earlier, in March, Amelia Gould, paralyzed after a stroke, had quietly died in her bed and was buried in the new cemetery the colony had purchased on Mount Scopus. The colonists sensed that her death had affected Anna deeply. She did not seem herself these days, and they heard she was not sleeping well. There were periods when she remained in her room and let Brother Jacob officiate at the morning prayer meetings. One morning not long after Sister Elizabeth's death, Edith Larsson, pregnant with her first baby, watched Anna enter the assembly looking pale and distracted. Edith and the others listened as Anna described a night of tossing and turning. Raising her voice, she declared: "The wrath of God is poured forth from nation to nation." Anna paused. Her followers waited intently. She had always told them that cleaving to national identifications was what caused "disunity," and disunity caused war. "Terrible times lie ahead of us. But no evil shall befall you if you love one another. This is the beautiful promise the Lord has given us."[16] There was a gentle sigh from the fellowship. Touched, vowing to pull together as never before, the members rose to sing a hymn. "It is my will," they sang sweetly, "that you love one another as I have loved you."[17]

The day that war was officially declared, November 2, the colony had some Germans and a French lady among the guests. At dinner that evening these citizens of newly declared enemy nations refused to speak. The next morning they departed abruptly, joining an exodus of tourists and businessmen from the city. "There, you see," Anna counseled the morning assembly. "So mighty is hatred. But what will love not do? Peace on earth and good will toward people—this is what we are called upon to make real."[18] The colonists admired their leader anew, and privately resolved to fulfill the ideal in the difficult days to come.

Yet no one dreamed the war would last. Bertha, recently returned from a lengthy camping holiday with fifteen friends, said she was sure it would be over by Christmas.[19] Nevertheless, she felt she should fetch her mother in the carriage from the hospice of the Augusta Victoria, where she had spent several weeks hoping to cure some mysterious aches and pains. Anna had put on a lot of weight over the past decade. She was now seventy-two, and while her doctors did not recognize it, she was showing early symptoms of diabetes—fuzzy vision, for which they gave her eyeglasses, a troubled stomach, and numbness in her feet. Given the sudden turbulence in Jerusalem, the Vesters felt Anna should be with their family of five children, Anna Grace, Horatio, Jock, Louise, and the baby, Tanetta, in the large house they had rented two minutes from the colony compound.

It was impossible to guess which powerful foe would triumph in the war, but it was hoped that no matter what the outcome, the colony would be secure. The Vesters had been embedded in local German society from the time of their betrothal. The German headmaster had been Frederick's best man when the German Lutheran Probst married them. The Probst also officiated at the seven succeeding colony weddings. The colony's choir leader was German, their dentist and doctor were German, and a German architect had been supervising the renovation of various colony buildings. Bertha and Frederick were on the German consul's official list, invited to all state functions of the Reich.[20] Yet they were unsympathetic to Germany's invasion of Belgium, and while Frederick's Swiss mother was pro-German "heart and soul," the Vesters felt torn.[21] It was reassuring to remember that the colony was on good terms with both the Turkish administrators and the local Arab populace. Furthermore, Bertha was American, and America was a nonbelligerent. They felt some confidence, therefore, that the colony would be regarded as neutral.

Jerusalem sprang alive, suddenly filling with German and Turkish officers, advisers, soldiers, and spies. Rumors abounded and conditions were confusing. British, French, and Russian nationals were advised to leave. The Turks confiscated Allied consulates and seized all documents that the consuls had not had time to burn. British and French were carefully watched, as well as Arabs who worked in British or French hospitals and schools. The Turks seized all large institutions—convents, church schools, and dormitories—to turn them into hospitals or to billet troops. Their resident monks and nuns were expelled, including the Carmelite nuns whose cloistered lives had been spent entirely indoors and who now gazed shyly at an unfamiliar world from the back of a cart on their way to the railroad station. When Canon Hichens of the Anglican cathedral and the British headmaster of St. George's School faced arrest, the Vesters took them in, and when they slipped to safety with the help of the American consul, Dr. Otis Glazebrook, Bertha and Frederick helped Glazebrook pack away and hide the cathedral's silver crosses, chalices, vestments, and carpets. As unobtrusively as possible, they also concealed valuables belonging to the Dominican fathers and the French École Biblique et Archéologique, the Sisters of St. Joseph, and Notre Dame de France—along with property deeds worth millions.

Money was impounded. Banks and foreign post offices closed. Mail was censored, and accurate information became difficult to come by. Although a number of Zionist leaders who were German or Turkish citizens felt safe in staying, thousands of other Jews left, many boarding a cruiser sent by America to evacuate them to Egypt. Any man forty-five years of age or younger was required to report for military duty whether or not he was in any condition to serve. Frederick Vester, who was not physically strong, had celebrated his forty-fifth birthday just three days before war started and should have been exempt. In an act of courage, Frederick and Bertha called at the Probst's open house packed with Germans and told him they were not in sympathy. The anger in the room was fierce when Frederick made his declaration. "I put my hand out to say goodbye to my hostess," Bertha said, "but she held her hand behind her. We got out immediately. If they could have annihilated us with looks, we should have been dead."[22] Frederick was left alone—at least for the time being.

Everyone hurried to lay in supplies, knowing that products like sugar, rice, canned goods, and staples from British-controlled Egypt would be cut off when the Allies blockaded the Mediterranean. Only Jaffa oranges, olive oil, and grain were local. At the colony, the sound of donkey and camel bells jingled around the clock as a line of wheat-laden animals streamed through the gate. A large room was cleared for grain storage, and the boys worked like stevedores hauling in huge sacks, never dreaming of the scope of the famine to come. Although previously the colony had not kept pigs in deference to the sensibilities of their Muslim friends, who considered pigs unclean, it was now decided to add them to a pen. Cows and chickens might be commandeered by Turkish soldiers, but surely not pigs.

But to the residents of Jerusalem what mattered at the moment was the arrival of the third member of Constantinople's triumvirate. Djemal Pasha had been given unfettered authority from Aleppo to the Sinai, including the *sanjak* of Jerusalem. Commander of the Ottoman Fourth

Army, in charge of organizing an attack on the Suez Canal—the "jugular vein" for British and Allied supply ships—Djemal wasted no time in taking over the Augusta Victoria, the kaiser's immense and hideous Teutonic palace serving as a hospice, commanding the high northern spur of the Mount of Olives. He made it his headquarters and personal suite, a deliberate affront to his German colleagues. With obsidian eyes and jet-black hair, wearing polished boots and a chestful of medals, Djemal was already viewed as a man without pity. It was said that he could dine with a guest in the evening and have him executed the following morning. Jerusalem awaited its commander-governor with dread.

Suffering

When we look the other way or justify oppres-
sion, there is damage not only to the oppressed
but also to the oppressors, no matter how seem-
ingly righteous their cause.

—James M. Wall

Events unfolded rapidly. Over one million men had been mobilized to defend the Ottoman Empire from simultaneous attacks
on distant fronts, and for a time the Turkish soldiers did well, demonstrating extraordinary valor. The Entente had assembled an armada in
the northern Aegean and launched what became the bloody Gallipoli
campaign to seize the Dardanelles. "It is clear that Constantinople must
be yours," King George V had genially assured Russia, Turkey's traditional enemy.[1] The tenacity of the successful Ottoman defense of the
straits under the command of a young colonel, Mustafa Kemal, caught
the Allies by surprise, and by mid-1916 they were forced to withdraw,
leaving nearly fifty thousand of their dead.[2] Although Enver Pasha's reckless campaign in eastern Anatolia against the czar's troops added catastrophic numbers to the Turks' losses at Gallipoli, in Mesopotamia the
Ottoman army held off a British attack aiming at Baghdad and Mosul's
valuable oil fields in the north, capturing an entire British army at Al Kut
in 1916.[3]

In Jerusalem, Djemal Pasha planned his Suez assault. He chose the
southern town of Beersheba as his assembly point, inland and safe from
Allied naval bombardments. His directives were immediate and harsh.

Draconian quotas were imposed on farmers, who had to deliver every-thing they had to the authorities, leaving scant stores to tide over their families. Farmers were soon drafted, leaving fields unattended and fruit rotting on the vine. The countryside was pillaged as Djemal requisi-tioned food, water, and animals for his army, ruthlessly cutting down thousands of trees for fuel. Elderly, even crippled Arabs, as well as Chris-tians and Jews—whom Djemal did not trust to fight—were forced into labor gangs to build roads or haul water on their backs like donkeys, un-til they dropped from exhaustion.

The colony, situated on the main artery, watched lines of troops passing on their way south to Beersheba. Since the railway from Con-stantinople was incomplete, men had to march on foot for hundreds of miles. Grace Whiting and several colony "sisters" waited in the road to offer water to shabby, ill-shod soldiers until officers interrupted with whips to force them on.[4] From their friends in the now-dormant tourist business, Rolla Floyd, Herbert Clark, and the agent for Thomas Cook & Son, they learned that all available tents were needed for an expanding tent city in Beersheba. The yard of the Big House suddenly became a dumping ground, commandeered by the authorities, to gather folding beds, tables, and chairs as well as the tents. Members helped repair the handsome, colorful canvases, pondering on the turn of fate befalling what had once sheltered the likes of Mark Twain, President Grant, the Prince of Wales, and the kaiser himself.[5]

From his arrival, Djemal Pasha made it clear that he had nothing but suspicion and contempt for the Arabs he governed—and they feared him. Osman Bey el-Nashashibi, a member of parliament, chaired the first meeting of Jerusalem's Arab notables. "Now we Arabs are all united under the Turks," he began graciously. With a vicious look, Djemal Pasha whirled on Osman Bey. "And who are you to say who is a Turk or Arab? You are all Turks!" he spat, and as the notables watched in horror, Djemal directed his aide-de-camp "to place that traitor in jail."[6] Merci-fully, friends persuaded him to relent, but he had set a tone that left the city shaken.

It was with considerable trepidation that Lewis Larsson and his young helper Lars Lind responded to a summons to the Augusta Victo-ria. Djemal Pasha had sent for photographers from the American Colony to take pictures of himself, medal bedecked, in the company of distinguished visitors. Lars shivered under the piercing glance of the dictator, whose "eyes were as implacable as the beady eyes of an unblinking viper."[7] The men did their job—evidently to his satisfaction, for before the war was over, they were called on many more times, and, as Lars noted, while they were not always paid, they were reimbursed often enough to bring a needed income to the colony. More important, their usefulness seemed to prevent the Turkish commander's fearsome ire from turning on their little group.

In Beersheba, preparations intensified. Thousands of donkeys, horses, and the finest camels from all over Syria had been commandeered for the assault. South of Beersheba, there was no water. The animals were given so little to drink or eat that the desert was soon littered with rotting carcasses. Not surprisingly, typhus, spread by lice festering on unwashed bodies, became epidemic. Lewis Larsson was brought along as official photographer when twenty Red Crescent nurses opened a clinic in Beersheba with equipment that Turkish quartermasters had randomly gathered from hospitals and pharmacies. When a German doctor opened the medical chests, he was stunned to find he had been provided microscopes and gynecological instruments.[8]

High in the sky overhead, British planes continually circled, out of range of rifle fire from below, constantly monitoring Turkish movements. Instead of strafing or bombing the installations, the pilots dropped leaflets written in Arabic assuring the Arab troops that the British were their true friends; the Germans and Turks were the deceivers. "The Turkish commanders," an observer noted, "soon announced that anyone [picking them up] would pay the death penalty. After that, when the little bundles dropped near them, the natives would run as if from a high explosive bomb."[9]

In Jerusalem, in mid-January, skirmishes broke out south of Gaza. The American Red Cross, recognizing the dearth of doctors in the Sinai operation, offered to send a medical mission that would be headed by Dr. Ward of the Syrian Protestant College in Lebanon, who stayed at the colony. When he left for the front, John Whiting, along with a number of colony nurses, volunteered to go with him, even though it meant leaving his pregnant wife, Grace. The party was flown deep into the desert, as far as Hafir el Aujah, and was there for the grand assault on the Suez Canal in late February and the chaos that followed.[10]

More than 20,000 troops out of an army of 150,000 had braved the sandy wastes, dragging parts for pontoon bridges and large cannons by hand after their mules had collapsed on the march.[11] The plan had been to lay the pontoons over the water to Ismailia on the Egyptian side. The attackers were to cross at night, but a delay became fatal. As dawn broke, the waiting British commenced a decimating bombardment. Some four hundred experienced Turkish infantry from Anatolia made it across, but as they clambered onshore, it was into the arms of the enemy. To the chagrin of the Ottoman commanders who were ready to throw more troops into action, not only did the Egyptians fail to heed the sultan's call for jihad, but their German counterparts insisted on a full retreat. It became a rout, with abandoned equipment and guns left to be picked up by the British.

John Whiting and the medical team witnessed the first night. They had seen thousands of camels being loaded with hospital and telephone supplies for the front. "Before midnight they were all back, had unloaded and were again loaded (amid the greatest confusion and growling) with food and water for the fatigued and defeated army. The lack of water must have been cruel as many soldiers paid a dollar for a drink."[12] Whiting flew back to Jerusalem to inform Consul Glazebrook that his team might be left stranded and that the consulate should prepare a rescue. "To my surprise," Whiting said, "I found Jerusalem trying to work up an enthusiasm over the great victory of having crossed the Canal!"

When the people of Jerusalem learned they had been deceived by a victory telegram sent from Djemal, and streams of wounded soldiers, deserters, and refugees poured into the city, an ugly mood of resentment against the Turkish-German leadership mounted. The anger against the Germans, however, was greatest. German residents heard talk of a massacre and stayed indoors. It was claimed that three German officers had been shot by their Turkish comrades during the retreat and a fourth committed suicide.[13] Relations between Turkish and German officers were to remain tense through the rest of the war. Fast's Hotel, the place for Germans to gather, drink beer, and sing patriotic songs, seldom saw Turkish officers. The battle-hardened Turks, underpaid with depreciated

Turkish paper currency, deeply resented being subordinated to untested and overconfident pink-faced German officers whose compensation was not only greater but given in gold.

Ever alert to subversion, Djemal evacuated coastal towns like Haifa, Gaza, and Jaffa, sending more refugees into the holy city. Jaffa's brave, muscular, and independent-minded boatmen, whom Djemal particularly distrusted, were banished to the Dead Sea and their boats seized to haul grain. Not long afterward, the hangings by the Jaffa Gate began. Despite the fact that capital punishment had been banned for decades by the Ottoman government, Djemal reinstituted it, with no appeal. Young men, a placard announcing *farrar*, or "deserter," displayed on their chests, were hanged weekly. Many Arab peasants attempted to escape the military dragnet, hiding in improbable places and brought food at night by their families. A woman whom the colony knew was frantic to save her son from being arrested. He had gone into the street without his *wasika*, or military pass. Although his mother rushed to bring the *wasika* to the military police, she arrived to see her son hanging dead. Even more shattering to the colony was the day another friend, the mufti of Gaza, was hanged with his son as a traitor. Crowds of Jerusalemites gathered to watch a scene the members found unbearable.[14]

As the residents cowered under a curfew and strict martial law, homeless and hungry vagrants roamed the streets, many gathering at the colony door or in front of the Vester store by the Jaffa Gate, which was still open, selling an occasional trinket to a German officer. There was no electricity. Candles and matches were scarce, and residents turned to the old way of striking a flint against steel. From the backs of closets, antique oil lamps were taken out and lit with sesame oil. The colony store had once sold them to tourists, but now they were grateful to have them for themselves as the only source of light. At night the streets were deserted and silent except for the clang of hobnailed boots ringing against the ancient stones.

For a time, although she was expecting her sixth child, Bertha had initiated a small embroidery and lace-making effort, hoping to offer a livelihood to women whose husbands had been drafted. With the United States still neutral, she thought she could sell their handiwork through friends in America if she could get it on an American ship. No ship came, and soon the women were too weak from malnutrition to continue. Impoverished, unable to feed their children, they looked to the colony. Every day colony "sisters" made rounds to check on as many as they could, bringing what food they could spare, tending the sick, and in the process exposing themselves to rampant disease, especially typhus, cholera, and smallpox. Money from several donors in America still came through via Dr. Glazebrook's consulate and helped buy the beans and lentils to keep great cauldrons boiling in the colony kitchen. Daily the members doled out soup to the crowds. Stirred by Anna's message to succor the helpless, the members realized this could well be their finest hour. "We thought conditions could not get much worse," Bertha wrote a supporter. But a year later she said, "We have learned differently."[15]

In March 1915, the sky suddenly blackened. A locust plague descended on Palestine. The colonists had seen minor infestations in the past, but never anything like this. Not for forty years had there been such a visitation of "flying pilgrims" from the Sudan, blanketing the earth, consuming not only the leaves of trees but the tender bark of branches, dooming fruit for the coming season. Colony members joined with every available man, woman, and child, rushing to the fields to clang pots and pans or beating the ground with carpets to scare the monstrous waves of insects, but it was no use. Every inch of ground for miles outside the city was covered with female locusts digging in the soil to deposit their egg packets. In fluttering multitudes, storks arrived to feast on the eggs until their bellies were too swollen for them to fly. After a pause of weeks, the insects incubated, and a new and more frightening swarm attacked the countryside. Djemal Pasha, recognizing the menace to his grain supply, ordered thousands of soldiers to dig trenches to bury the hatching insects.[16] He issued a decree that every man and boy in the city was to dig up half a kilo of locust eggs, a "stupid idea," as Lars Lind and Lewis Larsson agreed, hacking hopelessly at the hard dried ground with pickaxes. Instead, they made a meticulous photographic study of the devastated landscape, documenting the stages of the plague. The dictator heard about it and asked for copies, although he paid them nothing.

When the locust eggs hatched, the earth seethed once again as black larvae fed on early spring grasses and tender shoots. Not a leaf was left on the ancient olive trees in the Garden of Gethsemane. The people of Jerusalem waited in growing dread, watching the black horde move inexorably toward the city, finally entering through the Jaffa Gate. "They swarmed over the ramparts of the Tower of David until every stone of the sixty foot height was covered by the crawling mass," Lars Lind wrote later of the horrifying scene. "They crammed into David Street, thousands were mashed on the smooth cobble stones, rendering them dangerously slippery and creating a never-to-be forgotten stench."[17] Repelled and desperate, people barricaded themselves in their houses with sheets of tin or old planks. Even so, the undulating, rustling flow entered houses. There were stories of babies left unattended in their cradles whose eyes and faces were devoured before their screams could be heard.[18]

Finally, after three months, the developed grasshoppers flew off to other pastures. The Overcomers gathered to offer prayers and hymns in unison, helpless like everyone else before such devastation. Food had been scarce before, and now there was none. Not a tree stood on which a single leaf was left. For the colony, the people of Jerusalem, and Djemal Pasha's army, famine had been added to the ravages of war.

The colony guarded its grain store carefully. Two of the "sisters" knelt on the floor and ground the grain into flour by the same primitive methods of the ancients. None of the colonists had ever been fat, and some, like Sister Johanna Brooke and Brother Elijah, who were not among those served the better meals, were painfully thin. Only Anna had grown heavy. With all the fruit trees blighted and fresh vegetables nearly impossible to find—except expensively through the black market, or what could be coaxed from a tiny garden plot—many members became susceptible to illness. Grace Whiting, never very strong, had given birth to a sickly baby. To Anna, watching her worried daughter rock the little one, it was as if the fear and hunger she had escaped in Chicago had returned to haunt her old age.

One hot July morning in 1915, a boy raced into the upstairs salon, where Anna was resting. He carried a metal box, which he thrust into her hands. It was from the garden, he said excitedly, where he had been planting vegetables and his spade struck something hard. When he pried it open, he had found gold coins sparkling in the sun.[19] Without delay, Anna summoned the members. God had come to their aid, she announced, her voice trembling, holding the box before her. The Almighty had sent them a cache of solid gold at this dark hour. She would not allow them to spend it, she cautioned, until this sudden windfall could be explained.

The next day William Rudy asked to speak to Anna in private. Curious, Anna followed him as he led the way to a divan in the hallway, sinking heavily down beside him. Drawn and haltingly, the man she used to trust before all others—before young Vester came into her daughter's life—began a strange and awkward story. This was half the money from the sale of Olaf Larsson's house, he confessed in a hoarse whisper. Anna stared at Rudy wordlessly. He stuttered, trying to explain. Then suddenly, with a barely audible cry, as if to deflect the awful condemnation due him, Brother William collapsed on Anna's shoulder, toppling into her arms. Several members rushed to respond to Anna's alarmed shout, but it was too late.[20]

A doctor arrived and pronounced Rudy dead of "apoplexy." Dr. Glazebrook was called. "He left nothing of his own," the consul wrote on the death certificate, which he forwarded to the State Department, noting that the dead man's relatives had been duly notified.[21]

Anna was holding her Bible as the members filed into the meeting the following morning. It was clear to her, and she made it clear to her fellowship, that in their brother William, they had sheltered an "Ananias" in their midst. From the Acts of the Apostles, she read the story of Ananias and his wife, Sapphira, who had sold valuable property for the benefit of Christ's little community that held "all things in common." But when they kept back part for themselves, Saint Peter chastised them—and they fell dead.[22]

"Peter said, 'Ananias, why hath Satan filled thine heart to lie to the Holy Ghost, and to keep back part of the price of the land?' " The benign look with which she usually surveyed her fellowship was ominous behind the new spectacles.

" 'Thou hast not lied unto men, but unto God.' And Ananias hearing these words fell down, and gave up the ghost." Anna glanced fiercely over the assembly, then slowly and emphatically resumed: *"And great fear came on all them that heard these things."*

The room was silent. Old Otis Page, so often the brunt of Anna's rebukes, bowed his head. He and Rudy had come together from Chicago in 1881. Now, except for the little ones who had accompanied their parents, he, Anna, and Mary Whiting were all that were left of the original "apostles," and Mary, kept apart from her son, John, and daughter, Ruth, and told so many times that she loved flowers more than God, was just a broken, silent shadow. Otis had followed young Rob Lawrence's casket to his grave; he had known forty-three members now dead, including Lizzie, his wife, and Rudy was the forty-fourth to be gathered.[23] How long, wondered the aging believer, would it be before the great horn would blow, and would he live to see that blessed day?

"Confess your sins." Anna's voice rose. "And let this be a lesson to all who conceal parts of their lives and do not give themselves completely to God!"[24] A paroxysm of confession followed. Members stood, lacerating themselves. Some wondered if the war might be the result of their sinfulness. Others wept, a few admitting anger that one should get more bread than another. And then, somehow, the exercise turned on Anna's children. Why should so many privileges be granted Bertha and Frederick, or to the Whitings? "There is a gap," said one member fiercely. "Bertha and her girls get what they wish for, instantly. We have to beg humbly for the smallest thing."[25]

The outpouring increased in passion, and suddenly the members were attacking Anna herself. "Humility," she told them, holding herself steady, "is necessary for your spiritual growth."[26] Anna reminded her followers that it was not for them "to think," but "to believe and to have faith."[27] At last, she quieted them. The older members, chastened, agreed to soldier on. But there were others—and Anna knew she would have to remain alert—who would need to be carefully watched.

The meeting had been stressful, and Anna wondered if she had the strength to hold her band together. She had spent the night thinking about Brother William. She thought, too, of her longtime friend Amelia Gould. Could Amelia have been Sapphira, conspiring with Rudy to keep money from her?[28] After Horatio died, Anna had determined never again to lose control of the family purse. Hadn't she sensed that Brother

Rudy was faltering? Surely it was the Lord guiding her when she changed bursars. At the time she thought it a means to bind Frederick to her side. It seemed now that her intuition had saved her. Only the day before, she had sat with William Rudy and looked into his eyes. She had read his soul. Like Ananias, he had betrayed her, and, fittingly, he died.

As members resumed their duties, however cowed or chastised they felt, they could not suppress their relief, their excitement that the cache of golden coins would get them through this endless test of privation and illness. In their joy at the discovery of the coins, many believed that their quiet bursar had buried the cache as a hedge to protect them against an uncertain future. Together, pledged to communal sacrifice and charity, they girded themselves to endure terrible new developments. The Whiting baby died, and afterward, another "sister," and then Sister Johanna Brooke expired alone in her tiny room on the stair landing. The students who had loved her mourned, although at the assembly Anna exhorted them to rejoice. The next morning the colonists found three children huddled by their dead mother's body outside the compound door. They took them in.

Documents seized from the French Consulate in Beirut in 1914 appeared to have implicated numbers of Arab notables. Djemal instituted a reign of terror in Lebanon, hanging eleven Arabs in Beirut on August 28, 1915, and blockading the Lebanon Mountains so that countless numbers starved there. In May 1916, he ordered twenty-one more to be tortured and executed in Beirut and Damascus, including an Arab senator, three Arab parliamentary delegates, several leading journalists, and members of prominent families.[29] At least one, a friend of the colony, had escaped and was in hiding in Damascus.[30]

At the same time, trickling into Jerusalem came hollow-eyed, emaciated Armenians, bearing incredible tales. Uprooted from their villages in Anatolia in May 1915, suspected of collaborating with Russian field commanders, two million Armenians had been sent on a death march through murderous Kurdish territory, into Mesopotamia or the Syrian desert. Over a million had starved or perished of disease. As pitiful stragglers appeared in Jerusalem, the Overcomers did what they could for a few of them and were told that Djemal was one of those who had ordered what eventually came to be known as the Armenian genocide.[31]

Behind his back, Djemal was called *al-Saffah*, or "the blood shedder," and he took the precaution of guarding his headquarters with crack Anatolian troops and two huge field guns.[32] Yet his suspicions of the Arabs were not without foundation. For nearly two years, the British had been engaging in secret talks with the sixty-year-old sharif of Mecca, a direct descendant of the Prophet and guardian of the keys to Mecca and Medina.[33] Promised British support for his claim to the caliphate as "an Arab of true race," and told he would be ruler of an Arab nation if he would raise an Arab army against the Turks, Sharif Hussein ibn Ali was not truly an Arab nationalist. He loathed the CUP, to him a group of atheistic adventurers who ignored the Koran and disavowed the Sharia, or Islamic law. The sharif was an ambitious dynast hoping to acquire a hereditary kingdom for his family.[34] But out of promises made to him by the British high commissioner in Cairo came the Arab revolt that Djemal had feared. On June 5, 1916, Arab irregulars attacked the Turkish garrison in Mecca, and by July 6, with the help of a brilliant young British adviser, T. E. Lawrence, Aqaba fell, and wild tribesmen from the Hejaz were galloping north, blowing up the Turkish railroad. Soon to be a legend for his exploits in the Arab Revolt, Lawrence observed that Djemal Pasha "united all classes, conditions, and creeds in Syria, under pressure of a common misery and peril, and so made a concerted revolt possible."[35]

Yet Djemal did not harm the colony. He knew about its soup kitchen, where some nine hundred to one thousand persons were served daily, regardless of race or religion. He had learned that its spacious yard was filled with the weak and dying, laid gently beneath a shady tree until means could be found to bring them to a hospital. His staff had kept him informed of this odd group that had stayed apart from the missionaries, priests, and nuns of the organized orders that he had expelled. They called themselves "Christians" but did not proselytize; and their salon had been a favored gathering place for Turkish officials. One of Djemal's recent visitors, the famous Swedish explorer Sven Hedin, had told him how touched he had been to see the colony's hardworking Swedes and to meet its Norwegian leader. "She is heavily built and stands erect, quite large in size," Hedin reported. He was impressed to find her "humble and friendly to everyone, and always holds herself in the background even though she is the head."[36] Djemal decided to call on her himself.

For Anna and Bertha, the prospect of a visit from His Excellency was more than a little disquieting. Anna wondered what they could serve him with his tea. Bertha suggested they have the kitchen make gingerbread from carob syrup, the only sweet available. Apparently, the visit, one of several to come, was a success. The dictator arrived in his carriage, was hospitably received, and before long took Bertha's little daughter Louise on his knee, declaring that "children are a bit of heaven."[37] The ladies smiled politely. When he told them that he admired them more than any other Christian community he had ever seen, Bertha was emboldened. She confessed that her children had been disturbed by the noise coming from the nearby St. George's School, which had been requisitioned by the Turks as an ordnance factory. As Djemal Pasha well knew, the school was also used to punish prisoners, and frequently bastinado was the method employed, a singularly painful torture involving beating the naked soles of a victim's feet. Sensing that she was safe in persisting, Bertha said that she had found her little son Jock shaking his finger at the Turkish officer in charge and announcing the man would not get to heaven. Djemal Pasha listened quietly, then responded: "I shall not allow those children to witness such sights." Bertha concluded that the man had "a dual personality," but her family was no longer troubled by the ghastly shrieks from across the street.[38]

Equally a relief, the colony was allowed to keep its three camels, although the army was impounding all animals. Djemal gave orders that all the colony's wishes were to be met to the extent he could make it possible. Unlike the other residents of Jerusalem, they were allowed to buy cheap corn from across the Jordan River.[39] Nevertheless, misery surrounded them. Every morning pushcarts collected more bodies that had died the previous night. Desperate mothers offered to sell their babies for a pittance, just to get a meal. Young girls sold their bodies to soldiers in order to eat.

Unquestionably, Bertha shared a profound sympathy for the plight of the hungry despite being able to withdraw to her family and enjoy nutritious food in her large, well-appointed house on Nablus Road. At the zenith of her beauty, slim, self-confident, and imperious, entitled above others from youth, Bertha had a natural sense of her own superiority and a keen awareness of snobbery in others. Early in the war, as the shortages began, she found it droll that upper-class ladies begged to come on a different day or be permitted a separate door from that of their poorer neighbors. She called them "the bashful elite."[40] Now, she noted to an American supporter who had sent her $5,000, these ladies were as grateful as anyone else to stand in line to have their soup pails filled.[41]

Her sister and John Whiting also had a house of their own, opposite the Big House in the colony compound. Bertha and her brother-in-law, who continued as Glazebrook's vice-consul, used the considerable contacts they had developed to implore American friends for money to keep up the soup kitchen.

There was constant talk now that the United States would enter the war. Beyond their windows, the members heard the thunder of German iron-wheeled vehicles grinding against the pavement on their way south, where Field Marshal Edmund Allenby had taken over command of the Egyptian Expeditionary Force in June 1917. A tremendous Allied push north was expected at any moment. Consul Glazebrook called on Anna.

"I am leaving shortly," the consul announced. "For your safety, I suggest you leave yourself. It would be best for the whole Colony to go. To be here when a retreating Turkish army arrives could be unpleasant."

"Are you ordering me to leave?" Anna asked, squaring her shoulders and facing him sternly.

"I cannot order you, only suggest."

Anna looked him in the eye. "I left my country to be of service, and this is my supreme moment."[42]

It was a sorrowful day when the colony saw off the Glazebrooks and a few remaining Americans from the Quaker mission. Now, with all missionaries and church-supported doctors and nurses gone, the city was bereft of medical help. During March and April, the British had failed to break through the Ottoman-German defenses in two fierce battles at Gaza. British prisoners, unshaven and disheveled, were paraded through the streets, shorn of their tunics and boots. Crowds of Arabs watched silently, but did not jeer. The sight of both British and Turkish wounded, lying on stretchers outside overcrowded hospitals, provoked only pity. As with everyone, a sense of utter isolation descended on the Overcomers. All wondered, "How soon, how soon, before the British come?" Arab friends admitted they, too, prayed to Allah that a "Christian nation" would rescue them from their fellow Muslims.

On April 6, a courier arrived from Djemal Pasha, requesting the colony send representatives to the Augusta Victoria. "Naturally, it was a purely Spafford delegation that drove up in the Colony wagon to the Dictator's lair," noted Lars Lind wryly, controlling his resentment with difficulty.[43] Fearful they were to be expelled, many of the Overcomers felt bitter and hopeless, at a loss to imagine where they could flee. "We knew that whatever [the delegation] agreed to would be binding on the whole membership," Lars explained.[44]

"Djemal Pasha kept us waiting in the anteroom," Bertha wrote in her version of this important meeting.[45] Despite previous cordial relations with Anna and his help to the colony, according to Bertha, "he was not gracious."[46] She went on to describe how she stood boldly before him to propose the colony's services to nurse the wounded. "I must say that Djemal Pasha was taken aback." However, "he immediately regained command of himself and said with a look by which he meant to wither me, 'Today your country has been foolish enough to cut diplomatic relations with Turkey . . . and now, after hearing what I have said, are you still willing to nurse our wounded?' " Stunned to learn this news, Bertha described herself privately asking "for guidance." And then she replied coolly: "We have offered to nurse neither friends nor foes, but humanity—and our offer holds good."[47]

In Lars's version, the delegation returned with the news that they had been welcomed by Djemal. Through his interpreter, he had told them, "You have no doubt noticed the increasing flow of wounded to this city and the inadequacies of hospital facilities due to the closing down of foreign mission hospitals. I am asking if you would volunteer, in the cause of humanity, to reopen these hospitals and take charge of all the nursing facilities in the city." Simply, according to Lars—who mentioned no heroics on Bertha's part—the delegation had unhesitatingly affirmed the colony's willingness, and Djemal thanked them on behalf of his government. He then told them that early that morning he had heard that the United States was at war, and he realized they did not know this.

Under such circumstances, he asked, "will you still volunteer to perform this service?"[48] They agreed instantly, and Djemal thanked them. He then said that he would issue orders to hand over to the colony all hospitals and equipment, adding that his chief medical officer would give every assistance possible, as well as provide whatever supplies were available. In a final word he added, "From today, the situation is critical."[49]

The relief when the delegation returned with the news to the Big House "was immense," Lars remembered. The younger men of military age had been especially alarmed, aware they could be deported to the notorious prisoner-of-war camps in Anatolia, from which there was little prospect of returning alive. Others, who had devoted their lives to work in the holy city and meant to die there, felt once more that the Almighty supported them. And so, ironic though it was, men and women who had never had any professional medical training, who for years had renounced modern medicine altogether in favor of prayer and anointment with oil, who had allowed physicians on the premises only in the past decade after "Mother" had rescinded her rule against them, found themselves in charge of staffing and running five military hospitals and the Casualty Clearing Station.

Surrender

*The house of the tyrant collapses when the time
is right.*

—Arab proverb

There were no shirkers. Every member still fit enough to work converged on the requisitioned Grand New Hotel, given over by Djemal Pasha to be their central facility. It had been home to Dr. and Mrs. Merrill, then to Reverend Wallace; it was where Merrill had ordered Mary Whiting confined and where Selma Lagerlöf had stayed. Now filthy, crawling with vermin, the Grand New Hotel once again joined the colony in a new and formidable drama. The members attacked it with all their usual earnestness, and as Bertha supervised, every corner was scrubbed clean. To make room for as many beds as possible, they removed the largest pieces of furniture but left the ornate mirrors, chandeliers, and heavy marble washbasins. To banish hordes of bedbugs, they used kerosene, and when that ran out, they dismantled the iron bedsteads and passed each piece of frame through fire.[1]

Frederick Vester, regarded as a sensible businessman by his Turkish friends, had early joined the city government's Food Control Office. John Whiting, who had proved a diligent deputy consul, put his administrative skills toward directing the acquisition of medical equipment, stretchers, and supplies, sending members to gather what they could from the closed foreign-operated hospitals. A number of elderly Arab doctors who had not yet deserted helped other members to organize into medical units for assisting in surgery, anesthesia, wound care, and the use of such medicines as were available. They made notes on the doctors' instructions, and as most members had done at least some nursing over the years, they prayed they were up to the job.

Bertha was there when the first wounded arrived, directing them in Arabic to beds. A barefoot, ragged fellow lagged behind, looking bewildered as well as miserable. "What did you say?" he asked in English, surprising her that they had been sent a British soldier.[2] Bertha was sure it was a mistake, confident the Turks would not wish Allied prisoners of war to be treated by Americans. That evening the Vesters and Whitings conferred with Anna and Brother Jacob. Why not volunteer to take over the Casualty Clearing Station outside the walls by the Latin Patriarchate of Notre Dame? They might be able to identify, possibly hide, or at least protect the "Tommies," as British soldiers were known. Their offer was accepted. The job entailed bathing, delousing, shaving, providing hospital gowns, and directing patients, or more usually carrying them by stretcher, to one of the various hospitals. But with it came a new responsibility. The Casualty Clearing Station was also the morgue where the dead were sent. It would be up to the colony to organize proper burials, ensuring that a Jew was not buried by Muslims, nor a Muslim by Greeks or Latins. For the faithful of Jerusalem, getting this right was of paramount importance.

In short order, the American Colony was running makeshift hospitals in the Amdursky Hotel, the Greek Convent Hospital, the Convent of the Perpetual Adoration near the New Gate, the Italian Hospital, and the English hospital of the London Jews Society. Dedicated and willing as they were, the volunteers were not prepared for the suffering they now beheld.

Those wounded who made it alive to Jerusalem were almost all Anatolian Turks because so many Arab soldiers had deserted. These Turkish sons had endured transport on lurching camelback across the Sinai under a beating sun, then been transferred at Beersheba to a slow railroad fueled no longer with scarce coal but by wood from the forests once shading Palestine. By the time they arrived at the clearing station, they were often unconscious, and their wounds were hideous. When the colony staff cut off the stinking uniforms and removed the bandages, they saw maggots swimming in streams of pus. Usually the wounds were gangrenous. "Pansman, effendi," the soldiers pleaded to the one-eyed general practitioner, the lone remaining surgeon, "Mister bandager, cut if off." A heap of severed limbs rapidly filled the hospital courtyard like a giant stack of wood. With scarcely enough disinfectant and before antibiotics were introduced, many amputees died. Supplies soon dwindled. The lack of morphine especially grieved the struggling nursing staff. "We tore our room curtains into bandage strips, used our soft papers for cotton, and contributed our candles for night lights and such bits of kindling as we could scrape together for heating water."[3]

Lice presented a grave danger to the volunteers. These ubiquitous insects leaped into their clothes as they worked. And while periodically they hastily stripped, bathed, and changed, four of the Overcomers caught the typhoid fever that eventually killed more than 20 percent of the population during the war. Miraculously, the affected colonists survived. But for months they were bedridden, losing their hair, their hearts permanently weakened, which was a serious loss to the already undermanned, overworked, nearly sleepless team.

Lars Lind, his brother Olaf, Lewis Larsson, and others tried to persuade old friends to help them with the endless cleansing and bandaging, but they were always reluctant. The Arabs claimed they feared being taken prisoner along with the Turks when the British came. Jews and Armenians refused on principle to help Turks whether or not they were dying. Lars did finally inveigle their affable, six-foot-seven-inch neighborhood butcher, an Arab. But at his first look at a bandage coming off, he toppled over backward in a dead faint. "I cannot bear the sight of blood," weakly explained the butcher, who had slaughtered hundreds of sheep for the colony over the years.

Bertha stayed away from the harrowing sights of the operating and dressing rooms, saying, "Because of my young baby."[4] Instead, she assumed charge of housekeeping and supplies and visited the bed-lined corridors to cheer the patients, sometimes bringing her children to sing hymns. One day, however, she did happen to be at the clearing station, and glanced in at the morgue in time to see the presiding mullah dump the dead body of a handsome young soldier off his stretcher onto the floor. Furiously, she turned on the cleric. "No wonder there are so many deserters!" she exploded. "They make the supreme sacrifice, and you treat them like this!"[5] The mullah, incensed at being reproved by a woman, and an infidel to boot, responded rudely. It was not in Bertha's nature to tolerate such treatment. Immediately, she rushed to the Turkish medical headquarters to complain to the head officer. That same day, returning for lunch, Frederick informed her that she had stirred an uproar. The mullah was to receive sixty lashes and be made to sleep in the morgue for a week. She and Frederick hurried back to medical headquarters, where Bertha insisted that at least the beating be canceled even if he had to sleep in the morgue, a punishment for a superstitious mullah more onerous, perhaps, than a beating. With some satisfaction, she returned the following week to find the mullah pale, thinner, and no longer disposed to tangle with a female infidel like Bertha.

Her quiet sister, Grace, had never fully recovered from the death of her baby. She stayed in the compound and helped run the soup kitchen. Infrequently Anna called at the hospital as well. But she, too, was not herself these days. At her assembly, attended by mostly the old and infirm, as younger members had no time to spare, Anna predicted that Armageddon was at hand. Closing her eyes, lifting her powerful voice, she cried: "The conqueror must come through the southern gate, the gate of Love! If he comes through the northern gate—that will be the door of Doom."[6]

Then, in October, several German officers presented themselves at the compound. They wished to speak to Mrs. Spafford. She would have to close the soup kitchen; it was American propaganda. An hour later the Germans arrived at the hospital. The officer in charge was officious, impatient, striding through the beds, peering at the patients through his monocle. Turning to the worried group of Swedish and American male and female nurses, he announced that it was intolerable that Americans, with whom his country was at war, should be looking after Turkish wounded. To his accompanying officers, he said they must dismiss the hospital staff immediately, adding, "We will take the buildings of the American Colony as well. We shall need them for a convalescent hospital."[7] When he turned on the six American men, clearly of military age, and said they were to be deported as prisoners of war, the Overcomers were again suffused with dread.

Although Djemal Pasha was away, the Turkish governor of Jerusalem,

Izzet Bey, for whom Frederick Vester was working, intervened with the Germans. He pointed out that there was ample German property already vacant and that his administration could not do without the colony or the six young men, his most energetic helpers. He then talked with Frederick, who, as a German citizen, had been threatened with draft himself but exempted by a kindly doctor who declared him "unfit."

"What the Germans are really after," said Izzet Bey, "are the Colony pigs, cows, and horses—but chiefly the pigs. What started this war was pigs. Serbia is a pig-raising country, and Austria wanted their pigs. That is why the Austrians attacked in the first place. Now," he said, looking at Frederick with a twinkle in his eye, "I have told the Germans they may have your pigs, but nothing more. So when they come, let them take the pigs and be gone."[8] And so it was that twenty-one pigs were taken away on several military trucks. The colonists shook hands and heard no more threats of expulsion. Instead, they heard the boom of artillery approaching nearer every day.

In October 1917, satisfied that the massive Egyptian Expeditionary Force he had assembled was sufficiently irresistible, Field Marshal Edmund Allenby launched his great offensive. With twice as much infantry and ten times the cavalry of the Turkish-German defenders, this imaginative commander was "striding like a giant up the Holy Land."[9] Using tricks, feints, and surprises as well as sheer strength to keep the enemy off balance, Allenby had promised Jerusalem to Prime Minister Lloyd George as a Christmas present.[10] Steadily pushed back were fourteen Ottoman divisions and special troops from the German Asia Corps, commanded by General Erich von Falkenhayn, a man of such consummate arrogance that his co-commanders, Djemal Pasha and Mustafa Kemal, were unable to work with him. The Turkish troops had fought with exceptional courage, holding the line at Gaza through two previous battles, but now were "so physically weak that they could not even stand at parade, let alone march against the enemy," as Kemal reported to Constantinople.[11]

Beersheba had fallen to the British on October 3. On November 7,

Gaza was theirs as well. By November 9, Australian and New Zealand troops had reached Latrun at the base of the Jerusalem hills.

On that same day, November 9, in London, His Majesty's government made an announcement that would darken the lives of Palestine's Arabs into an unforeseeable future: the publication of the Balfour Declaration. Britain viewed "with favour the establishment in Palestine of a national home for the Jewish people, and will use its best endeavors to facilitate the achievement of this object." Although the announcement noted additionally "that nothing shall be done which may prejudice the civil and religious rights of existing non-Jewish communities in Palestine," the hearts of the Arabs sank low. Not long afterward, the Bolsheviks, in command of a tumultuous revolution in Russia, added to the Arabs' dawning sense of betrayal by disclosing secret agreements between the czar and the Great Powers to divide the Middle East. Specifically, the Bolsheviks let the shocking news be known that Sir Mark Sykes of Britain, secretly conferring with Georges Picot of France, had allotted between them most of the Ottoman Empire. When the telegram bearing this news was read to Jerusalem's Turkish guardians and Arab notables—and eventually circulated to an incredulous Arab public—they realized it contained no specific mention of Arab national aspirations, and draped their closed shops in black. It may not be surprising, therefore, that on the last day, as the British closed in on Jerusalem, Izzet Bey expelled forty Jews with American passports and a number of Zionists holding Turkish passports. And entering the telegraph office hammer in hand, he personally smashed the telegraph instruments.[12]

These extraordinary developments had not yet come to the ears of the colonists. Their concern was the closed soup kitchen and the desperate at their door when the grand mufti of Jerusalem, Kamil Effendi al-Husseini, called on Anna. Tall, kindly, a product of Al-Azhar University in Cairo, seat of Islamic scholarship, the mufti had often stopped on his way to his residence on the Mount of Olives to watch the long lines waiting for soup. Now, he asked Anna gently, would she be willing to have her people manage the distribution of food for the *d'ikieh* in the old arched souk? This was a *waqf*, or pious endowment, founded by a rich family over a thousand years earlier and had sustained the city's hungry ever since. At such a critical time, the mufti was concerned that temptations to graft or theft might compromise its invaluable service. Thus he turned to the colony, known to be neutral and above reproach. Sent by Anna to check it out, Bertha found "hundreds of clamoring and ragged skeletons clawing one another to reach the distributing center, and only being kept from tearing one another's clothes by police using whips."[13]

At the colony's soup kitchen, the scene had never been chaotic. But at the *d'ikieh*, Bertha saw a wild and threatening line stretching from the souk to the Damascus Gate. Not in the least daunted, she rose to her imperious best. The mufti, she said firmly, must dispense with the police and the whips. She lifted her skirts and scrambled on top of a wall. Loudly, she clapped her hands and demanded silence and attention. The crowd looked up, many recognizing the beautiful daughter of the American Colony who rode in an elegant carriage drawn by matching grays. Bertha spelled out her program. The American Colony was taking over; there would be no police, but supplicants must be orderly. "You will all get soup this way—even those at the end of the line," she promised, shouting from the top of the wall. That night two colonists volunteered to oversee the *d'ikieh*, and when the British came, the American Colony was serving up to six thousand recipients daily.[14]

In early December, the pounding of nearby cannon fire kept residents awake as a heated battle raged on Nebi Samuel, a strategic high point ten miles outside the city. The end was at hand. Everyone knew it. Izzet Bey arrived at Anna's gate, asking for her. In case Jerusalem was besieged, he confided, he had collected stores of food that were under lock and key. Would she be willing to supervise these precious stores? Anna was deeply moved at this final gesture of respect for herself and her people. As they stood together in the great salon, neither she nor Izzet Bey could guess how completely the lives of so many Arab and Turkish friends would be upended by coming events, nor how the city they all loved would soon be changed forever.

On December 8, 1917, the Turks began their evacuation from the city they had controlled for over four hundred years. The colonists watched Turkish soldiers, animals, stores, and equipment heading north for Jericho or Nablus. Only a skeletal guard remained in the silent streets to confront what everyone expected would be a fight to the finish within the walls. Turkish officers went through the wards, ordering out every patient who could hobble. Quickly, the nursing staff hid their three British "prisoners" in a small, out-of-the-way ward, praying they would be overlooked. The one-eyed Arab surgeon and other Arab attendants, fearing capture, slipped away. Still, all afternoon wounded kept arriving, filling up the empty beds.

Again Izzet Bey was at Anna's gate. Jerusalem may be bombarded, he cautioned hurriedly, and urged them to extinguish all lamps. They must stay in the basement that night. With no police in the streets, there was danger of looting. At last, bidding her a sorrowful adieu, he asked if he might borrow her carriage and the two grays, promising they would be returned. It was a favor Anna was glad to extend, and one of the young men volunteered to drive the departing governor north to safety, not to return until months later.[15] Anna then joined the Whitings and the Vesters at Bertha's house across from the deserted St. George's School. The rest of the membership descended to the basement of the Big House.

At the hospital, six young colonists, three Swedes and three Americans, including Lars Lind, agreed to remain on duty and let the others return to the Big House basement. They all feared an Allied bombardment. When the sun set, they bolted the door. There was no medicine left to dispense. The silence of the wards was broken only by the groans of men in pain. To pleas for morphine, they could offer only cups of water, walking quietly along dimly lit rows of beds, calming an agitated patient, putting a cooling cloth on a fevered brow. Before midnight, a deafening burst of gunfire rattled the windows, followed by flares lighting the black sky. Shortly afterward, they heard the clatter of horses' hooves and heavy boots. Looking down from the balcony, Lars Lind made out the tall figure of a mounted officer and troops entering the Jaffa Gate. A loud knocking on the hospital door sent him downstairs, where he begged the visitor in Arabic to be quiet. Outside stood a handsome young Turkish officer. In French, the officer said he had come to pick up his wounded subalterns, brought to the hospital that morning. He asked if Lars could please find their uniforms and get them dressed.

As the colonists scrambled to assist, locating crutches and clothes, the officer spoke wearily: "The artillery burst you just heard was to cover our withdrawal. By morning there won't be a soldier left when the British come for their battle for Jerusalem. We are the last to leave." With a sad smile, he bowed slightly. "Tcheckeradarum," or "Thank you," he said, then mounted his horse and vanished with his company into the night.[16] The little group watched him go, thrilled to know there would not be a street battle and moved to realize they were witnessing the end of an epoch.

At the first hint of dawn, a sleepless and exhilarated Lars stepped out on the balcony facing the city's ancient ramparts. He looked down at a vendor shuffling along with a tray of bread on his head. It seemed so normal. Just then, two bedraggled Turks carrying rifles walked through the Jaffa Gate. Lars watched them remove the vendor's loaves and cram them into their tunics. Not a word was exchanged. The vendor moved off. The soldiers shouldered their rifles and headed toward the Zion Gate. So began the extraordinary morning.

It was agreed that Lars should bring the news to the colony. Leaving the others with their patients and three very cheerful British wounded, he ran along the main road, muddy from nearly constant rain and gouged by heavy military vehicles, past the abandoned Turkish military headquarters, where telephone and telegraph lines dangled like spiderwebs. The air was bitterly cold, but the sun shone. He headed up Nablus Road and rang the bell at the Vesters' house. The Vesters and Whitings were already up; Anna emerged minutes later. Lars told them of the night's events. Anna turned to her daughters. Spontaneously bursting into the doxology as tears flowed down their cheeks, together they sang: "Praise God from whom all blessings flow . . . Praise him all creatures here below." The doorbell rang again. On the threshold stood the colony's long-time friend and near neighbor, the mayor of Jerusalem, Dr. Hussein Salim al-Husseini, accompanied by a small crowd.

"Mother," said the mayor, addressing Anna and waving a large brown envelope in his hand. "I am going out to Sheikh Badr to surrender the city."[17]

Lars raced on to the colony, whose members were just emerging from the basement. They had already heard from the mayor. The Husseini house was adjacent to the compound, so he had first stopped in on Lewis and Edith Larsson. Lewis, eager to capture the historic moment, grabbed his heavy photograph equipment and commandeered a young lad to help him carry it. He took his three-year-old son with him, too, and they all hurried on to join the mayor's group on Jaffa Road, dashing into the Italian Hospital on the way to snatch a bedsheet and fix it to a broom. Catching up with the mayor, the group was stopped with a cry: "Halt!" Two British scouts in shorts and helmets rose up from behind a rubble wall, pointing their rifles menacingly. The group put up their hands. Larsson waved his white flag, shouting in English.[18] They were not a very threatening-looking little assembly, the mayor in his red fez and frock coat, Lars, Lewis, and others in dark suits, the little boy wearing a white bonnet. The startled sergeants watched Hussein Effendi open his brown envelope and with great ceremony begin to translate the document of surrender. But, the soldiers explained, they were not authorized to accept the surrender; the mayor must wait for the commander in chief. However, they wouldn't mind sharing one of the mayor's cigarettes. Lewis clicked his camera shutter.

Next to arrive were two artillery officers, who also demurred on accepting the mayor's surrender but were interested to hear that the city was offering no resistance. By now, large numbers of soldiers were moving cautiously toward the city from several directions as men, women, and children were pouring into the streets, laughing, hugging, ecstatic to discover that friends they had given up for dead had merely been in hiding. A Lieutenant Colonel Bailey arrived. He, too, refused the mayor's proffered surrender, but radioed to the command center the news that the Turks had withdrawn. Finally, on a bony old horse, a brigadier general arrived, surrounded by infantry. Brigadier General C. F. Watson, commander of the 180th Brigade, was happy to accept the mayor's solemn speech of surrender as the crowd pressed close. He then put the document in his pocket and asked, "Where can a man get a good cup of tea?" Again Lewis clicked his camera.

Euphoric at what they had documented, the Swedes elbowed their way through shouting, dancing, clapping throngs to the photo studio and commenced to develop the negatives. In the meantime, General

John S. M. Shea, commander of the Sixtieth Division, delegated by Field
Marshal Allenby to receive the surrender of Jerusalem on his behalf, was
stuck in mud some twelve miles away. When his car finally reached the
city, it was late afternoon and street crowds had thinned. Looting of
abandoned buildings had begun, and there was still skirmishing in the
hills between entrenched Turks and the British. Nine of the colony windows were broken by shots from Mount Scopus. A stray bullet tore
through a dress lying on the bed of one of the Swedish "sisters," penetrating the mattress and lodging in the floor. No one was hurt. From her
daughter's house, Anna watched a bayonet charge.[19]

According to Bertha's account of this momentous day, she was walking toward the city walls when she spotted an official-looking car filled
with officers in red tabs and gold braid. She stood in the road and waved
it down. In the car was General Shea, who had finally arrived. Bertha described herself stepping on the running board and informing the general
that she needed food "for her men" immediately. Shea gave her his
promise, and in due course more food than they had seen in years arrived by truckload at the hospitals.[20]

At this point in Bertha's version, Mayor Husseini appeared. She introduced him to General Shea. As the mayor surrendered the city for a
fifth time, Bertha stood right next to the general and the mayor.

All versions written by members of the American Colony agree that
General Shea was in a furious state when he finally reached the holy city
and discovered that a subordinate had taken the historic surrender ahead
of him. Lars Lind reported that he demanded witnesses be corralled to
watch him stand on the steps of the Crédit Lyonnais for a reenactment
with the exhausted mayor—albeit without the surrender document now
secured in General Watson's pocket. "The Mayor was in a dither," Lars
remembered, "and the vast crowd could not make head or tail of the [re-
peated] pantomime."[21]

There was another reason for his irritation. At the highest levels of
government, the British had intended to make much of their gallant decision not to harm Jerusalem. Yet the surrender letter made clear that the
Turks had also resolved to protect Jerusalem's sanctity. "The Turkish
armed forces are being withdrawn in order to spare the Holy City," Izzet

Bey had written, "and the Turkish High Command hopes the British High Command will treat the Holy City with equal respect."[22] "It's a lie, a lie," Bertha had heard General Shea fume. But somehow, mysteriously, the original document given to General Watson never surfaced again. The British were free to broadcast to an appreciative world that Jerusalem had been saved entirely thanks to the restraint of His Majesty's government.

General Shea's irritation would also haunt Lewis Larsson and Lars Lind all their lives. Incredibly, he commanded them to destroy the negatives of the mayor's surrender to Watson. Although they managed to evade for a time this fatal sentence on the images that made them prouder than anything they had ever done, when Shea sent his aide-de-camp to enforce his order, they had no choice but to obey. Shea wanted only his moment at the Crédit Lyonnais to go down as history's record. But he allowed them to keep a copy of the mayor with the two sergeants and the white flag, which became one of the best-known and most published photographs of the war, credited to "The American Colony."

As for General Watson, every bit as disappointed as the two photographers to have his moment of glory erased, Lewis gave him the white bedsheet attached to the broomstick that Lewis had retrieved and hidden behind a bureau. In turn, Watson gave it to Lady Allenby, and today the flag of surrender behind which Lars and Lewis walked with the mayor of Jerusalem followed by a thrilled and smiling crowd rests safely in the Imperial War Museum in London.

Still, Mayor Husseini had not finished with his surrenders. Two weeks later, in a carefully orchestrated drama planned by Whitehall, Field Marshal Edmund Allenby, the tall, impressive leader of the "Last Crusade," as the British were fond of describing it, who could count Oliver Cromwell as his ancestor, slipped from the saddle of his horse and walked as humbly through the Jaffa Gate as the crisply uniformed head of a victorious army could manage. The contrast—intended—with the 1898 mounted entry of the soon-to-be-dethroned Kaiser Wilhelm in his ostentatious white and gold cape was duly recorded by the American Colony Photo Department, and forwarded to newspapers throughout the world.

By the end of September 1918, seventy-five thousand Turkish soldiers had surrendered to Allenby after he won the Battle of Megiddo on the plains of Armageddon, the last time cavalry was used in modern warfare. Anna was deeply satisfied by these biblical associations and assured her people that the prophecies would be fulfilled at last. But it was not to be quite as she anticipated. For soon into Jerusalem came Zionist organizers who were not religious—indeed many were atheists—and their purpose was political, not religious. They meant to fulfill the dream of a secular and socialist Jewish state, a safe and prosperous harbor for their abused brethren. As it turned out, it was a dream consistently supported by British policy under their mandate administration, despite opposition by Arabs, who were far less well organized and lacked the financial and political resources of their Zionist opponents.

Ten days later, on October 1, 1918, Damascus was occupied by the sharif's exultant Arab irregulars, prepared to make the ancient city the capital of the new Arab nation they had been promised by the British. They were forming their government when, two years later, in accord with the secret Sykes-Picot Agreement awarding Syria to France, a French army expelled them at gunpoint and they scattered, disappointed, furious, but helpless to oppose the will of the Great Powers. Ashamed of his part in the betrayal, Lawrence of Arabia withdrew from government service.

The late fall of 1918 saw the Ottoman government capitulate in defeat and a line of Allied warships stretch from the shores of Constantinople for sixteen miles westward into the Sea of Marmara. The victors, and for a time the new Turkish government, let the Ottoman dynasty keep its throne until 1923, when Mustafa Kemal, later known as Atatürk, became the first president of an independent Turkish nation in Anatolia. Not so fortunate were the Romanov czar and czarina, destined to die at the hands of the revolution, while the grand houses of Hohenzollern, Hapsburg, and the old kingdom of Bulgaria became just memories of a past glory.

As for the triumvirate, they fled to Berlin in 1918. By 1922, both

Talat Pasha and Djemal Pasha were dead, murdered by Armenian assassins. That same year Enver Pasha died fighting with the White Russians against the Red Army. When Anna heard the news of Djemal's murder, she bowed her head, remembering how he had protected the colony. Better than most, she understood how the demands placed on a dictator to achieve a higher good for his people could result in difficult but necessary measures.

The Lion and the Lamb

*An irresistible conflict between two national
communities, each demanding self-determination
within the narrow boundaries of one small
country, could not be healed or averted. The
Arab claim was based on Arabs having lived in
Palestine for over a thousand years: the Jewish
on ancient history, present memory and burning
faith . . . And the Palestine Administration, it
was said, was tossed in the turbulent waters between the Scylla of injustice to the Arabs and
the Charybdis of faith-breaking with the Jews.*

—Norman Bentwich

When the British arrived, Bertha embraced British officialdom
with open arms. It could even be said that it was her undoing. By
Christmas 1917, with Anna presiding benignly and her guests impressed
that they dined with a Jerusalem legend, the colony had entertained four
generals and twenty officers.[1] From that point on, Bertha's efforts never
flagged. At last, it seemed, she had come into her own.

With victory against the Turks assured, she spared no expense to
provide their British saviors lavish dinners, lunches, musicales, tennis,
and tea parties to entertain the officers—dipping deeply into the colony's
exchequer, which soon bulged with profits from the Photo Department
and the reopened colony store as soldiers asked for photos, souvenirs,
and antiquities to take home. The military administrators reciprocated,

turning to Bertha for advice on who was who in the conquered holy city that Britain intended to restore, refurbish, and transform into a "civil society." She helped to organize relief efforts in the Old City, joined by returning missionaries, the Hadassah medical units, and other women who earned the appreciation of Field Marshal Allenby. Lowell Thomas, a young and ambitious American journalist, came to the "open house" kept by Anna and Bertha, and shortly afterward T. E. Lawrence appeared as well, dressed in his Arab robes and soon to be made famous by Lowell Thomas as "Lawrence of Arabia."

An Arabic-speaking officer, Ronald Storrs, immediately recognized the value of relying on Bertha. A bachelor, Storrs had served as Oriental Secretary in Cairo, where he initiated the famous exchange with the sharif of Mecca that precipitated the Arab Revolt that was so well guided by Lawrence. Soon he would be knighted. Now he was Allenby's military governor. An enthusiastic aesthete, collector, and music lover, Storrs plunged into his duties in Jerusalem with relish, more interested in setting up the Pro-Jerusalem Society to protect the holy city's antiquities and giving interesting dinner parties than in the more dreary duties of controlling tensions between Arabs and Jews. Storrs relied heavily on Bertha to provide guest lists, later complimenting her in his memoirs for "all the advice and assistance which we never failed to receive in the early days when we knew nothing . . . from Mrs. Vester, the great-hearted and charming leader of the 'American Colony.' "[2]

Storrs admitted that he was never able to figure out just what beliefs her mother's sect held, but he wasn't sure it mattered. He also understood that "as the majority of members were Swedes or Norwegians, the name was not popular with the American Consulate."[3] But that didn't much matter, either, and Bertha's help did. It was especially useful that she could send one of the colony workers to do any manner of job at any time, including translating for the administrators—without the bother of having to compensate them.

Propelled by Storrs into the very center of a dizzying social whirl, thirty-nine-year-old Bertha rose gracefully in her enhanced position. She was happy to call Storrs "Pontius Pilate," an appellation he encouraged as he had a taste for the theatrical and, as a critic noted, "the limelight." Bertha responded wholeheartedly to the arch and quietly superior

Oxbridge mannerisms he and other Englishmen cultivated. She ordered new dresses and hats, and carefully glued the gold-edged invitations and calling cards into her "commonplace book." Her mother, always proud of her beautiful daughter, accepted her absences, although she was somewhat less happy that the young colony men were often too busy taking photographs, doing chores for the military, or working long hours at the store to attend the assemblies.

Another young officer, Charles Robert Ashbee, an architect who had served with Storrs in Egypt, joined him as civic adviser and secretary of the Pro-Jerusalem Society. "Life here is really amazingly interesting and picturesque," Ashbee wrote home after attending with Storrs the American Colony's Fourth of July festivities in 1918 "among generals, bishops, and the 'Best Society' of Jerusalem, 'all the world and his wife.' " Ashbee found the gathering "so absolutely, so naively American . . . We ate great swimming slabs of ice cream, and rose with our plates, and napkins folded in neat triangles, to the sound of 'Hail Columbia.' " He couldn't get over the sight of one of the colony girls representing Columbia in a pageant. "A dear, deadly earnest young woman, dressed in white, standing on a white box to make her taller," attended by "two little pages got up as Red Indians." The Swedish girl held a copy of the Declaration of Independence in one hand and "a sort of trident" in the other, with a crown of silver spikes on her head. Ashbee considered the colonists "splendid people," though he had heard the Anglicans "whisper this American 'freak colony' has a religion all of its own and follows some fanciful tradition of the Puritan fathers, enough to turn the colour of any Anglican Bishop's gaiters."[4]

Had she known his thoughts, Bertha would not have appreciated her pageant being viewed by this polished, urbane Englishman as something comical—and she hated the idea that her mother's fellowship was patronizingly discussed as a "freak" group, however much these officers seemed to admire her mother. There was little that she could do about it except to conduct herself with dignity, inviting them to select and elegant dinners at her house with several hired servants—paid for by the colony—and Swedish "sisters," who brought delicious food from the colony kitchen. It seems never to have occurred to Bertha that her exploitation of her mother's "evenly sheared sheep" was noted or resented.

During these fraught political days when people frequently invoked the image of "the lion lying with the lamb" in relation to Jews and Arabs, Bertha was always confident that among the docile lambs of the colony, she was the lion.

Still, despite the embrace of Storrs, Ashbee, Lawrence, Thomas, and others who shared their concerns about the rising vehemence between Arabs and Jews, all was not trouble-free. First of all, Frederick was a German, which did not sit well with the English. As soon as she could, Bertha wanted to obtain American citizenship for her husband. She solicited short tributes from Field Marshal Allenby and General Shea praising the Vesters' efforts to hide British soldiers and tend the sick and the wounded, but apparently asked for no mention of what other members had contributed. As the best way to obtain Frederick's U.S. citizenship, Bertha intended to travel to America, show the tributes to influential friends, and ask their help with her mother's old enemy the State Department. Her three oldest children, she told her mother, ought to be educated in good American private schools. She did not tell Anna yet that she was also toying with the idea of opening a store in New York, which she hoped would bring in still more profits and which would provide the needed excuse for frequent supervisory visits.

More immediately, however, Bertha and Frederick had a pressing worry. The British Custodian of Enemy Property threatened to confiscate the American Colony Store as German-owned. Frederick explained to the authorities that actually it was purely "a charitable institution . . . neither a partnership nor a share company and earnings are used for the members' living expenses and for charity."[5] For a time, helped by Ronald Storrs, the Vesters succeeded in ignoring the government's demand that the business be registered and proper records kept of income and expenditures. As a "charity," they also avoided paying taxes—but this could not continue forever, and a moment would come when the singular arrangement that put all the colony's earnings into Frederick's hands would become a problem.

In the meantime, the colony's old friend Professor Gustav Dalman, although a distinguished archaeologist, was no longer considered acceptable as a consul in the British occupation because he was German. The professor had represented the Swedish government for years, and had not only provided Swedish passports to the colony's Swedes, but to some degree restored the sense of national pride that Anna had tried to expunge. Now he suggested that Lewis Larsson be appointed to act for Swedish interests in Palestine. Both Lewis and Edith were delighted. With Anna's approval, Lewis accepted his credentials, along with a Swedish flag planted in his front yard, and Edith and Lewis were invited to all the official receptions, joining Bertha in Jerusalem's social stream.

To Bertha it was a cruel blow. She had no doubt that her husband was far more deserving and she far better suited to be a consular hostess. In time, it began to rankle so badly that she put forward Frederick's name for the vacant post of Danish consul. "She was so certain that his application would be accepted that she boasted that she would 'show the Larssons how to run a consulate,' " Lewis's son Theo Larsson remembered. "She even erected her own flagpole."[6] Unfortunately, Frederick was turned down.

Well before the colonists' own tensions echoed the political troubles surrounding them, the new caretakers of the holy city discovered just how full their hands had become. The old imperial order had collapsed. The mostly young British administrators assumed their duties in a mood of optimism and hope, confident that they could rebuild a Muslim world along Western democratic lines. The American president, Woodrow Wilson, had said, "The world must be made safe for democracy. Its peace must be planted upon the tested foundations of political liberty. We have no selfish ends to serve." Most of these youngish officials endorsed this lofty goal, even as the British government turned its attention to the oil deposits and strategic issues raised by the addition of some million square miles of former Ottoman territory stretching from Palestine through the Jordan desert, across the Euphrates and Tigris rivers to the foothills of the Zagros Mountains separating Iraq from Iran. Some, like the British architects of the Balfour Declaration, believed deeply in the right of the Jews to claim their ancestral home, while others, sympathetic to Arab fears for their own ancestral land, felt that the declaration had put Britain in an impossible bind.

In 1919, like the rest of the world, the colonists followed the extraordinary news coming out of Paris. Some ten thousand spokesmen for various constituencies had converged there for a peace conference aimed at settling the world's first global conflict. Representatives pored over maps, attempting to reconcile the demands of the ten thousand advocates. An Italian diplomat wrote that "a common sight at the Peace Conference in Paris was one or another of the world's statesmen, standing before a map and muttering to himself: 'Where is that damn'd?' while he sought with extended forefinger for some town or river that he had never heard of before."[7] The Middle East was especially unfamiliar. For a time David Lloyd George felt great frustration at not being able to locate the Dan of "from Dan to Beersheba," the biblical boundaries vaguely assumed to define the promised Jewish homeland.

Before President Wilson collapsed from exhaustion, he had made clear his opposition to the annexation of land as spoils of war. He also wanted to create a League of Nations as a forum for settling international disputes peaceably. For both the British and the French, the American president's insistence on the doctrine of "self-determination" of peoples was especially discomfiting as they knew perfectly well that the people of Greater Syria, Palestine, Jordan, and Iraq were interested in forming their own governments, not in having foreigners design them for their own purposes. Before he died, President Wilson appointed two friends, Henry King, the president of Oberlin College, and Charles Crane, a businessman from Chicago, to tour the former Ottoman lands and to assess their peoples' will. Not surprisingly, they learned that the vast majority wanted an Arab state in Greater Syria, including Lebanon and Palestine, and recommended this be done. The King-Crane Commission also recommended a drastic curtailment of the Zionist program, limiting it to an expanded Jewish community within the Arab state.[8] Such inconvenient conclusions were ignored as hostile to the aspirations of the Zionists, the British, and the French. After President Wilson's death, the United States withdrew from the League of Nations, and the British and French were free to assume their mandatory responsibilities. After the San Remo Conference in 1920, where Lloyd George and Clemenceau divided the Turkish spoils, the French drove out the Arabs and cut Lebanon from Syria. Britain won not only Iraq and Transjordan but also Palestine, and embarked on the impossible task of adjudicating the conflicting aspirations of the Zionists and the Arabs in a drama that would last twenty-eight bitter years.

A vigorously pro-Zionist observer wrote Lloyd George: "The Conference has laid two eggs, Jewish nationalism and Arab nationalism. They are going to grow up into two troublesome chickens; the Jews virile, brave, determined, intelligent; the Arabs decadent, dishonest and producing little beyond eccentrics, influenced by the romance and silence of the desert. In fifty years' time those Jews and Arabs will be obsessed with nationalism, the natural outcome of the [American] President's self-determination. A national home for the Jews must develop sooner or later into a sovereignty state." The writer added presciently, "Arab nationalism will also develop into sovereignty from Mesopotamia to Morocco. Jewish and Arab sovereignty must clash."[9]

As it happened, this letter read the future. It also reflected the dismissive attitude of the Zionists toward the Arabs as "decadent, dishonest," and eccentric. To Anna Spafford, her daughter Bertha, and the other members of the American Colony who had enjoyed the support and friendship of the Arabs, and who appreciated their traditions, attitudes, and habitual courtliness, these views were unfair. The colony had always been ecumenical. Jews and Arabs were their friends equally. They considered it shocking that the arriving Jews showed such little interest in trying to understand the customs, history, and especially the religion of the Arabs. Such willful ignorance, in the colonists' view, was arrogant and did not bode well for the future. But as the mandate got under way and Jewish immigrants bought up land and houses, it was quickly apparent that the Zionist dream did not include Arabs. While the colony remained close to such old Jewish friends as Eliezer Ben-Yehuda, the scholar who had dedicated his life to making Hebrew the living language for a united Jewish people, and continued to supply fresh bread to his family after his death in 1922, it distressed them that the new Zionist schools insisted on speaking only Hebrew and were for Jews alone.

Like the officers who frequented the colony, they disapproved of the self-segregation of the Zionists who were building hospitals, welfare agencies, and other institutions exclusively for Jews and creating a tax system for the Yishuv and, most alarmingly, a paramilitary force headed by a Russian firebrand named Vladimir Jabotinsky, who imported guns illegally while pro-Zionist officers in the administration looked the other way. The Zionist Commission, the colony believed, was rapidly becoming a state within a state, developing its own government and pressing the mandate authorities for road signs and public notices to be written in Hebrew. Dr. Chaim Weizmann, the brilliant head of the commission whose remarkably persuasive powers and closeness to members of the British cabinet had succeeded in obtaining the Balfour Declaration, officiated on July 24, 1918, at a ceremony on Mount Scopus dedicating the Hebrew University. The Vesters were among the socially prominent guests, including Field Marshal Allenby, who watched Dr. Weizmann lay out twelve foundation stones representing the twelve tribes of Israel. There was no record, however, that the man later considered the father of Israel ever called on Mrs. Anna Spafford or her daughter at the American Colony.

"The Arabs and the Jews don't love each other, and those people at home who talk so glibly of them lying down together like lions and lambs are ignorant of the real feeling here. The antagonism goes very deep, and the Jews are not as tactful as they might be in trying to make things easier," wrote Helen Bentwich, who joined her husband, Norman, in Jerusalem in January 1919, where Norman had arrived to take on the job of the mandate's first attorney general. The Bentwiches were liberal Jews and agreed that difficulty would come from the Zionists' conviction that "it was the duty of Lord Allenby and his staff to promote immigration and settlement of Jews on the land, to give Jews autonomy, and to make Hebrew an official language." Bentwich reflected unhappily, "If an officer resisted the pressure, he was regarded as an anti-Semite, or at least an enemy of Zionism." Increasingly it worried Bentwich that "more and more the two communities fostered 'apartheid.' "[10]

A year later, in 1920, Helen Bentwich's uncle, Lord Herbert Samuel, arrived to assume office as the first high commissioner of Palestine. His bulletproof car was escorted by motorcycle guards and armored trucks bristling with guns to protect him from the death threats that preceded him. The military occupation was ended, and Allenby departed for somewhat less volatile duties in Cairo. Lord Samuel was a fair-minded politician who wished to honor the mandate's responsibility to all the peoples of Palestine, tutor them in democracy, get the economy running smoothly, build power plants for electricity, and ensure a reliable water supply, and he genuinely believed he could promote the welfare of both Jew and Arab impartially. However, like Helen and Norman Bentwich, Samuel was a Jew and a Zionist, albeit of the same humane and tempered stripe. He had been the first Jewish member of the British cabinet, and now was the first Jew to govern Palestine in 1,850 years. He was convinced that the Jewish return would strengthen the British position in the Middle East. Although he was to court and charm the Arab aristocracy, the Arabs were aware that he had helped craft the Balfour Declaration. One of his first official acts was—"ingeniously," as Norman Bentwich put it—to issue a stamp that included "Eretz Israel" in Hebrew along with the name of Palestine in English and Arabic. It delighted the Jews. But the Arabs were enraged by such a formal recognition of the Jewish claim to Palestine. During the five contentious years that Samuel served, he could satisfy neither party. His fellow Jews assailed him for not doing enough; the Arabs for doing too little.

Helen and Norman Bentwich were frequent visitors to her uncle in his residence in the Augusta Victoria, no longer German or Turkish, but British "Government House." They never went to the American Colony, but they often met Bertha and Frederick at functions, where they kept their distance. Norman knew they "were anti-Zionist" and believed they "influenced visitors who stayed with them." Helen saw Bertha at the Women's Council, which provided medical help to women and children. Often, the Christian, Muslim, and Zionist ladies clashed over seemingly small things like whether or not to put "Eretz Israel" on the council's stationery. Helen conceded that Bertha "had a thorough knowledge of the Arab women and their problems and had given years of service to them. She played a large part in the social life of Jerusalem, after the arrival of the British." But, Helen thought, "although she was outwardly friendly, she, too, had no love for the policy of the Jewish Home."[11]

In her rooms at the colony, and often staying at Bertha's house nearby, Anna Spafford felt poorly. She was seventy-eight, and for some years now she had suffered episodes of headaches and drowsiness, followed by anxiety and confusion that sent her reeling to her bed. It was important to keep from her followers the extreme thirst she felt, the desperate hunger between meals, yet the peculiar satiety before she could finish her dinner. The weight she had carried for years was dropping off, her tender feet had developed nasty infections, and her eyes had become swollen, making it difficult to focus even through the spectacles she had been wearing for the past five years or so. Although she had her own porcelain commode and thus never had to resort to the ramshackle outhouses behind the Big House used by the rest of the members, she took care not to stray far lest the urgency to urinate embarrass her, although now that the colony could afford it, they were putting in modern plumbing as much for their guests as for the members. Bertha, Grace, and the dedicated "sisters" who looked after her were aware of Anna's increasing delicacy. Among themselves, the members whispered, but it seemed inconceivable that anything could daunt their leader. No one knew the problem was diabetes, which had still not been diagnosed by her doctor. The face that Anna showed them, with enormous effort, was the strong, confident, and commanding visage of a woman who talked with God.

Privately, however, Anna felt tremors of uncertainty. She had been sustained from the beginning in her faith that the return of the Jews would guarantee a glorious Advent. Yet just before Lord Samuel arrived at Easter, violent riots had broken out over the Wailing Wall in Jerusalem, provoked by a decision on the part of the grand mufti, Amin al-Husseini, to re-point the ancient stone blocks. An Arab mason, hanging high on a scaffolding, had succumbed to the temptation to drop blobs of mortar on the worshippers below. Jews and Arabs understood that the mufti was sending a bold message that the wall belonged to the Haram al-Sharif and not to the Jews. However, what the Zionists may not have grasped—or were indifferent to—was that the subterranean Mosque of Al-Buraq lay beneath the ancient stones into which Jews pressed their slips of paper, or that for five hundred years the area had been the inviolable Waqf of Abu Madian, and thus an area equally sacred in Muslim eyes. To the Zionists the importance of the Wailing Wall was not so much its function as a place of worship—many Zionists were atheists, and the movement was secular—but its powerful symbolic role as the heart of Judaism. They were ready to claim it no matter the cost, and the Arabs were prepared to do the same. In 1920, during the Nebi Musa festival when Arabs thronged the city, British police were unable to stop rampaging celebrants from turning on Jews and murdering large numbers in a spree of hatred. Although Vladimir Jabotinsky's paramilitary force was not allowed inside the walls, outside his armed followers fell murderously on Arabs. This ugly collision, coming on top of previous incidents, shook Anna profoundly.

"I was reading in the Old Testament this morning," she wrote in a rambling letter to her old friend Mary Miller in Chicago, "and was struck with the number of times God mentions Jerusalem . . . It seems to be the place on earth that God has chosen to work out his plan. And strange to say—now at this crucial time of the world, Jerusalem again comes up, and here again is a struggle over her. She is delivered from the Turk, but there is a strife over her. Whose is she to be? A bitter hatred has arisen between those in possession: the Arabs, and those to whom it was promised. The Jews claim they are the rightful heirs. The fight over possession has begun, and manifested itself in an attempt to massacre each other . . . Thank God the British . . . stand in the breach while God works out his will with his ancient people."[12]

Anna struggled to organize her thoughts. "God's mighty plan of Salvation," she told her friend, had been to lead the Israelites, "a peculiar people, a holy people, a prepared people," to Canaan, where they were to have been "perfected" and to have realized "a great work." But instead of embracing God "as their King and Bridegroom, married to his Will," the Israelites had been blind to the arrival of God's Son. Drawing as she always had on Horatio's theology, heavily influenced by Protestant evangelical messianism, Anna believed that when the Israelites failed to see Christ's divinity, God had turned to the Gentiles. But as Horatio's heretical teachings instructed, Anna believed that God had chosen the Overcomers instead of the organized church as the new "holy and peculiar people" to be "the Bride made one with Him and one another."[13]

Although Anna had added her own innovations over the years to what Horatio had preached, she had never departed from the central tenet holding that the Jews must eventually be converted. Now she felt that a climactic moment was at hand. "It seems to me we are reaching this time," she wrote portentously. "Is the judgment of blindness going to fall away from [the Israelites]? Will their eyes be opened? And by whom and where?"

Staring death in the eye in the privacy of her quarters, Anna wondered if God's—if her—message would be heard. If it were not, if the Jews refused to see the light, how could she continue to hope that the Messiah would return? Given the direction in which things were going in Jerusalem, that possibility seemed increasingly remote. Again, Anna felt she might be disappointed.

Then Anna suffered a stroke that paralyzed her right side. With her superhuman willpower, she regained her strength and was able to walk again with difficulty, continuing to take part in the morning meetings. Although it had shaken the fellowship, the colonists, like Anna herself, could not believe she could die. "Do you think that I am speaking for myself?" she reproved her followers. "Do you not think that God is leading me?" She reminded them of doubting Thomas, unable to believe that Christ had risen until he saw the marks on His hands and feet and felt the wound in His side.[14]

In 1921, as cars tooted, lorries rumbled, and motorcycles whizzed past bicycles in the crowded but much cleaner streets, visitors shopped in refurbished bazaars, and anyone, without paying a fee, could visit the Holy Sepulchre—still plagued by beggars, stray cats, and sectarian disputes—or stroll peacefully among the cypresses and pavilions on the Haram al-Sharif. At the colony, another Swedish "sister" died, and there were three weddings, including the marriage of John Whiting's sister, Ruth, to a Romanian member, Maurice Goldenthal. Bertha continued to attend balls, teas, and important functions and entertained a roster of celebrities that included Gertrude Bell, Lady Astor, Vita Sackville-West, Lord Northcliffe, Mrs. Holman Hunt, Mr. and Mrs. John D. Rockefeller, and many of archaeology's luminaries—to mention just a few in the limitless parade of famous names. But Zionists did not come to the colony, nor were they invited.

Frederick ran the colony store, still without government interference, continuing to sell vials of Jordan water, robes, jewelry, and antiquities and adding, very profitably, a franchise for Dodge cars, which flew from the showroom so fast they were obliged to telegraph to America for more. Given the frequency of motor accidents as enthusiasts drove with more abandon than caution, they also opened a mechanical department, and the colony boys added another trade to their repertoire of skills, handing over the profits to Frederick.

On the first of May, provoked by news that the Zionist Commission was demanding that Jews be privileged in acquiring land and wanted concessions for public utilities, and especially by the arrival of yet another wave of Jewish immigrants, violent riots broke out in Jaffa. A mob descended on an immigrant hostel in the burgeoning city of neighboring Tel Aviv and killed forty Jews. That night, as the riots and bloodshed spread to Jerusalem, Bertha threw a farewell dinner party for one hundred before she and Frederick departed for America. It was a grand occasion. Charles Ashbee was among those admiring "the customary musical grace, the customary good fare, and the sprite-like sisters that wait upon us. They flit through the great rooms like ministering angels. Theirs is a fine ideal of service, and one always feels rather humble when one goes to the American Colony, a feeling that intellect counts for so little after all.

"I was honored with a seat next to old Mrs. Spafford—'Momma'—the mother of it all. She is a wonderful old lady, and what a lot she must have weathered! She is very old and feeble now," said Ashbee, who had recently read Selma Lagerlöf's book. "I noted her still terrific underlip and chin—a characteristic of all the great 'religious.' "[15]

The Vesters' departure for America in 1921 became the first of regular trips. They put their three oldest children in private schools there, and Bertha enjoyed visits to wealthy friends with summer homes in places like North Haven, Maine, and the Adirondacks. The second year she left, she insisted that her sister move to the Big House to keep an eye on things. Even if Bertha had stayed back in Jerusalem in 1922, she could not have prevented a sequence of events that spelled the beginning of the end for her mother's dream. While she was abroad, a series of crises arose, and although Anna tried to lead her bewildered and increasingly roiled flock from her sickbed, her illness had now become the colony's real master.

Death

*Christian, Muslim, and Jew: there is no longer
any chosen people, nor any "dominating spirit,"
nor earmarked religion, nor Messianism. For
the Kingdom of Heaven is in one place only—
where Christ always told us it was—within
ourselves.*

—Charles Robert Ashbee

On March 16, 1922, Anna's daughters threw an elaborate eightieth birthday party for her, inviting two hundred of Jerusalem's finest. Lord Herbert Samuel could not attend, but he wrote a congratulatory letter to Bertha mentioning Mrs. Spafford's "higher ideals" and noting "the high esteem" in which she was held by "all sections of the varied community of Jerusalem."[1]

Buoyed by the attention, Anna improved. She sent a copy of Samuel's encomium to her friend Mary Miller, adding chattily that the colony was happy to put up Baron von Ustinov's widow, who had been so good to them in the past; the poor baron had died "from slow starvation having lost all to the Bolsheviks!" She had also heard that Dr. Hedges was dead. "Now his ill-gotten gains will not help him."[2] The euphoria, sadly, was soon spent. With Bertha away in America, Grace in charge, and old troubles resurfacing, Anna began a serious decline. She was extremely thin, unable to hold down her food, and often too weak to get out of bed. There were moments when she blacked out, but, characteristically, she tried to follow everything that was happening within the colony.

Grace wrote Bertha loyally, keeping her apprised of events. She saw to it that Anna was carried back and forth between a rented house by the sea at Jaffa and a house that the Vesters bought in Ain Karim in the hills outside Jerusalem. Frequently, it was Anna herself who asked for the change of scene, perhaps recognizing that it was just as well her followers did not see how debilitated she really was. Colonists were not encouraged to visit except for several devoted Swedes who nursed her. Her worshipful adopted son, Jacob, was almost constantly at her side, writing her letters when she was too weak and, when she felt strong enough, leafing through the Bible as they sought to discern God's will. And it was Jacob who conveyed Anna's messages to the assembly.

Anna knew her daughter's plans included staying for the summer in Lynn, Massachusetts, visiting Chicago, and taking the children to Niagara Falls. First, however, Bertha intended a holiday in Venice, the excuse being to check on "lace-making" should she revive the embroidery factory. Before she left, Anna had given Bertha a necklace as a peace offering to a girl who had angrily fled the colony and was working in Chicago. She also hoped that on her way to Niagara Falls, Bertha would stop in Buffalo and call on old Brother Baldwin's sons, who had escaped several years earlier and married former colony girls. She hoped Bertha would make peace with them, for she feared they were writing negative things to younger members.

Unfortunately, Bertha's visit to Buffalo was a disaster. The two families bore little love for Anna's spoiled daughter, whom they had been forced to wait on as children. Too many thrashings at Brother Jacob's hands, too many humiliations in the assemblies, and too many hungry days had left bitter memories of the Spafford leadership. While they made a show of welcoming Bertha, the stage was set for a confrontation. Bertha, contemptuous of their "secondhand furniture," their efforts to support themselves as photographers, their lack of social position, did not conceal her disapproval. "The Baldwins have made no impression in Buffalo," she wrote her mother witheringly. In Bertha's eyes, the Baldwins were "out to prove that we are wrong and they are right by succeeding."[3]

When one of the wives brought up some troubles that her sister-in-law was having with the colony in Jerusalem and remarked that she wished she could be with them in Buffalo instead, Bertha seized the occasion to storm out. "In one second Frederick and I were on our feet," Bertha wrote Anna. "We would not stay to hear such talk," noting with evident satisfaction that when she stalked out, Farida Baldwin's children "turned deathly pale."[4]

Bertha's strong suit had never been empathy. She was incapable of seeing that her visit was damaging to her mother's plan to placate rebellious members. It was the Baldwins who were at fault. "How precious are those who will let the sword pierce them," she wrote, invoking Anna's repeated injunction that her flock pierce themselves with a sword of self-abnegation.[5] Brittle and unbending, she would make no concession to dissidents however valuable it might be, for the deft "sword" that had molded Anna's submissive community was merely a cudgel in Bertha's hands.

In her bed at Jaffa, Anna worried. Old wounds were not being tended. Recently she had given permission for Olaf Lind, Lars's older brother, to accept a job as manager of Jerusalem's American Express office, where he was exposed to the many exciting business opportunities arising in postwar Palestine. Olaf proposed to the assembly a real estate deal of his own, but John Whiting had squashed the project as risky. The other members, knowing little of such matters themselves, agreed. Frustrated, Olaf was continuing to resist the decision. To Lewis Larsson, he complained bitterly, "I suppose if I should be a botanist then the Colony would think I was alright, pegging away at flowers all my life . . . I have a craving and talent for business, and to expand myself, and to make a lot of money." He protested, "If they could only realize it would be a splendid thing for the house."[6]

Adding to Olaf's agitation, he was in love with Bertha's seventeen-year-old daughter, Anna Grace, to whom he assumed he was betrothed. The previous year Anna had joined their hands and led them from the dining room, the usual signal that she wished them to marry.[7] However, either Anna Grace herself or her mother, or even possibly in an after-thought her grandmother, had decided that Olaf's younger brother Nils was a more reliable bet for a daughter of the First Family. The hurt added to Olaf's frustration.

In the assembly, members said he was flouting the principle of holding "all things in common," and suspected he was holding back a portion of his salary. Anxiously, Anna sent messages that she felt the disharmony. But by June, she was incoherent and delusional, and her doctors quietly told Grace that she was dying. Frantic, Olaf, fearing expulsion from the only family he knew, secretly paid a visit to "Mother" where he wept, repented, and declared he would do only what she wished. A group from the colony chorus traveled to Jaffa to sing to Anna outside her door. The doctors decided the malady was diabetes and put her on a regimen of oatmeal and butter every two hours, and the crisis appeared to have passed. Olaf returned to the assembly and plunged "the sword" into his breast. "Olaf broke," Brother Jacob recorded with relief.[8]

Grace was exhausted as she tried to keep the colony together. Despite Olaf's contrition, he had resumed wavering, while another member named Herbert announced he was leaving "because they taught him to hate his mother and . . . he would rather die than to think evil of her."[9] Worse, a former member living in New York, Enor Shelburg, was urging restless colonists to demand their fair share of the colony's profits. To Bertha, away in America, this presented the gravest threat of all.

But she did not come home. In part Bertha wished to raise money for her newly established American Colony Aid Association—caring for the forgotten, after all, was what had made her mother famous. It gave Bertha a position in the city, and if she could obtain financial backing, it could provide an income as well. Although she was detaching herself from her mother's religious notions, she believed that she was destined to be the leader of the fellowship that Anna had built.

The Vesters anticipated the need to formalize Frederick's control of the American Colony Store, recognizing that the Palestinian government would eventually oblige formal registration, although it would be exceedingly complicated. Bertha also wanted to get rid of uncooperative members, leaving only those who acceded to direction from Frederick and herself. She toyed with the possibility of relocating the assembly to New York if she could obtain citizenship for Frederick. With this in mind, she had found a location for her new store at 9 East Fifty-sixth Street.[10]

Anna was aware of her daughter's ambitious plans. They had discussed them together. Grace reported that their mother was still remarkably clear minded when it came to "spiritual matters," even though she
was now in nearly constant pain. Grace added that Anna had recently
said, "Something is ahead for us . . . We must be awake and not asleep.
It may be the time that God wants to send the ones ready to America."
When Anna mentioned to a member "that it might be possible that the
assembly would not remain in Jerusalem long," he had thought it very
strange and unsettling.[11]

In late August 1922, Anna sat up in bed and devoured a long, bitter-
sweet letter from Bertha in Chicago. The house on Monroe Street where
they had stayed during the Whiting trial, Anna read, "was as dilapidated
as ever," and Bertha had not been able to find any trace of Anna's beautiful home in Lake View. It had vanished as Chicago grew. Nor had she
delivered the necklace that Anna sent to the girl who had fled, Ellen Anderson, who had found work as a chambermaid but was not in town.
When Bertha met with Ellen's relatives, they said "hard things" to her
that made her "quite sick for a moment . . . the same old story. That we
did all kinds of wicked things." It was no better when she called on relatives of Otis Page, finding them drunk and disorderly, and accusing
Anna of being a tyrant.[12]

In a more encouraging vein, she wrote her mother that she was staying with a wealthy family who had a car and driver at her disposal. She
and Frederick had called on potential donors, visited Anna's simple Norwegian relatives and some of her aged classmates, and gone out to Lake
Forest to see Ferry Hall, where Horatio had sent Anna to school. But for
Anna, holding the pages in her trembling hand, her daughter's attendance at a Sunday service at the Fullerton church was what mattered
most:

> Ever so many people came up to speak to us when the service was
> over . . . It would have been amusing had it not been so terrible to
> see the change come over the different individuals when they heard

who I was. Some came over & shook hands warmly & said, "I remember your father, he was a grand man." Others said feebly, "I remember your father," and I knew just exactly by their tone of voice what special circumstance they were remembering.

I said quite strongly & without wincing, "So, do you remember when he was turned out of this church? Well, I thought you might like to hear that the wonderful work he was brave enough to break loose from here and start, is going on splendidly & growing daily & is now a living success."

I took their breath away a little at first. Several got away from us as soon as possible. They didn't want to hear of their victim being so successful.[13]

The pastor of the church took them to see McCormick Theological Seminary, on whose board Horatio had once served:

It was thrilling to be walking on the ground where you & Papa spent so much time. Where circumstances were brought to bear to cause our wonderful work to begin. Of course, such a crippled, cramped and narrow outlook on life as the Fullerton Avenue Church & McCormick Seminary, Miss Dryer & Co., could not satisfy such a marvelous hunger after the higher and nobler things of life, such an honest-seeking after Truth. Of course you and Papa had to break away & go to simple Jerusalem & the honest, noble & sincere desire & seeking brought its answer. How we bless you for this. How we love you for bringing the real things of life into our reach. How we admire you for your courage & how we realize that nothing but that same courage will complete the work your noble and Papa's noble spirits began. And we ask God as never before to endue us with a double portion of your spirit, our precious Mama. There is nothing so beautiful in all the world, under heaven, as your wonderful spirit.[14]

A few days after the visit to the seminary, as a guest of one of the colony's wealthy admirers, Bertha sank into a luxurious bed. "My mind would not cease to work after we retired. It was all so strange. Being in Chicago, enjoying the most courteous hospitality from these rich people, who acted as though they were having the rarest privilege to entertain us. And imagining the circumstances of our last sojourn in Chicago. The contrast was too great and my mind could not stop making comparisons & unraveling our course since we were last here."[15]

Bertha's tour of America confirmed her desire to move there and begin a new and better life for herself and her family. The wealth she had encountered, the modernity of escalators and air-conditioning, the welcome and respect she had been shown by prominent citizens, convinced her that she could rise above her parents' controversial past. She did not fear the angry former members living there, who lacked social position and worked in menial jobs and whom she was sure she could successfully avoid when she and Frederick established themselves as owners of a profitable store. The plan would require, of course, the cooperation of colony members, and while she had not worked out the details, Bertha was confident that she could persuade members remaining in Jerusalem to keep them supplied with antiquities and other salable Middle Eastern goods.

Still, the encounters with the colony's critics and disaffected had been unpleasant. While Bertha would always mythologize her dead father, her feelings toward her autocratic mother were more ambiguous. Anna's word was law, but her religious beliefs were peculiar, even fantastic, and as Bertha grew up and saw the ridicule they engendered, she had begun to disavow them silently, although not the work of her mother's community, which had always drawn praise from outsiders and which she herself had come to admire and wished to emulate. Her role as her parents' primary defender had always come at a cost, and Bertha wished to be free from it forever.

In its way, Bertha's childhood had been no easier than those of the other colony children. She had never been included in their special fellowship. While she ached over her parents' outcast status, in games when the children played "Overcomers" battling "Missionaries," her playmates knew she had to be assigned the winning part. But spoiled and privileged as she was, Bertha had found her royalty lonely. Even her timid sister,

Grace, had shared more fun and affection from the "sisters and brothers" than Bertha ever had. In her own way, therefore, Bertha had been as bruised as everyone else, although she never had to share their terror of being condemned and expelled. Because she was beautiful, charming, and intelligent, she had the necessary talents to realize many ambitions for herself and her family—but unfortunately she lacked her mother's remarkable charisma and especially her insight into character that had been such a powerful tool for Anna. Even had she wanted to, which she did not, she could not have imitated her mother's sibylic gifts, and by now too many of her contemporaries did not trust her. No wonder, then, that when the Vesters finally returned to Jerusalem in November 1922, Bertha found treasonable forces at work beyond her control. And the person who could have dealt with them had only five months to live.

During January 1923, Anna was carried into the assemblies on a chair but usually fell asleep. "I don't think I will die," she reiterated to the anxious assembly. "The resurrection is near, when we will have the dead back amongst us." But it was alarming to hear Anna begin making vague references to sins she claimed to have committed. No one in the assembly was sure what sins she was talking about, but her voice rose piercingly, and she shouted, "Sin must be rooted out!" Then, abruptly, Anna ceased to attend. Instead, Jacob conveyed her "message," and one in particular disturbed Edith Larsson. "God will be paying for our sins," Jacob read aloud, adding enigmatically: "This message fulfilled in 1896."[16] It shocked Edith, for that was the year her father and the Swedes had come to Jerusalem. Had their arrival been a punishment for Anna's sins? Hardly a member was not frightened by the disturbing message.

Anna was kept at Bertha's house. Grace went over daily, and Jacob now slept there as well. Bertha pursued a dizzying round of appointments, parties, teas, meetings—but kept a diary on her mother's condition. Her mother was having strange dreams. She talked to "Papa." She thought she had been left at the Damascus Gate and pleaded to be taken home. Bertha meticulously recorded the friends and important visitors who called, including Lady Samuel. But often now her mother recognized no one. Grace was taking her mother's decline badly. When Anna had another stroke on February 11, Grace suffered "spasms" and fainted in the salon.

On February 20, Bertha expelled Olaf Lind. She told him that as he was working independently of the colony, and had not put his earnings into it, his connection was severed. She told him to go to Frederick at the colony store. Olaf assumed he would receive a sum of money on the condition that he sign a statement renouncing further claims. Instead, Frederick informed him he would be given four days to gather his things and "to disappear."[17] Olaf consulted a lawyer, although it was a while before Bertha and Frederick heard about it.

On March 13, Brother Edward Baldwin died and was buried the next day. "Dear Bro. Edward!" Bertha recorded. "He knows it all now, and realizes with regret that sorrowing for oneself does not work redemption."[18] She had had enough of the Baldwins. It was time to rid the fellowship once and for all of the ungrateful and uncooperative.

March 16 was Anna's birthday, and clear headed that day, she asked that she be dressed in a favorite purple gown to receive the friends who came to call. Her visitors, Bertha noted with pleasure, included Lord Samuel's secretary, Brigadier General Sir Wyndham Deedes, a devout Christian Zionist interested in Anna's group. He was leaving shortly to help the poor in the London slums, and Bertha had arranged for the colonists to put together a beautiful book illustrating the Twenty-third Psalm as a going-away present. That night, Bertha's recently knighted friend Sir Ronald Storrs dropped in to join an amusing group for dinner. Upstairs in her room, Anna murmured about the Resurrection.

As she slipped from them, the watching family heard Anna talking in Norwegian. Feverish, she developed an ominous cough. Through the night of April 17, she sank into a coma. Grace and John Whiting joined Bertha and Jacob in an all-night vigil. At 4:00 a.m., Bertha went to her room to rest. At six, Frederick called her. "Our precious one was crossing to that 'Beautiful Land.' Oh! the crushing agony of seeing her go!" Bertha wrote in her diary. "But, for her who had inspired us, we would not disappoint her. She would have us meet her in Galilee and not mourn at the tomb." She and her sister had seen Anna dance when their father died. It was up to them to celebrate now, not to sorrow. "May her mantle fall on us," Bertha implored her diary, "and may we have a double portion of her spirit."[19]

All night the assembly had waited and prayed silently together. They had been warned by Bertha that the end was coming, yet believed in a miracle. Nothing was impossible for God, and Anna had said she would not die. As ever, they were prepared to believe in her as they did in the Lord himself.

Early that morning Bertha announced the dreadful news: "Mamma is now with Jesus." The room hushed. "[We] thought that the time for the resurrection was perhaps near." Edith recalled the extraordinary stillness as the fellowship shared an identical thought. "The Colony had lost its mother. What would happen now? Her daughter had neither the disposition nor the power which she had had. The ship had lost its rudder, and we did not know if it would sink or right itself."[20]

CHAPTER THIRTY

Epitaph

*Now faith is the substance of things hoped for,
the evidence of things not seen . . . These all
died in faith, not having received the promises,
but having seen them afar off, and were persuaded of them, and embraced them, and confessed that they were strangers and pilgrims on
the earth.*

—Saint Paul's Epistle to the Hebrews 11:1 and 13

The Overcomers filed past the open casket in a daze, staring at their leader's body lying on white silk. "She was perfectly beautiful in death. Every wrinkle removed, as all sorrow was washed away."[1] Trying to suppress their tears, they buried her on Mount Scopus, a simple stone marked "Mother" on her grave. Months passed. There was no sign of the millennium. The Messiah did not come; the prophecies remained unfulfilled. Bereft, the congregation floated, doing what they had always done. As they had been trained, they asked no questions; they tried not to think.

Three months later Frederick submitted a request to register the colony store as a business, not a charity, under the name of "Vester & Co., the American Colony Stores." Its two proprietors were Frederick Vester and John D. Whiting, and in their names were all the valuable properties. Soon the New York store opened, and Bertha insisted that the reluctant Whitings move there to run it. After a time they called Nils Lind to come. Married now to Anna Grace Vester, Nils was unable to prevent the store's losses from accumulating or his marriage from dissolving (it ended in divorce). In short order, the store was in debt to the American Colony for over $200,000.

Bertha and Frederick continued their frenetic social life, adding to their servants a white-coated butler. Bertha launched a School of Handicrafts and Dressmaking, and in due course opened the Anna Spafford Baby Nursing Home and Infant Welfare Center, staffed by a mix of dedicated Jewish and Arab doctors. She made it clear that she had little time or interest in conducting the assemblies. Indeed, she rarely attended. But for nearly seven years, she did all she could to maintain control over the still obedient Overcomers.

The morning meetings fell to Brother Jacob, often too choked with emotion to speak. Anna's acolyte for four decades, a gifted linguist and biblical scholar much admired in archaeological circles, Jacob never recovered from Anna's death. Distressed, he observed the smoking and cocktails, previously strictly forbidden by "Mother," that Bertha allowed in the upstairs salon and the free and easy behavior of her children, who were showing little aptitude for religion. When a widowed tourist offered to give $25,000 to build the colony a chapel as a more formal setting for their services, Bertha encouraged the gift by telling the widow that her son was taking theological courses in New York. The chapel was never built, and only the Vesters knew what happened to the $25,000.

Another ardent apostle of Anna's, Brother Elijah, the skeletal genius from Bombay whose inventions had been such a help to the colony, was as devastated as Jacob. Elijah had been with the colony nearly as long as Jacob, lovingly preserving Anna's "messages" in a book. Alarmed by Bertha's drift from her mother's teaching, and fearing that the fellowship would founder, he frequently reproved Bertha—as it turned out, once too often. One day she flew at him in a fury, snatched the precious book from his hands, and tore it to shreds. Elijah left the colony shortly afterward. Jacob loyally remained, unhappy but silent, until he was killed in an automobile accident in 1932. At his death, it was discovered that in the interim he had converted to the most despised of Anna's "pools of iniquity," the Roman Catholic Church.

As high commissioners came and went, none more able than the last to quell ever more violent Arab protests against ever greater numbers of

Jewish emigrants settling in Palestine, it was discovered that Frederick
had been dealing in stolen antiquities. One transaction in particular created a scandal that terminally soiled Frederick's reputation in important
circles. An ancient cartouche, in perfect condition, of the type issued by
the Pharaohs during the Israelite captivity in Egypt, was brought secretly
to the store. Frederick recognized its value, bought it, and sold it to Professor James Breasted, a renowned archaeologist at the University of
Chicago who published the acquisition. The cartouche was instantly recognized by the French archaeologist from whose dig in Byblos, Lebanon,
it had been stolen. The French governor of Lebanon demanded its return, and Frederick, threatened with imprisonment by the British high
commissioner's office, rushed to Chicago, where he persuaded Breasted
to sell it back to him for an undisclosed sum.

The transaction had been expensive for the American Colony but
cost the standing of the Vesters far more. At the same time, Olaf Lind
sued. He had suggested the American Colony declare itself a "charitable
foundation," with shares equally allocated. But Bertha would not hear of
it. Instead, she returned from one of her trips to New York with papers
that declared the colony a U.S. business corporation with herself, Frederick, John Whiting, and several unknown Americans as trustees. The
agreement she insisted that all the members sign was patently unfair and
additionally gave her the legal right to summary expulsion. The elderly
members signed, trusting her, but younger members were outraged.
They demanded equality as shareholders in the financial assets of the
colony and in its administration.

As a consequence, Bertha expelled a number of colonists. She persuaded others to return to their native lands. As these were generally
older couples who had long lost the initiative to make a living on their
own, their departures with a small monetary "gift," a disclaimer to
colony assets, and travel expenses left them in penury.[2] Bertha was apparently reconciled to supporting the oldest members, mostly in their
seventies or eighties and mostly spinsters. But it was critical to get rid of
the younger ones, especially those with children to feed, clothe, and educate. Although Olaf Lind was now exiled, he remained in Jerusalem
trying to persuade the Larssons to join his suit. Initially they resisted but
eventually came on board along with several others to make up a large

"minority" to Bertha's "majority." The insurrection that Anna had feared was in full cry.

By 1928, the level of fratricidal acrimony had become extraordinary. The Whitings were summoned home, and the ruinous New York store closed. When Bertha attempted to expel the Larssons, the rancor spilled out for all Jerusalem to witness, and soon the high commissioner's office instructed Attorney General Norman Bentwich to look into the situation. And once again, an American consul general, Paul Knabenshue, involved at the request of Lewis Larsson, found himself writing the U.S. State Department about the colony:

> My investigations have convinced me that, with few exceptions, the members of this colony are honest, kindly, moral, charitable, and law-abiding citizens, but that there are many indications that Mr. and Mrs. Frederick Vester and their family connections have been exploiting the Colony for their own personal benefit. Their rule of the Colony has had the appearance of a benevolent despotism. They have had most of the members, chiefly old men and women, absolutely within their power, and they have caused the expulsion from the Colony, from time to time, without compensation, of members who have attempted to dispute their authority . . .
>
> It is noticeable to every one in Jerusalem that the Vesters live better, dress better, and educate their children better than other members of the Colony . . . Mr. Vester is suspected of sharp practice in his business dealings in the operation of the Colony stores . . . In brief, the activity of the Vesters is considered by the people of Jerusalem, generally, as scandalous, particularly so as they are said to cloak their questionable actions under an outward guise of Christianity and charity which seems to have deceived many influential American tourists.[3]

The consul's conclusion was that "the American Colony has been a religious autocracy under Mrs. Spafford and since her death Mrs. Vester has been its tyrant."[4] There was no hope now that Frederick would get his American citizenship. Neither would the colony receive the U.S. consular protection Bertha and her mother had always craved. Instead, the colony was soon hopelessly split between the Vester-led majority of old Swedes and the dissident younger minority. Appalling accusations were hurled, every remembered injury, every old grudge, jealousy, or petty quarrel was aired vindictively. The lawyers tangled hopelessly in the deepening morass. In the colony, former roommates changed rooms as they could no longer stand being together. In the communal dining room, diners left their accustomed seats to sit with someone else. Finally, Attorney General Bentwich appointed C. H. Perrott, His Majesty's Crown prosecutor in Egypt, to come to Jerusalem and adjudicate the conflicting claims. To make matters even more complicated, Flora Page, whom Anna had always treated shabbily and forced into a loveless marriage, joined a number of others previously expelled as a third party. Bertha accused Flora of "immorality," and Flora returned the favor by suing her. As Mr. Perrott later told Lars Lind, whom he eventually appointed as the liquidator of the colony's properties: "Never in all my life have I had a more distasteful arbitration to perform and never have I dealt with such impossible people."[5]

The end was predictable. By 1930, after the catastrophic financial crash that plunged the world into the Great Depression, the once rich coffers of the colony were completely depleted by the enormous fees paid to lawyers or for travel expenses. Could Bertha have settled with Olaf Lind and the Larssons without a fight, they could all have done well. As it was in Perrott's settlement, the minority members received shares worth only $5,386.19 each for a lifetime's work.[6] There was virtually no cash left, so to compensate the Larsson family and their four young sons, Mr. Perrott awarded them Bertha's house. The photo studio that Lewis had spent years building went to G. Eric Matson. Lars Lind took his share in tires and rubber goods and eventually acquired the Goodyear Tire & Rubber franchise. Most significantly, the Vesters, the Whitings, and the "majority group" that had stayed loyal to Bertha received the Big House and other properties related to the tourist business, which was ultimately inherited by the Vester and Whiting children as the only progeny among the "majority."[7]

Under Bertha's direction, they struggled out of bankruptcy by carrying on the hotel business, but it was no longer a religious community.

Prayers were offered quietly by the old folks. Bertha neither interfered nor attempted to lead them. Instead, for the rest of her life, she dedicated herself to social work. It was her raison d'être, what she had to do if she were to live up to the towering figure that had been her mother; it was what eventually rehabilitated her reputation, and also, it was in social work that she genuinely believed.

The warring parties avoided each other after the breakup. The Larssons and others survived by taking in paying guests until various business opportunities materialized and they could improve their situation. As the years went on and Palestine was riven with strife, many scattered, most leaving for America or Sweden. All loved Jerusalem, and the majority would have preferred to stay there had they found remunerative work. As they went on with their lives, they looked back on the extraordinary experiences of their youth as something unique, amounting to something greater than the various individuals making up the colony's parts. True, there was bitterness, and some wounds never healed. Having suffered firsthand from a religious dictatorship, many of this younger generation were left without faith, distrusting religions of any kind. Yet the survivors seemed to agree that their fellowship had been very rare and special indeed, sharing punishments and pleasures as they labored together in the service of a common goal to help the poor and the needy. They mourned the breakup as a tragedy caused by human nature's inherent flaws, and all felt a lingering nostalgia for a lost comradeship.

In the years between the two world wars, as people everywhere struggled to lift themselves from the devastation of the Depression, those who remained endured difficult times. An Arab nationalist league, Thuwwar, was formed to mount a full-scale revolt against British rule. At one point Thuwwar took over the Old City, threatening the inhabitants with random kidnappings. A bomb was found outside the Larssons' house, where the district governor was lodging with his bodyguard. It was unsafe to walk alone at night or drive without a military escort. The British poured troops into Palestine, but the revolt took a heavy toll, with three thousand Arabs, two thousand Jews, and six hundred British killed.[8] By March 1939, the Arab leaders were in exile or under arrest, the economy in chaos. It was hard for the colonists to run their businesses.

In 1939 yet another commission—out of at least eighteen previous ones whose recommendations were never enforced—offered a reversal of previous British policy: "His Majesty's Government therefore now declare unequivocally that it is not part of their policy that Palestine should become a Jewish State."[9] The Zionists were incensed. The colonists saw it as a cynical effort to keep Muslims, furious at the betrayal of their fellow Arabs, from joining the Axis powers. Like others in Jerusalem, they wondered if it were not too late to reverse the Zionists' drive stimulated by the Balfour Declaration. Still, World War II brought a momentary lull where once again it was possible for Jewish and Arab ladies, their differences forgotten for the moment, to sit at the same table with Bertha and roll bandages for the Red Cross.

With Germany the enemy a second time, Frederick Vester gave up his German citizenship to become a Palestinian but had little time to enjoy his new status, as he died of a heart attack in January 1942. Bertha described their marriage as "thirty-eight perfect years together."[10]

The war ended in 1945. Bertha was a widow, and peace did not come to Palestine. Instead, the tragic conflict resumed with greater ferocity. The Nazis had done their best to exterminate the Jews. Now Jewish soldiers who had fought alongside the British turned against them, forming well-disciplined cadres passionately committed to righting the terrible wrongs of the Holocaust, determined to seize Palestine from the British and secure a Jewish homeland whatever the cost. Kidnappings, explosions, and assassinations became daily fare. Two militant groups, the Irgun, commanded by Menachem Begin, who later became prime minister of Israel, and the Stern Gang (after its founder, Abraham Stern), committed acts of sabotage and terror. In 1944 the Stern Gang assassinated the British minister of state for the Middle East, Lord Moyne. In 1946 the Irgun blew up the King David Hotel in Jerusalem, killing ninety-two persons, mainly British. Some victims had been friends of the colony, including an Arab and a Jew, business associates of Lewis Larsson. Everyone lived in fear.

On November 29, 1947, the General Assembly voted to approve the partition of Palestine with Jerusalem as an international city. White

House pressure together with pro-Zionist lobbies in the U.S. Congress had ensured the vote would go in favor of the Jews. As President Harry Truman said: "I have to answer to hundreds of thousands who are anxious for the success of Zionism. I do not have hundreds of thousands of Arabs in my constituents."[11] When the news was announced, because the head of the commission had been a Swede, the Arabs planted a bomb in the Larssons' house and came close to destroying it. Fortunately, the Larssons were in Sweden at the time, but later they returned, rebuilt, and struggled on.[12]

It was the massacre of Deir Yassin on April 9, 1948, that most appalled the former colonists. The little Arab village, just outside Jerusalem, was attacked at night by Irgun and Stern Gang commandos. A wedding party was rounded up against a wall and shot. Houses were ransacked and then dynamited. Women were raped, their bodies thrown down cisterns, and the skulls of their babies were crushed. A woman saw her pregnant sister killed and her stomach cut open with a butcher's knife.[13] Jewish loudspeaker trucks broadcast the horror, driving through Palestinian towns, promising more Deir Yassins to Arabs who did not leave. The Arabs heard the fearful message, and there was a general panic. Fifty thousand fled in three days.[14] The exodus that the Zionists had intended to precipitate—they called it "Plan D"—began in earnest. Hundreds of thousands more refugees, clutching what few belongings they could carry, poured out of the country to Jordan, Syria, Lebanon, Egypt, believing that soon they would be able to return to their homes.

Horrified and sick at heart, Bertha and the nursing "sisters" reopened the Anna Spafford Baby Nursing Home and Infant Welfare Center, which they had temporarily closed because of the warfare around it. They took in forty orphans from Deir Yassin. On April 13, the Arabs retaliated for the massacre, attacking a convoy going to the Hadassah Hospital on the road passing the American Colony. This provoked an intense campaign on both sides to control the Sheikh Jarrah district. As Arab fighters gathered in the colony's garden for a battle that would go on for weeks, Bertha pleaded with them to respect the colony's long history of neutrality. She took her petition to the Muslim Higher Committee, and although the guerrilla fighters departed the grounds, the colony buildings suffered extensive damage from artillery from both sides. Not a window was left intact. John Whiting was shot in the leg. One of the old Swedes was also hit, and three Arab staff were wounded. They survived, while two old people who passed away at this time were buried in the colony garden as it had been too dangerous to take them to the cemetery.

On May 14, 1948, the last British high commissioner, Sir Alan Cunningham, quietly departed from the Haifa harbor. According to one eyewitness: "The Union Jack was lowered and with the speed of an execution and the silence of a ship that passes in the night British rule in Palestine came to an end."[15] A few hours later in Tel Aviv, the head of the Jewish Agency, David Ben-Gurion, stood beneath a portrait of Theodor Herzl and proclaimed the independence of the state of Israel, which was promptly recognized by both the United States and the Soviet Union.

The next day units from the armies of Egypt, Syria, Lebanon, Transjordan, and Iraq invaded Israel, but were no match for the disciplined Haganah awaiting them. With the exception of Transjordan's Arab Legion, the invading troops were poorly equipped, poorly prepared, and poorly led. They were also outnumbered, fielding a combined force of 21,500 against the superbly prepared Haganah and its affiliated units of some 30,000.[16] The United Nations sent an envoy, Count Folke Bernadotte, a Swedish nobleman, to mediate between the warring sides. The count was delighted to find Lewis Larsson's son Theo ready and willing to act as his aide, especially as he spoke Arabic fluently. Bernadotte lodged at the American Colony and succeeded in getting a thirty-day cease-fire. On September 17, while riding in Theo's new Chrysler car, Bernadotte was assassinated by Jewish terrorists. To the relief of his parents, Theo was on another errand at the time. One of the plotters was Yitzhak Shamir, who went on to become a prime minister of Israel. The fighting resumed with brutal intensity. All the while, the Red Cross flag waved over the baby nursing home in the Old City, where tracer bullets lit the corridors by night and Bertha, the elder "sisters," and several doctors did their best for hurt and despairing Arab men, women, and children.

When the twelve-month conflict ended, the Old City was in Jordan's hands, but Israel controlled the western areas of Jerusalem outside the walls as well as having vastly enlarged the territory assigned it by the United Nations on the partition map. The Palestinians were left without a state, and over 700,000 Arab refugees were sent into diaspora. No reparations were paid them by Israel, and by 1954 their homes, orchards, vineyards, and arable lands were taken over by the Israeli "Abandoned Property" custodian to be sold to Jews. John Whiting died in 1951, having never fully recovered from his wound. Old Professor Dinsmore, who had educated so many Jews and Arabs as well as colonists, also died that year. Before long, given the ongoing difficulties and their dislike of Israel's discriminatory ordinances, all who had once been part of the colony were gone with the exception of Bertha.

She stayed on, angry at the fate of so many of her friends whose homes and livelihoods were destroyed and profoundly sad to see the old spirit of tolerance and respect between Christian, Jew, and Muslim vanish. Bertha excelled at anger, and she put it toward a good cause. For the rest of her life, she continued her trips to the United States to raise money for the baby nursing home and to sell native embroideries for the benefit of Arab women. A wealthy American, Georgiana Stevens, a board member of the venerable Foreign Policy Association, was one of many donors on whom Bertha regularly called. "She was very handsome, with tremendous style," Mrs. Stevens remembered. "She had no money, but she always made an excellent impression. She was the best beggar in the Middle East and told wonderful stories—the same stories of wars she had been through, but she told them brilliantly, year after year. I took her to the United Nations several times, and both Israelis and Arabs rushed to see her. They really admired her for her work."[17]

Bertha's energy was prodigious. The problem of miserable refugee camps crowded with 860,000 homeless Palestinians stoked her indignation.[18] She urged her important friends to use their influence to get the United States' help in implementing the United Nations' resolutions providing refugees with cash compensation for their lost properties. She believed that with such compensation the refugees would be returned to the general economy instead of festering in a despair that could only result in subversive violence. In 1954 she circulated a plea for funds to build a hospital for Arabs in Jerusalem as the only available one was eighteen kilometers away in Bethlehem. "We have got to do something to give confidence and bring back the friendship of the Arabs for America—which we have lost," she declared presciently. "It is urgently necessary that the Arabs become convinced of the often expressed American policy of neutrality between Israel and the Arab states . . . In the present strained situation, such aid cannot come too quickly, for the cleavage between East and West is dangerously sharp in this vital region."[19] Again and again, to anyone who would listen, Bertha insisted that Jerusalem be internationalized in the best interests of all parties, and out of respect for the three great monotheistic religions for which the city was sacred.

Through her efforts the American Colony Hotel prospered, and the Vester family opened a travel bureau in Amman, Jordan. Her oldest son, Horatio, who had become an English barrister, and his wife, Valentine Vester, a niece of Gertrude Bell's, left their London life to help her. At various times her other children also helped with the hotel and the baby nursing home. As it had for so long, the hotel maintained its reputation among Middle East cognoscenti for being a beacon of tradition, peace, beauty, and comfort—the only place to stay in Jerusalem. It was often said among those hearing the old stories: "If only the walls could speak."

Bertha wrote her memoirs. The American edition had a foreword by Lowell Thomas, and the English edition was introduced by Sir Ronald Storrs. Bertha, understandably, was her own heroine, and while she gave virtually no credit to the Swedes, and dismissed the breakup in a sentence or two, she used her book to redeem her parents and put the past to rest. "The old stories cropped up now and then," she noted ruefully, "but were turned aside with oh-that-used-to-be-looks, which hurt worse than the accusations when one thought of the robust Christianity of the Colony's founders which allowed 'no room for self-pity,' as Mother expressed it, at the most crucial moment of her life."[20]

Eschewing self-pity had become Bertha's coda. She was hard on herself and equally hard on her children and her contemporaries in the colony's second generation. The latter, she never forgave. Eric Dinsmore Matsson, Professor Dinsmore's grandson and the nephew of G. Eric Matson, who won the Photo Department, said that he was always welcome among former members but "Mrs. Vester almost spat when she saw me."[21] In 1947 Eric had tried to sue for his expelled mother's share, and thanks to the generosity of Bertha's son Horatio, it was arranged that he be given a share for his children. But as far as Bertha was concerned, Eric was still anathema.

Repeatedly she was written up in American newspapers. The "fabulous Mrs. Martha Spafford Vester," the *San Francisco Examiner* gushed inaccurately in 1955, marveling at Bertha's war stories and astonished at her courage: "There should be more Mrs. Vesters." *Look* magazine praised her "deep conviction that Jerusalem—a city sacred to the three great religious faiths—should be an international trust." The *Christian Science Monitor* called her an "artist, author, teacher, social worker, and humanitarian."

She attended church at St. George's Cathedral and became a respected friend of the new bishop. Bertha's attendance was a social concession, not an act of faith, and her abhorrence of crank religions remained ironclad. In 1952, noting in her diary that she was reading *Father and Son* by Edmund Gosse, she wrote: "What strange ideas some people have about religion." As if the past had been some sort of remote and distant fantasy, she mused, "We even were tainted in the early days."[22]

During the Six Days' War of June 1967, the American Colony Hotel was again in the middle of prolonged cross fire, and again it sustained considerable damage. On one day the area was captured by Israel, whose soldiers forced their way into the Big House and shot up every door. Another day it reverted to the defending Jordanians. In the end, the Israelis won that district and much else. In addition to gaining the sought-for goal of the West Bank, Israel was now the master of all Jerusalem. Finally the Old City lay under the Israeli blue and white flag, including the Holy Sepulchre and the sacred Muslim grounds of the Haram al-Sharif. As the hotel was also inside Israel, the gracious and long-serving Palestinian staff now welcomed visitors with the Hebrew greeting: "Shalom."[23]

The following year, on March 24, Bertha celebrated her ninetieth birthday. Both Jews and Arabs attended a grand reception for the last of the Overcomers to have disembarked at Jaffa in 1881. Residents turned out in force to honor her. She had much to be proud of. The children's clinic in the Old House that she started in 1925 was still operating—and continues to do so to the present day. The American Colony Hotel had become a cherished institution. From the Patriarch of Jerusalem she had received the Cross of the Holy Sepulchre "for her piety and good service," while King Hussein of Jordan had awarded her the Jordanian Star, the only Christian woman ever to have received that honor. Most touching of all, in the city of Jerusalem itself, despite the usual official reluctance to move even a stone, a cement ramp was built to partially fill a series of steps leading from Herod's Gate to the children's clinic so that the old lady might be wheeled up to visit her beloved babies.[24] She had steered those who still depended on her through perilous times without indulging in religious hypocrisy. If she had not been loved—even her children had found her remote and imperious—she was justly admired for her untiring efforts on behalf of neglected Palestinians, especially the children.

Bertha was unbending throughout her life. Like her mother, she had sought, and achieved, legitimacy. However, to be the high priestess of a marginal religious cult was not for her, and she was wise to see this. Instead, discarding the peculiar doctrinal wrappings that covered some very dubious practices, she took from her parents' teachings their ecumenical outlook and particularly their commitment to service, brilliantly fulfilling that entirely admirable portion of her inheritance. By honoring their memory with a lifetime of good works, Bertha had become anchored, justified, and at peace with herself. When she died two months after her birthday fete, the hotel's longtime Palestinian doorman told reporters, "She was like a queen."[25] Tributes came from little-known people as well as from Mrs. Franklin D. Roosevelt, various Morgans and Longfellows, churchmen, newspaper editors, scholars, university heads, and many members of the clergy, including the well-known preacher Harry Emerson Fosdick. They exceeded those that had come after Anna's death. For far more than her father, Horatio, and perhaps even more than her remarkable mother, Bertha had truly been an "overcomer."

Afterword

Today the American Colony Hotel flourishes. With its location at the border dividing Arab and Jewish Jerusalem, it continues to be particularly favored by journalists and diplomats as well as by representatives of organizations engaged in the multitude of issues that bring them to the holy city. Tourists also flock there, knowing they will be well cared for—if expensively, as it has become a five-star luxury hotel. In the summer of 2007, with his $8 million budget and staff of fourteen, the former British prime minister Tony Blair, the new envoy of the international Quartet of Middle East mediators, composed of the United States, the European Union, the United Nations, and Russia, chose the hotel as his headquarters. The sunny, flower-filled garden is invariably filled with known and not-so-well-known guests taking their breakfast or lunch, and most are aware that the door of room 16 by the splashing fountain is where the Israelis and the Palestinians, led by Yitzhak Rabin and Yasir Arafat, began their negotiations toward the Oslo peace accords in the early 1990s.

Twice a year, the colony's descendants who own shares in the hotel assemble for board meetings. They meet once in London, and when they gather a second time, in Jerusalem, they are welcomed by the aged but remarkably vigorous Valentine Vester, Bertha's daughter-in-law, who still presides over the hotel. The business is managed by a Swiss hotel company, and according to John D. Whiting's granddaughter, Wendy Whiting Blome, the families have seen their profits "go up and down" over the years as troubles have come and gone, yet "we don't think of selling it."[1] They are far too attached to the place and usually make time to visit Mount Scopus and wander in the shaded quiet of the American Colony

graveyard beside Hebrew University. In August 2006, the board organized a reunion, helping eighty descendants of shareholders with their
airfare to Jerusalem. "I saw first cousins I'd never met before, and many
Swedes that I didn't know. We felt it was important for the younger generation to see and feel the place, and become as passionate about it as we
are," Mrs. Blome remarked recently.[2]

She is also on the board of the Spafford Children's Center, the mod-
ern name for the clinic that Bertha founded in 1925. In London, Bertha
Vester's oldest granddaughter, Lady Djemila Cope, chairs a fund-raising
committee for the center in England, while in Bellevue, Washington,
Georgette Lind, wife of Nils Lind's son, and Bertha's daughter Anna
Grace, raises money in America. The clinic's Dutch director, Dr. Jantien
Dajani, a pediatrician who has been with the center for almost forty
years and is married to a Palestinian physician, supervises Muslim and
Christian doctors, nurses, and ancillary staff deeply committed to improving the health and well-being of children from a variety of religious
and ethnic backgrounds. They are open to all, they say, who need help.
In 2006, with the victory of the Hamas party, long designated as "terror-
ist" by the United States and some European countries, desperately
needed funds were withheld, resulting in a strike by unpaid Palestinian
government workers, including those in the health and education sectors. Many children were left without vaccinations, health care, or teachers, as the schools were temporarily closed. During the summer of that
year war broke out between Israel and Hezbollah in Lebanon, causing
further disruptions. Another continuing complication for the clinic has
been the towering cement wall being erected by the Israelis that cuts
Palestinian East Jerusalem from neighboring towns in the West Bank.
The wall isolates many Arab villages, preventing families from getting to
the main clinic inside the Old City, which still operates out of the Overcomers' original Old House near Damascus Gate. To reduce the problems resulting from this obstruction and Israeli military checkpoints, in
2005 the board decided to open two outpatient clinics in the West Bank,
one in Taybeh and another in Bethany. In addition, the Jerusalem clinic
offers group and individual counseling programs with a trained psychol-
ogist and an Expressive Arts Therapy program that encourages youngsters to reveal and confront feelings about their current hardships. It is

impossible not to be touched by a corridor hung with drawings describing the children's fear, depression, and encounters with violence.

Yet the center makes a point of staying rigorously away from incendiary political issues. Neither the hotel board members nor the center's board members make statements or take sides. "Our work and our commitment speaks for itself," said Mrs. Blome.[3] This was the ecumenical philosophy of Bertha Spafford, and her descendants strive to honor it, one of the reasons a neutral Swiss management firm runs the hotel. One is inclined to believe, however, that along with others in the region, they, too, hope that eventually the conflicts between Israel and the Palestinians will be resolved when the international community helps them toward a fair settlement to end the anguish of more than half a century.

Anna Spafford dreamed there would be peace between peoples, frequently declaring to her fellowship that "love could conquer disunity," and in many ways this is the American dream, rich with the conviction that there should be no distinctions between races, genders, ethnicities, or classes, with freedom and democracy available to all. If Anna herself was flawed, the message she conveyed to Selma Lagerlöf for world peace was sound. Anna, the Norwegian immigrant, had early fastened onto ideas that are deeply embedded in the American consciousness and abide today. Americans have long believed that sober living, frugality, and hard work will win success and fame, and be crowned with God's grace, and this continues to be true despite the country's excessive commercialism and a more relaxed moral atmosphere. Laziness was a sin to the evangelicals, and it is still viewed by many as a sin. In the madness of grief, Horatio upended this dearly held notion, stopped working, borrowed from others, and sank into debt. He wished to abandon personal ambition and attachment to material things, to found a collective where everything was held in common. This kind of experiment has been repeated in American history and even occurs occasionally today, despite being ridiculed and even causing alarm in the hearts of an industrious majority that extols acquisitiveness and is fiercely protective of private property rights. For Horatio, the liberty that counted was the freedom to save one's soul.

Anna accepted much that Horatio preached, and both believed in the necessity of returning the Jews to the land of their fathers in order to fulfill the ancient prophecies and hasten the Messiah's return. A theme for many Protestants since the Reformation, refined and developed by men like John Nelson Darby and Lord Shaftesbury in England, adopted by Dwight Moody's evangelicals in America, and pursued by William Blackstone and others, this idea is alive today among Christian Zionists who are closely connected to, and assiduously promote, Israel's interests.

Horatio's professional and personal failures, however, were a different matter for Anna; they shamed her. What infuriated Consul Merrill about Horatio's indebtedness and refusal to work also troubled his wife, and when the Swedes arrived and the colony was put on a sturdy economic footing, she felt vindicated, respectable, and powerful at last. In this, she was like any other American who deeply believes that only individual achievement and the acquisition of wealth, coupled with good works, can justify one's life and bestow God's grace.

There are neither villains nor saints in this story. The Spaffords, the Swedes, and others who joined the colony wanted to be right with their fellow man, and especially they wanted to be right with God. Perplexed, fearful of the future, swept by events out of their control, they did their best under the circumstances. The Spaffords in particular had to find a way to overcome crippling emotional wounds, while the Swedes and other members were overly susceptible to strong religious influences, paying the price in their captivity to Anna, who was hardly the first, and certainly will not be the last, to use religion as a tool in the service of goals having more to do with Caesar than with God. If there is a lesson to be learned from this small slice of history, surely it is the importance of thinking for oneself lest one be victimized. Still the colony left a legacy of generosity to the people they served, and Bertha and her descendants have carried it on. And if anything is true about Americans, and fits their ideal of the American dream, it is their inclination to think of themselves as ready and willing to help others in the service of making the world a better place.

Acknowledgments

The idea for this book originated during visits to London beginning in 1989 when I was tracking the life of Dame Freya Stark for a biography that became *Passionate Nomad*. A Swedish businessman, Theo Larsson, regaled me with stories not only about Dame Freya but also of growing up in Jerusalem. He explained that his was the third generation of a singular group that had come to the Holy City to await the Second Coming, but that had evolved into the famous American Colony Hotel. Their history, he said, was far more complicated than hotel guests usually understood.

Intrigued, I spent the month of December at the American Colony Hotel in 2000 and discovered that in fact it was a fascinating story. Many Jerusalemites helped me, but I must thank especially Shimshon and Bilhah Arad, Helen Dudman, Professor Ruth Kark, Munther Fahmi, and of course Valentine Vester, the grand doyenne of the hotel, and her courtly staff. The second intifada had begun, a difficult if interesting time, so I was very happy when Tim and Wren Wirth joined me and Wren kept me company for a week. On visits to Jordan, Karen and Mohammed Asfour introduced me to Palestinians who had fled during the wars and had their own memories of the colony.

Back home in the United States, I realized that various critical materials were written in Swedish, and as I wondered how to get them translated, I met Peter Scott-Hansen, a multilingual neighbor in Boca Grande, who, to my everlasting gratitude, agreed to have a look. He quickly became as fascinated by the colony's history as I was, and not only did he translate what was needed, but he and his wife, Christian, have become close friends and have supported this endeavor in countless ways.

In addition to Peter's invaluable help, Toni Vanover, of the Boca Grande Community Center, showed me how a first-class librarian can use the library system to uncover almost anything for a needy biographer. Toni went far out of her way to procure an astonishing number of books, periodicals, and newspaper articles. When it came to furnishing a complete bibliography and especially to correcting footnotes, on her own time Toni sleuthed what must have seemed an infinity of dropped page numbers, omitted article titles, or overlooked dates. I can never thank her enough.

At the Library of Congress, I am grateful to Barbara Bair in the Manuscript Division for her guidance and insights, and to Barbara Natanson and Arden Alexander in Prints and Photographs. In Minnesota, the historian Gary Bakko of Goodhue County and, in Chicago, the historian Barry Smith of the Lincoln Park Presbyterian Church both graciously responded to many queries with fresh materials. Also in Chicago, I got help from Christine Reynen, the Newberry Library, and the Moody Bible Institute, while from Kentucky the Asbury Theological Seminary sent materials. From Kansas, help came from Phyllis Bell of Lebanon and from Darel Miller and Doris Chamberlin of Smith Center. From Amman, Odd Karsten Tveit gave me permission to quote from his own fine study of the colony, written in Norwegian.

Descendants of the colony were very good to me, patiently sharing what they could: Norman and June Baldwin; Alvin, Gladie, and Ron Yantiss; Furman and Peg Baldwin; Roweyda Pearse; Sally Whiting and her children, John Whiting and Wendy Whiting Blome, who provided important family documents and put me in touch with Georgette Lind, Djemila Cope, Frederick Matsson, and Tim Ward. Three other descendants, John Larsson, the redoubtable and delightful Mugs Matson, and her cousin Cecily Dewing, provided valuable manuscripts.

I was given encouragement by many journalist friends and others with business in Jerusalem who all love staying at the American Colony Hotel and wanted to know more of its story. Still others too numerous to mention contributed, especially Alison and Charlie Buckholtz, Tim Beeken, Tom Groom, and Betsy Birch. Pamela Peabody and Joan and Talcott Seelye gave me books; Jennone Walker translated; Condit Eddy looked up his grandfather's diary; Ted Curtis, John Spofford, Bill and Polly Spofford, Alice Gorman, Daly Walker, Lucinda Sullivan, Tom and Alix Devine, Janet Wallach, Doyen McIntosh, Susan Ackerman, Barclay and James Larsson, Dr. Phyllis Magrab, and Barbara Porter all advised, and my honorary godson, Joe Arcidiacano, took a photograph for the dust jacket.

Needless to say, no book would have happened without my brilliant editor, Nan A. Talese, or an agent as rare as Lynn Nesbit. It has been wonderful to have them at my side, as it was to profit from the astute pencil of Luke Epplin, the consistent help of Ronit Feldman, and the meticulousness of my copy editor, Ingrid Sterner. But finally, I have to thank my family. Over the seven years that it took to write this book, my Internet-savvy son, Tom, my daughter, Julia, and her husband, Brian, never failed to encourage me, while my talented daughter-in-law, Jan, read and commented on the manuscript with keen understanding in all its stages. My husband, Bob, an amusing and patient counselor who never lost faith and even washed dishes occasionally, showed consistent and buoying interest. Together, their faith and enthusiasm propelled me forward.

Notes

Chapter One: A Beginning

1. Rogers, *Domestic Life in Palestine,* 3; Straiton and Straiton, *Two Lady Tramps Abroad,* 76.

2. Bloom, *American Religion,* 61.

3. From what has been called ever since the Great Disappointment, the Seventh-Day Adventists and, in the twentieth century, the Jehovah's Witnesses are directly descended.

4. Ibid.

5. For this concise definition of the apocalypse, I am indebted to *Webster's Third New International Dictionary of the English Language* (Springfield, Mass.: Merriam-Webster, 1993), 100.

6. "Taking his cue from Christ's prophetic Sermon on the Mount, John Winthrop wrote in 1630 of an anticipated American destiny while he was still in transit on the Atlantic voyage: 'For wee must Consider that wee shall be as a Citty upon a Hill.' " "Dead Sea, Sodom, Gomorrah," 187, quoted in Davis, *Landscape of Belief,* 15.

7. Vester, *Our Jerusalem,* 56.

8. See excellent treatments of this theme, from which I have drawn the generalized description of the American Protestants' first encounter with the Holy Land, in Davis, *Landscape of Belief,* and Vogel, *To See a Promised Land.*

9. Elliott, *Remarkable Characters and Places of the Holy Land,* quoted in Vogel, "Zion as Place and Past," 9.

10. Samuel Clemens, *Traveling,* 302, quoted in Vogel, "Zion as Place and Past," 145, quoted in Davis, *Landscape of Belief,* 51.

11. Current Events, *New York Times,* Sept. 4, 1881, 10.

12. Clemens, *Traveling,* 302, quoted in Vogel, "Zion as Place and Past," 145, quoted in Davis, *Landscape of Belief,* 51.

Chapter Two: Anna

1. Tveit, "Anna's House," 7.

2. Tveit writes there were four Øglende children on the *Norden* manifest yet

no further mention of others except Anne and Rachel later on. Gary Bakko, a historian of Norwegian immigration, finds documentation for only two children by Lars's first wife. The mystery still remains.

3. Tveit, "Anna's House," 7.

4. Hokanson, *Swedish Immigrants in Lincoln's Time,* 47.

5. Ibid., 48.

6. Ibid.

7. Tveit, "Anna's House," 7; Johnson, *Goodhue County, Minnesota,* 111–30.

8. Dedman, *Fabulous Chicago,* frontispiece.

9. Pierce, *As Others See Chicago,* 184.

10. Ibid., 164.

11. Robertson, *Chicago Revival,* 10.

12. Gary Bakko, historian, Goodhue County, Minn.

13. Pierce, *As Others See Chicago,* 184.

14. Vester, *Our Jerusalem,* 13.

15. The Minnesota Territory was claimed at the expense of the Sioux and Dakota tribes, consistently cheated of almost all their ancestral lands. Zebulon Pike of Pike's Peak fame, representing the U.S. government, despite knowing that the hundred-thousand-acre parcel now the site of the Twin Cities was worth $200,000, paid the Dakotas $2,000.

16. Johnson, *Goodhue County, Minnesota,* 35.

17. Ibid., 37.

18. Ibid., 58.

19. Ibid., 39.

20. Ibid., 43.

21. Mrs. Ely was probably the wife of a partner in a clothing store, Ely Brothers, which in 1869 sold out to journeymen tailors who wanted to create a tailors' cooperative. Pierce, *From Town to City,* 182.

22. Vester, *Our Jerusalem,* 16.

23. Johnson, *Goodhue County, Minnesota,* 114.

24. A Kansas law still today allows children as young as twelve to marry. Indeed, according to the August 30, 2005, *New York Times,* 150,000 babies a year are born to a minor parent.

25. Vester, *Our Jerusalem,* 14–15.

26. Johnson, *Goodhue County, Minnesota,* 56, 57.

27. Gary Bakko, historian, Goodhue County, Minn.

28. Vester, *Our Jerusalem,* 14.

29. Gary Bakko, historian, Goodhue County, Minn.

30. The census was doubtless taken that year, as the state was to become official in 1858. Edward gave his age as twenty-one, probably in order to be able to vote. Information from land records researched by Gary Bakko.

31. Vester, *Our Jerusalem,* 15.

32. Ibid., 15–16.

33. Chicago newspapers described her working as "a servant girl." It makes sense that Anna did work at fifteen, as she had no other source of income. However, her daughter Bertha, powerfully motivated to polish her mother's image, never mentions this. On the other hand, that "working as a waitress" came from the Larsson family, one of Bertha's bitter enemies, somewhat tarnishes the veracity of this description. Larsson, *Seven Passports for Palestine,* 9.

34. Vester, *Our Jerusalem,* 16.

Chapter Three: Spafford

1. Vester, *Our Jerusalem,* 12.

2. Findlay, *Dwight L. Moody,* 56–57.

3. Bradford, *D. L. Moody,* 37.

4. Evensen, *God's Man for the Gilded Age,* 30.

5. Findlay, *Dwight L. Moody,* 73.

6. Ibid., 82.

7. According to an obituary, "The Singular Life—History of a Native of Lansingburgh," *Troy (N.Y.) Daily Times,* Oct. 24, 1888, Horatio's father was Horatio Gates Spafford, LL.D., a historian of Lansingburgh. His mother was Elizabeth Clark Hewitt, formerly of Canaan, New York. His brother was Julius Gates Spafford of Adams Basin, New York; his sisters were Margaret W. Lee and Eureka Perry, while his cousins were the Honorable Edward A. Stevenson of Idaho and the Honorable Charles C. Stevenson of Nevada—both deceased by the time of the obituary. Horatio also had a niece who was "a well-known author," Mrs. Rev. G. R. Alden, signing her work as "Pansy." What contact Horatio maintained with his brother and cousins is unclear, but it would seem he cut himself off from his New York roots.

8. Tveit, "Anna's House," 12.

9. Ibid., 13.

10. Vester, *Our Jerusalem,* 17. Many years later, Anna's daughter visited the school and noticed that someone had scratched the initials "HS-AL" on a dormitory window and realized Anna had done this with her diamond engagement ring.

11. Tveit, "Anna's House," 13; Vester, *Our Jerusalem,* 17.

12. Vester, *Our Jerusalem,* 16.

13. Lind was later incorporated in the medical school of Northwestern University.

14. Evensen, *God's Man for the Gilded Age,* 8.

15. Findlay, *Dwight L. Moody,* 86.

16. Vester, *Our Jerusalem,* 18.

17. Chamberlin, *Chicago and Its Suburbs,* 351.

Chapter Four: Thrilling Ideas

1. Ward, Burns, and Burns, *Civil War,* xix.

2. Ibid., 186.

3. Smith, *Revivalism and Social Reform in Mid-Nineteenth Century America,* 25.

4. The First Great Awakening burst over the country in the 1730s, and its standard-bearers were Jonathan Edwards and George Whitefield. After the American Revolution came the Second Great Awakening, which stirred the eastern churches and bent to bring the frontier to the churchgoing fold. Its great leaders were the Yale president Timothy Dwight, Charles Grandison Finney, and Peter Cartwright. Martin E. Marty, foreword to *Dwight L. Moody,* by Findlay.

5. Ibid., 126.

6. Sandeen, *Roots of Fundamentalism,* 30, 31, 32.

7. Ibid., 31.

8. Marsden, *Fundamentalism and American Culture,* 46, 54, 70.

9. Sandeen, *Roots of Fundamentalism,* 63.

10. Tuchman, *Bible and Sword,* 177.

11. Charles Dickens admired Lord Shaftesbury, and if he did not support all of Shaftesbury's ideas, he did say that the Lodging House Act, one of the peer's many reform works, "was the finest piece of legislation ever enacted in England up to that time." Ibid., 178.

12. Vester, *Our Jerusalem,* 23.

13. Findlay, *Dwight L. Moody,* 124.

14. Evensen, *God's Man for the Gilded Age,* 29.

15. Findlay, *Dwight L. Moody,* 227.

16. Evensen, *God's Man for the Gilded Age,* 14, 41.

17. Robertson, *Chicago Revival,* 197.

18. Findlay, *Dwight L. Moody,* 127.

19. Ibid., 129.

Chapter Five: The Calamity of the Age

1. Cromie, *Great Chicago Fire,* 9.

2. Ibid., 240.

3. Ibid., 126.

4. Eyewitness account of Alexander Frear in Pierce, *As Others See Chicago,* 201.

5. Vester, *Our Jerusalem,* 5.

6. Ibid., 6.

7. Evensen, *God's Man for the Gilded Age,* 129.

8. Chamberlin, *Chicago and Its Suburbs,* 233–34.

9. Cromie, *Great Chicago Fire,* 246.

10. Moody and Goss, *Echoes from the Pulpit and Platform,* 55.

11. Lyman Abbott, introduction to ibid., 29.

12. Vester, *Our Jerusalem,* 27.

13. *Mary F. Murphy and Anna Spafford v. Dr. Samuel P. Hedges, et al.,* IL, G-142175 (Ill. Circuit Court, Chancery Court, Cook County, Feb. 8, 1896). Testimonies of Anna Spafford, Feb. 8, 1896; Samuel Hedges, June 1, 1897; and Daniel W. Whittle, Aug. 24, 1897.

14. *Murphy v. Hedges,* master's report.

15. Wilkie, *Chicago Bar,* 84.

16. "Cooke, Jay," in *The New Encyclopædia Britannica,* 15th ed.

17. Vester, *Our Jerusalem,* 29.

Chapter Six: Collision at Sea

1. I found it very confusing to track the correct number of passengers and crew on board as the *Ville du Havre* sailed from New York. There were many conflicting accounts. No one knew there were stowaways when they left. An editorial, "The Ville du Havre," in the *Chicago Tribune,* published on December 4, 1873, days after the initial reports, gives the number of lost as 226 with 87 saved. Counting the stowaways, which not all papers mentioned, would bring the total to 319 people. If there were 157 guests, 150 crew, 5 officers, Captain Surmont, and the 6 stowaways, the number adds up to 319 people aboard when the ship left New York.

The three Frenchmen had been attending one of the first gatherings of the Evangelical Alliance in New York.

2. Weiss, *Personal Recollections of the Wreck of the Ville-du-Havre and the Loch-Earn,* 99–101. I hope the reader will forgive me for slightly modifying this exchange.

3. The following action and the dialogue between Weiss, Anna, and her daughters are taken from ibid., 111–17.

4. Vester, *Our Jerusalem,* 33.

5. Ibid., 133.

6. The papers mostly agreed that the number of people saved was eighty-seven, with the breakdown of passengers, captain, officers, and crew as I have given it in the text, quoting from "The Loss of the Ville du Havre," *New York Times,* Dec. 2, 1873. The *Chicago Tribune* gave a slightly lower number for the crew: fifty-two men, not fifty-four, as others reported. As I mentioned in note 1, the confusion over numbers was considerable.

7. The company that owned the *Trimountain* could not collect its insurance against a delivery delay.

8. It is troubling to know that Mrs. Bulkley also made it clear in her letter that she regarded the management of the *Ville du Havre* as disorganized from the very start of the voyage. In her view there were constant problems that she and others noticed. The newly remodeled ship had engine problems only a few days after they sailed; during the storm, the roof leaked; but, worse, "there seemed no organized discipline on board." At the time of the collision, she was again appalled yet said that she continued to hope "that under all this outward confusion there must be some organized system going on for our rescue." Obviously, there was not. It is hard not to wonder why the Frenchmen, so curious about cultural comparisons, would not have recorded the Americans' disdain for European inefficiency. Neider, *Great Shipwrecks and Castaways,* 214.

9. Vester, *Our Jerusalem,* 40.

10. The full text reads: "Saved alone: what shall I do. Mrs. Goodwin children Willie Culver lost go with Lorriaux until answer reply Porclain 64 Rue Aboukir Paris. Signed Spafford." Anna Spafford to Horatio Spafford, telegram, Dec. 1, 1873, ACJC.

Chapter Seven: "You Must Give Yourself to My Work"

1. Vester, *Our Jerusalem,* 41.

2. Ibid.

3. Ibid., 22.

4. Ibid., 41.

5. Ibid., 42.

6. Moody and Goss, *Echoes from the Pulpit and Platform,* 362. There seems to be a difference of opinion on when Moody left to meet Anna in London, whether before or after her stay in Paris. Moody himself remembered it as a meet-

ing in Liverpool. Bertha Spafford Vester, Anna's daughter, wrote in her book that both her parents were met by Moody after Paris, and in London. Following Moody's tour schedule as best I could, I have concluded that Moody saw Anna before she went to Paris. Whatever the actual fact, the essential truth is that Moody's concern was for Anna. She was the mother of the lost girls, and presumably the more vulnerable. Moody, who used the shipwreck story in his sermons, never mentions talking to or comforting Spafford.

7. This exchange is excerpted from Moody's sermons in ibid., 362; Vester, *Our Jerusalem*; and conversations Anna had with Selma Lagerlöf, "Svensk kultur-mässa," *Dagens Nyheter,* Aug. 27, 1925.

8. Vester, *Our Jerusalem,* 48–49.

9. According to Ira Sankey's memoir, Horatio composed this hymn in 1876, when Moody and Sankey "were entertained" at the Spafford home for several weeks. Sankey, *Sankey's Story of the Gospel Hymns,* 119. Although Bertha Vester, the Spafford's daughter, remembered it differently, as told above, perhaps her father first had the idea on that transatlantic voyage and wrote the final version in 1876, as Sankey says. Sankey's original manuscript was destroyed, and he had to recall his stories from memory, and therefore may have gotten some details confused. In any event, Horatio's hymn was put to music in 1876 by Philip P. Bliss, a talented evangelical composer, and friend of the Spaffords and Moodys before Bliss was killed in a railway accident. More than a hundred years after the hymn was written, Horatio's great-granddaughter heard it sung by Luciano Pavarotti and Plácido Domingo at a huge outdoor concert in Bath, England, in 2002.

10. Anna Spafford to Horatio Spafford, Nov. 28, 1873, Holt-Atherton Special Collections, University of the Pacific Libraries, Stockton, Calif.; "The Ville du Havre," *Chicago Daily Tribune,* Dec. 18, 1873.

Chapter Eight: Return to Chicago

1. *Chicago Herald,* 1885, Vester scrapbook, ACJC.

2. "When Peace Like a River," *Chicago Daily Tribune,* Sept. 28, 1902.

3. Ibid.

4. Vester, *Our Jerusalem,* 48.

5. Vester Papers, ACJC.

6. Records of the Foreign Mission Society of the Fullerton Avenue Presbyterian Church, Chicago, Nov. 1879, minutes, courtesy Barry Smith, church historian, Lincoln Park Presbyterian Church, Chicago.

7. Vester, *Our Jerusalem,* 44.

8. Goodwillie, "Early Days in the Fullerton Avenue Presbyterian Church."

9. Ibid.

10. "Why the Commune Is Possible in America," *Chicago Tribune,* May 24, 1874; Robertson, *Chicago Revival,* 22.

11. Robertson, *Chicago Revival,* 17.

12. Ibid., 17.

13. Ibid., 25.

14. Ibid., 26.

15. A brilliant lecturer concerned with improving the status of women, Miss Willard joined Susan B. Anthony in the suffrage movement. Ultimately, she abandoned the emphasis on drink as the source of society's ills, recognizing that poverty, appalling working conditions, and discrimination were the real problems.

16. It was Miss Willard who helped a well-known writer of religious tracts, Hannah Whitall Smith, the author of *The Christian's Secret of a Happy Life* (1875), to compile a file on religious fanatics, which included the "Overcomers."

17. Vester, *Our Jerusalem,* 48.

18. Ibid., 50.

19. Job 40:4 and 42:6, Horatio Spafford's underlined Bible, ACJC.

20. Vester, *Our Jerusalem,* 55.

21. Evensen, *God's Man for the Gilded Age,* 65, 66.

22. Ibid., 73, 76.

23. Evensen tells us that in all the excitement, few of Philadelphia's black citizens seem to have made it into the gigantic auditorium. One middle-aged black lady did, however. So moved was she mid-sermon that she jumped up and hollered: "Glory, glory!" Instantly, it was reported, thousands of women stood, looking anxiously about, "many fearing fire." Moody immediately called for the audience to rise and sing, while the unfortunate enthusiast was bustled from the auditorium. Ibid., 88.

24. Ibid., 95.

25. *Jubilee History of the Fullerton Avenue Presbyterian Church,* 8.

26. Goodwillie, "Early Days in the Fullerton Avenue Presbyterian Church," 161. The evangelicals' letters home, the careful reports about their missionary undertakings, their descriptions of the inhabitants they were striving to bring to Christ, were to have a stupendous, almost incalculable impact on shaping America's opinion of other cultures. In the Middle East, for example, the cultural insensitivity, historical ignorance, and often downright antagonism of many missionaries toward those they had come to convert produced in due course extremely negative stereotypes of Turks, Arabs, and Eastern rite Christians. Even today, images of "the unspeakable Turk," "the filthy Arab," and "the mendacious

Armenian"—who later became "the piteous Armenian"—are difficult for Americans to discard. At the end of the nineteenth century, as the Ottoman Empire cautiously undertook to reform and modernize itself, the brethren's meddling, particularly among the fractious and independent-minded Christian Armenians of Anatolia, spurred revolts that helped to destabilize that great polyglot empire and contributed to its demise. Nevertheless, missionaries kept coming, supported by the U.S. State Department, which often trembled at the pressure exerted on U.S. foreign policy by these virtuous churchmen. It would be only a few more years before Horatio and Anna Spafford themselves would see the necessity of heeding the Holy Land's siren call—but when they went to Jerusalem, they elected to be different. As part of their deviant new creed, they chose not to proselytize and thus made fast friends with many grateful ethnic and religious groups, but especially with Muslims, for whom conversion was a capital offense.

27. "The Fullerton Avenue Church," *Chicago Daily Tribune,* July 8, 1876.

28. Ibid.

29. *Mary F. Murphy and Anna Spafford v. Dr. Samuel P. Hedges, et al.,* IL, G-142175 (Ill. Circuit Court, Chancery Court, Cook County, Feb. 8, 1896).

30. Robertson, *Chicago Revival,* 63.

31. This is the thesis that Darrel Robertson offers in his excellent book on the revival, from which I have enormously profited.

32. Robertson, *Chicago Revival,* 153.

33. Ibid., 141, 140.

Chapter Nine: The Overcomers

1. "A Singular Sect: The 'Overcomers,' a New Religious Sect, Makes Its Appearance in Chicago," *Daily Inter Ocean,* Aug. 17, 1881.

2. Edith Larsson, *Dala-Swedes in the Holy Land,* 84.

3. Hannah Whitall Smith, *Religious Fanaticism,* 207, 208–9.

4. Hannah Whitall Smith, a prominent Philadelphia Quaker whose devotional tract *The Christian's Secret of a Happy Life* was enjoying immense popularity, had met the group on a trip to Chicago. They begged her to join them, but she declined. Rational, thoughtful, and sympathetic to "dear deluded saints" of every stripe, Mrs. Smith began to investigate "fanatic" groups and eventually wrote a book about those she had encountered, to be published by her granddaughter after her death, when no reputations might be harmed. Horatio's group, with whom she kept up—helped by Francis Willard—was "one of the strangest," Mrs. Smith wrote in *Religious Fanaticism,* 208–9.

5. "A Singular Sect."

6. "Cash for a Colony," *Chicago Daily News,* March 9, 1894.

7. Smith, *Religious Fanaticism,* 209–10.

8. Vester, *Our Jerusalem,* 51.

9. "A Singular Sect."

10. *Chicago Daily Tribune,* April 8, 1884.

11. *Mary F. Murphy and Anna Spafford v. Dr. Samuel P. Hedges, et al.,* IL, G-142175 (Ill. Circuit Court, Chancery Court, Cook County, Feb. 8, 1896), testimony, 210, 212.

12. Anna Spafford, diary, July 20, 1878, ACJC.

13. Ibid., Aug. 8, 1878.

14. Ibid.

15. Vester, *Our Jerusalem,* 55.

16. *Murphy v. Hedges,* testimony, Anna Spafford, Feb. 8, 1896.

17. Ibid.

18. "A Singular Sect."

19. *Murphy v. Hedges,* testimony, Trypema C. Rounds, June 16, 1897.

20. *Murphy v. Hedges,* testimony, Dr. Hedges, June 1, 1897.

21. Ibid.

22. Ibid.

Chapter Ten: "Amelikans" in Yerushalayim

1. Gilbert, *Jerusalem,* 131.

2. Armstrong, *Jerusalem,* 336.

3. Lind, "Jerusalem Before Zionism," 14.

4. Lind, "Return of the Gaddites," 151.

5. A delightful image partially borrowed from Lind, "Jerusalem Before Zionism," 44.

6. Lind, "Return of the Gaddites," 151.

7. Lind, "Jerusalem Before Zionism," 25.

8. "Coming into Jerusalem by the Damascus Gate, 14 March, 1882, I noticed two unfamiliar objects standing out above the city walls against the evening sky. Upon inquiry I found they were ventilating pipes. A family (American, I believe) had taken a house there, as they thought the day of judgment was at hand, yet wished to have a sanitated house meanwhile." Cecil Torr, *Small Talk at Wreyland: The Journal of an English Country Gentleman* (Cambridge, U.K.: Cambridge University Press, 1918), quoted in Ashbee, *Palestine Notebook,* 179.

9. Kiser, *Monks of Tibhirine,* 136.

10. Lind, "Jerusalem Before Zionism," 44.

11. Ibid., 42.

12. John 15:5.

13. "Holy City Their Home," *Chicago Daily News,* May 15, 1895.

14. Vester, *Our Jerusalem,* 64.

15. "Is on Its Last Legs," *Chicago Daily Tribune,* Oct. 18, 1894.

16. "Holy City Their Home."

17. Acts 14.

18. "Holy City Their Home."

19. Ibid.

Chapter Eleven: The Gadites

1. The notion that nationals residing in a foreign land should be judged by their own laws dates back to the Byzantine era. The Ottomans granted this privilege first to the French in 1535, to the Austrians in 1625, to the English in 1675, and then to others. It was accorded the United States in 1830. For the Ottomans it constituted a solution to a problem arising from Ottoman law: that an infidel had no right to own property or to legal protection. To make it practical, therefore, to trade with non-Muslim nations, the empire adopted this solution to maintain trade relationships without breaking its own laws. By the nineteenth century, however, the nations that benefited from these "capitulations" had taken such severe advantage of the system and offered no reciprocal relief that a weakened Turkey feared for its sovereignty. Capitulations were officially rejected by Turkey in 1914.

2. Kelk to U.S. Consul Edwin S. Wallace, Dec. 7, 1897, USNA, RG 84.

3. Ibid.

4. Sheean, *Personal History,* 348–49.

5. John Franklin Swift, *Going to Jericho; or, Sketches of Travel in Spain and the East* (New York: A. Roman, 1868), 249, quoted in Vogel, *To See a Promised Land,* 81.

6. Gilbert, *Jerusalem,* 163–64.

7. Armstrong, *Jerusalem,* 352. The period of 1882–84, when about eight thousand European Jews established agricultural settlements in Palestine, marked the first aliyah, or wave of immigration, that culminated in the establishment of Israel.

8. Peters, *Jerusalem,* 583.

9. In 1839 the London Society for Promoting Christianity Among the Jews (familiarly called the London Jews Society) had been given permission to work in Jerusalem. It was the first major presence of a Protestant group, although the

French had made it clear for some time that they sponsored the Latins, just as the Russians had declared that they were protectors of the Orthodox. The society established a hospital near the Jewish Quarter as well as various farms outside the city where it was hoped that Jews could learn agriculture and be weaned from dependence on the *haluka,* the alms collected in the Diaspora to maintain a Jewish community in Jerusalem. A Protestant bishop opened a school for both Jewish and Arab children. These efforts were humanitarian in intention, but their primary purpose was to remove any impediment to the fulfillment of the prophecies, and accordingly were resented by the Orthodox Jewish establishment. This prompted the British Jewish philanthropist Moses Montefiore, as well as the Rothschild family, to counter with Jewish welfare establishments of their own such as hospitals and training schools for Jews, as they, too, considered the *haluka* an unhealthy custom. In turn, as philanthropy became more aggressive, it became more divisive. Both the Greek Orthodox Church and the Roman Catholics felt compelled to open schools as well. While this competition to educate the people and ameliorate their poverty did much to improve the appalling conditions in Jerusalem and helped thrust the city into modernity, it did nothing to cool the fierce religious antagonisms between the different faiths.

10. Vester, *Our Jerusalem,* 103.

11. Lind, "Return of the Gaddites," 153.

12. A Pentateuch is a scroll containing the first five books of the Old Testament used in a synagogue for liturgical purposes. It is also known as the Torah. This scene and dialogue are quoted from ibid., and Vester, *Our Jerusalem,* 135–40, gives a similar account.

13. Today, Israelis are deeply indebted to Ben-Yehuda and the other visionaries who devoted their lives to the task of making Hebrew their common language.

14. Moses William Shapira, a Russian Jew living in Jerusalem, an amateur scholar and antiquities dealer, was alleged to be the thief who apparently cannibalized the scroll and sold part of it to the British Museum. The fraud was exposed by the French orientalist Charles Clermont-Ganneau in 1885, and Shapira committed suicide. See a fuller description of the theft and the controversy that followed in Dudman and Kark, *American Colony,* chap. 6.

Chapter Twelve: Bad News and Good Works

1. *Mary F. Murphy and Anna Spafford v. Dr. Samuel P. Hedges, et al.,* IL, G-142175 (Ill. Circuit Court, Chancery Court, Cook County, Feb. 8, 1896), Exhibit C.

2. Vester, *Our Jerusalem,* 58.

3. *Murphy v. Hedges,* Exhibit D.

4. *Murphy v. Hedges,* master's report.

5. U.S. Consul Selah Merrill to State Department, report, July 8, 1901, USNA, RG 84.

6. *Chicago Herald,* 1885, scrapbook, ACJC.

7. Vester, *Our Jerusalem,* 128.

8. Merrill to State Department, report, July 8, 1901.

9. Vester, *Our Jerusalem,* 94.

10. Ibid., 114.

11. Ibid., 115.

12. Horatio Spafford to H. S. Beebee, printed in *Chicago Herald,* 1885, scrapbook, ACJC.

13. Kelk to U.S. Consul Edwin S. Wallace, Dec. 7, 1897, USNA, RG 84.

14. Vester, *Our Jerusalem,* 93.

15. Ibid., 94.

16. Ibid.

17. Jacob had been intrigued by talk of a subterranean tunnel in the Ophel Hill running from a spring at the Virgin's Well, the presumed site of the first Jebusite settlement, to the Pool of Siloam. The tunnel was described in the Old Testament as the work of King Hezekiah to divert water from the Assyrian armies of Sennacherib, massing to attack Judah. He and a somewhat reluctant friend attached candle floats around their necks and, beginning at opposite ends, agreed to meet in the middle. Jacob waded through the icy water and, when his candle went out, felt his way by the ancient chisel marks on the wall. Deep inside, he stumbled, fell, and, regaining his balance, detected curious markings suggesting an inscription. When he emerged at the other end and found his friend had given up and left, Jacob hurried to tell his headmaster, Dr. Conrad Schick, a well-regarded Swiss Protestant archaeologist in charge of excavations for the British Palestine Exploration Fund. Dr. Schick was soon able to confirm that Jacob had located a landmark in the rediscovery of biblical Jerusalem: a description of Hezekiah's tunnel cutters meeting from two ends, and the longest single document ever found in ancient Hebrew. Tragically, even as Dr. Schick was filing his report, an antiquities thief tried to pry the inscription from its rock face, and it broke into several pieces. The Turkish government quickly confiscated this valuable artifact and sent it to Istanbul, where it is today.

18. Baldwin, "From the Damascus Gate," 22.

19. Strachey, *Eminent Victorians,* 171. Strachey's biographical sketch of Gordon is famously scalding.

20. Charles Gordon to R. H. Barnes, June 6, 1883, Boston Public Library, quoted in Vogel, *To See a Promised Land,* 155.

21. Strachey, *Eminent Victorians,* 242.

22. An admirer of Gordon's bought it and donated it to Cuddesdon College, England, in Gordon's name.

Chapter Thirteen: Friends and a Foe

1. The story of the Adams Colony, and the genial rogue who led it, is only one of the many preposterous but true tales of hopeful believers frustrated by the realities of the Holy Land in the nineteenth century, although perhaps the best known, as Mark Twain wrote about it. Parsons, *Letters from Palestine,* 4–11.

2. Ibid., 66.

3. Ibid., 75–76.

4. *Our Rest and Signs of the Times* 10, no. 7 (July 1883).

5. Parsons, *Letters from Palestine,* 67.

6. Silberman, "Curiosities of the Holy Land," 7.

7. Ibid., 5.

8. Merrill to State Department, June 15, 1883, USNA, RG 84.

9. Ibid.

10. Bross was quoting Virgil's *Aeneid:* "Facilis descensus averno," or "Easy is the way down to the Infernal Regions," or, more vernacularly, "The road to hell is easy."

11. Bross to Merrill, July 7, 1883, USNA, RG 84.

12. Gould to Merrill, July 16, 1884, USNA, RG 84.

Chapter Fourteen: Overcoming Temptation and the Dangers of Attachment

1. "On Holy Paths."

2. "Warns All Against the Spaffordites," *Chicago Journal,* Dec. 24, 1897.

3. Spafford to H. S. Beebee, printed in *Chicago Herald,* 1885, scrapbook, ACJC.

4. Vester, *Our Jerusalem,* 201.

5. A. Hastings Kelk to U.S. Consul Wallace, Dec. 7, 1897, USNA, RG 84.

6. "On Holy Paths," 13.

7. Many letters about Lizzie Page, written between 1888 and 1901, are in State Department archives. According to the list of American Colony dead compiled by John Whiting's son, she died at Ain Karim of tuberculosis in April 1888. John D. Whiting, Record of American Colony Deaths, John Whiting Collection, Library of Congress.

8. Lind, "Jerusalem Before Zionism," 32.

9. Merrill to State Department, July 8, 1901, USNA, RG 84.

10. "On Holy Paths," 12.

11. Rahbek and Bähncke, *Faith and Fate in Jerusalem,* 33–34.

12. Parsons, *Letters from Palestine,* 55.

13. Alice E. Davis to U.S. Consul Edwin S. Wallace, Dec. 6, 1897, USNA, RG 84.

14. Ibid.

15. Vester, *Our Jerusalem,* 154, 155.

16. Newspaper accounts, Vester scrapbook, ACJC.

17. The novel Gillman wrote was *Hassan, a Fellah.*

18. Newspaper accounts, Vester scrapbook, ACJC.

Chapter Fifteen: Struggling On

1. Baron von Ustinov was an eccentric Russian and the grandfather of the actor Peter Ustinov who remained a friend of the American Colony all his life.

2. Vester, *Our Jerusalem,* 48, 157.

3. Curtis, "100 Years of Blessing."

4. "Chicago's Come-Outers," *Chicago Evening Journal,* May 4, 1889.

5. Vincent, "Study in Social and Religious Life in Modern Jerusalem."

6. *Wallace v. D. Appleton & Co.* (U.S. Circuit Court, Southern District of New York). Testimony of Mary Whiting, Sept. 9, 1908.

7. "Cash for a Colony," *Chicago Daily News,* March 9, 1894.

8. "Holy Lives."

9. Ibid., and other similar articles.

10. Morgan, "Letters from Palestine."

11. Ibid.

12. Ibid.

13. Amelia Gould, will, May 1891, drawer 18, 1887–93, "Amelia Gould" file, ACJC.

14. William Rudy to John Gould, May 26, 1891, ACJC.

15. Lind, "Jerusalem Before Zionism," 37, 39.

16. An article about Jacob's being "the whipper" reveals the harsh treatment of the "second class" children in the colony, which interviews with colony descendants confirmed (Marbourg, "Separate the Men and Women!"). Most damaging, however, is the testimony of Constantine Antoszewsky (Aug. 13, 1900, USNA, RG 84). It should be noted, on the subject of whipping, that even today, particularly in rural parts of America's South and lower Midwestern states, corporal

punishment has long been practiced and is a legal tool in schools, according to the *New York Times,* in a front-page story by Rick Lyman, Sept. 30, 2006. The *Times* observed also that a paddle with holes was favored in order to make the punishment more painful.

17. Rahbek and Bähncke, *Faith and Fate in Jerusalem,* 33–34.

18. Merrill to State Department, dispatch enclosing sworn testimony of Constantine Antoszewsky, Aug. 15, 1900, USNA, RG 84.

19. Rahbek and Bähncke, *Faith and Fate in Jerusalem,* 33–34.

20. "Life in the Colony," *Chicago Tribune,* April 18, 1895.

Chapter Sixteen: The Whiting Affair

1. Merrill to State Department, Aug. 13, 1900, USNA, RG 84.

2. Merrill to State Department, Nov. 15, 1884, USNA, RG 84.

3. Merrill to State Department, Oct. 3, 1891, USNA, RG 84.

4. Lingle to Merrill, July 10, 1893, USNA, RG 84.

5. Merrill to Lingle, July 20, 1893, USNA, RG 84.

6. Lingle to Merrill, July 31, 1893, USNA, RG 84.

7. Moore to Merrill, report, Aug. 11, 1893, USNA, RG 84.

8. Merrill to State Department, Aug. 19, 1893, USNA, RG 84.

9. Lingle to Merrill, Aug. 15, 1893, USNA, RG 84.

10. Merrill to State Department, Oct. 9, 1893, USNA, RG 84.

11. Merrill to State Department, report, Aug. 19, 1893, USNA, RG 84.

Chapter Seventeen: The Trial

1. "Cash for a Colony," *Chicago Daily News,* March 9, 1894.

2. Ibid.

3. Ibid and "Heirs to a Fortune," *Boston Daily Globe,* March 12, 1894.

4. "Is on Its Last Legs," *Chicago Daily Tribune,* Oct. 18, 1894.

5. "That New Jerusalem," *Chicago Evening Journal,* March 2, 1895.

6. Myers, "Unscrupulous 'Overcomers' Left Trail of Graft, Grief, and Heartbreak at Lebanon."

7. *Mary F. Murphy and Anna Spafford v. Dr. Samuel P. Hedges, et al.,* IL, G-142175 (Ill. Circuit Court, Chancery Court, Cook County, Feb. 8, 1896). Testimonies of Anna Spafford, Feb. 8, 1896, and Samuel P. Hedges, June 1, 1897.

8. Ibid.

9. *Murphy v. Hedges,* master's report, June 16, 1899.

10. "Asks for a Guardian," *Chicago Daily Tribune,* April 17, 1895.

11. Ibid.

12. Ibid.

13. "Life in the City of Zion: Lizzie Aiken Tells of the Queer Doings of Mrs. Spafford in Old Jerusalem," *Chicago Daily News,* May 14, 1895.

14. Ibid.

15. Ibid.

16. "Colony Is a Winner," *Chicago Daily Tribune,* May 15, 1895.

17. For decades, families back in Kansas would shake their heads over the "great swindle" that had so bitterly divided them, that caused the hair of one father to "turn white overnight." Eventually they learned enough of the truth to call the adventure "the trail of heartbreak." Myers, "Unscrupulous 'Overcomers' Left Trail of Graft, Grief, and Heartbreak at Lebanon."

Chapter Eighteen: The Chicago Swedes

1. "Parousia," from the Greek word for presence, and meaning "the Second Coming."

2. Rahbek and Bähncke, *Faith and Fate in Jerusalem,* 60.

3. Ibid., 54–55.

4. Ibid.

5. Ibid.

6. Larsson, *Dala-Swedes in the Holy Land,* 22.

7. Rahbek and Bähncke, *Faith and Fate in Jerusalem,* 61.

8. Ibid., 54.

9. Larsson, *Dala-Swedes in the Holy Land,* 23, 37.

10. Larsson, *Seven Passports for Palestine,* 11.

11. Tveit, "Anna's House," 94. Italics mine.

Chapter Nineteen: The Swedes from Nås

1. Larsson, *Dala-Swedes in the Holy Land,* 42.

2. Rahbek and Bähncke, *Faith and Fate in Jerusalem,* 68.

3. Ibid., 69.

4. Lind, "Jerusalem Before Zionism," 67.

5. Whiting, Record of American Colony Deaths, John Whiting Collection, Library of Congress.

6. Rahbek and Bähncke, *Faith and Fate in Jerusalem,* 87.

7. Ibid., 89. The letter was written by fifteen-year-old Karin Mockelin, who quickly lost five of her family.

8. Lind, "Jerusalem Before Zionism," 28.

9. Vester, *Our Jerusalem,* 176.

10. Larsson, *Dala-Swedes in the Holy Land,* 48.

11. Ibid.

12. Ibid., 79.

13. Baldwin, "From the Damascus Gate," 27.

14. There were many distinguished graduates of the school while it flourished before World War I: Among them were Musa al-Alami and his sister, who married Jamal el-Husseini, secretary of the Arab National Party and later secretary to King Ibn Saud. Musa became a barrister at Cambridge University and aide-de-camp to High Commissioner Sir Arthur Wauchope, then founder of Boys Town, Jericho. Akram Rikabi became secretary of agriculture under successive Syrian administrations.

15. Larsson, *Dala-Swedes in the Holy Land,* 56.

16. Lind, "Jerusalem Before Zionism," 40.

17. Ibid.

18. Ibid., 28.

19. Ibid.

Chapter Twenty: A Cemetery War Begins

1. *Wallace v. D. Appleton & Co.* (U.S. Circuit Court, Southern District of New York), 55. Testimony of Furman O. Baldwin, Sept. 8, 1908.

2. Wallace, "Some of the Peculiar People of Jerusalem."

3. The son of the consul was an unruly and rather disagreeable boy, Rudolf Hess, who as an adult became a Nazi intimate of Hitler who parachuted into Britain in a wild attempt to organize an underground support movement. He was caught, imprisoned, and at the end of World War II tried as a war criminal. Apparently, Brother Rudy was one of the few who were able to pacify the lad when his parents came to call. This is only one of many examples of the historical figures whose lives touched Anna's and the colony.

4. "Tells Secrets of the Colony," *Chicago Journal,* Dec. 16, 1897.

5. Gertrude Bell, the traveler who as Oriental secretary under Sir Percy Cox after World War I helped determine the boundaries of present-day Iraq, visited this school shortly after it was founded and formed a pleasant acquaintance with Bertha.

6. Wallace to State Department, Aug. 16, 1897, USNA, RG 84.

7. Later it emerged that when the child was only sixteen months old, she had been beaten or whipped, although not by her parents. It was the custom for men to be asked to whip girls who were unrelated to them on their naked bodies, but the parents were never told who had administered the punishment. From a sworn statement by Constantine Antoszewsky, March 10, 1900, and forwarded to the State Department by Selah Merrill, USNA, RG 84.

8. Ibid., 38–39, 62.

9. Sept. 12, 1897. These events have been reconstructed from Wallace's dispatches to the State Department, April through December 1897, as well as from testimony gathered in *Wallace v. D. Appleton & Co.*

10. Vester, *Our Jerusalem*, 202.

11. Bertha Vester tells of this interview in *Our Jerusalem* (197–207) and gives her version of the cemetery scandal, which she described as "a plot." I have laboriously stitched together this very complicated story with its accusations and counteraccusations from Mrs. Vester's self-serving account, newspaper articles, State Department archives, Dudman and Kark's *American Colony*, an interview with Condit N. Eddy, and *Wallace v. D. Appleton & Co.* None of the Swedes—Edith Larsson, Lars Lind, nor various others (Baldwin or Rahbek and Bähncke's *Faith and Fate*)—mentions the controversy. I am convinced the following account is the actual truth.

12. Whiting, Record of American Colony Deaths, John Whiting Collection, Library of Congress.

13. The colonists were kept in the dark when dead members were buried on the properties of Arab friends. Later, some were apparently retrieved from their secret hiding places when the colony finally purchased a cemetery on Mount Scopus. Lind, "Jerusalem Before Zionism," 75–78.

14. Syria was a huge Ottoman province before World War I. In 1920, the French drove out the Arabs who had converged on this beloved Arab heartland to build a new and modern Arab nation. The British had promised it to them—a message confirmed by T. E. Lawrence—as the just reward for their help in the famous Arab Revolt against the Turks. But the secret Sykes-Picot Agreement required this promise to be broken. The French came in and by force expelled the Arabs in a betrayal they never forgot. Then the French divided Syria and made Lebanon an independent state with Beirut as its capital.

15. Archaeological findings have since relocated the site to Mount Ophel, not Zion, and indicate the town predated David, who had seized a settlement of an earlier indigenous people. Armstrong, *Jerusalem*, 362.

16. Merrill to State Department, report, Nov. 12, 1898, USNA, RG 84.

17. Wallace to State Department, report, Aug. 16, 1897, USNA, RG 84.

18. Alley, "Spaffordism."

19. "Tells Secrets of the Colony."

20. Wallace to State Department, report, Nov. 3, 1897, USNA, RG 84.

21. Note, n.d., responding to dispatch from Wallace, April 19, 1897, USNA, RG 84.

22. Note, n.d., during this period, USNA, RG 84.

23. "Say Sect Is a Fraud," *Daily Inter Ocean,* Dec. 16, 1897.

24. "Just from Jerusalem," *Harvey (Ill.) Tribune-Citizen,* Sept. 4, 1897.

25. "Still Long for the Holy Land," *Chicago Daily News,* Dec. 15, 1897.

26. "Say Sect Is a Fraud."

27. "Says Spaffordites Are Persecuted," *Chicago Journal,* Dec. 15, 1897.

28. Ibid.

29. Constantine Antoszewsky, sworn statement, Aug. 13, 1900, USNA, RG 84.

30. Larsson, *Dala-Swedes in the Holy Land,* 96.

Chapter Twenty-one: The Sultan, the Emperor, the Zionist—and Buried Bodies

1. Armstrong, *Jerusalem,* 352.

2. Tveit, "Anna's House," 79.

3. Gilbert, *Jerusalem,* 221.

4. Merrill to State Department, report, March 5, 1899, USNA, RG 84.

5. Ibid.

6. Ibid.

7. Sick and exhausted from his efforts to convince the Great Powers and his own divided people, Herzl died in 1904, and any realistic chance of a place other than Palestine as acceptable for a Jewish homeland died with him.

8. Mulhall, *America and the Founding of Israel,* 49.

9. Repressive measures against the Armenians, and the zealotry of the sultan's Kurdish special forces in eastern Anatolia, the *hamidiyya,* had resulted in an uprising that ended with some hundred thousand dead between 1894 and 1895. When Greek and Armenian revolutionaries sparked a rebellion in Crete in 1896, supported by the Greek government, the Turks invaded Greece, which capitulated to the far stronger Turkish army in 1897. Palmer, *Decline and Fall of the Ottoman Empire,* 175–88.

10. Finkel, *Osman's Dream,* 494–502.

11. The Hejaz Railway from Damascus to Medina (it was recognized to be unwise to carry it on down to the door of Mecca) was finally completed in 1908. The railway was to carry pilgrims on their hajj, and from all over the empire the faithful donated what they could in this tremendous effort, raising over 100 million pounds. For the Turks, who ever needed to keep a vigilant eye on their Arab population, lest modern ideas of nationalism spark rebellion, the railway was also a fast way to carry troops to put down an endless revolt in Yemen. The Baghdad

Railway was not completed until 1917, partly as a result of the many and varied obstacles that the British and French managed to put in its path. By then, the Hohenzollern rule was about to end.

12. There was a beautiful symmetry, as Frederick was Hohenstaufen and Wilhelm was a Hohenzollern descendant. Palmer, *Decline and Fall of the Ottoman Empire*, 189.

13. *Wallace v. D. Appleton & Co.* (U.S. Circuit Court, Southern District of New York). Testimony of Furman O. Baldwin, Sept. 8, 1908.

14. *Wallace v. D. Appleton & Co.*, testimony, Edward F. Baldwin, July 28, 1908.

15. Vester, *Our Jerusalem*, 204.

16. Merrill to State Department, Aug. 10, 1900, report to Merrill by Constantine Antoszewsky, USNA, RG 84.

17. *Wallace v. D. Appleton & Co.*, testimony, Edward F. Baldwin, July 28, 1908.

18. Ismail Bey Husseini (superintendent of public instruction) to the U.S. president, Sept. 27, 1897, republished in *Appleton's Magazine*, Dec. 1906.

19. *Wallace v. D. Appleton & Co.*, testimony, Edward F. Baldwin.

20. The colony did succeed in bringing attention to the "scandal" in some newspapers, but nothing much came of it. An investigation by the British naval commander Ottley of Her Majesty's sloop *Nymphe* meeting with Turkish authorities concluded that "the alleged desecration" of the graves of "British officers" may "be considered satisfactorily closed." Newspaper article, March 10, 1898, Anna Spafford's scrapbook, ACJC. There were also short pieces in the *Chicago Record* on March 2, 1898, and March 3, 1898, reporting that the field secretary of the American Board for Missionaries denied the colony's accusation that the mission sold the cemetery to raise money as "too ridiculous." It seems that only the American Colony wished to pursue the matter.

21. *Wallace v. D. Appleton & Co.*, testimony, Edward F. Baldwin, July 28, 1908.

22. Merrill's dispatches to the State Department through 1900, USNA, RG 84.

23. Vester, *Our Jerusalem*, 204.

24. Merrill to State Department, Nov. 12, 1898, USNA, RG 84.

25. In a tragic footnote to the royal exit, Ismail Bey lost his pretty daughter. The evening after the child presented her gift to the kaiserin—who gave her a diamond pin in the shape of the imperial eagle—her dress caught on fire from a lit candle. Bertha Spafford happened to be with the Husseinis at the time and rushed to roll her in a rug. Although the kaiser sent his personal physician, and Bertha stayed with her through the night, Ismail Bey's daughter died before dawn, leaving her father grief-stricken and reconsidering the power of the "evil eye."

26. "Pilgrim in Palestine: Details of Kaiser Wilhelm's Journey to Jerusalem," *Washington Post,* Nov. 6, 1898; "The Kaiser at Jerusalem," *New York Times,* Oct. 31, 1898.

27. Vester, *Our Jerusalem,* 185.

28. Dudman and Kark, *American Colony,* 156.

29. Gilbert, *Jerusalem,* 225, 227.

30. Ibid., 227.

31. Aaronsohn, *With the Turks in Palestine,* 19.

32. Larsson, *Dala-Swedes in the Holy Land,* 84.

33. Lind, "Jerusalem Before Zionism," 99.

Chapter Twenty-two: The Novelist

1. See Larsen, *Selma Lagerlöf;* Maule, *Selma Lagerlöf;* Edström, *Selma Lagerlöf.*

2. Constantine Antoszewsky, sworn statement, March 5, 1900, USNA, RG 84.

3. In Stockholm on August 26, 1925, before an international assembly of church leaders, the Swedish royal family, and the archbishop of Sweden, Selma Lagerlöf told Anna's story and urged "unity" between Christians and non-Christians at a time when society was struggling to recover from World War I.

4. Rahbek and Bähncke, *Faith and Fate in Jerusalem,* 83.

5. Vester, *Our Jerusalem,* 188.

6. Rahbek and Bähncke, *Faith and Fate in Jerusalem,* 76.

7. Ibid., 85.

Chapter Twenty-three: The New Dispensation

1. Lind, "Jerusalem Before Zionism," 105.

2. Merrill to State Department, forwarding statement by Constantine Antoszewsky, Aug. 13, 1900, USNA, RG 84.

3. Larsson, *Dala-Swedes in the Holy Land,* 35.

4. Lind, "Jerusalem Before Zionism," 147, 148.

5. Ibid., 151.

6. Furman Baldwin to Mr. Gelat, vice-consul, statement, July 14, 1901, USNA, RG 84.

7. Merrill to State Department, July 9, 1901, USNA, RG 84.

8. Larsson, *Dala-Swedes in the Holy Land,* 65.

9. The two Americans were E. K. Warren of Michigan, inventor of the "featherbone," and a Mr. Hartshorn from Boston. Lind, "Jerusalem Before Zionism," 143.

10. In her memoir, Bertha Spafford gives the date of her wedding as March 1, 1904. One would think that the bride should know, but as she frequently played loose with facts, I have chosen to give the date provided by Lind, "Jerusalem Before Zionism," 143. On the other hand, Lars was only thirteen at the time, so perhaps he is the one in error!

11. Ibid., 153.

12. Tveit, "Anna's House," 130.

13. Ibid., 137. Quoted from a documentary film, *Dreams of Jerusalem,* by Mia Gröndahl, Swedish Television, Malmö, Production 30–96/0180.

14. Furman Baldwin's first wife was Eva Henwood; his second was Farida Naseef, whose fascinating private memoir, "From the Damascus Gate," was kindly shown to me by his son.

Chapter Twenty-four: Triumph

1. Larsson, *Dala-Swedes in the Holy Land,* 122.

2. Lind, "Jerusalem Before Zionism," 161.

3. Ibid., 137.

4. Larsson, *Dala-Swedes in the Holy Land,* 121.

5. "On Holy Paths," 122.

6. Ibid., 139–42.

7. The Feast of the Prophet Moses was initiated by the Turks, ever suspicious of Russian intentions. At Easter as many as fifteen thousand Russians could arrive, and the Turks feared the possibility of these "pilgrims" actually being undercover troops aiming at conquest. As the Koran holds Moses in high regard, an annual festival was devised honoring Moses and attracting thousands of Muslim worshippers as a counterweight. The long parade to a tomb on the purported site of the prophet's grave in the Judaean wilderness was a fantastic affair featuring dervishes, bandoliered horsemen, penitents flaying their flesh, banner bearers, and hawkers of festival food. Christians, Jews, and other infidels wishing to observe the frenzied commotion were cautioned to keep a low profile.

8. Ford, "Our American Colony at Jerusalem."

9. In 1900, the United States was one of the last to form a society dedicated to the study of the Holy Land. England was the first, forming a society as far back as 1585. It was the British Palestine Exploration Fund, chartered in 1865, that undertook the first scientific study of Palestine from climate measurements to archaeology and created the maps that proved invaluable to Field Marshal Allenby in his Eastern campaign in World War I. The American Schools of Oriental Research was organized and supported by a group of American colleges and univer-

sities to send students to Jerusalem under a resident professor. Since that time, ASOR scholars have contributed to many important archaeological discoveries as well as to other disciplines that have illuminated both the ancient and the modern Middle East.

10. Ibid.

11. *Wallace v. D. Appleton & Co.* (U.S. Circuit Court, Southern District of New York). Testimony of Gustav Herman Dalman, Sept. 15, 1908.

12. One of the buried dead was the mother of William M. Thomson, who had written the enormously successful *Land and the Book,* widely read and admired. It would have been a great embarrassment for Eddy and the Presbyterian board if Reverend Thomson chose to make an issue of the cemetery or join the protests of the American Colony. He apparently did not.

13. Ford, "Our American Colony at Jerusalem."

14. In a telephone interview on December 7, 2006, Eddy's grandson, Condit N. Eddy, looked up his grandmother's diary for me and found no mention of the *Appleton's* article. Her concern, clearly, was the sudden death of her husband. However, there was an entry for 1902 mentioning that he had been "sent to U.S. on a committee to the State Department." Then, in 1903, another brief note: "W. had to go to Jerusalem that fall, as he did frequently during several years on the business of the cemetery." Unfortunately, that was all Mrs. Eddy had to say about the issue.

15. George Wheeler to Merrill, May 30, 1906, State Department dispatch, July 7, 1906, USNA, RG 84.

16. Adelaide Merrill to State Department, Aug. 20, 1906, filed under "Jerusalem," USNA, RG 84.

17. Van Atta, *History of the First Presbyterian Church of Greensburg.*

18. Ibid., 124.

19. Ibid.

20. Merrill must have found some irony in knowing that this was the very place where the French government had imprisoned Alfred Dreyfus, an act of such supreme injustice that Theodor Herzl launched his titanic effort on behalf of his co-religionists.

21. "Liked Jerusalem, but Glad to Be Home Again," *Boston Sunday Herald,* Aug. 18, 1907.

22. *Wallace v. D. Appleton & Co.,* Opinion of Hon. John R. Hazel, Judge, April 16, 1909.

23. This is the last sentence in a passage winding up her account of the long antagonism describing a cordial encounter between Anna and Mrs. Merrill at the

home of a mutual friend in Jerusalem in 1910, when Dr. Merrill, according to Bertha, recognized their carriage and waited outside rather than going into the house. "At last Dr. Merrill entered with some belated guests. His agonized behavior was disconcerting to witness," remembered Bertha. "He wrote on a pad but was careful not to let the pad out of his hands." Vester, *Our Jerusalem*, 207. If the two ladies did in fact meet, and doubtless they did, it was not in 1910, as by then the old scholar had been dead and buried for a year.

Chapter Twenty-five: War

1. Lars Lind writes that he had longed to have a pet dog to love and look after. Only when he was in his teens was he allowed to keep a mongrel that had detached itself from the packs of feral dogs; he brought the dog home, and it became a beloved mascot for him and the other boys.

2. Lind, "Jerusalem Before Zionism," 276–77.

3. John Whiting was in charge of ordering hundreds of shoes from England for the members. Among his papers are the numbers of orders for specific sizes. John Whiting Collection, Library of Congress.

4. Larsson, *Seven Passports for Palestine*, 15–16.

5. The CUP saw parliament merely as "an extension of the modern bureaucratic apparatus under the control of an enlightened governing elite." Finkel, *Osman's Dream*, 512.

6. Palmer, *Decline and Fall of the Ottoman Empire*, 219.

7. Larsson, *Dala-Swedes in the Holy Land*, 133.

8. Ibid., 86.

9. Ibid., 87.

10. The Entente was unwilling to jeopardize their alliance with Russia by colluding with the Young Turks. They were not sure exactly who they were or what they were about. It was said in the British Foreign Office that they were "a collection of Jews and gypsies." Fromkin, *A Peace to End All Peace*, 43.

11. Palmer, *Decline and Fall of the Ottoman Empire*, 221.

12. Smith, *Palestine and the Arab-Israeli Conflict*, 38.

13. Fromkin, *A Peace to End All Peace*, 54–58.

14. Palmer, *Decline and Fall of the Ottoman Empire*, 226.

15. Cleveland, *History of the Modern Middle East*, 145.

16. "On Holy Paths," 17; Rahbek and Bähncke, *Faith and Fate in Jerusalem*, 113.

17. Ibid.

18. Ibid.

19. Vester, *Our Jerusalem*, 253.

20. Lind, "Jerusalem Before Zionism," 280.

21. Vester, *Our Jerusalem*, 233; Lind, "Jerusalem Before Zionism," 280.

22. Vester, *Our Jerusalem*, 234.

Chapter Twenty-six: Suffering

1. Palmer, *Decline and Fall of the Ottoman Empire*, 227.

2. The Gallipoli campaign cost the lives of thirty-four thousand British and ten thousand French soldiers, but the Turks lost twice as many men. When the Allies retreated, they left food and equipment sufficient to sustain four Turkish divisions for months. With the final defeat of the empire, Kemal went on to become Atatürk, the master, creator, and first president of modern democratic Turkey.

3. Cleveland, *History of the Modern Middle East*, 143.

4. Vester, *Our Jerusalem*, 235.

5. Lind, "Jerusalem Before Zionism," 303.

6. Ibid., 297.

7. Ibid.

8. Aaronsohn, *With the Turks in Palestine*, 41.

9. Ibid., 42.

10. John D. Whiting to William Coffin, July 17, 1919, John D. Whiting Collection, Library of Congress.

11. Aaronsohn, *With the Turks in Palestine*, 42–43.

12. John D. Whiting to William Coffin, July 17, 1919, John D. Whiting Collection, Library of Congress.

13. Aaronsohn, *With the Turks in Palestine*, 44–46.

14. Ibid., 301.

15. Bertha quotes from her letter to Edward F. Loud, of Oscoda, Michigan, who sent money himself and raised more from friends. Vester, *Our Jerusalem*, 240.

16. Aaronsohn, *With the Turks in Palestine*, 51.

17. Lind, "Jerusalem Before Zionism," 324.

18. Aaronsohn, *With the Turks in Palestine*, 51.

19. Rahbek and Bähncke, *Faith and Fate in Jerusalem*, 118.

20. Lind, "Jerusalem Before Zionism," 28.

21. I saw the death certificate and verified that Mr. Rudy's "effects" were pitifully few—a monocle, a picture of a female relative, notations about some land he had purchased in Chicago, about which there appeared to be a dispute with the seller. Also, there was a notebook with biblical citations. Glazebrook to State

Department, "Report of the Death of an American Citizen," Aug. 9, 1915, USNA, RG 84.

22. Acts 5:1–11.

23. John D. Whiting, Record of American Colony Deaths, ACJC.

24. Rahbek and Bähncke, *Faith and Fate in Jerusalem,* 119.

25. Ibid.

26. Ibid.

27. Ibid.

28. Lars Lind recorded that after Rudy died, Anna persisted in linking Amelia Gould and Rudy as Sapphira and Ananias. Lind, "Jerusalem Before Zionism," 28.

29. Today, in both Lebanon and Syria, May 6 is commemorated as Martyrs' Day.

30. The escapee was Haj Hassan Hammad, a notable from Nablus, summoned to Aley, forty miles west of Damascus, along with other notables to a "conference." Tricked, they were summarily tried and hanged, but Haj Hassan, through an accident to his carriage wheel, learned what had happened and, making his way to Damascus, hid with a friend, whose daughter he took as a second wife, and did not emerge until the war's end. His Nablus family thought he was dead, until he returned home with a second family. Lind, "Jerusalem Before Zionism," 306–8.

31. This issue has been endlessly debated between Turkey and Armenian survivors, with Turkish historians arguing that the numbers have been vastly inflated by Armenian lobbyists and insisting that it was a decision not to exterminate their Armenian minority but to secure eastern Anatolia from plots by Armenian revolutionaries, or *dashnaks.* The Armenians were Christian, like the Russians, and this affinity definitely inspired sympathy between them as well as active disloyalty to the Ottomans. If, as the Turks say, it was a tragic but unintended consequence of war, it was a tragedy of unprecedented proportion.

32. Cleveland, *History of the Modern Middle East,* 145.

33. These secret discussions were initiated at the suggestion of Lord Kitchener, secretary of war in Asquith's government. He cabled Ronald Storrs, later military governor of Palestine but at the time Oriental secretary in Cairo, to inform the sharif that he would have British support in a revolt. It was further promised that the British had no designs on Arab territories after the war and would repay the sharif by helping to establish Arab independence "without any intervention in your internal affairs" (Smith, *Palestine and the Arab-Israeli Conflict,* 43). These were essentially the same promises given in the famous and much

disputed correspondence with High Commissioner Henry McMahon, and are the basis of the Arabs' claims to having been betrayed.

34. Ibid., 151.

35. Palmer, *Decline and Fall of the Ottoman Empire*, 234.

36. From a description by Sven Hedin, one of the great explorers of central Asia, on his visit to the colony in 1916. He was deeply moved to see the "Dala-people" as industrious and serious as they were back home, and liked the atmosphere enormously, especially Sunday service, when the "female choir sang an exquisitely beautiful and wistful hymn" followed by a performance by the children. Sven Hedin, *Till Jerusalem* (Leipzig: F. U. Brodhaus, 1918), quoted in Rahbek and Bähncke, *Faith and Fate in Jerusalem*, 116.

37. Vester, *Our Jerusalem*, 249.

38. Ibid.

39. Rahbek and Bähncke, *Faith and Fate in Jerusalem*, 118.

40. Vester, *Our Jerusalem*, 241.

41. Ibid.

42. Rahbek and Bähncke, *Faith and Fate in Jerusalem*, 113; Vester, *Our Jerusalem*, 242.

43. Lind, "Jerusalem Before Zionism," 345.

44. Ibid.

45. Vester, *Our Jerusalem*, 243.

46. In her book *Our Jerusalem*, Bertha says nothing of the help Djemal Pasha gave the colony. And in this account, written for British and American readers, not for Turks, she may well have embroidered her boldness in the exchanges with the dictator.

47. Ibid.

48. Lind, "Jerusalem Before Zionism," 345.

49. Ibid.

Chapter Twenty-seven: Surrender

1. Lind, "Jerusalem Before Zionism," 348.

2. Vester, *Our Jerusalem*, 244.

3. Lind, "Jerusalem Before Zionism," 347.

4. Vester, *Our Jerusalem*, 245.

5. Ibid., 244.

6. Rahbek and Bähncke, *Faith and Fate in Jerusalem*, 123.

7. Lind, "Jerusalem Before Zionism," 351.

8. Ibid., 352.

9. Storrs, *Orientations*, 318.

10. Fromkin, *A Peace to End All Peace*, 308.

11. Palmer, *Decline and Fall of the Ottoman Empire*, 238.

12. Gilbert, *Jerusalem*, 50.

13. Vester, *Our Jerusalem*, 247.

14. Ibid.

15. In fact, some months later the young man returned with the carriage.

16. Lind, "Jerusalem Before Zionism," 360.

17. Bertha always claimed that the mayor sang the doxology with them. Lars Lind is emphatic in his own memoir that this educated Muslim, whose family had provided the Big House, could never have committed such a heresy, praising "Father, Son, and Holy Ghost," and that Bertha's account was "pure fantasy." Whatever the truth, it was a very exciting moment for everyone.

18. In the many subsequent accounts of the surrender of Jerusalem, including that of *One Palestine, Complete,* by Tom Segev, the mayor had first bumped into a cook and a private, out to find eggs for their major's breakfast, and the mayor had attempted to surrender to the bewildered soldiers. If this actually happened, the incident occurred before Lewis and Lind got there. It does seem a bit far-fetched, as Mayor Husseini was a sophisticated man who spoke English; surely he would have known they were inappropriate recipients.

19. Vester, *Our Jerusalem*, 258.

20. Ibid., 257–59.

21. Lind, "Jerusalem Before Zion," 368–69.

22. Lars Lind, a friend of the son of the mufti who had written Izzet Bey's lost surrender letter, was able to obtain a copy of this historic document. Following the usual course of the colony members, he gave it to Bertha for safekeeping. A few years later, when Bertha was in the United States to put her children in school, she also wanted to obtain U.S. citizenship for her husband. She arranged an appointment with Charles Evans Hughes, at that time the secretary of state, and later chief justice of the Supreme Court. She gave Lars's letter to him as a gift, without consulting Lars, who was very upset at what he regarded as a typical example of Bertha's exploitation of the members. The letter, written in Arabic, and thus unintelligible to most Americans, vanished in Hughes's files and, as far as I know, has never resurfaced.

Chapter Twenty-eight: The Lion and the Lamb

1. Vester, *Our Jerusalem*, 263.

2. Storrs, *Orientations*, 483.

3. Ibid., 482.

4. Ashbee, *Palestine Notebook*, 7, 9.

5. Matsson, *American Colony of Jerusalem*, 41.

6. Larsson, *Seven Passports for Palestine*, 18.

7. Fromkin, *A Peace to End All Peace*, 400.

8. Smith, *Palestine and the Arab-Israeli Conflict*, 62.

9. Colonel R. Meinertzhagen (later chief political officer for the British mandate of Palestine) to Lloyd George, March 1919, quoted in Bentwich and Bentwich, *Mandate Memories*, 35.

10. Bentwich and Bentwich, *Mandate Memories*, 45, 46, 87.

11. Ibid., 73, 65.

12. Spafford to Miller, April 28, 1920, ACJC.

13. Ibid.

14. Larsson, *Dala-Swedes in the Holy Land*, 125.

15. Ashbee, *Palestine Notebook*, 178.

Chapter Twenty-nine: Death

1. Samuel to Vester, March 10, 1922, ACJC.

2. Spafford to Miller, March 13, 1922, ACJC.

3. Vester to Spafford, Sept. 15, 1922, ACJC.

4. Vester to Spafford, Sept. 4, 1922, ACJC.

5. Ibid.

6. Grace Whiting to Bertha Vester, Oct. 30, 1922, ACJC.

7. Olaf Lind to Anna Grace Vester, May 15, 1924, ACJC.

8. Jacob Eliahu Spafford to Nils Lind, June 19, 1922, ACJC.

9. Grace Whiting to Bertha Vester, Nov. 9, 1922, ACJC.

10. This may have been the second location for the store, as apparently it was moved after a few years of operation and before it went bankrupt.

11. Grace Whiting to Bertha Vester, Nov. 9, 1922, ACJC.

12. Vester to "Our very precious ones at home," Aug. 21, 1922, ACJC. I have corrected Bertha's spelling mistakes in order for the text to read more smoothly.

13. Ibid.

14. Ibid.

15. Ibid.

16. Larsson, *Dala-Swedes in the Holy Land*, 125, 126.

17. Payron, "A Self-Elected Regent in the 'Dala Colony.' "

18. Vester, diary, March 14, 1923, ACJC.

19. Ibid., April 17, 1923.

20. Larsson, *Dala-Swedes in the Holy Land,* 127.

Chapter Thirty: Epitaph

1. Bertha Vester, diary, April 17, 1923, ACJC.

2. Lind, "Jerusalem Before Zionism," 532.

3. Knabenshue to State Department, Jan. 20, 1930, Records of the United States Consulate in Jerusalem, Palestine, Confidential Correspondence, 1920–35, USNA, RG 84.

4. Ibid.

5. Lind, "Jerusalem Before Zionism," 553.

6. Ibid., 556.

7. Although Vester and Whiting descendants own the hotel shares today, through the kindness of Horatio Vester, Bertha's oldest son, who became an English barrister, children of Eric D. Matsson and Rachel Dinsmore were allowed a share as well. Horatio was making up for what he thought was his mother's wrong when Bertha expelled Rachel.

8. Cleveland, *History of the Modern Middle East,* 241.

9. Ibid., 242.

10. Vester, *Our Jerusalem,* 323.

11. Oren, *Power, Faith, and Fantasy,* 484.

12. One of the old Swedish ladies loyal to Bertha at the American Colony, seventy-eight-year-old Nanny Holmström, sent a letter to President Truman. "Alas, Mr. President," Nanny wrote, "I am sorry to tell you that we live with bombs that have smashed our windows and we are in danger of flying bullets at all hours . . . You have contributed to the creation of this mess, so I implore you to kindly help in solving it. This crisis, this cruel, barbaric wave of pure hatred can only be helped by a miracle . . . If you insist on a division, then it will have to reach up as high as the sky, for no amount of cement or stone, borders or agreements will solve this problem. It can only be done with the help of mutual consent. Mr. President, the whole thing has been tragically destroyed by you." Nanny Holmström to President Harry Truman, Feb. 19, 1948, quoted in Rahbek and Bähncke, *Faith and Fate in Jerusalem,* 146.

13. Collins and Lapierre, *O Jerusalem,* 275.

14. Smith, *Palestine and the Arab-Israeli Conflict,* 143.

15. Cleveland, *History of the Modern Middle East,* 247.

16. Cleveland noted: "The legend of a defenseless, newborn Israel facing the onslaught of hordes of Arab soldiers does not correspond to reality." Ibid., 249.

17. Mrs. Harley Stevens, interview by author, June 2, 2000.

18. This was the number of refugees in 1954. Now that number has grown to nearly 2 million.

19. Vester, "What Is the American Colony?" To make her point, she quoted from an article Mrs. Harley Stevens had written in the *Foreign Policy Bulletin,* July 15, 1952.

20. Vester, foreword to *Our Jerusalem.*

21. Eric D. Matsson, nephew of G. Eric Matson, telephone interview by author, June 2000.

22. Vester, diary, Jan. 4, 1952, ACJC.

23. Rahbek and Bähncke, *Faith and Fate in Jerusalem,* 149.

24. Antar, "Story of Bertha Vester," 24–33.

25. Rahbek and Bähncke, *Faith and Fate in Jerusalem,* 149.

Afterword

1. Telephone interview with Wendy Whiting Blome, Nov. 16, 2007.

2. Ibid.

3. Ibid.

Bibliography

Books and Essays

Aaronsohn, Alexander. *With the Turks in Palestine*. Boston: Houghton Mifflin, 1916.

Aburish, Said K. *Children of Bethany: The Story of a Palestinian Family*. London: Bloomsbury, 1988.

Adams, Charles J., and Mircea Eliade. *The Encyclopedia of Religion*. Vol. 2. New York: Macmillan, 1995.

Andrews, Fannie Fern. *The Holy Land Under the Mandate*. New York: Houghton Mifflin, 1931.

Ariel, Yaakov. "American Dispensationalists and Jerusalem, 1870–1918." In *America and Zion: Essays and Papers in Memory of Moshe Davis*, edited by Eli Lederhendler and Jonathan D. Sarna. Detroit: Wayne State University Press, 2002.

————. *On Behalf of Israel: American Fundamentalist Attitudes Toward Jews, Judaism, and Zionism, 1865–1945*. Brooklyn, N.Y.: Carlson, 1991.

Armstrong, Karen. *Jerusalem: One City, Three Faiths*. New York: Knopf, 1996.

Ashbee, C. R. *A Palestine Notebook, 1918–1923*. Garden City, N.Y.: Doubleday, Page, 1923.

Attwater, Donald. *The Penguin Dictionary of Saints*. London: Penguin, 1965.

Bentwich, Helen. *If I Forget Thee: Some Chapters of Autobiography, 1912–1920*. London: Paul Elek, 1973.

Bentwich, Norman De Mattos, and Helen Bentwich. *Mandate Memories, 1918–1948*. New York: Schocken Books, 1965.

Bernstein, Peter L. *Wedding of the Waters: The Erie Canal and the Making of a Great Nation*. New York: Norton, 2005.

Bierman, John, and Colin Smith. *Fire in the Night: Wingate of Burman, Ethiopia, and Zion*. New York: Random House, 1999.

Bishop, Isabella Lucy Bird. *The Aspects of Religion in the United States of America*. New York: Arno, 1972. First published 1859 by Sampson Low.

Bloom, Harold. *The American Religion: The Emergence of the Post-Christian Nation*. New York: Simon and Schuster, 1992.

Blyth, Estelle. *When We Lived in Jerusalem*. London: J. Murray, 1927.

Bradford, Gamaliel. *D. L. Moody: A Worker in Souls*. Garden City, N.Y.: Doubleday, Doran, 1928.

Carmody, Denise Lardner, and John Tully Carmody. *Exploring American Religion*. Mountain View, Calif.: Mayfield, 1990.

Carruth, Gorton. *The Encyclopedia of American Facts and Dates*. 9th ed. New York: HarperCollins, 1993.

Chamberlin, Everett. *Chicago and Its Suburbs*. Chicago: Hungerford, 1874. Reprint, New York: Arno, 1974.

Cleveland, William L. *A History of the Modern Middle East*. 2nd ed. Boulder, Colo.: Westview, 1999.

Collins, Larry, and Dominique Lapierre. *O Jerusalem*. New York: Simon and Schuster, 1972.

Coüasnon, Charles. *The Church of the Holy Sepulchre in Jerusalem*. The Schweich Lectures of the British Academy, 1972. Translated by J.-P. B. and Claude Ross. London: Oxford University Press for the British Academy, 1974.

Cromie, Robert. *The Great Chicago Fire*. New York: McGraw-Hill, 1958.

Cummings, Jonathan. *A Tour of the Holy Land and Six Weeks in Jerusalem in the Interest of the Nation of Israel*. Cambridgeport, Mass.: Harvard Pub. Co., 1890.

Davis, John. " 'Each Mouldering Ruin Recalls a History': Nineteenth-Century Images of Jerusalem and the American Public." In *America and Zion: Essays and Papers in Memory of Moshe Davis,* edited by Eli Lederhendler and Jonathan D. Sarna. Detroit: Wayne State University Press, 2002.

————. *The Landscape of Belief: Encountering the Holy Land in Nineteenth-Century American Art and Culture*. Princeton, N.J.: Princeton University Press, 1996.

Dedman, Emmett. *Fabulous Chicago*. New York: Random House, 1953.

Dudman, Helga, and Ruth Kark. *The American Colony: Scenes from a Jerusalem Saga*. Jerusalem: Carta, 1998.

Edström, Vivi. *Selma Lagerlöf.* Translated by Barbara Lide. Boston: Twayne, 1984.

Eliade, Mircea, ed. *The Encyclopedia of Religion*. New York: Macmillan, 1993.

Elliott, Charles Wyllys. *Remarkable Characters and Places of the Holy Land: Comprising an Account of Partriarchs, Judges, Prophets, Apostles, Women, Warriors, Poets, and Kings*. Hartford, Conn.: J. B. Burr, 1868.

Elon, Amos. *Jerusalem, City of Mirrors*. London: Weidenfeld and Nicolson, 1990.

Evensen, Bruce J. *God's Man for the Gilded Age: D. L. Moody and the Rise of Modern Mass Evangelism*. New York: Oxford University Press, 2003.

Findlay, James F., Jr. *Dwight L. Moody: American Evangelist, 1837–1899*. Chicago: University of Chicago Press, 1969.

Finkel, Caroline. *Osman's Dream: The Story of the Ottoman Empire, 1300–1923*. New York: Basic Books, 2006.

Finnie, David H. *Pioneers East: The Early American Experience in the Middle East*. Cambridge, Mass.: Harvard University Press, 1967.

Fogarty, Robert S. *All Things New: American Communes and Utopian Movements, 1860–1914*. Chicago: University of Chicago Press, 1990.

Foster, Lawrence. *Religion and Sexuality: The Shakers, the Mormons, and the Oneida Community*. Urbana: University of Illinois Press, 1984.

Freeman, Charles. *The Closing of the Western Mind: The Rise of Faith and the Fall of Reason*. New York: Knopf, 2003.

Fromkin, David. *A Peace to End All Peace: Creating the Modern Middle East, 1914–1922*. New York: Henry Holt, 1989.

Galanter, Marc. *Cults: Faith, Healing, and Coercion*. New York: Oxford University Press, 1999.

Geldbach, Erich. "Jerusalem in the Mind-Set of John Nelson Darby and His Fundamentalist Followers." In *Jerusalem in the Mind of the Western World, 1800–1948*, edited by Yehoshua Ben-Arieh and Moshe Davis. Westport, Conn.: Praeger, 1997.

Gilbert, Major Vivian. *The Romance of the Last Crusade: With Allenby to Jerusalem*. New York: William B. Feakins, 1923.

Gilbert, Martin. *Jerusalem: Rebirth of a City*. New York: Viking, 1985.

Gillman, Henry. *Hassan, a Fellah: A Romance of Palestine*. Boston: Little, Brown, 1898.

Goodrich-Freer, Adela M. *Arabs in Tent and Town*. London: Seeley, Service, 1924.

Gorenberg, Gershom. *The End of Days: Fundamentalism and the Struggle for the Temple Mount*. Oxford: Oxford University Press, 2002.

Graham, Stephen. *With the Russian Pilgrims to Jerusalem*. London: Macmillan, 1914.

Greenberg, Gershon. *The Holy Land in American Religious Thought, 1620–1948: The Symbiosis of American Religious Approaches to Scripture's Sacred Territory*. Lanham, Md.: University Press of America, 1994.

Griswold, Mrs. Stephen M. *A Woman's Pilgrimage to the Holy Land; or, Pleasant Days Abroad, Being Notes of a Tour Through Europe and the East*. Hartford, Conn.: J. B. Burr and Hyde, 1872.

Handy, Robert T. "Holy Land Experiences of Two Pioneers of Christian Ecumenism: Schaff and Mott." In *Contemporary Jewry: Studies in Honor of Moshe Davis*, edited by Geoffrey Wigoder. Jerusalem: Institute of Contemporary Jewry, Hebrew University of Jerusalem, 1984.

Haslip, Joan. *The Sultan: The Life of Abdul Hamid.* London: Cassell, 1958.

Hastings, James, ed. *Encyclopedia of Religion and Ethics.* Vol. 6. Edinburgh: T. & T. Clark, 1908–26.

Henry, Marie. *The Secret Life of Hannah Whitall Smith.* Grand Rapids, Mich.: Chosen Books, 1984.

Hodgkin, Thomas. *Letters from Palestine, 1932–36.* Edited by E. C. Hodgkin. London: Quartet Books, 1986.

Hokanson, Nels. *Swedish Immigrants in Lincoln's Time.* New York: Harper and Brothers, 1942.

Holmes, Reed M. *The Forerunners: The Tragic Story of 156 Down-East Americans Led to Jaffa in 1866 by Charismatic G. J. Adams to Plant the Seeds of Modern Israel.* Independence, Mo.: Herald, 1981.

James, Lawrence. *Imperial Warrior: The Life and Times of Field-Marshal Viscount Allenby, 1861–1936.* London: Weidenfeld and Nicolson, 1993.

Jenkins, Philip. *Mystics and Messiahs: Cults and New Religions in American History.* Oxford: Oxford University Press, 2000.

Johnson, Frederick L. *Goodhue County, Minnesota.* Red Wing, Minn.: Goodhue County Historical Society Press, 2000.

Jubilee History of the Fullerton Avenue Presbyterian Church: Written for the 50th Anniversary. Chicago: The Church, 1914.

Kaganoff, Nathan M., ed. *American Presence.* Vol. 1 of *Guide to America–Holy Land Studies.* New York: Arno, 1980.

Kark, Ruth. *American Consuls in the Holy Land, 1832–1914.* Detroit: Wayne State University Press, 1994.

———. "From Pilgrimage to Budding Tourism: The Role of Thomas Cook in the Rediscovery of the Holy Land in the Nineteenth Century." In *Travellers in the Levant: Voyagers and Visionaries,* edited by Sarah Searight and Malcolm Wagstaff. London: Libri Books, 2001.

Kark, Ruth, and Michal Oren-Nordheim. *Jerusalem and Its Environs: Quarters, Neighborhoods, Villages, 1800–1948.* Jerusalem: Hebrew University Magnes Press, 2001.

Keith-Roach, Edward. *Pasha of Jerusalem: Memoirs of a District Commissioner Under the British Mandate.* London: Radcliffe, 1994.

Kesaris, Paul, and Robert Lester. *Confidential U.S. Diplomatic Post Records: Middle East, Jerusalem.* Frederick, Md.: University Publications of America, 1984.

King, Philip J. *American Archaeology in the Mideast: A History of the American Schools of Oriental Research.* Philadelphia: American Schools of Oriental Research, 1983.

Kiser, John. *The Monks of Tibhirine: Faith, Love, and Terror in Algeria.* New York: St. Martin's, 2002.

Klatzker, David E. "American Christian Travelers to the Holy Land, 1821–1939." Ph.D. diss., Temple University, 1987.

———. "Sacred Journeys: Jerusalem in the Eyes of American Travelers Before 1948." In *Jerusalem in the Mind of the Western World, 1800–1948,* edited by Yehoshua Ben-Arieh and Moshe Davis. Westport, Conn.: Praeger, 1997.

Krakauer, Jon. *Under the Banner of Heaven: A Story of Violent Faith.* New York: Doubleday, 2003.

Lagerlöf, Selma. *The Holy City: Jerusalem II.* Translated by Velma Swanston Howard. Garden City, N.Y.: Doubleday, Page, 1918.

———. *Jerusalem: A Novel.* Garden City, N.Y.: Doubleday, Page, 1915.

Larsen, Hanna Astrup. *Selma Lagerlöf.* Garden City, N.Y.: Doubleday, Doran, 1936.

Larsson, Edith. *Dala-Swedes in the Holy Land.* Translated by Peter Scott-Hansen. Privately published, 2005. Originally published as *Dalafolk i Heligt Land.* Stockholm: Natur och Kultur, 1957.

Larsson, Theo. *Seven Passports for Palestine: Sixty Years in the Levant.* Pulborough, U.K.: Longfield, 1995.

Lipman, V. D. *Americans and the Holy Land Through British Eyes, 1820–1917: A Documentary History.* London: V. D. Lipman, in association with the Self Pub. Association, 1989.

Luckhoff, Martin. "Prussia and Jerusalem: Political and Religious Controversies Surrounding the Foundation of the Jerusalem Bishopric." In *America and Zion: Essays and Papers in Memory of Moshe Davis,* edited by Eli Lederhendler and Jonathan D. Sarna. Detroit: Wayne State University Press, 2002.

Luke, Harry, ed. *Cook's Traveller Handbook: Jerusalem and Judea.* London: Simpkin, Marshall, Hamilton, Kent & Co. T. Cook & Son, 1924.

Malone, Dumas, ed. *Sewell-Trowbridge.* Vol. 9 of *Dictionary of American Biography.* New York: Charles Scribner & Sons, 1935, 1936.

Mandel, Neville J. *The Arabs and Zionism Before World War I.* Berkeley: University of California Press, 1976.

Marsden, George M. *Fundamentalism and American Culture: The Shaping of Twentieth Century Evangelicalism, 1870–1925.* Oxford: Oxford University Press, 1980.

Massey, W. T. *How Jerusalem Was Won.* London: Constable, 1919.

Matson, Olaf G. *The American Colony Guide-Book to Jerusalem and Environs.* Jerusalem: Vester, 1925.

Matsson, Eric Dinsmore. *The American Colony of Jerusalem: A Brief Historical Outline.* Menton, France: E. D. Matsson, 1992.

Maule, Harry E. *Selma Lagerlöf: The Woman, Her Work, Her Message.* Garden City, N.Y.: Doubleday, Page, 1926.

Merrill, Selah. *East of the Jordan: A Record of Travel and Observation in the Countries of Moab, Gilead, and Bashan During the Years 1875–1877.* New York: Charles Scribner's Sons, 1881.

Minor, Clorinda. *Meshullam! or, Tidings from Jerusalem.* Published by the author, 1851. Reprint, New York: Arno, 1977.

Moody, Dwight Lyman, and Charles F. Goss. *Echoes from the Pulpit and Platform.* Hartford. Conn.: A. D. Worthington, 1900.

Moody, Paul D. *My Father: An Intimate Portrait of Dwight Moody.* Boston: Little, Brown, 1938.

Mulhall, John W. *America and the Founding of Israel: An Investigation of the Morality of America's Role.* Los Angeles: Deshon, 1995.

Neider, Charles, ed. *Great Shipwrecks and Castaways: Authentic Accounts of Disasters at Sea.* New York: Dorset, 1952.

Newton, Frances E. *Fifty Years in Palestine.* Wrotham, U.K.: Coldharbour Press, 1948.

O'Brien, Conor Cruise. *The Siege: The Saga of Israel and Zionism.* New York: Simon and Schuster, 1986.

Oliphant, Laurence. *Haifa; or, Life in Modern Palestine.* New York: Harper & Bros., 1887.

Oren, Michael B. *Power, Faith, and Fantasy: America in the Middle East, 1776 to the Present.* New York: Norton, 2007.

Palmer, Alan Warwick. *The Decline and Fall of the Ottoman Empire.* New York: M. Evans, 1992.

Parsons, Helen Palmer, ed. *Letters from Palestine, 1868–1912, Written by Rolla Floyd.* Privately published, 1981.

Peters, Francis Edwards. *Jerusalem: The Holy City in the Eyes of Chroniclers, Visitors, Pilgrims, and Prophets from the Days of Abraham to the Beginnings of Modern Times.* Princeton, N.J.: Princeton University Press, 1985.

Pierce, Bessie Louise. *From Town to City, 1848–1871.* Vol. 2 of *A History of Chicago.* New York: Knopf, 1937.

———. *Rise of a Modern City, 1871–1893.* Vol. 3 of *A History of Chicago.* New York: Knopf, 1956.

———, ed. *As Others See Chicago: Impressions of Visitors, 1673–1933.* Chicago: University of Chicago Press, 1933.

Rahbek, Birgitte, and Mogens Bähncke. *Faith and Fate in Jerusalem.* Unknown translator. Originally published as *Tro og Skaebne I Jerusalem.* Copenhagen: Hasler, 1997. Courtesy of John Larsson.

Robertson, Darrel M. *The Chicago Revival, 1876: Society and Revivalism in a Nineteenth-Century City.* Metuchen, N.J.: Scarecrow, 1989.

Rockwell, A. Lovell, and Daniel Goodwin. *In Memory of Mrs. Agnes Goodwin, the Wife of Daniel Goodwin Jr., and Her Children, Goertner and Lulu: Who Passed from Earth with the Sinking of the Steamer "Ville du Havre."* Chicago: Lakeside, 1874.

Rogers, Mary Eliza. *Domestic Life in Palestine.* 1862. London: Kegan Paul International, 1989.

Rohl, John C. G. *The Kaiser and His Court: Wilhelm II and the Government of Germany.* Translated by Terence F. Cole. Cambridge, U.K.: Cambridge University Press, 1994.

Samuel, Horace B. *Unholy Memories of the Holy Land.* London: Leonard and Virginia Woolf, 1930.

Sandeen, Ernest R. *The Roots of Fundamentalism: British and American Millenarianism, 1800–1930.* Grand Rapids, Mich.: Baker Book House, 1970.

Sanders, Ronald. *The High Walls of Jerusalem: A History of the Balfour Declaration and the Birth of the British Mandate for Palestine.* New York: Holt, Rinehart, and Winston, 1983.

Sankey, Ira D. *Sankey's Story of the Gospel Hymns and of Sacred Songs and Solos.* Philadelphia: Sunday School Times, 1906.

Scofield, C. I., ed. *The First Scofield Study Bible.* Iowa Falls, Iowa: World Bible Publishers, 1986. Based on the 1909 ed.

———. *The Scofield Reference Bible.* New York: Oxford University Press, 1996. Based on the 1909 ed.

Segev, Tom. *One Palestine, Complete: Jews and Arabs Under the British Mandate.* Translated by Haim Watzman. New York: Metropolitan Books, 1999.

Sheean, Vincent. *Personal History.* Garden City, N.Y.: Doubleday, Doran, 1934.

Sinclair, Andrew. *Jerusalem: The Endless Crusade.* New York: Crown, 1995.

Smith, Charles D. *Palestine and the Arab-Israeli Conflict.* New York: St. Martin's, 1992.

Smith, Hannah Whitall. *Religious Fanaticism: Extracts from the Papers of Hannah Whitall Smith.* Edited by Ray Strachey. London: Faber and Gwyer, 1928.

Smith, Logan Pearsall, ed. *Philadelphia Quaker: The Letters of Hannah Whitall Smith.* New York: Harcourt, Brace, 1950.

Smith, Timothy L. *Revivalism and Social Reform in Mid-Nineteenth Century America.* New York: Abingdon, 1957.

Socin, Albert, and Immanuel Benzinger. *Palestine and Syria: Handbook for Travellers.* 3rd ed. Leipzig: K. Baedeker, 1898.

Stirling, Walter Francis. *Safety Last.* London: Hollis and Carter, 1953.

Storrs, Sir Ronald. *Orientations.* London: Ivor Nicholson & Watson, 1937.

Strachey, Barbara. *Remarkable Relations.* New York: Universe Books, 1982.

Strachey, Lytton. *Eminent Victorians.* Edited by John Sutherland. New York: Oxford University Press, 2002. First published 1918 by G. P. Putnam's Sons.

Strachey, Ray. *Shaken by the Wind.* New York: Macmillan, 1928.

Straiton, M. S., and Emma Straiton. *Two Lady Tramps Abroad: A Compilation of Letters Descriptive of Nearly a Year's Travel in India, Asia Minor, Egypt, the Holy Land, Turkey, Greece, Italy, Austria, Switzerland, France, England, Ireland, and Scotland by Two American Ladies.* Flushing, N.Y.: Evening Journal Press, 1881.

Thomas Cook Ltd. *Cook's Tourists' Handbook for Palestine and Syria.* London: T. Cook & Son, 1876.

Thomson, William M. *The Land and the Book.* New York: Harper and Brothers, 1880, 1885.

Thubron, Colin. *Jerusalem.* London: Century, 1969.

Tibawi, A. L. *American Interests in Syria, 1800–1901: A Study of Educational, Literary, and Religious Work.* Oxford: Clarendon, 1966.

———. *Jerusalem: Its Place in Islam and Arab History.* Beirut: Institute for Palestine Studies, 1969.

Trench, Charles Chenevix. *A Life of General Charles Gordon.* New York: Norton, 1978.

Tuchman, Barbara. *Bible and Sword: England and Palestine from the Bronze Age to Balfour.* New York: New York University Press, 1956.

Tveit, Odd Karsten. "Anna's House: An American Jerusalem Saga." Translated by Peter Scott-Hansen. Privately published, 2006. Corrected version May 9, 2007. Originally published as *Annas Hus: En beretning fra Stavanger til Jerusalem.* Oslo, Norway: Cappelen, 2000.

Twain, Mark. *The Innocents Abroad.* New York: Signet Classic, 1966. First published 1869 by American Publishing Co.

Van Atta, Robert B. *History of the First Presbyterian Church of Greensburg, Pennsylvania, 1788–1988.* Greensburg, Pa.: The Church, 1988. Courtesy of the parish office.

Vester, Bertha Spafford. *Flowers of the Holy Land.* Kansas City, Mo.: Hallmark Cards, 1962.

———. *Our Jerusalem: An American Family in the Holy City, 1881–1949.* Garden City, N.Y.: Doubleday, 1950.

Vilnay, Zev. *Legends of Jerusalem, the Sacred Land.* Vol. 1. Philadelphia: Jewish Publication Society of America, 1973.

Vogel, Lester I. *To See a Promised Land: Americans and the Holy Land in the Nineteenth Century.* University Park: Pennsylvania State University Press, 1993.

———. "Zion as Place and Past, an American Myth: Ottoman Palestine in the American Mind Perceived Through Protestant Consciousness and Experience." Ph.D. diss., George Washington University, 1984.

Ward, Geoffrey, Ken Burns, and Ric Burns. *The Civil War: An Illustrated History.* New York: Knopf, 1990.

Weiss, N. *Personal Recollections of the Wreck of the Ville-du-Havre and the Loch-Earn.* New York: Anson D. F. Randolph, 1875.

Whittle, D. W., and P. P. Bliss. *Memoirs of Philip P. Bliss.* Introduction by D. L. Moody. New York: A. S. Barnes, 1877.

Wilkie, Franc B. *The Chicago Bar.* Author's ed. Chicago: Published by the author, 1872.

Articles in Periodicals

Antar, Elias. "The Story of Bertha Vester." *Saudi Aramco World,* July/Aug. 1967.

Broder, Jonathan. "A Family, a Colony, a Life of Good Works in the Holy City." *Smithsonian,* March 1997.

Ford, Alexander H. "Our American Colony at Jerusalem." *Appleton's Magazine,* Dec. 1906.

Goldman, Shalom. "The Holy Land Appropriated: The Careers of Selah Merrill, Nineteenth Century Christian Hebraist, Palestine Explorer, and U.S. Consul in Jerusalem." *American Jewish History,* June 1997, 151–72.

Gronback, Jakob H. "Lewis Larsson: A Swede in Jerusalem in the First Half of the Twentieth Century." *Scandinavian Orientalist Studies.* Living Water, Copenhagen, 1990.

Hobart, George S. "The Matson Collection: A Half Century of Photography in the Middle East." *Quarterly Journal of the Library of Congress* 30, no. 1 (1973).

"Holy Lives: A Visit to the 'American' Sect in Jerusalem." Signed by I. H. *Public Ledger* (Winter 1890).

Kark, Ruth. "Millenarism and Agricultural Settlement in the Holy Land in the Nineteenth Century." *Journal of Historical Geography* 9, no. 1 (1983).

———. "Post Civil War American Communes: A Millenarian Utopian Commune Linking Chicago and Nås, Sweden, to Jerusalem." *Communal Societies* 15 (1995): 75–113.

————. "Sweden and the Holy Land: Pietistic and Communal Settlement." *Journal of Historical Geography* 22, no. 1 (1996): 46–67.

Kark, Ruth, and Yaakov Ariel. "Messianism, Holiness, Charisma, and Community: The American-Swedish Colony in Jerusalem, 1881–1933." *Church History* 65, no. 4 (1996): 641–57.

Lind, Nils E. "The Return of the Gaddites: Reminiscences of the American Colony and the Yemenite Jews in Jerusalem." *Palestine Exploration Quarterly* (July–Dec. 1973).

Our Rest and Signs of the Times 10, no. 7 (July 1883). Archive: 1983–002, Miscellaneous: From Jerusalem. "Spaffordites." Box 8, folder 19. Asbury Theological Seminary Archives. Wilmore, Ky.

Payron, E. "A Self-Elected Regent in the 'Dala Colony,' " *Bonniers Veckotidning,* Aug. 26, 1924.

"Public Opinion: Fanaticism as a Source of Crime." *American Journal of Sociology,* Nov. 9, 1899.

Shamir, Milette. "Our Jerusalem: Americans in the Holy Land and Protestant Narratives of National Entitlement." *American Quarterly* 55, no. 1 (2003): 29–60.

Shilo, Margalit. "Self-Sacrifice, National-Historical Identity, and Self-Denial: The Experience of Jewish Immigrant Women in Jerusalem, 1840–1914." *Women's History Review* 11, no. 2 (2002).

Vester, Bertha Spafford. "Jerusalem, My Home." *National Geographic,* Dec. 1964.

————. "What Is the American Colony?" Jerusalem: Greek Convent Press, n.d.

Vincent, John H. "A Study in Social and Religious Life in Modern Jerusalem." *Independent,* March 7, 1889.

Wallace, E. S. "Some of the Peculiar People of Jerusalem," *Congregationalist,* Feb. 6, 1896.

Articles in Newspapers

Alley, T. J. "Spaffordism: A Conclusive Expose of the Spaffordite Fraud." Sept. 28, 1897.

Badner, Jenny. "Let's Talk Shop." *Jerusalem Post,* Aug. 27, 1999.

Boston Daily Globe, "Heirs to a Fortune," March 12, 1894.

Boston Sunday Herald, "Back in America After 40 Years Exile," July 9, 1922.

————, "Liked Jerusalem, but Glad to Be Home Again," Aug. 18, 1907.

Chicago Daily News, "Cash for a Colony," March 9, 1894.

————, "Holy City Their Home," May 15, 1895.

————, "Life in the City of Zion: Lizzie Aiken Tells of the Queer Doings of Mrs. Spafford in Old Jerusalem," May 14, 1895.

————, "Still Long for the Holy Land," Dec. 15, 1897.

Chicago Daily Tribune, "Americans at Ancient Jerusalem," Dec. 23, 1896.

————, "Asks for a Guardian," April 17, 1895.

————, "Colony Is a Winner," May 15, 1895.

————, "The Fullerton Avenue Church," July 8, 1876.

————, "Her Rescued Transferred to the Trimountain, and Taken to Bristol," Dec. 2, 1873.

————, "Holy City Crusader Here," June 28, 1903.

————, "Home Founded by Spaffords Is Refuge for Sick," Feb. 26, 1928.

————, "In Real Estate Circles," Aug. 31, 1902.

————, "Is on Its Last Legs," Oct. 18, 1894.

————, "Lake View," Nov. 14, 1875.

————, "Make the Start for Jerusalem," March 6, 1896.

————, "Middle East Friends, Near East Society Will Have Tea Friday," March 19, 1952.

————, "Not a Cent to Them," Oct. 15, 1894.

————, "The Overcomers," Sept. 21, 1882.

————, "Overcomers Off for the Holy Land," March 5, 1896.

————, "Overcomers Wroth at Yantis," Jan. 15, 1898.

————, "Pilgrims Sail for Jerusalem," March 8, 1896.

————, "Sensational Evidence in the Overcomers Case," April 19, 1895.

————, "Spafford's Name in Court Again," April 28, 1895.

————, "When Peace Like a River," Sept. 28, 1902.

Chicago Evening Journal, "Chicago's Come-Outers," May 4, 1889.

————, "That New Jerusalem," March 2, 1895.

Chicago Journal, "Cash Is Needed by the Spaffordites," Dec. 20, 1897.

————, "Says Spaffordites Are Persecuted," Dec 15, 1897.

————, "Tells Secrets of the Colony," Dec. 16, 1897.

————, "They Claim Title to Valuable Land," Jan. 5, 1898.

————, "Warns All Against the Spaffordites," Dec. 24, 1897.

Chicago Times, "The Calamity Has Thrown a Pall of Mourning over Chicago," Dec. 2, 1873.

————, "Casualties," Dec. 8, 1873.

Chicago Tribune, June 30, 1874.

————, "Life in the Colony: Sensational Evidence in the Overcomers Case," April 18, 1895.

————, "Ville du Havre," Dec. 3, 1873.

————, "The Ville du Havre," Dec. 4, 1873.

————, "The Ville du Havre," Dec. 20, 1873.

————, "Why the Commune Is Possible in America," May 24, 1874.

Dagens Nyheter, "Sven kulturmassa inför ekumenmötet dr. Lagerlöf talar," Aug. 27, 1925.

Daily Inter Ocean, "Horror," Dec. 2, 1873.

————, "Pith of the News," Aug. 16, 1881.

————, "Pith of the News," Aug. 17, 1881.

————, "Say Sect Is a Fraud," Dec. 16, 1897.

————, "A Singular Sect: The 'Overcomers,' a New Religious Sect, Makes Its Appearance in Chicago," Aug. 17, 1881.

————, "The Ville du Havre Disaster," Dec. 4, 1873.

Dammann, Tom. "A Hotel with Elegance." *Christian Science Monitor,* Nov. 10, 1981.

Evening Post, "Jerusalem of To-Day," July 7, 1884.

Feron, James. "Stopping at a Pasha's Palace." *New York Times,* Nov. 4, 1984.

Gillon, Philip. "Even Tourists Can Relax." *Jerusalem Post,* Sept. 24, 1971.

Greensburg (Pa.) Daily Tribune, "Rev. Wallace Ends Pastorate," Sept. 20, 1907.

Harper's Weekly, "The Loss of the Ville du Havre," Dec. 20, 1873.

Harvey (Ill.) Tribune-Citizen, "Just from Jerusalem," Sept. 4, 1897.

Heron, Frances D. Review of "Chicagoan's 65 Years in Jerusalem." *Chicago Daily Tribune,* Feb. 12, 1950.

Lebanon Times, "Glimpse in the Past: The Overcomers," Nov. 9, 1961.

Marbourg, Nina. "Separate the Men and Women!" *San Francisco Chronicle,* Nov. 16, 1919.

Miller, Lucy Key. "Front Views and Profiles." *Chicago Daily Tribune,* Dec. 8, 1949.

Minneapolis Sunday Tribune, "A Little America Close by Jerusalem's Wall," July 4, 1920.

Myers, Ray. "Unscrupulous 'Overcomers' Left Trail of Graft, Grief, and Heartbreak at Lebanon," *Smith County (Kans.) Pioneer,* Jan. 16, 1953.

New York Observer, "Death of Emile Cook," Feb. 24, 1874.

New York Times, "The Chicago Fire," Oct. 11–15, 1871.

————, "Current Events," Sept. 4, 1881.

————, "The 'Jerusalem Colony' Starts," March 6, 1896.

————, "The Kaiser at Jerusalem," Oct. 31, 1898.

————, "The Loss of the Ville du Havre," Dec. 2, 1873.

————, "Our Scandinavian Accessions," Feb. 23, 1880.

————, "Pilgrims Sail for Jerusalem," March 8, 1896.

O'Brien, William. "An American Colony of Saints." *Westminster Gazette,* Sept. 16, 1907.

Ozanne, Julian. "Gateway to Palestinian Contacts." *Financial Times,* May 30, 1994.

Peale, Norman Vincent. "White Mother of Mercy Honored by the Arabs." *Chicago Tribune,* Sept. 21, 1963.

Shore, T. E. Egerton. "The House of the Peace of God; or, The American Colony at Jerusalem." *Christian Guardian* (1895).

Smith County (Kans.) Pioneer, "Lebanon People Who Went to Jerusalem 62 Years Ago Were Dupes of Schemers," Jan. 2, 1958.

————, "The Overcomers," Jan. 6, 1898.

Stephens, Bret. "Palestine: The Dream and the Nightmare." *Wall Street Journal,* Sept. 20, 2000.

Thomas, Lowell. "Holy Land's Turbulence Lives in U.S. Woman's Memory." *Washington Post,* Nov. 27, 1938.

Troy (N.Y.) Daily News, "The Singular Life—History of a Native of Lansingburgh," Oct. 24, 1888.

Veysey, Arthur. "Arab Hospital Has Old Ties with Chicago." *Chicago Tribune,* June 25, 1967.

Washington Post, "Come 5,000 Miles to Become Naturalized as Americans," July 16, 1922.

————, " 'Overcomers' in Jerusalem," Dec. 23, 1896.

————, "Pilgrim in Palestine: Details of Kaiser Wilhelm's Journey to Jerusalem," Nov. 6, 1898.

————, "William II in Jerusalem," Oct. 31, 1898.

Unpublished Manuscripts

Baldwin, Farida Naseef. "From the Damascus Gate." Buffalo, N.Y., 1946.

Curtis, William E. "100 Years of Blessing." AMF anniversary booklet. AMFI, 1987.

Goodwillie, James G. "Early Days in the Fullerton Avenue Presbyterian Church." Nov. 18, 1914. Courtesy of Barry Smith, church historian, Lincoln Park Presbyterian Church, Chicago.

Hellsman, Erika Lind. "The Fish in the Sarcophagus." N.d.

Lind, Anna Grace Vester. "The House on the Wall." Courtesy of Helga Dudman. N.d.

Lind, Lars E. "Jerusalem Before Zionism." Courtesy of Cecily Dewing. N.d.

Morgan, R. C. "Letters from Palestine: 'Jerusalem—the Americans.'" 1891? Lacking source. Archive: 1983-002, box 8, folder 19, "Spaffordites," Hannah Whitall Smith Papers. Courtesy Asbury Theological Seminary, Wilmore, Ky.

"On Holy Paths: Jerusalem in Prose." Translated by Laura Petri. Originally published På Heliga Vägar (Stockholm, 1931). Gift of Mrs. Larsen, wife of Swedish consul. Jerusalem National and University Library. Department of Manuscripts and Archives.

Roelhe, Emil. Travel letter. Jerusalem, July 1, 1931.

Silberman, Neil Asher. "Curiosities of the Holy Land: The Rev. Selah Merrill and Politics of the Ottoman Empire." Branford, Conn., 1998.

Ward, Frieda. "Account of the 1967 War." N.d.

Archives

American Colony in Jerusalem Collection, 1786–2006 (bulk 1870–1968). Manuscript Division, Library of Congress, Washington, D.C. Cited in notes as ACJC.

Andrews, Fannie Fern, and Jacob Eliahu Spafford. Correspondence. Schlesinger Library, Radcliffe Institute, Harvard University.

Circuit Court, Cook County, Chicago. Courthouse records: *Lingle v. Whiting*: P11-6785; *Lingle v. Rasmussen*: G-137955; *Schoebohn v. Hedges*: G-169494; *Murphy v. Hedges*: G-142175.

Culver, William B., Memorial Scrapbook of Shipwreck of *Ville du Havre*, 1873. Holt-Atherton Special Collections, University of the Pacific Libraries, Stockton, Calif.

Dispatches from United States Consuls in Jerusalem, Palestine, 1856–1906. Record Group 84. U.S. State Department. United States National Archives, Washington, D.C. Cited in notes as USNA, RG 84.

Moody Bible Institute, Crowell Library and Learning Center, Chicago.

Mott, John R., Papers. Yale Divinity School Library, Special Collections.

Records of the United States Consulate in Jerusalem, Palestine, Confidential Correspondence, 1920–35. Record Group 84. United States National Archives, Washington, D.C.

Smith, Hannah Whitall. Papers. Archive: 1983-002, Miscellaneous: From Jerusalem.

Smith County Pioneer Archives. Smith Center, Cedarville, Kans.

Spafford, Anna, to Rev. Jacobsen. Letter. Decorah, Iowa, Aug. 1, 1894. St. Olaf College, Northfield, Minn.

"Spaffordites." Box 8, folder 19. Asbury Theological Seminary Archives, Wilmore, Ky.

U.S. Circuit Court for the Southern District of New York Law Case Files. Entry 25 1790–1912, *Edwin S. Wallace v. D. Appleton & Co.* Boxes 6 and 7.

Whiting, John D., Papers, 1890–1970 (bulk 1904–64), box 6, John Whiting Collection. Manuscript Division, Library of Congress. Donated by Wendy Whiting Blome and John F. Whiting.

Private Collections

Baldwin, Edward F., Letters. Furman Baldwin. Private Collection.

Baldwin, Ella Amelia. Diary. Alvin Yantiss. Private Collection.

Interviews by the Author

Aburish, Said, by telephone, Oct. 25, 2000, London.

Aghazarian, Albert A., Oct. 8, 2000, Bir Zeit University, Jerusalem.

Bailey, Clinton, Oct. 10, 2000, Jerusalem.

Baldwin, Furman, and Pat Baldwin, Dec. 2000, Cornwall, N.Y.

Baldwin, Norman, and June Baldwin, June 2003, Savannah, Ga.

Barwick, Jack, Nov. 2004, N.H.

Blome, Wendy Whiting, Jan. 2005, McLean, Va.

Di Giovanni, Jannine, Oct. 16, 2000, Jerusalem.

Dudman, Helga, Oct. 19, 2000, Tiberias, Israel.

Eddy, Condit N., Dec. 7, 2006, Chevy Chase, Md.

Even, Gokhan, Oct. 7, 2000, Jerusalem.

Franji, Mrs. Hanna (Mary), Oct. 9, 2000, Jerusalem.

Getman, Thomas, Oct. 16, 2000, Jerusalem.

Gittan, Dr. Seymour, Oct. 6, 2000, Jerusalem.

Gröndahl, Mia, Oct. 10, 2000, Jerusalem.

Hammond, Corinna Findley, April 2005, Boca Grande, Fla.

Hart, Mrs. Parker (Jane), June 3, 2000, Washington, D.C.

Kark, Ruth, Oct. 5, 2000, Jerusalem.

Karmi, Dr. Hasan S., Oct. 12, 2000, Amman, Jordan.

Khoury, Dr. Sami, Oct. 12, 2000, Amman, Jordan.

Kilgore, Ambassador Andrew, Dec. 2003, Washington, D.C.

Kosinski, Claire, Oct. 15, 2000, Jerusalem.

Larsson, John, by telephone, May 2000, Stockholm, Sweden.

Larsson, Theo, 1989, 1993, London.

Majaj, Betty, Oct. 5, 2000, Jerusalem.

Matson, Margaret "Mugs," by telephone, Jan. 2004.

Matsson, Eric Dinsmore, by telephone, June 4, 2000, Stockholm, Sweden.

O'Connor, Father Jerome Murphy, Oct. 19, 2000, École Biblique, Jerusalem.

Parker, Ambassador Richard B., Dec. 2003, Washington, D.C.

Pearse, Mrs. Charles (Roweyda Baldwin), and John F. Whiting, Dec. 2000, Secane, Pa.

Sawualha, Mrs. David (Ann), Oct. 13, 2000, Amman, Jordan.

Stevens, Mrs. Harley (Georgiana), July 31, 2000, San Francisco.

Vester, Valentine, Oct. 20, 2000, Jan. 2005, Jerusalem.

Waheeb, Dr. Mohammed, Oct. 16, 2000, Amman, Jordan.

Whiting, John, Dec. 2000, Lancaster, Pa.

Whiting, Mrs. John (Sally), Wendy Whiting Blome, and John F. Whiting, Dec. 2000, Philadelphia.

Wilcox, Ambassador Philip C., Dec. 2003, Washington, D.C.

Wilson, Mrs. Evan (Leila), June 16, 2000, Washington, D.C.

Wooten, James, Oct. 19, 2000, Jerusalem.

Yantiss, Alvin, and Gladdie Yantiss, July 10, 2002, N.H.

Zaghari, Ibrahim, Oct. 17, 2000, Jerusalem.

Zilka, Morris, Oct. 6, 2000, Jerusalem.

Index

Abdul Hamid II, Sultan, 93–94, 190,
    200–201, 202, 210, 232, 233, 234,
    236
Abraham, 80, 99, 104
Abu Yusuf, Sheikh, 104–5
Acts, Book of, 4*n*, 252–53
Adams, George J., 125
Adamson, Amelia, xiv, 186, 192–93, 211,
    230
Adamson, John, xiv, 186, 192–93, 194,
    211, 230
Addams, Jane, 160
Age to Come (paper), xiv, 138
Aiken, Annie, xiii, 90, 140, 156, 193
    AS and, 149–50, 164, 172
    trial testimony of, 161–65
Al-Azhar University, 265
Al-Buraq, 92, 110
Alexander II, Czar of Russia, 10
al-Husseini, Amin, 283
al-Husseini, Hussein Salim, 268–69,
    270
Allenby, Edmund, 257, 264, 271, 272,
    275, 281
Alley, T. J., xiv, 192
Alliance Israélite Universelle, 114, 140
American Baptist Home Mission Society,
    159
American Colony, 6–8, 94–108
    Arab relations with, 103–5, 110, 111,
        115, 120, 146–47, 149–50, 156,
        160, 242, 280
    Bezetha house of, 100–102, 110, 112,
        114–15, 119–24, 126–27, 133–40,
        143, 153, 180, 218–19, 309, 312
    Big House of, 173, 174–76, 181–82,
        196, 206, 222, 236, 246, 257, 259,
        267, 283, 286, 301, 308
    British soldiers hidden by, 261, 267, 268
    celibacy instituted in, 136–37, 149,
        161–62, 163, 172, 173, 174
    charity and hospitality of, 7, 112–15,
        118–19, 126–27, 134–36, 143,

    145, 163, 184, 209, 250, 254, 255,
        259–63, 265–66, 274
    confession of sins in, 192, 195, 219,
        253, 290
    contribution to the social and political
        life of Jerusalem by, 7–8, 103–5,
        178–79, 180–81, 183–84, 221–22
    criticism of, 7, 150, 151, 152–56, 163,
        183–84, 186–87, 191–96, 211,
        219–20, 224–25, 227, 228, 231,
        291
    daily routine in, 176–77, 179, 181–82
    defiance and insurrection in, xiv, 182,
        186, 192–95, 211, 215, 219–20,
        299–302
    division of assets in, 301, 307–8,
        310–11
    early financial straits of, 105, 115,
        116–18, 130–33, 135, 144, 145,
        153, 162
    expulsion and escape from, xiv, 150,
        172, 186, 220, 225, 234, 290, 295,
        299, 300, 301
    fictionalized account of, 212–13
    holiday celebrations of, 178, 183,
        221–22, 226, 276
    hymn singing of, 104, 105, 109, 140,
        144, 171, 176, 178, 241
    illness and death in, 135, 137, 138–41,
        142, 145, 147, 177, 188, 240–41,
        252, 253, 285, 295, 296
    immoral practices ascribed to, 7, 153,
        192, 193, 211, 225, 291
    Jewish relations with, 110–15, 118,
        119–22, 160, 179, 280
    makeshift hospitals run by, 259–63,
        267–68, 270
    medical policy in, 139, 177, 222, 259
    prayer meetings of, 103–5, 115, 144,
        148, 169, 180, 192, 219, 241, 298
    press coverage of, 144–45, 157,
        158–59, 160, 161, 164, 165, 171,
        192, 208, 220, 226–30

profitable businesses established by,
7–8, 178–79, 184, 187, 196,
208–9, 216, 222, 235, 238
raising and discipline of children in,
119, 148, 177–78, 179–82, 211,
214
school conducted by, 120–22, 124,
140, 160, 164–65, 180–82, 235
temporary U.S. passports issued to,
236–37
thriving and expansion of, 7, 147, 160,
162, 165, 168–76, 183, 208–9,
221–22, 227
unmarked graves of, 138, 140, 146,
153, 188, 189
work and productiveness of, 103, 119,
137, 174, 178–79, 184, 187, 208–9
See also Overcomers
American Colony Aid Association, 290
American Colony Hotel, 213, 246, 301,
307, 308, 309, 310–11
origins of, 7–8, 126–27, 179, 196
American Colony Photo Department,
208, 216, 238, 246–47, 271, 274,
301, 307
American Palestine Exploration Society,
128
American Schools of Oriental Research,
224
American University of Beirut, 235
Anderson, Ellen, 291
Anna Spafford Baby Nursing Home and
Infant Welfare Center, 298, 304
anti-Catholicism, 74, 75
Antichrist, 37, 75, 127, 144
anti-Semitism, 200, 207–8, 281
Antoszewsky, Constantine, 211
Appleton's Magazine, 226–29, 231
Arabic language, 100, 104, 112, 114,
119, 125, 237, 247, 261, 267, 305
Arabi Pasha, 184
Arab Legion, 305
Arabs, 92, 94, 96, 198
American Colony relations with,
103–5, 110, 111, 115, 120,
146–47, 149–50, 156, 160, 242,
280
effendi class of, 120, 149, 174, 203
Jewish relations with, 197–98, 275,
277, 278, 280–84, 286, 302–7
nationalism of, 280, 283–84, 302–3
Turkish conscription of, 210, 246, 249
See also Muslims

Arafat, Yasir, 310
archaeologists, 9, 98, 109, 110, 119, 122,
124, 128, 129, 142, 189
Armageddon, 10, 37, 263
Armenian genocide, 201, 236, 254–55
Arminianism, 35, 75–76
Arminius, James, 35
Armour, Philip, 30, 70
Arthur, Chester, 128
Ashbee, Charles Robert, 276–77, 286,
287
Astor, Lady, 285
Atatürk, Mustafa Kemal, 245, 264, 272
Augusta Victoria, Empress of Prussia,
185, 205–8

Babylonian captivity, 99, 114
Badr, Sheikh, 268
Baghdad Railway, 240
Baldwin, Edward F., xiii, 147, 148, 154,
183, 188, 202, 204, 295
Baldwin, Farida, 288–89
Baldwin, Furman, 202–3, 216–17, 220,
288–89
Balfour Declaration, 265, 278, 281, 282,
303
Ballou, Annie, 70
Baptist Church, 4, 5, 6, 12
Barnum, P. T., 25, 74
Baybars, Sultan, 1
bedouins, 109, 113, 146, 198, 218
Beebee, H. S., 67–68
Begin, Menachem, 303
Bell, Gertrude, 285, 307
Ben-Gurion, David, 305
Bentwich, Helen, 281–82
Bentwich, Norman, 281–82, 300, 301
Ben-Yehuda, Eliezer, xiv, 114–15, 207,
280
Bergheim, Samuel, 130
Bernadotte, Folke, 305
Besant, Walter, 108
Bible, 3, 33–35, 48, 72, 116
inerrancy of, 36, 75
prophecies of, 37–39, 96, 104, 160,
189, 272
reading and study of, 2, 8–9, 13, 26,
80, 121, 122–23, 167, 181, 223,
252–53
scientific analysis of, 142
See also New Testament; Old Testa-
ment; Torah
Bismarck, Prince Otto von, 184

Black Hand, 240
Blackstone, William E., xv, 84, 143–44, 313
Blackstone Memorial, xv, 84, 144
Blair, Tony, 310
Bliss, Philip P., 84
Blome, Wendy Whiting, 311, 312
Blyth, George Francis Popham, 184, 194, 202, 203
Bolshevik Revolution, 265, 272, 287
Bowman, H. H., 158, 161, 195
Brandeis, Louis D., 144
Breasted, James, 299
British Army, 184, 245, 255, 261, 264–65, 269–72, 274–78
British Custodian of Enemy Property, 277
British-Israelite theory, 38
British mandate, 7, 280, 281–82
British Palestine Exploration Fund, 128
Brooke, Clara Johanna, xiii, 121–22, 155, 181–82, 186, 202, 235, 251, 254
Bross, William, 130–31
Bulkley, Lallie, 60
Bulkley, Mary Adams, 59–60
Bull Run, First Battle of, 31
Burton, Sir Richard, ix
Byzantium, 91, 93, 96

Calvinism, 16, 31, 35, 75
Casualty Clearing Station, 259–63
Chautauqua movement, 145
Chicago, Ill., 14–36, 69–79, 142, 291–93
  business and social leaders of, 24, 30, 31, 32, 43–44, 70, 102
  churches of, 15, 31–32, 43, 44, 70, 75–79
  city council in, 70, 71
  City Hall in, 14–15, 70
  European immigrants in, 15–16, 24, 25–26, 70, 71, 72
  great fire of 1871 in, 43–48, 62, 68, 69, 70, 72
  growth and prosperity of, 14, 33, 43
  industry and trade in, 14, 42, 47, 70
  North Side of, 15, 44
  poverty and unemployment in, 30, 48, 70, 72, 78
  rebuilding of, 46–47, 48, 70
  saloons and brothels in, 29, 44, 71
  South Side of, 31, 43, 166

Chicago, University of, 152, 158, 299
Chicago and Rock Island Railroad, 16–17
Chicago Daily News, 30, 157, 164
Chicago Daily Tribune, 24, 30, 47, 68, 70, 76, 161, 171
Chicago Hebrew Mission, 144
cholera, 15, 16, 134, 250
Christ Church, 109, 184
Christianity, 96–97, 134
  conversion of Jews to, 9, 37, 38, 109, 111–12, 119, 122, 284–85
  Holy Week in, 223–24
  See also Protestantism; *specific Christian sects*
Christian science, 6
Christian Science Monitor, 308
Churches of Christ, 6
Churchill, Winston, 240
Church of England, 40, 184, 242–43
  reform movement of, 35–36
Church of the Dormition, 190, 207
Church of the Holy Sepulchre, 95, 96–97, 98, 101, 223, 285, 308
Church of the Redeemer, 190, 207, 218
Civil War, U.S., 30, 31, 33–34, 48, 51, 103, 125, 128
Clark, Herbert, 223, 246
Clemenceau, Georges, 279
Cleveland, Grover, 183, 196
Closing of the Western Mind, The (Freeman), 134
Committee of Union and Progress (CUP), 232, 236, 237, 240, 255
communism, 109, 193
Confederate Army, 31
Congregationalist Church, 6, 23, 26, 128
Connecticut Mutual Life Insurance Company, 87
Constantine I, Emperor of Rome, 96, 190
Constantinople, 91, 96, 185, 191, 198, 200–201, 203, 205, 207, 232, 236, 237, 245
  Sublime Porte of, 92, 184, 239
Cook, Émile, 54, 56, 65
Cooke, Jay, 50–51, 74
Cope, Lady Djemila, 311
Crimean War, 93, 111
Crozer, John P., 49
Crusades, 92, 97, 98, 174, 189, 190
  Fourth, 96
  Sixth, 202
Cunningham, Sir Alan, 305

Daily Inter Ocean, 67, 89, 116
Dajani, Jantien, 311
Dakota Indians, 17
Dalman, Gustav, 226, 236, 277
Darby, John Nelson, xv, 36–37, 38, 39, 40, 73, 77, 313
Darwin, Charles, 36
Darwinism, 38, 142
Davis, Alice E., xiv, 138–39
Dead Sea, 113, 249
Dearborn Academy, 18, 19, 21, 22, 45
Deedes, Wyndham, 295
Deir Yassin massacre, 304
Democratic Party, 70, 196
Depression, Great, 301, 302
Deutsche Palastina Bank, 208
dhimmis, 92, 104
Dickinson, Charles M., xiv, 204–5, 227
Dickson, John, 202, 203, 229
Dinsmore, John, xiii, 180, 235, 237, 306, 307
Dinsmore, Mary, xiii, 180
Dinsmore, Ruth, xiii, 180
dispensational premillennialism, 36–37, 40–41, 77, 144
Dixon, Johnny, 165
Djemal Pasha, 237, 239–40, 243–50, 254–56, 260, 263, 264
    American Colony and, 255–56, 258–59, 273
    murder of, 273
    terror reign of, 247, 249, 254–55
Dome of the Rock, 94, 95, 97, 99–100
Domesday Book, 28
Douglas, Stephen, 44
Drake, Herbert, xiii, 123–25, 138, 145, 188
Drexel, Anthony J., 73–74
Dreyfus, Alfred, 200
Dryer, Emma, 71
Dunn, Mrs., 135–36

East of the Jordan (Merrill), 128
ecstatic experience, 36, 80, 142–43, 168
Eddy, William K., xiv, 190–91, 202, 204, 207, 225–26, 227
Egypt, 38–39, 113, 184, 201, 243
    Israelite captivity in, 299
    plagues of, 123, 172
Egyptian Expeditionary Force, 257, 264
Egyptian Mamluks, 1, 92, 98
Eliahu, Jacob, 122–23, 155, 162, 188, 202–3, 222, 261, 290, 294

converts gathered by, 162, 175–76
relationship of AS and, 122, 137, 146, 148, 149, 158, 160, 174, 177, 288, 298
Spafford adoption of, 122, 175, 288
talents of, 122, 175, 298
Elkan, Sophie, 211–12
Ely, Sarah, 18, 22, 29
Emancipation Proclamation, 34
End Times, 9–10, 114, 115
England. *See* Great Britain
English Mission Hospital, 228
Enver Pasha, 232, 233, 237, 239, 245, 273
Episcopal Church, 6
Eretz Israel, 282
Erie Canal, 3, 5, 14
Eucharist, 104, 134
European Union, 310
evangelism, 4, 24–26, 34–40, 142–43, 284, 312, 313
    churches of, 70, 71, 166–72
    values and beliefs of, 6, 7, 24, 25–26, 31, 35, 39–40, 71, 73

Falkenhayn, Erich von, 264
Farwell, John V., 30, 74
Father and Son (Gosse), 308
Feast of the Tabernacles, 112
Felton, Lew, 160
Field, Marshall, 70
Fillmore, Millard, 16–17
First Presbyterian Church (Greensburg), 229–30
Floyd, Docia, xiv, 126, 141–42, 145
Floyd, Rolla, xiv, 125–26, 127–28, 141–42, 145, 180, 222, 246
Ford, Alexander Hume, 224–25, 226–29, 230, 231
Fosdick, Harry Emerson, 309
France, 50, 62, 184, 240, 272
Franciscan monks, 97, 101
Francis Ferdinand, Archduke of Austria, 240
Franson, Frederick, 166–67
Frederick II, King of Prussia, 202
Frederickson, Charles, 27
Frederickson, Rachel Lawson, 14, 16, 18, 27, 28–29, 112
Freeman, Charles, 134
Fuller, George A., 147
Fullerton Avenue Presbyterian Church, 48, 68–69, 86, 103, 291–92

HS's falling out with, 75–77, 79, 84
fundamentalism, 175
Fundamentalism and American Culture
(Marden), 4*n*

Gadites, 114–15
Gallipoli, Battle of, 245
Garden of Gethsemane, 251
Garfield, James A., 10, 128
General Missionary Convention (London), 144
George V, King of England, 245
German Archaeological Institute, 226
German Asia Corps, 264
Germany, Imperial, 200–202
    colonial ambitions of, 184–85, 201–2
    Turkish alliance with, 208, 239, 240,
        247, 248–49, 257, 263–64
Gillman, Henry, 140
Glazebrook, Otis, 242–43, 248, 250,
    252, 257
Goeben (ship), 240
Goldenthal, Maurice, 285
Goodwin, Agnes, 50, 51, 56, 65
Goodwin, Daniel, Jr., 50, 53, 62, 63,
    65–66, 67, 79
Goodwin, Goertner, 50, 79
Goodwin, Julia, 50
Goodwin, Lulu, 50
Gordon, Charles George "Chinese," xiii,
    123–24, 125
Gosse, Edmund, 308
Gould, Amelia, xiii, xiv, 89, 90, 103,
    119, 120, 121, 130, 131–32, 145,
    177, 202, 253
    financial support of Overcomers by,
        102, 115, 118
    illness and death of, 240–41
    William Rudy and, 102, 146, 147–48,
        159, 253
Gould, John S., xiv, 131–32, 148, 159
Grand New Hotel, 154–55, 183,
    211–12, 260
Grant, Ulysses S., 51, 74, 246
Great Britain, 35–40, 69, 71, 103, 184
    Palestine occupation by, 7, 269–72,
        274–78, 280–81, 284, 302–3, 305
    in World War I, 240, 245, 257, 261,
        264–65, 269–72
    Zionist policy of, 265, 272, 279–82,
        303
    See also British Army; London; Scotland

Greek Orthodox Church, 96, 97
Greeley, Horace, 17
Green, Hetty, 87, 117
Grey, Sir Edward, 239

Habib, Elias, xiii, 95, 96–97, 98, 100,
    112, 120, 202
Hadassah, 275
Haganah, 305
haluka, 95, 152
Hamas, 311
Hanson, Katrina, 194
Haram al-Sharif, 94, 97, 110, 186, 222,
    283, 285, 308
Harrison, Benjamin, 133, 144
Hebrew language, 114, 115, 122, 124,
    128, 207, 280, 281
Hebrew University, 281, 311
Hedges, Rachel, 89
Hedges, Samuel, xiii, 49–50, 62, 75, 86,
    88–90, 116–18, 144, 161, 287
Hedin, Sven, 255–56
Helena, Roman Empress, 96
Herod, King of Judea, 99, 110
Herzl, Theodor, 144, 197, 200, 207–8,
    210, 305
Hezbollah, 311
Hichens, Canon, 242
Hiram of Tyre, 1–2
Hohenzollern (yacht), 206
Holocaust, 303
Holy Spirit, 4, 35, 39, 81, 127
Hull House, 160
Hussein, King of Jordan, 309
Hussein ibn Ali, Sharif, 255
Husseini, Ismail Bey, xiv, 185–86, 203–4,
    206, 228
Husseini, Kamil Effendi al-, 265
Husseini, Rabbah Daoud Amin Effendi
    al-, 174
Husseini family, 120, 174, 185–86,
    203–4

Imperial War Museum, 271
Irgun, 303, 304
Islam, 105, 233
    "capitulations" granted in, 92, 93
    founding of, 99
    sacred places of, 92, 94, 95, 97,
        99–100, 110
    See also Muslims
Israel (ancient), 122
    tribes of, 38, 113–15, 123, 281

Israel (modern), 303
　Arab wars against, 305–6, 308
　1948 creation of, 7, 305
"It Is Well with My Soul" (Bliss and Spafford), 61, 64, 84
Izzet Bey, 264, 265, 266, 267, 270–71

Jabotinsky, Vladimir, 280–81, 284
Jaffa, 1–3, 116, 122, 127, 141–42, 145, 172, 249
　harbor of, 1–2, 8, 125–26, 130, 176
Jarrah, Sheikh, 174
Jerusalem, 3, 6–8, 10–11, 57, 87–90
　Arab quarter of, 100–102, 109, 143
　Christian quarter of, 95
　1516 Ottoman capture of, 92
　Food Control Office in, 260
　gates of, 10, 98, 99, 100, 102, 112, 128, 140, 172, 176, 180, 205, 207, 222, 249, 266–68, 271, 309
　growth and modernization of, 197
　holy sites of, 2, 94–100, 101, 104, 108, 110, 124, 130, 207, 308
　Jewish quarter of, 101, 111
　multiple destructions of, 47, 97, 110
　Old City of, 100–102, 222, 275, 302, 305, 308, 311
　as "Old Zion," 6, 9, 37, 111
　Ottoman district of, 111
　religious diversity and tension in, 7, 95, 145, 197–98, 223–24
　squalor and filth of, 11, 94, 98–99, 138, 197, 207
　Turkish evacuation of, 266–68, 269
　Turkish seizure of property and institutions in, 242–43, 244, 264
　Via Dolorosa in, 97–98
　Wailing Wall in, 95, 110, 207, 283
　walls of, 91, 95, 101, 110
　in World War I, 241–44, 246–50, 255–72
Jerusalem (Lagerlöf), 212–13
Jerusalem, the City of Herod and Saladin (Besant and Palmer), 108
Jerusalem, U.S. Consulate in, 128–29, 150, 152, 187, 188–92, 216–17, 275
　cemetery war of AS and, 187–96, 202–5, 217, 225–26, 227, 230–31
　consuls and vice-consuls of, xiv, 108–9, 119, 126, 128–33, 138, 140, 150, 183–200, 202–5, 211, 216–17, 224–25, 227, 228, 231

Jesus Christ, 10, 72, 124
　Crucifixion of, 96, 97, 104, 123
　healing power of, 83, 106, 117, 118
　life of, 8, 96, 97–98, 99, 112
　Resurrection of, 2, 97, 285, 295
Jesus Is Coming (Blackstone), 144
Jewish Agency, 305
Jews
　agricultural settlements of, 95, 198, 208
　American Colony relations with, 110–15, 118, 119–22, 160, 179, 280
　Arab relations with, 197–98, 275, 277, 278, 280–84, 286, 302–7
　Ashkenazic, 110, 180, 218
　assimilation of, 152
　as Chosen People, 152
　Christian conversion of, 9, 37, 38, 109, 111–12, 119, 122, 284–85
　Ethiopian, 111
　Polish, 111
　Russian, 95, 110, 111, 198, 199
　Sephardic, 110, 122, 180, 218
　stereotypes of, 207–8
　trades of, 95, 113, 115
　U.S. passports sought by, 199
　Yemeni, 112–15, 118
　See also Palestine, return of Jews to; Judaism
John, Gospel of, 105
Johnson, Bertha, 65, 86
Jonsson, Jon, 212, 219–20
Jordan River, 73, 224, 256
Joseph of Arimathea, 124
Joshua, 114
Judaism, 112, 113, 283
　holy days of, 110, 112, 223
　Orthodox, 37, 99, 110, 122, 179
　reform, 110
Judea, 101
Judenstaat, Der (Herzl), 200
Juzdar, Ali Bey, xiv, 101, 115, 153

Kaminitz Hotel, 150
Karin, Lisslasses, 169
Kelk, A. Hastings, xiv, 109, 121, 122
King-Crane Commission, 279
King David Hotel, 303
King David's Tomb, 104
Knabenshue, Paul, 300
Kohlsaat, Judge, 165

Koran, 237, 239, 255
Kurds, 95, 236, 254

Lagerlöf, Selma, 210–13, 219, 228, 260,
    286
Lake View, Ill., 43–47, 49–50, 52, 53,
    121
    chapel and congregation at, 76, 77,
        79, 80–84, 86–90, 102, 103, 105,
        117
    Spafford home in, 32, 34, 43, 44–45,
        49, 68, 71, 87, 88, 89–90, 117,
        130, 159, 160–61, 291
Larsson, Edith, xiv, 215, 221, 237–39,
    241, 269, 278, 294, 296
    childhood of, 177–78, 179, 181
Larsson, Hannah, 179
Larsson, Lewis, xiv, 238–39, 250, 262,
    271, 278, 289, 299–300, 303
    photography of, 238, 246–47, 269–70,
        301
Larsson, Mathilda Helgsten, xiv, 168,
    169–70, 172, 174, 177–78, 179,
    221, 223, 237
Larsson, Olof Henrik, xiv, 167–71,
    173–75, 177–79, 188, 237, 294
    gold left by, 194, 252
    illness and death of, 223
    power struggle of AS and, 169, 171,
        174, 175, 179, 211–12, 222–23
Larsson, Theo, 269, 278, 305
Larsson, Tipers Lars, 171
Last Supper, 168, 189
Lawrence, Rob, xiii, 49, 90, 119, 122,
    135, 253
Lawrence, T. E., 255, 272, 275, 277
Lawson, Edward, 14, 16, 17, 19–20, 21
Lawson, Hans, 16, 72
Lawson, Lars, 13–14, 16–20, 214
Lawson, Rachel. See Frederickson, Rachel
    Lawson
Lawson, Tanetta, 13–14, 16, 72
Lawson, Victor, 30
League of Nations, 279
Lebanon, 184, 189, 201, 235, 254, 279,
    305, 311
Lee, Margaret "Maggie," xiii, 49–50,
    80–82, 90, 135, 145, 188, 189
    "signs" and "visions" of, 81, 105,
        106–7, 192
Lee, "Mother" Ann, 5
Lincoln, Abraham, 9, 29, 33, 34, 43–44
Lincoln Park, Ill., 32, 43, 46, 47, 61

Lind, Anna Grace Vester, 222, 242, 289,
    297–98, 311
Lind, Eric, xiv, 202, 220
Lind, Georgette, 311
Lind, Lars, xiv, 181–82, 220, 246–47,
    250–51, 258–59, 262, 267–71,
    301
Lind, Nils, xiv, 289, 297–98, 311
Lind, Olaf, xiv, 262, 289–90, 295,
    299–300
Lind University, 29
Lingle, David, xiv, 152–55, 158, 228
Lingle, Regina, xiv, 146, 150, 157–58,
    161–62
Lloyd George, David, 264, 279, 280
Loch Earn (ship), 57–59
London, 2, 36–38, 62–63, 90, 102, 229,
    271, 295, 310
London Jews Society, xiv, 109, 111–12,
    119, 194, 261
    Mission School of, 112, 121, 122, 140
Lorriaux, Théophile, 53–58, 60, 62, 65
Lusitania, 58
Lutheran Church, 12, 13, 18, 20–21, 70,
    218, 222, 242

McCormick, Cyrus H., 30, 44, 46, 70
McCormick Theological Seminary, 292
McKinley, William, 196, 230
Maimonides, Moses, 33
Marsden, George M., 4n
Matson, Eric Dinsmore, 307–8
Matson, G. Eric, 301, 307
Matsson, Gastgifvar Mats, 171, 188,
    191
Matthew, Book of, 72, 136, 181
Mecca, 92, 201, 255, 275
Medill, Joseph, 30, 47
Medina, 92, 255
Mediterranean Hotel, 11, 94–95, 99,
    100, 106
Megiddo, Battle of, 272
Mehmed II, Sultan, 91
Mehmed V, Sultan, 236
Merrill, Selah, xiv, 128–33, 138, 140,
    150, 152–56, 179, 183, 189, 190,
    196–200, 216–17, 218, 227–30,
    237, 260, 313
    American Colony criticized by, 151,
        152–56, 163, 193–94, 196, 211,
        223, 224–25, 228, 231
    archaeological work of, 128–29, 133,
        189, 224, 230

illness and death of, 228–30, 231
"Jewish Question" considered by,
    198–200
Merriman, Caroline, xiii, 90, 102, 119,
    135
Messiah, 2, 5, 6, 9, 33, 65, 88, 100, 111,
    120, 215, 297, 313
    See also Second Coming
Methodist Church, 4, 6, 12, 26, 145,
    170, 195
Meyers, Elijah, xiii, 148, 208, 251, 298
Meyers, Joseph, 162
millennialism, 6, 9, 10, 39, 48, 65, 111,
    125, 138, 163, 165–67, 233
Miller, Halsey, 45
Miller, John A., 147
Miller, Mary, 45, 68, 284, 287
Miller, William, 5
Mills, Luther Laflin, 162–63
Minnesota Territory, 16–22, 23, 27
missionaries, Protestant, 7, 12, 28, 75,
    104, 109, 111–12, 121, 135–36,
    179, 209, 257, 293
Mission of Terra Santa, 202–3
Montefiore, Moses, 95
Moody, Dwight Lyman, xv, 44, 48,
    62–63, 166–67, 313
    AS and, 48, 63, 71–72, 88, 142–43
    business pursuits and investments of,
        25, 26–27, 30–31, 46, 48, 74, 79
    charismatic and flamboyant style of,
        25, 30, 39–40, 63, 73, 74
    HS and, 25–27, 30–31, 33–36,
        83–85, 88, 143
    minimal education and theology of,
        25, 34, 41
    preaching and doctrine of, 25, 29–30,
        39–40, 48, 73, 77–78
    religious zeal of, 25–27, 29–30, 33–36,
        39–41, 48, 63
    revivals of, 30, 34, 39–40, 69–70,
        73–79, 142–43
    Sunday school teaching of, 25–26, 30,
        143
    wealthy patrons of, 30, 34, 73–74, 78,
        79
Moody, Emma, 44
Moody, William, 84
Moody Bible Institute, 71
Moore, Franklin T., 154
Morgan, J. P., 74
Mormons, 5, 12
Moses, 104, 113

Mosque of Al-Buraq, 110, 283
Mosque of Omar, 130, 143
Mosque of the Tomb of David, 189
Mount Bezetha, 100, 120, 126, 133, 134,
    143, 153, 155–56, 180, 218–19
Mount Moriah, 99
Mount of Olives, 2, 94, 99, 101, 105–6,
    110, 205, 265
    Augusta Victoria hospice on, 205, 241,
        244, 246–47
Mount Scopus, 101, 270, 281
    American Colony cemetery on, 131,
        240–41, 297, 310–11
Mount Zion, 187–91, 207
    American cemetery on, 140, 142,
        187–91, 202, 204–5
    British cemetery on, 190–91, 202–4,
        225–26
Muhammad (Prophet), 92, 99, 104, 110,
    174, 233, 234
Murphy, Mary, 49, 89, 117
Muslim Higher Committee, 304
Muslims, 82, 103–5, 113, 124, 143, 197,
    233
    relations of Jews and, 92, 104, 180–81,
        197–98
    See also Islam

Napoleon I, Emperor of France, 201
Napoleon III, Emperor of France, 184
Napoleonic Wars, 12
Nebi Musa festival, 223, 284
New Haven Theological Seminary, 128
New Testament, 9, 37
New York, N.Y., 14, 51–52, 54, 69, 74,
    290, 299
New York Herald, 73
New York Stock Exchange, 51, 301
New York Times, 10
New-York Tribune, 17
Nicholas I, Czar of Russia, 93
Nicholas II, Czar of Russia, 265, 272
Nicolet, Mademoiselle, 50, 52
Norden (ship), 14
Northern Pacific Railroad, 51
Northwestern Christian Advocate, 26
Northwestern University, 71
Noyes, John Humphrey, 5

Øglende, Anne Tobine Larsdatter. *See*
    Spafford, Anna Tubena Lawson
Øglende, Bjarne Lars Larsen. *See* Lawson,
    Lars

Øglende, Edvard. *See* Lawson, Edward
Øglende, Gurine Tobine Andersdatter. *See* Lawson, Tanetta
Øglende, Rachel. *See* Frederickson, Rachel Lawson
Old Testament, 37–39, 104, 189, 284
O'Leary, Mrs., 43
Osman I, 91
Osman Bey el-Nashashibi, 246
Ottoman Empire
    Arab revolt against, 255, 275
    decline of, 7, 92–94, 111, 184, 201, 239
    ethnic groups and states of, 92, 93, 94, 95, 233
    German alliance with, 208, 239, 240, 247, 248–49, 257, 263–64
    laws and courts of, 132, 152, 154, 188, 190, 235, 249
    1908 Young Turks revolt against, 232–33
    Palestine ruled by, 6–9, 38, 91–94, 104, 120, 129, 130, 132, 143, 152, 188, 198, 227–28
    parliament of, 236, 240, 246
    postwar division of, 265, 279–80
    reforms instituted in, 232–34, 239–40
    Sunni Islam embraced by, 82
    World War I surrender of, 272–73
    See also Turkey; Turkish navy; Turkish soldiers
Ottoman Fourth Army, 243–44
Our Jerusalem (Vester), 231, 307
Our Rest and Signs of the Times (periodical), xiv, 126–27
Overcomers, 3, 6–8, 9–11, 80–91, 94–115
    advanced "Saints" among, 10, 82, 84, 86, 87, 90, 117, 120, 126, 135, 137
    as "Bride" of Christ, 10, 80, 82, 83–84, 87–88, 105
    Chicago departure of, 1, 2, 3, 6, 10, 11
    "dispensations" of, 10, 80, 88
    faith healing belief of, 83, 106, 117, 118, 127, 132
    rebuff and ridicule of, 3, 7, 11, 82, 106, 121, 126–27, 130–33, 138, 143–44, 147
    See also American Colony

Page, Flora, xiii, 102–3, 123, 301
Page, Lizzie, xiii, 102–3, 119, 137–38, 163, 202

Page, Otis, xiii, 102–3, 119, 137–38, 182, 202, 253, 291
Palestine, 1–3
    British occupation of, 7, 269–72, 274–78, 280–81, 284, 302–3, 305
    famine in, 251, 256
    as Holy Land, 8–9, 127, 128, 133, 142, 160, 185, 191
    Jewish agricultural settlements in, 95, 198, 208
    1915 locust plague in, 250–51
    1947 partition of, 303–4, 306
    Ottoman rule of, 6–9, 38, 91–94, 104, 120, 129, 130, 132, 143, 152, 188, 198, 227–28
    return of Jews to, 6, 7, 9, 37, 38, 72, 82, 84, 95, 110–15, 118, 129, 143, 152, 160, 197–200, 280, 283, 298–99
    sacred sites of, 8–9, 94–100, 101, 108, 110, 124, 128, 223–24
    segregation of religions as protected groups in, 129, 143, 223–24
Palmer, Edmund, 162–64
Palmer, Edward Henry, 108
Palmer, Potter, 43, 46–47
Palmerston, Lord, 38
Panic of 1857, 27
Panic of 1873, 50–51, 62, 64, 69, 70, 74
Panic of 1893, 167
Parham, Charles F., 4n
Paris, 52, 62, 65, 68, 200
Paris Peace Conference of 1919, 278–79
Parousia of Christ, 166
Passover, 223
Paul, Saint, 9, 37, 106, 136, 297
pentecostalism, 4–6, 36, 147
Perrott, C. H., 301
Peter, Saint, 2, 252
Philadelphia, Pa., 15, 50–51, 69, 73–74
Plutarch's Lives, 123
Plymouth Brethren, xv, 6, 37, 40
postmillennialism, 35
preacher-prophets, 3, 4, 5
predestination, 35, 75, 166
Presbyterian Board of Missions, xiv, 187–88, 189, 190, 202, 225–26, 227
Presbyterian Church, 4, 6, 24, 26, 44, 75, 147
Princeton Theological Seminary, 191
Pro-Jerusalem Society, 275, 276
Protestantism, 3–6, 313

fundamentalist vs. liberal, 26
schisms in, 4–6, 26
taboos of, 15, 23–24
traditional mainstream, 4, 6, 11, 35, 41
See also missionaries, Protestant; *specific sects and movements*
Public Ledger (periodical), 74
purgatory, 10, 82
Puritanism, 15, 35

Quakers, 12–13, 257

Rabin, Yitzhak, 310
"Rapture," 37, 144
Reaper Works, 44, 46, 70
Red Crescent, 247
Red Cross, 247–48, 303, 305
Reformation, 313
Relief and Aid Society, 70
Republican Party, 23, 24, 70, 129, 196
Revelation, Book of, 37, 80, 127
revivalism, 4–6, 23, 30, 34, 39–40,
    69–70, 73–79, 142–43, 169
Robertson, William, 58–59
Roman Catholic Church, 15, 36, 70, 71,
    96–97, 190, 202, 298
  religious orders of, 97, 101, 242, 243
Roman Empire, 99
Roosevelt, Eleanor, 309
Roosevelt, Theodore, 230
Rothschild, Baron, 95
Rudy, William, xiii, 89, 90, 103, 135,
    161, 177, 184, 186–87, 195, 208,
    253–54
  Amelia Gould and, 102, 146, 147–48,
    159, 253
  death of, 252, 254
  financial responsibilities of, 102, 115,
    118, 132, 147–48, 158, 159, 165,
    180, 194–96, 252
  gold buried by, 195–96, 252
Russia, 10, 111, 184, 240
  pogroms in, 95, 111, 198
Russian Orthodox Church, 224

Sabbath, 18, 25, 67, 70, 77
Saladin, 174, 186
Samuel, Lady, 294
Samuel, Lord Herbert, 281–82, 283, 287
Sanhedrin, 112
Sanitary Commission, U.S., 34
Sankey, Ira, xv, 73, 74, 77, 78, 79, 142–43
San Remo Conference of 1920, 279–80

Satan, 10, 37, 75, 82, 109, 127, 177, 188
Savignoni, Dr., 202–3
Schaff, Philip, 67
Schick, Conrad, 124
School of Handicrafts and Dressmaking,
    298
Scotland, 38–39, 62–63
Second Coming, 5, 35, 37, 39, 65,
    75–76, 82, 87, 99, 105–6, 175, 313
  delay of, 117, 120, 215, 234, 297
  pinpointing the date of, 39, 84, 166–67
  signs of, 6, 9, 80, 143
Second Great Awakening, 35
Second Presbyterian Church (Chicago),
    31–32, 44
Shaftesbury, Anthony Ashley Cooper, 7th
    Earl of, xv, 37–38, 73, 109, 313
Shakers, 5
Shakespeare, William, 123
Shamir, Yitzhak, 305
Shea, John S. M., 270–71
Shuni, Rabbi, 112–14
Simpson, Jenny, 22, 27
Sims, Aunty, 45, 48–49, 63, 68, 83
sin, 75
  confession and repentance of, 9, 35,
    40, 48, 56, 192, 195, 219, 253, 290
  punishment of, 82, 83, 181, 189
  redemption of, 65, 82
Sioux Indians, 17
Six Days' War of 1967, 308
slavery, 26, 27
  abolition of, 33, 34
smallpox, 119, 134, 177, 250
Smith, Charles Piazza, xv, 38–39, 48, 84,
    166
Smith, Joseph, 5
Solomon, 2, 99
Spafford, Anna Tubena Lawson, xiii, 3, 6,
    12–23
  blue eyes and blond hair of, 3, 8, 13,
    27, 29, 31, 50, 137, 160, 162, 167,
    170, 176, 192
  breaking of family ties ordered by, 178,
    186, 187, 192–93, 212, 214–15,
    234
  as "Bride" of Christ, 105, 186
  cemetery war of, 187–96, 202–5, 217,
    225–26, 227, 230–31
  character and personality of, 22, 27,
    29, 62–63, 68, 82, 119–20,
    136–43, 146, 181–82, 196, 209,
    212, 214–15, 256, 294

charm and beauty of, 8, 11, 27, 107,
    167, 294
childhood and adolescence of, 13–14,
    16, 17–23, 27–29, 215
converts recruited by, 162, 168–76,
    193, 196
criticism and denouncement of,
    194–95, 211–13, 291
death of, 213, 295–96, 298, 300,
    309
depressions of, 72, 86, 87
education of, 18, 19, 21, 22, 29, 235
establishment churches rejected by, 18,
    21, 22, 27, 34, 97, 121, 189, 298
ill-fated ocean voyage of, 52–59, 62,
    63–64, 67, 146, 168, 226
illnesses of, 49–50, 55, 136, 241–42,
    282–83, 285, 286, 287–88, 290,
    294–95
manifestations and messages of, 89–90,
    102, 105, 106–7, 120, 127, 141,
    148, 149, 163, 168–69, 172,
    215–18, 288, 290, 294, 298
marriage of, 31–32, 44
motherhood of, 8, 32, 34, 43, 44–46,
    48, 49–50, 53, 55–57, 79, 85, 86,
    88, 119–20, 135, 141
musical talent of, 18, 22, 27, 32, 149
names and chores assigned by, 103,
    119, 176, 179, 181, 186
Norwegian ancestry of, 12–14, 16, 18,
    20–21, 27, 29, 32, 63, 107, 214
physical appearance of, 8, 176, 212,
    251, 255–56, 283
power and authority of, 82, 85–86,
    103, 105–7, 119–20, 127, 135–36,
    147, 149–50, 155, 161–65,
    173–75, 179, 181–82, 208–12,
    214–21, 234–35, 313
religious beliefs of, 62–63, 68–69, 86,
    88, 241, 284–85, 293, 294, 312
religious fear inculcated by, 181–82,
    209, 210, 214–15, 238
sanctioning of marriages by, 217–19,
    234, 238–39, 289
sexual and marital edicts of, 151,
    161–62, 163, 172, 173, 174, 186,
    187, 192, 195, 212, 215–21
shunning by, 220, 223
trial testimony of, 163–64
Spafford, Annie (daughter), 34, 44–45,
    48, 50, 53, 56, 60, 61, 63, 68, 143,
    149

Spafford, Bertha. See Vester, Bertha
    Hedges Spafford
Spafford, Elizabeth "Bessie," 34, 44–45,
    48, 50, 52, 53, 55–56, 60, 61, 63,
    68, 143, 149
Spafford, Eureka, 49
Spafford, Grace. See Whiting, Grace Spaf-
    ford
Spafford, Horatio Gates, xiii, 3, 6,
    291–92, 309
  as the "Branch," 105, 106–7, 127
  character and personality of, 23–24,
    25, 27, 28, 49, 61–62, 64–65,
    67–69, 312–13
  Christian theology of, 23–24, 30,
    33–39, 62, 65, 68, 75–84, 88, 89,
    104, 109, 114, 117, 119, 121, 127,
    135–37, 284, 312–13
  criticism of, 76, 83–85, 117, 119, 121,
    126–27, 130–33
  famous poem of, 61, 64, 84
  financial problems of, 46, 48, 49,
    51–52, 61–62, 64–65, 80, 83,
    84–90, 116–18, 130–33, 185, 312,
    313
  illness and death of, 138–41, 142, 161,
    223, 227, 253, 296
  land investments of, 26–27, 29, 31,
    32, 43, 47, 51, 61
  law practice of, 8, 23, 24, 25, 28, 29,
    33, 36, 47, 49, 50, 51, 83, 130
  misuse of funds by, 49, 64–65, 84–85,
    87, 88, 89, 117, 132
  political interests of, 23, 24, 29
  rambles and meditation of, 118, 120,
    135, 136
  relationship of AS and, 8, 27–29,
    31–32, 48–55, 60, 61–62, 65–66,
    72–73, 80, 85–87, 136–40, 148–49
  revelations of, 10, 80, 85, 88, 130–31,
    136–37
  teaching of, 22, 26, 27, 114, 121, 185
Spafford, Horatio Goertner Goodwin,
    79, 85, 86, 149
Spafford, John, 28
Spafford, McDaid, and Wilson, 33
Spafford, Maggie, 34, 44–45, 48, 50, 52,
    53, 60, 61, 63, 68, 143, 149
Spafford, Tanetta, 43, 44–45, 48, 49, 50,
    53, 55, 56–57, 60, 61, 63, 103,
    143, 149
Spafford Children's Center, 311
"Spaffordite Fraud, The," xiv, 192

Spiritualism, 4, 6, 139
Spofforth, Gamelbar de, 28
Star of Bethlehem, 82
State Department, U.S., 190, 196, 199,
    217, 230, 277
    investigation of cemetery scandal by,
        204–5
    reports on American Colony to,
        108–9, 129–30, 152, 154–56,
        186–87, 193–94, 211, 225, 227,
        300
Stavanger, Norway, 12–14
Stephen, Saint, 189–90
Stern, Abraham, 303
Stern Gang, 303, 304
Stevens, Georgiana, 306
St. George's School, 242, 256, 267
stock market crash of 1929, 301
Storrs, Sir Ronald, 275–77, 295, 307
St. Paul's Church, 43
Strand, Alvilde, 187
Strand, Axel, 187, 202, 205
Sudan, 124, 250
Suez Canal, 184, 244, 245, 248
Suleiman the Magnificent, 92, 98
Supreme Court, U.S., 74, 144
Surmont, Marius, 54, 55, 56, 59
Swedish Evangelical Church, xiv, 166–72,
    175
    Nås congregation of, 169–71, 173–74,
        175–77, 211, 212–13, 238
Sykes-Picot Agreement, 265, 272
Sylvester, Mary, xiii, 102, 103, 105, 202,
    205
Sylvester, William, xiii, 103, 106, 127,
    142, 188, 202
Syria, 184, 189, 190, 204, 237, 238, 247,
    255, 272, 279, 305
Syrian Protestant College, 154, 235, 247

Talat Pasha, 237, 273
Talmud, 95, 152
temperance movement, 26, 70–72, 77, 78
Temple Mount, 94, 95, 143
Temple of Solomon, 2, 99, 110
Thackeray, William Makepeace, 182
Thomas, Lowell, 275, 277, 307
Thomas Cook & Son, 8, 10–11, 125–26,
    205–6, 223, 246
Thuwwar, 302
Tilda, Sister, 178
Tipers, Karin, 212, 219–20
Titanic, 58

Titus, Emperor of Rome, 99
Tocqueville, Alexis de, 4, 8–9
Tomb of Simon the Just, 112
Torah, 95, 113, 115
Transjordan, 113, 279, 305
Treasury Department, U.S., 47
Trimountain (ship), 58–59
Trinity, 105, 142
Turkey, 93, 111, 122, 199, 258
    independent, 272
    See also Ottoman Empire
Turkish navy, 239–40
Turkish soldiers, 8, 94, 95, 96, 97, 101,
    153, 178, 198, 201, 237, 239, 242,
    245, 248–49, 261–62, 267–68
Twain, Mark, 9, 11, 246
Tweed, William Marcy, 74

Union Army, 31, 33
Union Pacific Railroad, 51
United Nations, 303, 305, 306, 310
United States
    European migration to, 3, 5, 13–16,
        17, 24–26, 70, 71, 72
    industrialization of, 3, 5, 23
    poverty and unemployment in, 3, 30,
        48, 51, 70, 72, 78, 125
    as Promised Land, 13
    religious awakenings in, 3–4
    social and economic upheavals in, 3, 5,
        27, 50–51, 62, 64, 69, 70, 74, 167,
        301, 302
    westward migration in, 3, 14, 17
    in World War I, 258, 263
Urquhart, William, 59
Ustinov, Baron von, 142, 287

Valparaiso, Ind., 82, 89, 117
Vanderbilt, Cornelius, 74
Van Dyne, F., 193
Vanity Fair (Thackeray), 182
Vester, Anna Grace. See Lind, Anna Grace
    Vester
Vester, Bertha Hedges Spafford (daugh-
    ter), xiii, 177, 256–58, 312
    ambitious plans of, 290–91, 293,
        297–98
    anti-Zionism of, 282, 285
    AS and, 185, 222, 234, 241–42, 256,
        266, 276, 288, 292, 293–96, 302
    character and personality of, 186, 206,
        256–57, 262–63, 276, 278, 289,
        293–94, 306, 307–8

childhood and adolescence of, 86, 87,
  88, 90, 106, 119, 121, 135,
  139–40, 141, 143, 148, 159, 163,
  164, 288, 293–94
diary of, 294, 296, 308
education of, xiv, 121, 148, 235
exploitation of American Colony
  charged to, 295, 298, 299–301
Frederick Vester and, 159, 172, 185,
  186, 202, 207, 215–16, 218–19,
  221, 241–43, 252, 253, 263, 289,
  291, 295, 298, 303
gala wedding of, 218–19, 222,
  226–27, 242
gradual assumption of American
  Colony leadership by, 213, 234,
  260–63, 266, 270, 275–78,
  290–91, 295, 297–98, 301–2
honors accorded to, 308–9
memoirs of, 231, 307
motherhood of, 222, 242, 249–50,
  253, 262, 286
Muslim girls' school headed by,
  185–86, 203, 206
ninetieth birthday of, 308–9
social prominence and agenda of, 221,
  231, 235, 278, 281, 282, 285, 286,
  294, 298
social work of, 302, 303, 306–7
widowhood of, 303, 304, 306–9
Vester, Frederick, xiv, 159, 172, 208, 216,
  264
death of, 303
financial and management responsibilities of, 208–9, 222, 234, 235, 254,
  277, 285–86, 290, 295
German connections of, 241, 242,
  243, 277–78, 303
illegal antiquities sale of, 299, 300
Vester, Horatio, 242, 307, 308
Vester, Jock, 242, 256
Vester, Louise, 242, 256
Vester, Tanetta, 242
Vester, Valentine, 307, 310
Vester & Co., American Colony Stores,
  208–9, 222, 235, 249, 274, 290,
  297–98, 300
Victoria, Queen of England, 184
Ville du Havre, S.S., 50
Anna Spafford's ill-fated voyage on,
  52–59
collision and sinking of, 55–59, 62,
  63–64, 67, 146, 168, 226

survivors of, 57–60, 62, 66
Vincent, John Heyl, 145

Wadi al Joz, 120
Wall, James M., 245
Wallace, Edwin S., xiv, 183–89, 190–96,
  198–99, 202, 204, 205, 207, 236,
  260
American Colony criticized by,
  183–84, 186–87, 191–95, 196, 227
congregations of, 229–30, 231
death of, 231
Wanamaker, John, 73–74
Wanamingo, Minn., 17, 19–20, 21
Waqf of Abu Madian, 283
Watson, C. F., 269, 270, 271
Weiss, Nathaniel, 54–57, 65
Weizmann, Chaim, 281
West Bank, 308, 311–12
Wheeler, George, 228–29
Whiting, Grace Spafford (daughter), xiii,
  88, 121, 135, 148, 202, 216, 286,
  287, 291, 295–96
childhood of, 90, 120, 121, 135, 141,
  143, 148, 159, 163, 177, 186, 294
John Whiting Jr. and, 217, 231, 246,
  247, 257, 297
motherhood of, 247, 251, 254, 263
Whiting, John, xiii, 103, 105, 106–7,
  115, 137, 146, 158, 188
Whiting, John, Jr., xiii, 253, 289, 295,
  297, 299
childhood of, 121, 135, 137, 146, 148,
  153–54, 157–59, 164–65, 177
marriage of; see Whiting, Grace Spafford
rescue efforts for, 153, 154, 157–59,
  164–65
shooting and death of, 305, 306
vice-consul appointment of, 231–32,
  247–48, 257, 260
Whiting, Mary E. Lingle, xiii, 102, 103,
  115, 119, 137, 145–46, 177, 182,
  253
rescue efforts for, 146, 150, 153–55,
  157–65, 192, 193, 228, 260, 291
Whiting, Ruth, xiii, 103, 253, 285
childhood and adolescence of, 121,
  137, 146, 148, 153, 154, 157–59,
  164–65, 177, 194, 195
marriage of; see Goldenthal, Maurice
rescue efforts for, 153, 154, 157–59,
  164–69

Whittle, D. W., xv, 62, 84–86
Wilhelm II, Kaiser, 184–85, 190, 191, 200–202, 236, 239, 240
    Jerusalem visit of, 201–2, 205–8, 246, 271
Willard, Frances, 71
Wills, Mrs. J. P., 49, 84, 87, 89, 117
Wilson, W. H., 157
Wilson, Woodrow, 278, 279
Wilson's Creek, Battle of, 31
Winterstein, P. H., xiv, 126–27, 133
Woman's American Baptist Foreign Mission Society, 159
Woman's Christian Temperance Union (WCTU), 71–72
World's Sunday School Convention, 217–19
World War I, 231, 241–50, 255–73
    events leading to, 240
    in Jerusalem, 241–44, 246–50, 255–72
    Ottoman surrender in, 272–73
    U.S. in, 258, 263
    See also Germany, Imperial
World War II, 7, 231, 303

Yale University, 128
Yemen, 112–15
    Arab revolts in, 210, 237
Yishuv, 280
Young, William C., 75, 76
Young Ladies' Seminary at Ferry Hall, 29
Young Men's Christian Association (YMCA), 142
    Boston, 24
    Chicago, 24–26, 30–31, 41, 44, 46, 48, 77, 84
    Christian Commission of, 33–34
    London, 39

Zionism, 7, 37, 84, 111, 199–200, 207–8, 234, 279–82
    British policy on, 265, 272, 279–82, 303
    Christian, 295
    U.S. policy on, 129, 144, 199, 200, 303–4
Zionist Commission, 281
Zionist Congress, 200